For Bert Emeney who
first started me on
language studies,
Bob

To my old friend Bert.
Hans

THREE KEYS TO LANGUAGE

THREE KEYS TO LANGUAGE

BY

ROBERT M. ESTRICH & HANS SPERBER

The Ohio State University

RINEHART & COMPANY, INC.

Library of Congress Catalog Card Number: 52-5586

INTRODUCTION

"THE NEW barbarian . . . more learned than ever before, but at the same time more uncultured. . . ." In these words, Ortega y Gasset characterizes—or annihilates—the modern scholar. He bases this indictment on the lack of common intellectual experience among the educated specialists of our time. Our higher education produces lawyers, doctors, and hundreds of other varieties of specialist but not culture if, by this word, we understand "the essential system of ideas concerning the world and man, which belong to our time."

Perhaps Ortega's words sounded revolutionary when they were first uttered (1930), but they have become almost commonplace. There is not a dean's office in the country where the problem of universality as against specialization of knowledge has not been the subject of lengthy and, we profoundly hope, fruitful discussions. But theory is a long way ahead of practice. Everybody is in a fair way of being convinced that the fences by which the vast field of knowledge is divided into cucumber beds and cabbage patches ought to give way. But as yet they stand as firm and forbidding as ever, and mere discussion will hardly remove them. In our opinion they will never be breached until someone is resolute enough to lay hands on that part of the fence that serves to limit his own backyard.

This is what we are trying to do with the field of language. We wish to stress the connections with such neighboring disciplines as the history of culture, of religion, political history, sociology, and psychology, rather than to emphasize the unavoidable distinctions in material and method. We also want to show how much linguistic studies stand to gain from these contacts. As a consequence, we have tried to present our matter in a way accessible to workers outside the field and, for that matter, to any interested person.

We doubt that Ortega is necessarily right in equating specialist with barbarian but, if he is, we should like to avoid being unreconstructible barbarians. We accept willingly any useful stimulus that workers in neighboring fields may have to offer. Yet, in one way, we are resolved to use the specialist's technique: the outside help we look for should not consist of theoretic generalities but should help to solve our individual problems. The reader will soon realize that our approach to the theory of our own field is very cautious. We do not attempt conclusions without having discussed characteristic examples on which they may be based. Therefore the outside information we want must itself be specific. General statements about the nature of primitive religion, for instance, do not help us. But the fact that under religious or superstitious impulses a member of some African tribe will change his name, and thorough information about the circumstances in which this happens, can be illuminating.

No desire to be fashionable, however, led us to our method. Close collaboration between the study of language and other fields is not to us a matter of fashion but a necessity. Whether a linguist, by ignoring the traditional frontiers of his domain, can make a valid contribution to a "system of ideas concerning the world and man" remains to be seen. One thing, however, is certain. Language, a function growing out of life, reflecting every phase and aspect of life, and influencing life, cannot be treated as a subject independent of the realities it represents. The alliance of history, sociology, and psychology with linguistics, therefore, may provide the key to any kind of linguistic problem, be it a detail of etymology or the intricate play of language and thought upon each other.

We have often been able to practice the collaboration we believe in because fortunately we could use the collections of the *Dictionary of Political Words and Phrases,* a project now in progress under the sponsorship of the Graduate School of the Ohio State University. We find it a pleasant duty likewise to acknowledge our debt to the English Department of the Ohio State University, and especially to its chairman, Professor James F. Fullington, who with his usual grace and generosity has given us help, time, and the gift of his own interest. To record the help of Professor Stanley K. Coffman, now of the University of Oklahoma, Travis Trittschuh, Nancy Mason Dasher, whose editorial experience and skill has improved our manuscript throughout, and Alice Estrich and Anna Luise Shearer, is to record our gratitude and their excellence.

R.M.E.
H.S.

Columbus, Ohio
March, 1952

CONTENTS

THREE KEYS TO LANGUAGE

Chapter One

WORD-TABOOS AMONG PRIMITIVE PEOPLE

IN language, many things can be made clear by a study of typical speech situations. By this term we mean situations in life which make it necessary that something should be said or, on the other hand, that some things should *not* be mentioned. Situations of the first type, and speech reactions resulting from them—e.g., your "Hello!" in meeting a friend or your "Thanks!" when somebody has done you a favor—are so extremely common, and in many cases so commonplace, that they do not appear very suitable to stimulate linguistic thinking. On the other hand, those of the second type—speech situations involving a "Don't!" —are often of a more striking nature and therefore provide a much more suitable starting point for the understanding of language and its ways.

We begin our investigation, therefore, with an analysis of a few situations of the "don't" type.

The following passage is taken from Stephen Powers' description of the habits of the Wintūn, an Indian tribe in California:

The name of the dead is never mentioned more, forever and ever. He has gone to the sky, he has ascended *ol'-lel hon ha'-ra,* and gone to the Happy Western Land. Standing beneath the blue, broad vault of heaven, little groups of mourners with bated breath and whispering voices will point out to one another imaginary "spirit-roads" (*klesh yem'-mel*) among the stars. With vague longings and futile questionings they seek to solve the time-old mystery of death and the grave. But the name is heard no more on earth. If some one in a group of merry talkers, assembled to while a weary hour and patter the gossip of the *campoody,* inadvertently mentions the name, another in a hoarse whisper cries out *"Ki-dach'-i-da!"* ("It is a dead person!") and straightway there falls upon all an awful silence. No words can describe the shuddering and heart-sickening terror which seizes upon them at the utterance of that fearful word.[1]

The customs of primitive peoples frequently exhibit features which, if not devoid of a logic of their own, still strike the modern mind as nearly unintelligible. Properly understood, they are based upon unexceptional logic, but the results to which this logic leads are surprising to minds used only to the ways of Western European culture. We know, for instance, of tribes that would not permit their chief to have his hair cut unless he had first dined on human meat. Elsewhere it is strictly forbidden to spill royal blood, but this inhibition applies only in its literal sense: a chieftain may not be stabbed, but it is quite permissible to starve or burn him to death, since this can be done without bloodshed. Compared to these and similar customs, of which any number can be found described in Sir James Frazer's standard work *The Golden Bough,* the name-taboo of the Wintūn appears neither nonsensical nor inaccessible to modern feeling.

In fact, our experience warns us that we ourselves can act in a very similar fashion. Here is an illustration from the story of so typically modern a figure as a great physicist. Marie Curie, after the death of her husband,

> . . . took a singular decision: that of never speaking of their father to the orphans. This choice was, above all, due to a physical impossibility in her. Until the end of her days it was with the greatest difficulty that Marie could pronounce "Pierre" or "Pierre Curie" or "your father" or "my husband," and her conversation, in order to get round the little islets of memory, was to employ incredible stratagems. She

[1] Stephen Powers, *Tribes of California, Contributions to North American Ethnology* (Washington: United States Department of the Interior, 1877), III, 240.

did not judge this silence to be blameworthy with regard to her daughters. Rather than plunge them into an atmosphere of tragedy, she deprived them, and deprived herself, of noble emotions.[2]

The historical perspective which this anecdote opens is matched only by the questions it arouses. Is it that the people whom we sometimes haughtily call primitive are capable of just as fine emotions as the most sophisticated moderns? Or do we humbly have to recognize the fact that even the most sophisticated modern still has a fund of primitive reactions within himself? Reactions so primitive that they make one doubt whether a few thousand years mean very much in the progress of human development. The answer to both questions must probably be "yes." But whatever it is, the example shows the potentialities of the study of language as a most fertile source for the study of human behavior.

If the similarities are striking, the differences between "primitive" and "modern" people are no less revealing: among ourselves, as well as among the Indians, we find the same tendency to speak in a subdued voice, the same silence produced by any tactless reference to the deceased, the same likelihood that the ideas and utterances of the bereaved will circle around the mysteries of life and death. On the other hand, there are differences that should not be overlooked. Among the Indians the name of the dead is strictly and lastingly *tabooed,* while among ourselves the inhibition can be broken or rather circumvented by the use of certain linguistic precautions, phrases like "our unforgettable friend Charles," "die selige Marie," "Simon Glendinning, that is now happy." [3] In any case, our own unwillingness to use a deceased person's name will soon wear out so that after a comparatively short time the inhibition will have disappeared. Also among civilized people the reaction against a blunder will be much less violent. An inconsiderate reference to a dead person might cause an embarrassed

[2] Eve Curie, *Madame Curie,* trans. by Vincent Sheean (New York: Doubleday & Company, 1937), p. 268. Reprinted by permission of Doubleday & Company, publishers.

[3] Sir Walter Scott, *The Monastery,* Chap. 4.

silence, but certainly no "shuddering and heart-sickening terror," much less any punitive act of the sort described in the following passage:

[Among the Karok in California] the highest crime one can commit is the *pet-chi-é-ri,* the mere mention of the dead relative's name. It is a deadly insult to the survivors, and can be atoned for only by the same amount of blood-money paid for willful murder. In default of that they will have the villain's blood.[4]

The main difference, however, appears to be one of motivation rather than of gradation. What deters us against indiscreet use of a dead person's name is the fear that in doing so we may cause pain by reviving the sense of loss, or the unwillingness to revive our own or another's painful memories and thereby prolong the period of depression. The whole question is a matter of social tact or, as with Mme Curie, educational tact combined with an acute sense of personal loss. But there is today no penalty attached to a breach of such tact except that one may incur the disapproval of sensitive people. Primitive peoples, on the other hand, are afraid of much more serious consequences than those resulting from a *faux pas:*

It is easy to arrive at some of the motives which render the savages so averse to speak of the dead. In one instance, when one of the Kŭrnai was spoken to about a dead friend, soon after the decease, he said, looking round uneasily: "Do not do that, he might hear you and kill me." [5]

From this report and an abundance of similar ones, it becomes clear that the avoidance of a dead person's name, as practiced by the natives in all parts of the world, arises from the same motive that dominates their whole behavior after a death has occurred: the fear that the spirit of the deceased may return and harm the survivors. Under no conditions does the native want to excite the attention of a ghost by pronouncing

---

[4] Powers, *op. cit.*, p. 33.

[5] A. W. Howitt, "On Some Australian Beliefs," *Journal of the Anthropological Institute of Great Britain and Ireland* (London: 1884), XIII, 191.

his name. From the same motive, he will also endeavor to render himself unrecognizable, or at least inconspicuous, by cutting his hair, by changing into a less colorful attire, or by plastering himself with mud. (Numerous examples are given in Frazer's *The Golden Bough* and *The Fear of the Dead in Primitive Religion*. The analogy with modern customs, like the wearing of black, and of arm bands, and of veils, is obvious.) Very likely the survivor will also deposit the deceased's most valued possessions in the grave so that the ghost will have no need to come and get them—a widespread custom to which we are indebted for large parts of the material on which the science of archaeology is based.

It is not too early to state two important theoretical conclusions: (1) Speech in a given situation is only a part of a general reaction made by the person involved. The work of such anthropologists as Bronislaw Malinowski, Clyde Kluckhohn, and Ruth Benedict has shown that each detail of behavior in a given culture is a part of a cultural nexus. Every detail of what is said is conditioned, therefore, by the characteristics of the situation, many of which have no direct connection with language. On the other hand, the same motives that affect man's linguistic reactions will also condition his nonlinguistic behavior. The man who holds the door open for an elderly gentleman and at the same time says, "After you, sir," is doing two different things with exactly the same motivation. (2) Analogies to similar speech situations in the speech reactions of different persons or peoples do not necessarily show that the reasons are identical. The reactions of modern and of primitive mourners are in many respects the same, but the motivation is entirely different: among civilized people, fear of appearing inconsiderate; among the aborigines, fear of ghosts. Such change of motivation is typical. Similar changes will appear in subsequent problems throughout this book.

Not only the name-taboo in general, however, but also several connected features have undergone a change of motivation. Take, for instance, the tendency to speak in subdued tones for some time after a death has occurred. To the native, this is not, or at least not exclusively, a matter of tact but part of the precautions which are necessitated by the possibility that the ghost might be listening:

Of the tribes on the Lower Murray we are told that when a person dies "they carefully avoid mentioning his name; but if compelled to do so, they pronounce it in a very low whisper, so faint that they imagine the spirit cannot hear their voice." [6]

Having now discovered the forceful character of primitive name-taboo, we may expect that the consequences to language of a man's death will not be exhausted by the impoverishment resulting from the mere avoidance of his name. Every element in language more or less connected with the name of the deceased may fall under a secondary taboo. Here is a supposedly accurate translation of what a member of the Masai tribe in Southern Africa had to say about the taboo in question:

On the death of a child, or a warrior, or a woman amongst the Masai, the body is thrown away, and the person's name is buried, i.e. it is never again mentioned by the family.

Should there be anything which is called by that name, it is given another name which is not like that of the deceased.

For instance, if an unimportant person called Ol-onana (he who is soft, or weak, or gentle) were to die, gentleness would not be called en-nanai in that kraal, as it is the name of a corpse, but it would be called by another name, such as epolpol (it is smooth).

And if anybody of that kraal were to ask for news of the great medicine-man Ol-onana, he would call him Ol-opolpol.

If an elder dies leaving children, his name is not buried, for his descendants are named after him.[7]

---

[6] G. F. Angas, *Savage Life and Scenes in Australia and New Zealand* (London: 1847), I, 94, quoted in James G. Frazer, *The Golden Bough,* 3d ed. (London: Macmillan & Co., 1914), III, 351.

[7] A. C. Hollis, *The Masai* (New York: Oxford University Press, 1905), pp. 304–305. By permission of Oxford University Press. Notice the difference in tone between this report and the quotation from Powers given on page 1. Hollis says nothing but what his native informants told him and, insofar as this is possible in translation, he uses their proper words. Powers, on the other hand, in describing the natives' reactions, produces a mixture

Before we discuss the main portions of this report, we wish to call attention to its last sentence in which it is stated that the name-taboo does not apply to the families of prominent persons. Among these, evidently, motives of family pride get the better of fear, and the name of the deceased, far from being suppressed, is perpetuated by being conferred on younger members of his family.

Here, for the first time, we come into contact with the social side of linguistic behavior. It is not only the speech situation that matters, but also the rank of the persons concerned. In fact, as the preceding example shows, similar speech situations may lead to entirely different speech reactions, according to the social standing of the speaker and of the persons spoken of. The great of this world have prerogatives, here as well as in other fields of behavior—a fact which language quickly and constantly reveals. To digress for a moment into another word-taboo, that against profanity, Shakespeare shows accurate understanding of the social implications of speech when he has Hotspur tease that great lady, his wife, for swearing with the tame gentility of the middle classes:

> Hear! you swear like a comfit-maker's wife! . . .
> Swear me, Kate, like a lady as thou art,
> A good mouth-filling oath, and leave 'in sooth,'
> And such protest of pepper-gingerbread,
> To velvet-guards and Sunday citizens.[8]

Returning to the Masai name-taboo, we learn that linguistic etiquette is not satisfied in suppressing the name of a dead person merely as a proper name. Since it is a widespread custom to use designations of animals, things, and abstract qual-

---

of facts and personal impressions that, artistic though it may be, does not carry a guarantee of absolute reliability. It is of the utmost importance, of course, that a student of linguistics, as well as any other scientific worker, be aware of the specific character of each of his sources. In the main, he will prefer matter-of-fact reports to descriptions tinged by the personal feelings of the author. But it would be a mistake to consider sources of the latter sort as altogether devoid of scientific value.

[8] Shakespeare, *Henry IV, Part I,* Act III, scene 1, lines 252–261.

ities as personal names—English family names like Bird and Wolfe, or first names like Rose, Violet, Grace offer modern examples—the name-taboo would be incomplete and ineffective if the dangerous word were continued in its nonpersonal function. How, indeed, in hearing the accustomed sound of his name, should the defunct Mr. Ol-onana (Softy) know that no allusion to his person is intended but that simply something soft is spoken of? On the other hand, while it is certainly possible to avoid all talk about a dead person, it is hardly feasible to create a state of things in which a language would be without a word for the idea of softness or gentleness. A substitute word must therefore be found, and an easy way of achieving this aim consists in letting a word of similar meaning, but of different sound, replace the tabooed one—for a short period of time or, as the case may be, permanently. If the latter be true, the vocabulary of the language in question will have undergone a durable change. It is important to note in this connection that linguistic changes may be caused by reasons which, in themselves, have nothing to do with language—a fact that may sound paradoxical but is of great theoretical importance.

Although linguistic details have to be isolated, they are still part of a general picture, most meaningful when seen as an integrated part of a total social context. In our next example, which deals with the complicated and far-reaching name-taboos of the Zulu, we are happy to have the details we are seeking appear in their setting:

> "There are three kinds of *Hlonipa* [the native word for taboo, derived from a word meaning 'shame' and indicating that 'they are ashamed, or too polite, to use the names of great people, or such others as they pay respect to, in the common speech of every day']—the *family,* the *tribal,* and in the case of the Zulus, the *national.* The first is confined to the women, as far as speech is concerned. They will not mention the name of their father-in-law, and they hide, or appear to hide, whenever they come in contact with their son-in-law. . . .
>
> "All the females in any way related to the girl's family will call her husband *Umkweniana,* but never by his name; and when he has

children grown up they will call him father of So-and-so. They think it is not respectful to call him by his name, and this is the case also with all young persons to old ones. The son-in-law too will not call his mother-in-law by her name, but simply mother, and the wife is generally called So-and-so of So-and-so, child of her father.

. . . . .

"The higher the rank of the parties the more strictly is the etiquette observed. At the king's kraal it is sometimes difficult to understand his wives, as they *Hlonipa* even the very sound of the name of the king's fathers, his and their brothers back for generations. They will not say *wenzani* ('What are you doing?') but, *wenkani,* because the sound of the *z* comes in *Enzenzengakona* . . .—Panda's [the king's] father. The same with water—*amanzi.* They call it *amandambi.* . . .

. . . . .

"The tribal *Hlonipa* is a much simpler affair. It is merely that no individual of any of the tribes which now constitute Zulu will use the name of their chief or his progenitors, as far as they remember, in the common parlance of every day. As, for instance, the Zungu tribe say *mata* for *manzi* (water), and *inkosta* for *tshanti* (grass), and *embigatdu* for *umkondo* (assegai), and *inyatugo* for *enhlela* (path), because their present chief is *Umfan-o inhlela*—his father was *Manzini,* his grandfather *Imkondo,* and one before him *Tshani;* the national *Hlonipa* is all the tribes omitting the king's name. . . . For instance, the root of a tree they call *nxabo*—whereas the true name is *impando.* Also the hill now known as *Entabankulu* was *Empandwene.*" [9]

Among the most interesting implications of Leslie's report is this: the name-taboo starts out as a merely negative factor in the development of language; but since it necessitates numerous substitute words, it becomes a stimulating force and produces a creative attitude toward language. The final result of the word coining provoked by it is, among the Zulu and, without doubt, among many other peoples, a large stock of

[9] David Leslie, *Among the Zulus and Amatongas,* 2d ed. (Edinburgh: 1875), quoted by J. G. Frazer, *Anthologia Anthropologica: The Native Races of Africa and Madagascar* (London: Humphries & Co., 1938), pp. 74–76.

synonyms; and since, in the case of tribal word-taboos, the range of prohibition is geographically restricted, there arise local differences within the national vocabulary, somewhat comparable in this respect to the dialects of modern languages.

The way in which this coining of new expressions works is not, according to Leslie, easily observed, since the custom of Hlonipa is a very ancient one, which usually makes available a ready-made substitute when it becomes necessary to taboo a certain word. Still, he gives a few useful hints on this subject.

. . . I claim that the practice [of Hlonipa] is one of great antiquity, as the language, at this present time, almost presents the phenomenon of a double one. There is scarcely a word in it applicable to a proper name—at least so far as I have enquired—which has not its corresponding *Hlonipa;* and in a case in which it might happen so—I have never heard of one which did—those interested should gather together and decide what they were to say.

As one of Panda's sisters, who is an old woman and well versed in the etiquette, described to me—some might propose one name, the others might object, saying that it was not a nice one . . . and at last they would agree to call him So-and-so.

If they could, they would find a word as near as possible to the meaning of that which they had laid aside. . . . As for example, *empise* (a wolf) they call *engadule,* because he is a great traveller—to *gadula* means to wander—or *umdela-'btonga,* one who despises sleep, because of his nocturnal habits. . . . *Idtsbe,* a stone, they called *egaio,* which may be translated "the grinder," because they grind their corn on stones. But on the other hand, they call *implisio,* the heart, *inkeddamu. Inhlela,* a path, *inyatugo inkomo.* . . . In all these latter *Hlonipa* names, I can discover no connection at all with the real ones. And a greater proof and one which to my mind is incontestable, is that all the different tribes in Zululand have different *Hlonipa* terms for the same words. Thus *mandambi* is the king's kraal *Hlonipa* for water, because of the same sound as in *manzi* being in *Ensenzangakona,* the name of Panda's father. *Mahda* is the Ziangu *Hlonipa* for water, because of Manzini, the father of their present chief. . . . And that has caused the language to be not only a double one, as I have said, but in the case of multitudes of words, they have three or four to express the same meaning. . . .[10]

[10] *Ibid.,* pp. 76–77.

You will probably have to read these last excerpts twice, since the quotation is condensed and loaded with strange words; but it will pay to do so, in order to achieve a thorough grasp of the matter: Almost every detail of this description can help us to understand important features in modern language. The close connection between speech and social institutions, the splitting up of a language into dialects, the formation of a rich supply of synonyms—all these problems are of the greatest importance to our own speech, and much more will have to be said about them as our investigation progresses. In Leslie's description of the Zulu name-taboo and its consequences may be discovered the very roots of these phenomena or, let us say, one of their roots, since any feature of language may be the result of several concurrent developments.

Note that in modern language, social speech conventions, dialects, and synonyms are three strictly different things. All three, however, have a common root in a more primitive stage: the conditions created by the necessity of avoiding certain words are apt to influence language in all of these several aspects.

Again and again, as this book proceeds, we shall find that the beginnings and causes of apparently disconnected features in language can be shown to be closely interrelated. It is essential that we learn to think of language not as an accumulation of isolated facts, nor of sharply defined groups of facts such as word-formation, syntax, and so on, but as a complicated maze of interlocking phenomena, within which every change is likely to produce influences in many different directions. All deeper understanding of language, and much of the fascination of linguistic studies, depends on the ability to trace such hidden connections. It is evident, however, that this aim cannot be reached by studying language in its modern forms only. Hence the emphasis that the science of linguistics puts on the historic development of the several languages.

With these things in mind, we will not be surprised to find that the avoidance of dead people's names is only a special case among a great mass of word-taboos observed among primitive tribes. Our last quotations have already shown that the names of living people as well as of dead ones may not be pronounced by members of their family, and that—naturally, since the tribe is nothing more than an enlarged family—the names of chieftains are conscientiously avoided by all members of their clan. It is not difficult to understand this extension of the name-taboo from the dead to the living. The connecting link can be found in a widespread unwillingness to mention the names of men engaged in war or in other dangerous enterprises, since, for all the speaker knows, they might already be dead. It is a well-known fact, moreover, that superstitious precaution, once established, is frequently carried further than mere logical thinking appears to warrant. The atmosphere, once established, creates an ever-widening circle of taboo. Since in many cases the use of a proper name is believed to be dangerous, and since the boundary line between permissible and prohibited uses of a person's name is often hard to define, it is considered safest to avoid personal names as much as possible, particularly those of prominent people. Among many native tribes these precautions are carried so far that no man would willingly reveal his own name to a stranger. In this case, the motivation may be different, although still closely connected with superstitious fear: curses and acts of black magic are considered more dangerous if the enemy is in a position to name his intended victim. That the names of gods and demons are included in the name-taboo need hardly be mentioned. Dangerous animals and, of course, sacred animals are likewise unmentionable. The following example shows how the atmosphere of taboo speech, once established, will affect a great many words that have no direct connection with the original sphere of the taboo. When engaged in the important business of gathering camphor, the Malay people use a special vocabulary, in which words related not only to this occupation but also to a great many others are replaced:

It would seem that the Malay Taboo languages resort occasionally to Arabic (*e.g. kĕlbu,* "heart," for "life"), Sanskrit (*e.g. bayu,* "wind"), and archaic Malay (*e.g. hulu,* "head"; *tohok,* "spear") . . . hence, doubtless, the acceptance in the Camphor Taboo of such words as *sĕngkrat,* "rhinoceros"; *sīap,* "cold"; *jokūt,* "pig," and the like, which are reported to be still preserved among some of the Jakun tribes in their everyday speech.[11]

As with other features of taboo language, this use of the foreign substitute extends into more civilized cultures. To take obvious examples, our own sensibilities are not shocked by any reference to body parts, processes, and functions so long as they are named by Greek and Latin words; the use of the native equivalents is usually forbidden in polite society. With much the same motivation we have also borrowed many a French word such as *liaison, gigolo,* and even *fille de joie* to describe amiably situations and people by which or by whom we would have to be offended if we named them in English.

To sum up, now, at the very outset of our investigation, we hope we have made a good case for the general viewpoints stated in our preface. It would be impossible to understand primitive word-taboos without considering a psychological motive—fear—behind language inhibitions. It would be equally impossible to overlook the many social implications of name-taboo. And finally the fact that our modern attitude appears to be connected in direct line with primitive usage makes a historical look at the problem essential.

[11] C. O. Blagden and W. W. Skeat, *The Pagan Races of the Malay Peninsula* (London: Macmillan & Co., 1906), II, 423–424.

Chapter Two

PRIMITIVE WORD-TABOOS AMONG CIVILIZED NATIONS

THE layman may wonder why university catalogues are full of such courses as Anglo-Saxon, Old French, Sanskrit, and other dead forms of speech. Is the scholar, in his choice between scientific progress and scientific traditions, vacillating—if not outright conservative? Some things in language, however, can be understood only by the use of historical methods. If the language reactions of a modern woman like Mme Curie are essentially the same, under certain conditions, as those of primitive women, then it is language which is conservative, not the student thereof. The connection between what we have learned about word avoidance in the speech of primitive peoples and the residuum of similar habits in our own speech may be further clarified by a few references to European folklore, ancient and modern.

The Eddic poem dealing with Sigurth's (Siegfried's) slaying of the dragon begins as follows:

> Sigurth and Regin went up to the Gnita Heath and found there the tracks of Fafnir [the dragon] where it was his wont to go for water. There dug Sigurth a great ditch and hid himself in it. Now when Fafnir left his lair on the gold, he spewed poison and it flowed from above on Sigurth's head. But when Fafnir crept over the ditch, Sigurth

thrust his sword into the dragon's heart. Fafnir shook himself and beat (the ground) with his head and his tail. Sigurth lept out of the ditch, and they saw one another. Fafnir said:

"Thou fellow bold,—what thy father's kin?
Youth, from what house doest hail?
In Fafnir's blood thy brand is reddened,
In my heart standeth thy steel."

Sigurth withheld his name; for it was the belief in olden times that the words of a doomed man had great might, if he cursed his foe by name. He said:

"Stag I am hight, homeless I wandered,
I am a motherless man;
No father had I as folks do else:
Ever fare I unfriended." [1]

The Icelandic original of this poem has come down to us in a thirteenth-century manuscript. But probably the lay, before being taken down in writing, had been in oral circulation for several hundred years. It may be more than a thousand years old. It reveals habits like those discussed in the preceding chapter. When the author of the prose narrative linking the lyrics says that "it was the belief in olden times . . . ," he seems to imply that, by around 1250, the Germanic people had outgrown such beliefs. Yet traces of these ways of thinking and acting are still to be found in remote corners of the Germanic world. Scandinavia, the home of the Eddas, although at present notably progressive, was only a few years ago full of these traditions:

Formerly it was very common among our [Norwegian] fishermen that they while fishing on the sea, never gave a thing its right name, but applied invented names both to men and animals, which now have gone out of use or at least are not used except by way of fun. Thus, they called a priest "Sidkofte" [longfrock] . . . a cow "Sidhale" [longtail], a horse "Fiirfötting" [fourfooting], etc. . . . [2]

---

[1] Lee M. Hollander, trans., *The Poetic Edda* (Austin: University of Texas Press, 1928), pp. 261–262. Reprinted by permission of the University of Texas Press, publishers.

[2] Translated from H. Ström, *Beskrivelse over Söndmöre,* I, 536, as quoted by Jakob Jakobsen, *Det norröne Sprog paa Shetland* (Copenhagen: W. Prior, 1897), p. 83.

Similar customs are reported from other northern countries. Especially rich is the material from the Shetland Islands, collected and discussed by Jakob Jakobsen in the study from which we have just quoted.[3] He gives hundreds of "lucky words" (substitute words replacing tabooed ones) used by fishermen while engaged in their trade. Most of these terms are clearly of Scandinavian origin, although the Norwegian dialect originally spoken on these islands has long ago been superseded by Scottish idiom. The parallel to what Skeat tells us about the Malayan "camphor language" is striking. Here as well as there, taboo language preserves words from an older language kept alive by their superstitious and, perhaps, religious connotations, in accordance with the conservative tendency of both superstitious and religious language. It is important to notice that neglect of these superstitions is punished. Probably a fisherman would not himself be conscious of a religious thought in dealing out a box on the ear (a situation described in our next quotation), but such drastic punishment for violating the taboo strongly suggests that behind it lies a blurred memory of religious dread. Also, in Northern Europe as well as among the Malay tribes, the speech prohibitions are not general ones but apply only to men engaged in the pursuit of certain types of work; clearly, there exists a connection between taboo language and professional language. Jakobsen further points out that taboo speech in the Shetlands is different in the several islands of the group, thus contributing, as among the Zulus, to the development of local dialects. Jakobsen suggests that

> . . . sea-terms have probably from the beginning been some sort of religious words. Since the sea, which was believed to be under the protection of special divinities, was an element upon which the fisherman, in a certain way, could be considered an intruder, it must have been of importance to show respect to the sea demons, in order to propitiate them: to neglect this would cause, according to the superstition, bad success in fishing, if nothing worse. Only one generation ago the observance of these customs was insisted on with great strictness on Shetland. To name the priest, the cat, the knife, the end of

[3] *Ibid.*, pp. 82 ff.

the fishing line etc. by their proper names, was a transgression which frequently led to instant punishment (for instance, a box on the ear) of the thoughtless young man who in this way spoiled the day's fishing.[4]

If this theory be correct, the analogy between the language of Scandinavian fishers and of aboriginal tribes is indeed a close one.

What a mine of folklore the novels of Sir Walter Scott are, every lover of his work knows. As a simple realist, he is informed and accurate. And, for the student who prefers to get his material from fact rather than from fiction, Scott often gives in a note the direct evidence upon which he has based a scene. Here is a dialogue between a man and his wife on their way through a region believed to be a favorite haunt of the fairies.

"But let us go our way; the trash that is left I can come back for. There is nae ane to stir it but the good neighbours, and they—"

"For the love of God, goodman," said his wife, in a remonstrating tone, "haud your peace! Think what ye're saying, and we hae sae muckle wild land to go over before we win to the girth gate."

The husband nodded acquiescence; for it was deemed highly imprudent to speak of the fairies, either by their title of *good neighbours* or by any other, especially when about to pass the places which they were supposed to haunt.[5]

If it be doubted that there is a good deal of folkloristic truth behind this piece of fiction, it is removed by Scott himself, who, in a note, tells the following story:

This superstition continues to prevail, though one would suppose it must now be antiquated. It is only a year or two since an itinerant puppet show-man . . . brought a complaint of a singular nature before the author, as Sheriff of Selkirkshire. The singular dexterity with which the show-man had exhibited the machinery of his little stage, had, upon a Selkirk fair-day, excited the eager curiosity of some mechanics of Galashiels. These men, from no worse motive that could be discovered than a thirst after knowledge beyond their sphere, committed a burglary upon the barn in which the pup-

[4] Jakobsen, *loc. cit.*

[5] Sir Walter Scott, *The Monastery,* Chap. III.

pets had been consigned to repose, and carried them off in the nook of their plaids, when returning from Selkirk to their own village.

"But with the morning cool reflection came." The party found, however, they could not make Punch dance, and that the whole troop were equally intractable; they had also, perhaps, some apprehensions of the Rhadamanth of the district; and, willing to be quit of their booty, they left the puppets seated in a grove by the side of the Ettrick, where they were sure to be touched by the first beams of the rising sun. Here a shepherd, who was on foot with sunrise to pen his master's sheep on a field of turnips, to his utter astonishment, saw this train, profusely gay, sitting in the little grotto. His examination proceeded thus:—

Sheriff.—You saw these gay-looking things? what did you think they were?

Shepherd.—Ou, I am no that free to say what I might think they were.

Sheriff.—Come, lad, I must have a direct answer—who did you think they were?

Shepherd.—Ou, sir, troth I am no that free to say that I mind wha I might think they were.

Sheriff.—Come, come, sir! I ask you distinctly: did you think they were the fairies you saw?

Shepherd.—Indeed, sir, and I winna say but I might think it was the Good Neighbours.

Thus unwillingly was he brought to allude to the irritable and captious inhabitants of fairy land.[6]

Doubt of religion as the creative force behind the taboos of the Shetland fisherman hardly holds here. Some may prefer to call avoidance of the names of fairies and other such beings superstitious rather than religious, and with this we would not quarrel. But we would point out that the line separating the two is very indefinite. Superstition is often religion on a lower level.

The Shetland example has brought us to the problems of professional language. The speech habits of similar occupations show similar features. It is only natural that the language of hunters and hawkers, as it has persisted from the Middle Ages

[6] *Ibid.*, Note D.

into our own time, offers striking resemblances to the speech of the Shetland fishers—whether in its outward aspects only or by virtue of an organic connection remains to be decided. In speaking of the actions of animals, of the parts of their bodies, of the methods of chasing them, and so on, a person skilled in venery or falconry will refuse to use the common vocabulary. Instead, special terms are used which are not found in everyday speech or which, in common language, have a different and usually less specific meaning. Great emphasis has been put, at least in Europe, on the necessity for every adept of these pursuits to learn this professional terminology correctly.

The *Book of St. Albans,* for instance, a treatise on hawking, hunting, and heraldry published in 1486, not only opens with a chapter on "the maner to speke of hawkis fro an eeg to thei be habull to be takene," but again and again warns the reader not to use unprofessional terms:

> And we shall say that hawkis doon Eyer, and not brede, in the woodes. And we shall say that hawkys doon draw when they bere tymbering to their nestes, and nott they beld ne make ther nestes. And in the tyme of their loue they call, and not kauke. (Fol. a2)
>
> Here shal ye vnderstonde furthermore other maner of termys that belong vn to hawkis for to commende them for diuerse of theyr propirteis.
>
> First ye shall say This is a fayr hawke, an hudge hauke a long hawke, a short thike hawke, & say not this is a grete hawke. also ye shall say this hawke has a large beke Or a shortt beke, and call it not bille. (Fol. a6)
>
> . . . in kyndeli spech ye shall say youre hawke hath Nomme or seesid a fowle and not take it. (Fol. a7) [7]

In spite of the outward similarity of this terminology to the primitive word-taboos maintained by hunters and fishers in Scandinavia and elsewhere, we cannot assert with absolute confidence that the language of falconry, as documented by the *Book of St. Albans* and other sources, has its origin in speech inhibitions arising from superstition. It is entirely possible and

[7] Dame Juliana Berners, *The Boke of Saint Albans,* reproduced in facsimile (London: Elliot Stock, n.d.).

indeed probable, but if so, evidently the original motive has been forgotten. Neither in the *Book of St. Albans* nor, so far as we know, in any similar work do we find any indication that the insistence on a special terminology arises from the fear of offending a supernatural power. On the other hand, it is not simply a specialized and technical terminology of the sort that every professional group is bound to use. It is evidently intended to win the approval of the listeners, in whose eyes the correct manner of using professional speech is a proof of thorough craftsmanship and of good standing in the aristocratic circle of hunters and hawkers. The full aristocratic significance of this vocabulary is made clear by Sir Thomas Malory's comment about Sir Tristram, who, according to the legend, was not only a mighty hunter but

> . . . began good measures of blowing of beasts of venery, and beasts of chase, and all manner of vermin, and all these terms we have yet of hawking and hunting. And therefore the book of venery, of hawking, and hunting, is called the book of Sir Tristram. Wherefore, as meseemeth, all gentlemen that bear old arms ought of right to honour Sir Tristram for the goodly terms that gentlemen have and use, and shall to the day of doom, that thereby in a manner all men of worship may dissever a gentleman from a yeoman, and from a yeoman a villain. For he that gentle is will draw him unto gentle tatches, and to follow the customs of noble gentlemen.[8]

Whether it will last "to the day of doom" is a matter for conjecture, but it is true that such social evaluation of hunting terminology and its correct use still persists in England and elsewhere, in communities in which hunting remains an aristocratic sport.

German hunters used to be severe in enforcing the correct use of their professional vocabulary:

> Every mistake in the language of hunters and in hunting actions and usages was formerly at big hunts punished by the blow of the hunting knife, and even now if a hunter makes such a mistake this

---

[8] Sir Thomas Malory, *Le Morte Darthur* (London: Macmillan & Co., 1925), Book VIII, Chap. III.

punishment ought rightfully be laid upon him. To do so one proceeds in the following way: the delinquent has to lie down over [the carcass of] a hunt-worthy hart or a big sow and receive three licks or blows with the hunting knife on his posterior, either from the master of the hunt or from a master forester, according to his rank. . . . Afterwards the culprit has to give thanks for just punishment by bowing to the hunting company.[9]

The existence of an elaborate ritual, as well as the fact that higher rank evidently does not exempt the offender from undergoing a drastic punishment, is certainly in favor of the theory, first illustrated by the similar practices of the Shetland fishermen, that more serious considerations than mere social usage have been active in creating this ceremonial. In other words, these factors appear to favor the derivation of modern hunting language from word-taboos based on superstition. It is, however, clear that to Hartig the correct handling of this terminology is a matter of social prestige and, therefore, another example, like the illustration from the life of Mme Curie, of changing motivation behind a continued taboo practice. Clearly, taboos tend to become matters of social relation when they lose their original meaning:

Therefore I strongly recommend not only learning . . . the language of the hunting art but also always speaking it correctly, because it unquestionably belongs to venery and no writing on hunting can thoroughly be understood without it, and furthermore because it is the means by which in social intercourse one proves oneself *an accomplished hunter* [als gebildeten Jäger].[10]

It is only natural, in a country where hunting has never been the privilege of the rich alone, and where the use of a special terminology of field sports has carried social distinction only among a few small groups, that this part of the vocabulary should be less richly developed. Both that fact and the reaction of the professional to it is evident in the following quotation:

[9] Translated from Georg Ludwig Hartig, *Lehrbuch für Jäger und die es werden wollen* (Vienna: Schaumburg und Compagnie, ca. 1810), II, 260.

[10] *Ibid.*, I, 10 (translated).

It has been suggested . . . that the appropriate sporting nomenclature and terms are so little understood, or so much neglected here, that a brief compilation of the most remarkable in general use, would be an addition to this work, not unacceptable to the sporting world of America.[11]

---

[11] H. W. Herbert, *Frank Forester's Field Sports of the United States, and British Provinces, of North America,* 6th ed. (New York: Stringer & Townsend, 1848), II, 311.

Chapter Three

WORD-TABOOS ON HIGHER CULTURAL LEVELS

ONE thing stands out very clearly from our illustrations: the survival or disappearance of the hunting vocabulary is not decided by forces within language. The recent House of Commons Bill for the Protection of Animals (Hunting and Coursing Prohibition) was a phase of the current social and political struggle in Great Britain over aristocratic privilege. If this attack ever succeeds (introduced in 1948–1949, the bill was defeated February 25, 1949), then hunting language is doomed. As long as it fails, privileged people and rural people in England will go on emphasizing their social standing or their rural culture by using a vocabulary of their own.

Similarly, factors outside language influence that province of language which, up to our own day, preserves more word-taboos than any other—the religious, in which a struggle similar to that over hunting words has been going on for centuries. The conflict is not primarily between upper and lower classes, it is true, but rather between the conservative spirit and the spirit of rebellion. The second Biblical commandment, which forbids us to take the name of God in vain, although interpreted with varying degrees of stringency, is still an active force in our speech habits, both positively and negatively.

We have pointed out above that taboos are apt to extend their scope. Religious taboos are no exception. It is often hard to decide whether, in a certain case, a word should be avoided or whether, considering the circumstances, its use might be deemed legitimate. In cases of this sort, the conscientious believer will usually find it safe to make the prohibition an unconditional one. The Old Testament's attitude in regard to the name of the deity offers a very good example. Although it is only the "vain" use of God's name that is forbidden, its avoidance in the Hebrew Bible is so scrupulous that we do not know the actual Hebrew word for God. *Adonai* (the Lord), *Jehovah* (probably transformed from an expression meaning "He who is"), and all the other synonyms are clearly substitute words. The practices of the New Testament and later Christian usage are much less strict, but remnants of the old prohibition still persist. Many persons find the exclamation "God be praised" objectionable (not, of course, when uttered in thanksgiving or prayer or in a sermon, but whenever introduced into everyday speech), while these same persons may have no scruples at all against the expression "The Lord be praised." It is evident that the substitute word "the Lord" is under a less stringent prohibition than the undisguised name of God.

Perhaps not in many recent books, but certainly in works printed during the nineteenth century and earlier—and often during the first quarter of the twentieth—you will find typographical evidence of the prohibition in question, in that the word *God* is replaced by *G—d, G—,* or just by a dash:

> The duchess, who did not love hypocrisy, would not actually assent to this, but she said nothing. "I suppose my sister-in-law would not object, Augustus?" "G— Almighty only knows," said the younger brother. The duchess, grievously offended by the impropriety of this language, drew herself up haughtily.[1]

In the spoken language, other methods of disguise are used to alleviate the offense, methods with which we are already familiar from our discussion of the Zulu word-taboo:

---

1 Anthony Trollope, *The American Senator,* Chap. LX.

when the word *Wenzani,* water, by its similarity to a given name, becomes unusable to a Zulu woman, a very slight distortion, *wenkani,* is considered sufficient to circumvent the prohibition. A similar thin disguise, applied to the holy names in English, has given rise to an amazing variety of expletives expressing anger, astonishment, or admiration, all of which can be easily recognized as distorted forms of God, Lord, Jesus, and so on. The following short list might be enormously multiplied: *Gad, Egad, Gosh, Golly, Ods* are all derivatives of God; *Law(s) Lawsy, Lawk, Lack* are some of the veiled forms of Lord; *Jeminy, Jings, Jingo, Gee, Jeez,* and probably *Jabers,* of Jesus (also *Jehosaphat,* originally a Biblical name, now used as a substitute for the more sacred name. As a substitute its strength is reinforced by the phonetic lengthening of the first syllable). The number of these corruptions becomes legion if we include phrases derived from obsecrations like *God's blood, God's body, God's wounds,* and so on. *Ods bodikin, Swounds, Swoons, Gadzooks, Gadsbud* may stand for all the rest of them. There is hardly any English play, from Shakespeare to Sheridan, that does not offer contributions to this list, and, skipping a century and a half, few since *What Price Glory* and *Diamond Lil* that could not further enrich it.[2]

Some of these forms combine the principle of distortion with that of abbreviation; they not only disguise the forbidden word by changing one or two sounds, but, from an objectionable two-word combination like "God's wounds," they eliminate the element that might provoke censure, thus letting the innocent second part do duty for the whole phrase. The practice can be shown to be an old one. Chaucer makes his drunken Miller swear "By armes and by blood and bones." [3] That these words

[2] Much more of this sort is to be found in H. L. Mencken, *The American Language,* 4th ed. (New York: Alfred A. Knopf, 1943), pp. 311 ff., and especially *Supplement One* (1945), pp. 661 ff. The studies of Eric Partridge are also valuable, as are such books as Lester V. Berrey and Melvin Van Den Bark, *The American Thesaurus of Slang* (New York: Thomas Y. Crowell Company, 1942). But the most genuine enlightenment is to be had from listening to people talk.

[3] *Canterbury Tales* (ed. Robinson), A, 3125.

have to be taken as equivalents of "God's arms," and so on, is clear in itself, and becomes evident from other passages in which the full phrases are used. "The Pardoner's Tale" contains, among other interesting remarks about violations of the second commandment, the following sample of a conversation among gamblers:

> "By Goddes precious herte," and "By his nayles,"
> And "By the blood of Crist that is in Hayles,
> Sevene is my chaunce, and thyn is cynk and treye!"
> "By Goddes armes, if thou falsly pleye,
> This daggere shal thurghout thyn herte go!" [4]

One might wonder why it should be considered less objectionable to say "Gosh" than "God," when everybody knows that the corrupted form stands for exactly the same idea as the word one is afraid to pronounce. Does not the mutilation of a holy word rather add to the offense than alleviate it? That such practices may appear satisfactory to primitive peoples is easily understood; they do not think of their demons as omniscient divinities, and therefore it is entirely logical that by changing its customary phonetic form, they should hope to fool a spirit whose name must not be pronounced. But this way of thinking is certainly not that of the higher religions.

We know by now that our modern language preserves many a primitive feature for whose explanation we must go back to much lower strata of linguistic development. It is entirely possible that our way of circumventing word-taboos by distortion and mutilation is nothing but residue from earlier periods, which, from a more modern point of view, has become meaningless. On the other hand, there may be factors involved that make our procedure less preposterous than it would appear at a first glance.

An episode in Sterne's *Tristram Shandy* seems to offer a hint in this direction: Two French nuns are left stranded in a coach drawn by mules that refuse to acknowledge any stimula-

[4] *Ibid.*, C, 651–655.

tion unless it is couched in terms of such coarseness that no lady, and least of all a nun, could bring herself to utter them. Finally the older nun finds an ingenious device:

Now I see no sin in saying, *bou, bou, bou, bou, bou,* a hundred times together; nor is there any turpitude in pronouncing the syllable *ger, ger, ger, ger, ger,* were it from our matins to our vespers: Therefore, my dear daughter, continued the abbess of *Andouillets*—I will say *bou,* and thou shalt say *ger.* . . . And accordingly the abbess, giving the pitch note, set off thus:
Abbess, Bou— bou— bou—
Margarita, —ger, —ger, —ger.[5]

The entire passage, Chapters 20–25, should be read. Its calculated and evasive treatment of tabooed expressions not only throws much light on the social meaning of taboo, but also brilliantly exhibits the function of taboo as a source of wit and humor. The application to our problem here, however, is this: any speech act, if it is not a monologue, is carried out by at least two persons, the speaker who utters certain sounds and the listener who takes these sounds to mean something. In most cases, this second part is so well prepared by the fact that the sounds uttered by the speaker have a traditional meaning that the completing role of the listener is of a receptive rather than of an active character. It is different, however, in cases where the produced sound in itself is nonsense (i.e., void of traditional meaning), or ambiguous (capable of conveying two or more traditional meanings). Under circumstances of this sort, the listener has to decide what to make of the spoken sound group. His collaboration is essential to the completion of the act of meaningful speech. In fact, whether a given use is profane may depend not upon the speaker but upon the hearer. Colley Cibber's plaintive remark about Jeremy Collier's attack upon his first play as profane is not wholly casuistical:

. . . he has shewn more Zeal than Justice, his greatest Charge against it is, that it sometimes uses the word *Faith!* as an Oath, in the dia-

[5] Laurence Sterne, *Tristram Shandy,* Book VII, Chap. 25.

logue: But if *Faith* may as well signify our given Word, or Credit as our religious Belief, why might not his Charity have taken it in the less criminal Sense? [6]

Now Chaucer's Miller, in swearing by "armes and by blood and bones" certainly commits only half a profanity. It is certain that he intends to procure himself the satisfaction an angry man may derive from uttering a round oath. On the other hand, his words are not in themselves objectionable. They become so only if his listeners choose to supply the suppressed words "God's" or "Christ's," and if they do, they make themselves accessories after the fact, thereby depriving themselves of their right to take offense. So neither hearer nor speaker is entirely responsible for the profane expression, just as, in a more literal way, Sterne's two nuns bring out the obscene word by pronouncing one innocent syllable each.

This trick of cutting the responsibility in half by forcing, or at least inviting, the listener to share it is not restricted, of course, to religious word-taboos. Many things that from social or political reasons are considered unmentionable can still be expressed by way of allusion or ambiguity, a technique that will be exemplified in later chapters.

The device, however, works satisfactorily only as long as it is new. For reasons much discussed but not yet sufficiently explained, the word *bloody,* in England, is considered extremely coarse. Many substitutes have been introduced, mostly words beginning with *bl-* like *blooming, blamed, blistering,* or words connected by similarity of meaning like *sanguinary.*[7] The first persons to introduce these words must certainly have profited from the mechanism just described, since the replacing words were at once close enough to the forbidden one to suggest it to the minds of the listeners, and vague enough to avoid offense. The more they were used, however, the less usable they became;

---

[6] *An Apology for the Life of Mr. Colley Cibber Written by Himself,* ed. by Robert W. Lowe, 2 vols. (London: Nimmo, 1889), I, 274.

[7] The many theories concerning *bloody* are summarized and criticized by Mencken, *The American Language,* pp. 311 ff., and *Supplement One,* pp. 678 ff.

from being euphemisms they turned into mere synonyms which, if not quite as bad as *bloody,* could not altogether fail to be infected with the rudeness of the word they were intended to avoid. Nowhere is the point made clearer than in the many stories resulting from Gilbert and Sullivan's use of the title *Ruddygore* (and nowhere is the unsubstantial quality of the taboo-avoiding mechanism made more apparent than in their prompt reaction to criticism by changing the title to *Ruddigore*). The sense of shock that gripped Victorian England at Gilbert's daring is evident in the reproof administered by the *Graphic,* January 29, 1887, over the

> . . . not very happily selected title. . . . The sterner and less mealy mouthed sex, safe in the club smokingroom, might pass such a name with a smile. But it is different in the case of ladies, to whom Savoy operas largely appeal, and on whose lips such a title would scarcely sound pretty.[8]

The result of wearing out euphemisms is a constant demand for new substitutes and a considerable word coining activity. A limited number of word prohibitions may give rise to almost innumerable substitutes and, thereby, to a considerable enrichment of the vocabulary.

So far this chapter has been more or less slanted to illustrate individual psychology, but the problem is as much a matter of the group as it is of the individual, a fact clearly evident in the different reactions to profanity made by different generations. We are not concerned to give a history of swearing, but we would like to indicate a few signposts along the way. What happens to language reflects, in a very close way, the general development of society and its culture, as the attitude of different periods toward the use or misuse of religious terms exemplifies. It can easily be shown that epochs dominated by religious feelings have been much more strict in their rejection of any abuse of religious phrases than is ours at the present. We certainly do not find it objectionable if a dramatic author makes one of

---

[8] Quoted in Isaac Goldberg, *The Story of Gilbert and Sullivan* (New York: Simon and Schuster, 1928), p. 349.

his characters utter a prayer couched in Biblical terminology—to our knowledge the language of St. John Irvine's *John Ferguson* has not been criticized. Two hundred years ago, this identical procedure was considered a liberty deserving severe censure, if not everywhere, at least in Scotland. When in 1756 the first performance of John Home's tragedy *Douglas* caused the literary circles of Edinburgh to hail the arrival of a new epoch in Scottish belles-lettres, a strong, church-minded party denounced, for participation in an ungodly act, not only the author but even persons who had done little more than take an interest in the performance. From a libel, directed against one of the author's friends, we quote:

> . . . the said Mr. Alexander Carlyle did, without necessity, keep company, familiarly converse, and eat and drink with West Diggs (one of the actors on the unlicensed stage or theatre at the head of the Canongate of Edinburgh, commonly called the Concert-hall) . . . the said Mr. Alexander Carlyle did, without necessity . . . converse in a familiar manner with the said West Diggs, or with Miss Sarah Ward, an actress on the said theatre . . . persons that do not reside in his parish, and who, by their profession, and in the eye of the law are of bad fame, and who cannot obtain from any minister a testimonial of their moral character . . . and he, the said Mr. Alexander Carlyle, did not only appear publicly in the said unlicensed theatre . . . and did there witness the acting or representation of the foresaid tragedy called *Douglas,* when acted for hire or reward, in which the name of God was profaned or taken in vain by mock prayers and tremendous oaths or expressions such as—"by the blood of the cross," and "the wounds of Him who died for us on the accursed tree." [9]

Some sixty years earlier Jeremy Collier, in his treatise *A Short View of the Immorality and Profaneness of the English Stage,* had severely criticized the way in which the playwrights of his time made light of the language of religion—with much better reason than Home's adversaries, since the freedom with which Restoration comedy used objectionable words is apparent even to the most broad-minded reader. What is remarkable

[9] *The Autobiography of Dr. Alexander Carlyle of Inveresk,* ed. by John Hill Burton (London: T. N. Foulis, 1910), pp. 335–336.

to our feeling is not so much his criticism in itself but the touchiness with which he reacts against words that to us have ceased to be subject to taboo prescriptions, as for instance *martyr* and *inspiration*.[10]

There are other points in Collier's criticism of the stage that deserve attention. The same abuses that provoke his indignation when they occur in the works of his contemporaries he judges with leniency when encountered in the old classics, or even in the works of the Elizabethan poets. It is true that Sir John Oldcastle (in the play of the same name, which Collier attributes to Shakespeare) swears with the most debauched of Wycherly's or Congreve's rakes and their foolish imitators. But such liberty, and similar transgressions of the older poets, Collier finds excusable on the grounds that it is in keeping with the general character of the persons introduced by the author.

This argument is very close to the defense used by Arthur Hopkins on the program note of Maxwell Anderson and Laurence Stallings' *What Price Glory*, when he produced the play in 1924—a time when the American public was not yet prepared to accept uninhibited speech: [11]

> *What Price Glory* is a play of war as it is, not as it has been presented theatrically for thousands of years. The soldiers talk and act much as soldiers the world over. The speech of men under arms is universally and consistently interlarded with profanity. Oaths mean nothing to a soldier save a means to obtain emphasis. He uses them in place of more polite adjectives.
>
> The authors of *What Price Glory* have attempted to reproduce

---

[10] Jeremy Collier, *A Short View of the Immorality and Profaneness of the English Stage* (London: 1698). See pp. 74 and 82.

[11] According to Arthur Train, *Yankee Lawyer* (New York: Charles Scribners Sons, 1943), p. 204, "Goddamn was first heard on the American stage in Clyde Fitch's 'The City' in 1909." Mr. Train further illustrates the verbal taboos of the era by commenting, "Those were the days of propriety in speech. No gentleman referred in the presence of a lady to any major part of the human anatomy below the neck, 'damn' was printed '———' or 'dash,' used vocally it was good for a sure-fire, if nervous, laugh at any time on the theatrical stage, while 'a good goddamn' would have brought the police."

this mannerism along with other general atmosphere they believe to be true. In a theater where war has been lied about, romantically, effectively—and in a city where the war play has usually meant sugary dissimulation—*What Price Glory* may seem bold. The audience is asked to bear with certain expletives which, under other circumstances, might be used for melodramatic effect, but herein are employed because the mood and truth of the play demand their employment.[12]

To return to Collier, he clearly has introduced an artistic principle, which, if impartially applied to his own contemporaries, would exonerate them from most of the accusations of which Collier finds them guilty. This inconsistency is interesting because it provides another example of the manifold influences of social factors upon language. Collier's two-faced view of the subject is not essentially different from the following observations about Ibsen's *Ghosts,* found in a modern American humorist:

> Wrongdoing is surely never so objectionable as when it is indulged in by common people and talked about in ordinary language, and the language of this play is not stage language at all. Immorality such as one gets in Shakespeare is of so elevated a character that one accepts it, the language having a grandeur incomparably above what any person was ever capable of in private life, being always elegant and unnatural.[13]

In others words, a person's speech habits are not, and have never been, judged exclusively by their intrinsic merits, but also by the social standard of the speaker. What may appear objectionable when uttered by the average citizen may be approved of and even imitated if the speaker or writer is a famous poet or a person of high social position. Of course, social position works two ways. If you and I say, "S.O.B.," no one minds. When the President of the United States applied the initials to a well-

12 Maxwell Anderson and Laurence Stallings' *What Price Glory* (New York: Harcourt, Brace and Company, 1924).

13 Harry Leon Wilson, *Ruggles of Red Gap* (New York: Doubleday, Page & Company, 1915), p. 160.

known news commentator (February 22, 1949), they caused a tempest of criticism and defense. The question of the degree to which changes in language are caused by a tendency of the lower classes to pattern their speech on that of privileged individuals is an important one, and will be discussed later.

It should also be noted that, in regard to profane language, our judgment depends on the character and status not only of the speaking persons but also of the persons before whom the breach of etiquette is committed. Again we quote from Collier, who is well aware of this point:

> *3dly,* Swearing in the *Playhouse* is an ungentlemanly, as well as an unchristian Practice. The *Ladies* make a considerable part of the *Audience.* Now Swearing before Women is reckon'd a Breach of good Behaviour, and therefore a civil Atheist will forbear it. The custom seems to go upon this Presumption; that the Impressions of Religion are strongest in Women, and more generally spread. And that it must be very disagreeable to them, to hear the Majesty of God treated with so little respect. Besides: Oaths are a boisterous and tempestiuous sort of conversation; Generally the effects of Passion, and spoken with Noise, and Heat. Swearing looks like the beginning of a Quarrel, to which Women have an aversion: As being neither armed by Nature, nor disciplin'd by Custome for such rough Disputes. A Woman will start at a Soldiers Oath, almost as much as at the Report of his Pistol; And therefore a well Bred Man will no more Swear, than Fight in the Company of Ladies.[14]

Swearing before ladies, and by ladies, is, of course, a topic that would richly deserve special treatment because of its implications for the history of both manners and language. The following quotations may suffice to give the reader an idea of the fluctuations which have taken place in the last few centuries.

We saw in Chapter I how Shakespeare describes a great nobleman teasing his wife by protesting the mild, middle-class flavor of her oaths. A lady should be able to swear like a lady—resoundingly.

At the end of the eighteenth century, the great lady still

[14] Collier, *op. cit.*, pp. 59–60.

accepted her privileges, but occasionally perhaps with a little reluctance. Georgiana, Duchess of Devonshire, in a letter (March 20, 1784) to her mother, the Countess Spencer, at a time when England's politics were at fever pitch, tells the story that at the opera one evening,

The Duchess of Rutland said D—— Fox, upon which Colonel St. Leger with great difficulty spirited up Lady Maria Waldegrave to say D—— Pitt.[15]

In contrast, we have already seen, in Trollope's amused description from *The American Senator,* how easily the antipathies of a Victorian duchess could be aroused by a casually profane remark. To emphasize that this was not just a matter of a shift in aristocratic prejudice, here is another quotation from the same author:

He was much given to profane oaths; but knowing that manners required that he should refrain before ladies, and being unable to bring his tongue sufficiently under command to do so, he was in the habit of "craving the ladies' pardon" after every slip.[16]

To complete the Victorian picture, we give a little scene from a mid-nineteenth century American writer.

There was an angry start in one or two of the seats; one man caught at the swinging side-strap and half rose, a husky voice began, "It's a d—d"—and then all as suddenly subsided. Every eye was turned to an insignificant figure in the back seat. It was a woman, holding a child on her lap, and gazing out of the window with her sex's profound unconcern in politics. Clarence understood the rude chivalry of the road well enough to comprehend that this unconscious but omnipotent figure had more than once that day controlled the pas-

[15] We may be permitted to doubt that the high-spirited Georgiana actually wrote "D——." But this letter has to be quoted from the edition prepared by a later Duchess of Devonshire for *The Anglo-Saxon Review,* II (September, 1899), 73. In 1899, even scholars were still employing the tricks of typography to circumvent taboos. It is amusing to note that exactly ten years later Walter Sichel in his *Sheridan* (Boston: Houghton Mifflin Company, 1909), II, 55, could print the story with the offending word spelled out in full.

[16] Anthony Trollope, *The Three Clerks,* Chap. IV.

sions of the disputants. They dropped back weakly to their seats, and their mutterings rolled off in the rattle of the wheels.[17]

It is an entertaining observation that profane speech, being largely conditioned by social influences, is subject to fashions just as is any other social phenomenon. The following quotation is evidently colored by a satirical tendency and must therefore be taken with a grain of salt. Nevertheless, it is safe to assume that it is based on factual observations.

Acres: . . . Then if I can find out this Ensign Beverley, odds triggers and flints! I'll make him know the difference o't.
Absolute: Spoke like a man! But pray, Bob, I observe you have got an odd kind of a new method of swearing—
Acres: Ha! ha! you've taken notice of it—'tis genteel, isn't it!—I didn't invent it myself though; but a commander in our militia, a great scholar, I assure you, says that there is no meaning in the common oaths, and that nothing but their antiquity makes them respectable;—because, he says, the ancients would never stick to an oath or two, but would say, By Jove! or By Bacchus! or By Mars, or By Venus! or By Pallas, according to the sentiment; so that to swear with propriety, says my little major, the "oath should be an echo to the sense"; and this we call the *oath referential* or sentimental swearing—ha! ha! 'tis genteel, isn't it?
Absolute: Very genteel, and very new, indeed!—and I daresay will supplant all other figures of imprecation.
Acres: Ay, ay, the best terms will grow obsolete— Damns have had their day.[18]

No attempt can be made here to discuss fully the social conditioning of bad language and its avoidance. The laws governing speech behavior, although for the most part unwritten, are extremely complicated. The same strong word, for instance, that an author might use in his book without incurring censure would certainly cause him to be taken off the air if he were to utter it in a radio speech. The reason for this apparent inconsistency lies in the fact that the spoken word is much more likely to make a strong impression than the printed. The social

---

[17] Bret Harte, *Clarence,* Argonaut Edition, XVIII, 30.
[18] Richard B. Sheridan, *The Rivals,* Act II, scene 1.

factors are also reinforced by economic considerations. The greater the audience, the greater the probability that some sensitive persons might take offense, and among these persons some might be influential enough to constitute a threat to a commercial organization dependent for its income on the largest possible number of listeners.

Again, the code of book language appears to be less rigid than that of magazine style. We happen to have before us as we write a copy of a novel that has been prepared for publication in a periodical—we do not know whether by the authors themselves or by the publisher. The first part of the story deals with the life of gold miners, and, in rendering their speech, the authors have made free use of oaths and other vulgarisms. This realistic feature is consistently toned down, however, in the magazine version. Instead of "Go to hell," it reads "Go to blazes"; "I don't give a damn," has been replaced by "I don't care"; and instead of "What th' hell!" we find "What of it?" Probably the authors' reason for expurgating their book has to do with the different literary training of book readers and magazine readers. This latter group would not, as the former is expected to do, condone the liberties the author is taking on the plea that, as an artist, he has a perfect right to make his characters speak as they would in actual life. In other words, an artistic principle has been sacrificed to the general moral code —without, as it would seem in the case in question, any appreciable damage to the literary value of the work.

In thus presenting many examples for analysis, we are not attempting to exhaust an inexhaustible subject; we wish rather to show how many interlocking motivations are involved in a single linguistic phenomenon. A conspicuous problem, however, still remains. From the oldest times profanity has been menaced with heavy sanctions, beginning with the Old Testament law that blasphemers shall be stoned to death down to the English Profane Oath Act of 1745, which directs that the offender be brought before a justice of the peace and fined five shillings, two shillings, and one shilling, respectively, according as he be a gentleman, below the rank of a gentleman, or a common laborer, soldier, and so on (social conditioning, again). In modern times the stigma of bad manners has been added to such legal consequences of profanity. How, then, is it to be explained that the habit of swearing has withstood until this day all the efforts directed against it?

It cannot justly be argued that although theft and murder, too, have been legally forbidden for ages, there still exist thieves and murderers. In these cases, it is evident that the criminal has a chance of remaining undetected, and that his crime may be rewarded by very palpable advantages, whether these consist in a material gain or in the satisfaction of a successful vengeance. Such advantages, however, are not apparent in profanity. If they do exist, they must be much more deeply hidden.

In attempting an answer to this question, we may glean a hint from the effusions of one of Shakespeare's contemporaries. It is interesting in many respects (among others, it may throw some light on the still debated derivation of *bloody,* used as an oath):

> . . . He that can lashe out the bloudiest othes, is coumpted the bravest fellowe: For (saie thei) it is a signe of a coragious harte, of a valiaunt stomacke, & of a generoseous, heroicall, and puissant mynde. . . . At euery other worde, you shal heare either woundes, bloud, sides, harte, nailes, foote, or some other parte of Christes blessed bodie, yea, sometymes no part thereof shalbe left untorne of these bloudie Villaines. . . . When thou swearest by his bloud, thou swearest by his life. . . . Therfore, learne this, and beware of swearyng, you bloudie Butchers. . . . What kinde of punishment would you haue appointed for these notorious bloudy swearers?
>
> . . . . .
>
> There was a certaine young man . . . who was alwaies a filthie Swearer. His common othe was by "God's bloud." The Lorde willying his conuersion, chastised him with sicknesse . . . but all chastisementes and louyng corrections of the Lorde, al freendly admonitions, and exhortations of others, he vtterly contemned, stil perseuering in his bloudie kinde of swearyng. . . . At the last, the people perceiuing his ende to approach, caused the Bell to toll. Who, hearyng the Bell toll for him, rushed vp in his bed very vehemently, saiyng: "Gods

bloud, he shall not haue me yet" . . . and thus ended this bloudie Swearer his mortall life, whose Judgment I leaue to the Lord.[19]

If this be a correct picture of how the average English person around 1600 felt in regard to profanity, it certainly indicates what advantages a man of that period could expect from using bad language. It is true that his swearing would degrade him in the eyes of a minority of persons of strict views. But if, on the other hand, the great majority would consider his profanities as "a signe of a coragious harte, of a valiaunt stomacke [which in our modern slang might be aptly rendered by *guts*], and a generoseous, heroicall, and puissant mynde," he might still feel that, in the end, the balance of social gains and losses would be in his favor.

This, of course, does not explain why profanity ever came to be considered as proof of a strong character. But, looking at the problem from a historical point of view, it is not hard to find an answer. There can be no doubt that, whatever may have been the views of a few advanced and spiritual minds, religious feeling in the Middle Ages was largely based on fear of punishment. Why else should medieval sermons and treatises contain such an abundance of tales about the terrible retributions with which sinners were visited, either in this world or the next? Stubbes's story about the man who suffered a terrible death after having uttered a blasphemy is just as characteristic of this kind of literature as is, on a higher level, Dante's *Inferno*. With these facts in view, it is easy to see why a swearer would be held in awful respect: his very transgression proved him to be a man who was afraid of nothing between heaven and earth, and, if he was a sinner, he was at least not a contemptible one. One can also understand that swearing was, according to many testimonials, most common among the class whose profession it is to be brave, the military class. Survivals of these conditions can be traced down to our own times: witness the expression "to swear like a trooper," or Arthur Hopkins' note, quoted above, to *What Price Glory*. We may also point to the fact that the

---

19 Phillip Stubbes, *Anatomy of Abuses,* New Shakespeare Society Edition (London: 1583), pp. 132–135.

very strict regulations against the use of profane words in broadcasts were considerably relaxed during World War II, at least in regard to rendition of actual or fictitious utterances of soldiers.

This, however, is only one side of the problem. Another aspect may be illustrated from a satirical essay by Swift in which he proposes *The Swearer's Bank,* in which the fines for profane speaking should be deposited for the benefit of the public finances. After having suggested that persons should not be fined who indulge in strong language after having received an attorney's bill, he continues:

> The medicinal use of oaths is what the undertaker would by no means discourage, especially where it is necessary to help the lungs throw off any distilling humour. On certificate of a course of swearing prescribed by any physician, a permit will be given to the patient, by the proper officer of the bank, paying no more than sixpence.[20]

The idea that swearing may be used for medicinal purposes will puzzle only those rare individuals who have never in their lives been so angry that they felt that any attempt to suppress their emotion would do them physical harm. In such situations some persons may vent their feelings by smashing a piece of crockery or by slamming a door, but the large majority will probably resort to the remedy prescribed by Swift's doctor. At this point we are not yet prepared to enter into a discussion of the general functions of language. But we may state that one of these functions, and a basic one, is its use as an outlet for bottled-up feelings. It is, however, a matter of experience that not every category of words is equally suitable for this purpose. When the urge arises to use language as a safety valve for one's feelings, the pressure will naturally escape in a direction where under normal conditions a conventional barrier prevents free uttering; in fact, it is the breaking down of this barrier that causes the unmistakable feeling of relief that commonly follows an outbreak of this sort. It is therefore easy to understand why the vocabulary of profanity is a preferred and

---

20 *The Works of Jonathan Swift,* Scott Edition (Boston: Houghton Mifflin Company, 1883), VI, 289–290.

effective means of staging an emotional explosion. We have to acknowledge, then, a second reason for the persistence of the habit of swearing and admit that it probably always will resist all attempts to eradicate it.

Social aspects of linguistic action have emerged so clearly from the materials previously considered in this book that we now have to ask ourselves whether emotional swearing—i.e., swearing as a release—is an exception. On the surface it may appear to be merely a personal matter, without any social implication. A man may certainly indulge in swearing for his own exclusive benefit, even if no other person is present. But it must not be overlooked that profanity uttered in the presence of others may very well relieve not only the swearing person himself but also those of his listeners who, without having entirely lost their power of self-control, may be on the verge of a similar outbreak. They will find the strain on their feelings removed by what they hear almost as effectively as by what they might have said; one might say that they have done their swearing by proxy. James Redpath, a pious abolitionist traveling in the pre-Civil War South, found himself forced to walk from Wilmington to Charleston, South Carolina, following a railroad track across particularly difficult swamps. The record of his temptation is a valuable witness to our point:

> . . . I trudged on—only losing my temper on one occasion, when I came to a horrible piece of work over a horrible swamp. My carpet bag incommoded me so much in walking, and once or twice, in leaping, so nearly caused me to lose my balance, that in a mild and genial temper, and with soft words of valedictory regret, I pitched it (with an unnecessarily extravagant expenditure of energy) at the flabby black bosom of the swamp, and then and there entertained the sinful desire that some person of profane habits were present, as I would willingly have given him half of my cash to have done a little swearing on my private account—a mode of relief which my habits and taste would not permit me to indulge in.[21]

---

[21] James Redpath, *The Roving Editor* (New York: A. B. Burdick, 1859), p. 134.

Even physical violence was not an entirely adequate outlet for Redpath's feelings. He would have rejoiced in profanity —provided it could have been had without sin. In situations of this sort, few persons will be inclined to be hard on a man who has prevented them from committing what they would probably consider a serious transgression. Incidentally, this accounts also for the general opinion that profane language caused by strong emotions is more excusable than habitual swearing in cold blood.

To return now from swearing to religious prohibitions in general, still another instigation to neglect speech inhibitions based on religious motives arises from the fact that occasionally human beings rise to a height of power and importance that makes their subordinates blur the distinction between divine beings and mortals. The old idea that kings and princes share the characteristics of the god or gods from whom they derived their lineage, or, according to a less naïve idea, exalted position, regularly goes hand in hand with a tendency to address such persons in terms that otherwise would be reserved for religious use. We need not go back to very remote times in order to find examples. The flatteries, for instance, that Spenser addressed to Queen Elizabeth were frequently couched in the phraseology of religion:

. . . O Goddesse heavenly bright,
Mirrour of grace and Majestie divine. . . .[22]

. . . . .

To such therefore I do not sing at all,
But to that sacred saint my soveraigne Queene,
In whose chast brest all bountie naturall
And treasures of true love enlocked beene . . .
To her this song most fitly is addrest,
The queene of love, and prince of peace from heaven blest.[23]

Public characters and the ideas or institutions they stand for may likewise, in the eyes of their supporters, assume such supreme importance that, in alluding to them, terms of religious

[22] Edmund Spenser, *Faerie Queene,* Proem of Book I, stanza 4.

[23] *Ibid.,* Proem of Book IV, stanza 4.

origin will be used, a practice which leads to further disregard of the boundaries between religious and profane language:

> The vernal sun new life bestows
> Even on the meanest flower that blows;
> But vainly, vainly may he shine
> Where Glory weeps o'er Nelson's shrine,
> And vainly pierce the solemn gloom
> That shrouds, O Pitt, thy hallowed tomb![24]
>
> Lächelnd steigt der süsse Frühling nieder,
> Doch er findet seine Brüder nie
> In Ilissus' heil'gem Tale wieder—
> Ewig deckt die bange Wüste sie.
>
> Mich verlangt ins bessre Land hinüber,
> Nach Alcäus und Anakreon,
> Und ich schlief' im engen Hause lieber
> Bei den Heiligen in Marathon!
> Ach! es sei die letzte meiner Tränen,
> Die dem heil'gen Griechenlande rann,
> Lasst, o Parzen, lasst die Schere tönen,
> Denn mein Herz gehört den Toten an.[25]

The degree and tempo by which such "ideological" uses of religious words applied to worldly matters finally destroy the taboo surrounding them, depend largely on the more or less dignified character of the spheres to which they are transferred. As soon as their use becomes "misuse," the tempo of their deterioration is accelerated. This is illustrated in the following quotations. The first is from Simms's *The Partisan,* a description of a Revolutionary War site:

> The sands have drunk deeply of holy and hallowed blood—blood that gave them value and a name, and made for them a place in all human recollection.[26]

To a few severely religious people, the phrase "holy and hallowed blood" will show a lack of respect for a religious sym-

---

[24] Sir Walter Scott, *Marmion,* Introduction to Canto I, stanza 5.

[25] Hölderlin, *Griechenland.*

[26] W. G. Simms, *The Partisan* (New York: 1882), Chap. XXI.

bol. Most readers, however, if they pay any attention to it at all, will let the patriotic feeling expressed by these words stand as an excuse for the infringement upon religious inhibition.

In marked contrast is a quotation from the *Autobiography* of Theodore Roosevelt:

> Afterwards this tenement-house cigar legislation was declared invalid by the Court of Appeals in the Jacobs decision. . . . The Court of Appeals declared the law unconstitutional, and in their decision the judges reprobated the law as an assault upon the "hallowed" influences of "home." . . . The judges who rendered this decision were well-meaning men. They knew nothing whatever of tenement-house conditions; they knew nothing whatever of the needs, or of the life and labor, of three-fourths of their fellow-citizens in great cities. They knew legalism, but not life. Their choice of the words "hallowed" and "home," as applicable to the revolting conditions attending the manufacture of cigars in tenement-houses, showed that they had no idea what it was that they were deciding. Imagine the "hallowed" associations of a "home" consisting of one room where two families, one of them with a boarder, live, eat, and work! [27]

Roosevelt's irony and scorn make perfectly evident the fact that the appearance of the word *hallowed,* in a legal document dealing with tenement conditions and with the hygienic handling of tobacco and, second, in a social context which many Christians would feel to be a direct violation of the spirit of Christianity, cannot fail to take away from the dignity of the word, and to contribute to the breaking up of the taboo protecting it.

The tradition of the lover idolizing the object of his affections reveals still another field in which the use or misuse of religious terminology is extremely frequent. One example from Elizabethan English must stand for many:

> *Gwydonius* wakened out of his musing slumber . . . seeing before his eies his gorjeous Goddesse, the verie Saint, at whose shrine he was offering up scalding sighs, farre fetcht sobs, plaints, praiers,

[27] *Theodore Roosevelt: An Autobiography* (New York: Charles Scribner's Sons, 1914), pp. 82–83. Reprinted by permission of Charles Scribner's Sons, publishers.

and protestations . . . so *Gwydonius* seeing the incomperable beautie of his best beloued *Castania,* was so astonished, yea, so inchanted with the rare perfection of this heauenlie *Pallas,* that as one besotted he sate senselesse, not beeing able to vtter one word, vntill at length reuiued with the view of her cheerefull countenance, hee repaide her with this pleasant answere.[28]

The tendency to describe beloved persons in terms originally reserved for religious use has produced lasting effects in the development of the English vocabulary, as well as that of other languages. *To adore,* for instance, means, by etymology, "to pray to" (from Latin *ad* = "to" and *orare* = "to pray"). The following examples illustrate the most important stages in the development of the word, and its gradual sliding over into the worldly sphere:

For they came to adore and worship the King of kings in their proper persons, by the star that led them, and by the prophet that enseigned and taught them.[29]

Lo! here I lend thee this sharp-pointed sword;
Which if thou please to hide in this true breast,
And let the soul forth that adoreth thee,
I lay it naked to the deadly stroke,
And humbly beg the death upon my knee.[30]

We have every reason to suppose that the original meaning of "to adore" was still strongly felt by Shakespeare. Richard, in speaking this tirade, assumes the attitude of prayer. Earlier he has called Anne an angel and spoken of her "divine perfection," and immediately afterward of her "heavenly face."

Miss Shepherd is a boarder at the Misses Nettingalls' establishment. I adore Miss Shepherd. She is a little girl, in a spencer, with a round face and curly flaxen hair. The Misses Nettingalls' young

[28] Robert Greene, "The Carde of Fancie," *The Life and Complete Words in Prose and Verse of Robert Greene, M.A.,* Grosart Edition (London, 1881–1883), pp. 72–73.

[29] *The Golden Legend . . . as Englished by William Caxton,* Temple Classics Edition, I, 52.

[30] Shakespeare, *Richard III,* Act I, scene 2, lines 175–179; Richard's wooing of Lady Anne.

ladies come to the Cathedral too. I cannot look upon my book, for I must look at Miss Shepherd. When the choristers chaunt, I hear Miss Shepherd. In the service I mentally insert Miss Shepherd' name; I put her among the Royal family.[31]

The religious connotations are less marked and, at any rate, much less serious than in the preceding example. Note the strong undercurrent of persiflage. Note also that the insertion of Miss Shepherd's name in the service means that she is prayed for, not prayed to.

In colloquial use today, any connection of the word *adore* with religious ideas seems to have entirely disappeared. To "adore" a musical comedy, a fashion in hats, the color red, or butterscotch are alike possible in youthful, feminine, and enthusiastic speech.

One factor that appears to be very active in depriving religious words of the taboo protection that surrounds them is the leniency with which a breach of language etiquette is usually judged if it is clear that the transgressor means no real harm but intends to speak in a facetious way. Cases of this sort belong, however, to a much wider group. They will be treated in the chapter dealing with the linguistic technique of humor.

---

[31] Charles Dickens, *David Copperfield,* Chap. XVIII.

Chapter Four

MORE TABOOS IN MODERN SPEECH

ONCE more we turn to Jeremy Collier:

> In *Love Triumphant, Carlos* is by the Constitution of the Play a Christian; and therefore must be construed in the sense of his Religion. This Man blunders out this horrible expression. *Nature has given me my Portion in Sense with a P—— to her etc.* The *Reader* may see the Hellish Syllable at Length if he pleases.[1]

The modern reader may well be at a loss to supply the suppressed word, but the "hellish syllable" is used quite freely in Shakespeare's works and does not appear to have been particularly objectionable to the censors of his period. As far as we know, the expurgator of the Folio Edition has not changed it in a single instance. In Dryden, it is printed in full, in *Love Triumphant* as well as in other places: *pox!*

That names of dangerous diseases should be used in curses is not to be wondered at; *plague* and *murrain,* for instance, are used by Shakespeare in this function, as well as *pox*. That, as such, they may be subject to all sorts of restrictions is no less natural. The restrictions against *pox* are multiple: the taboo against cursing is probably as strong as the taboo against disease words, and stronger than either is the taboo against sex expressions. It must be pointed out, however, that like other

[1] Jeremy Collier, *A Short View of the Immorality, and Profaneness of the English Stage,* p. 82.

word-taboos these restrictions can be traced back to primitive languages:

> Among the Gayos of Sumatra it is forbidden to mention the name of small-pox in the house of a man who is suffering from the disease; and the words for ugly, red, stinking, unlucky, and so forth are forbidden under the same circumstances. The disease is referred to under the title of "prince of the averters of misfortune." [2]

There is no law that forbids modern man's speaking of diseases by their proper names. Yet, as soon as a dangerous disease threatens the life of a beloved person, we are very apt to relapse into a way of behavior similar to that of the primitive:

> My brother Henry had left Cambridge and was ill. My younger sister was ill. And though as yet we hardly told each other that it was so, we began to feel that that desolating fiend, consumption was among us . . .
>
> Then, by degrees, an established sorrow was at home among us. My brother was an invalid, and the horrid word, which of all words was for some years after the most dreadful to us, had been pronounced. It was no longer a delicate chest, and some temporary necessity for peculiar care,—but consumption! The Bruges doctor had said so, and we knew that he was right.[3]

Let us recall what we have found in similar cases: the reactions of modern people—Mme Curie, for instance—and of savages in situations involving basic human motives are, at least outwardly, much the same. Here as well as there we find a reluctance to pronounce the name of the disease, and the consequent necessity to invent substitute words—the "prince of the averters of misfortune" among the Sumatran tribe, a "delicate chest" in the Trollope family. But we have already seen that similarity of behavior does not necessarily indicate iden-

---

[2] J. G. Frazer, *The Golden Bough,* ed. cit., III, 410, as quoted from C. Snouck Hurgronje, *Het Gajoland en zijne Bewoners* (Batavia: 1903), pp. 311 ff.

[3] Anthony Trollope, *Autobiography,* World's Classics Edition, p. 25.

tity of motives. A characteristic difference in the choice of substitute words gives us a valuable clue. The expression a "delicate chest" merely disguises and mitigates the truth, the Gayos' "prince of the averters of misfortune" goes further: its tone is conspicuously flattering. Why should a disease be paid a compliment? Evidently because it is believed to be the work of a demon whose good will might be secured if he finds himself addressed in terms of adulation. This idea of the nature of disease, very common among primitive peoples,[4] is not as remote from our modern state of mind as one might be inclined to think. And it can hardly be doubted that even among our contemporaries not a few will avoid the names of dangerous diseases, mainly from superstitious motives, vaguely fearing that the mention of the disease might bring added peril. The recent discreet publicity campaign to break the taboo surrounding the word *cancer* is an effort to attack these fears. In the highly educated Trollope family, however, such primitive thoughts and feeling appear to be out of the question. They do not avoid the word *consumption* because they fear that the use of that word might turn a delicate chest into an attack of mortal disease, but because they fear that from a personal point of view, the use of the correct term would change their suspicions into a hopeless and cruel certainty. As long as veiled expressions only are used, each member of the circle is at liberty to take a more or less optimistic attitude. After the ominous word is spoken, there is no escape from the tragic fact.

It is an essential truth about language that words and facts are not two separated worlds. Facts, of course, create words; they constantly have to be spoken of, and, if the existing vocabulary does not fit them, new expressions become imperative. Words can also produce and influence facts, not merely because they can convey orders but in many subtler ways. Until now, we have only hinted at the historical background of language. But from these hints it should already be clear that the connection between linguistic and historical facts is most significant. To understand our own attitude toward censurable words, we must

[4] Frazer, *loc. cit.*, pp. 105 ff.

go back to the views of remote generations from whose ways of thinking and feeling our own are inherited. Whether an expression should be banned from everyday speech because it occurs in the Bible, or whether it should be considered more obnoxious to swear in the presence of women than of men is clearly not a matter of language alone but of cultural standards in general. On the other hand, the study of language, while based on the history of culture, is in itself capable of helping our understanding of the cultural structure of periods gone by.

Let us turn to the modern English vocabulary that deals with illness and death. Even to the most superficial observer it is evident that some of the words are euphemistic; they are clearly substitute words that attempt to cover up rather than to reveal unpleasant conditions. The word *disease* is perhaps the clearest example. Its literal meaning is "a state of lacking ease," just as *disorder* means lack of order. *Distemper,* although less perspicuous, has a similar origin; its primary meaning is a "faulty mixture" (from Latin *temperare,* "to mix"). The word is connected with the theory, current in classic and medieval medicine, that one's health depends on the correct mixture of certain basic elements in the body. These elements are called *humores* in Latin, *humors* in English (it is an easy as well as a correct guess that the same theory has played a part in the history of the word *humor*). An *invalid* originally meant a person who is not strong (from Latin *validus,* "strong"). *Valitudinarian* is derived from Latin *valitude,* "health." We should expect that a word of this origin would refer to a healthy person, not one in bad health. The solution is this: illness in Latin can, by first step toward euphemism, be described as *infirma valetudo,* "weak health," or *imbecilla valetudo,* "unstable health"; in the second phase, these expressions were curtailed so that their characteristic part was dropped while their innocent part, *valetudo,* remained—a technique we have already seen in operation in the shortening of such phrases as *God's blood* to *blood,* and the like. *Imbecilla* is also involved in the taboo against unpleasantness. Thus, it developed a meaning diametrically opposed to the original one. In a similar way, *influenza* has become the name of an illness; it is the Italian equivalent of *influence,* of course, and its present meaning must have originated in a fuller phrase containing the word for *bad,* a reference to the bad influence of adverse stars or tainted air on the health of human beings. In this case, too, only the neutral part of the expression remained, while its unambiguous adjective was eliminated.

Just as clearly euphemistic in their origin are a number of words describing mental disease. *Insane, deranged, unhinged, cracked* are so transparent that no explanation is needed. *Crazy* is derived from *craze,* a fissure or crack, which makes its original meaning identical with that of *cracked. Barmy* is clearly connected with *barm,* "froth" or "ferment"; thus its primary meaning is fermenting in a state of agitation. *Lunatic* means susceptible to the influence of the (full) moon, Latin *luna.* That it too, from the beginning, was a mitigated expression becomes evident from the fact that a lunatic, in the original sense, while becoming "unsettled" (another euphemism) in the days of full moon, might be normal during the intervening period:

> Of cheer nor colour to no man he was lik
> And eueri moneth onys lunatik.[5]

We have already noticed that taboo language, in its tendency to avoid direct and too easily understandable expressions, frequently borrows words from foreign idioms. A good illustration of this procedure is offered by the American slang term *loco,* which is the Spanish word for *mad.*

The terminology centering around the idea of death presents probably the most impressive example of the extraordinary power of taboo to stimulate word production. *Decease* (ultimately from Latin *decedere,* "to go away"), *demise* (from French *demettre,* "to release," "discharge"), *departure, release, end; to expire, to breathe out, to pass away, to be taken away, to close one's eyes, to pay one's debt to nature, to be gathered to one's fathers, to go to rest, to slumber one's last sleep,* and many other synonyms are so clearly of euphemistic origin that no

[5] Lydgate, *Fall of Princes,* Book VII, stanza 116.

discussion is needed. Again, we have not a few expressions in which the veiling tendency is combined with a touch of humor—misplaced humor, if you like, but still humor. To this group belong *to pop off, to hand in one's checks* or *one's dinner pail, to be dead as a doornail* or *a doorpost* or *mutton, to go to Davy Jones's locker,* and the like.

Note also that the word *die* itself was not originally an English word. It does not occur in Anglo-Saxon, but was borrowed from a Scandinavian dialect during the Middle English period—another example of the use of foreign words for euphemistic purposes.

It would be easy to expand such word lists almost at will. But these will suffice to show that today's English vocabulary—and, we may add, that of other modern languages as well—contains a surprisingly large number of words that reflect an attitude toward death and illness which, by its whole tenor, belongs to a period when the fear of these evils was stronger and less intermittent than now, a period when mankind had no effective means to fight disease and thereby to postpone death. The same necessity to illuminate the present state of language by reference to its past will occur again and again; no generation creates an entirely new language but only makes comparatively slight additions to the means of expression inherited from its predecessors.

We conclude our discussion of word-taboo with a few examples of the frequent cases in which a word not falling under any general taboo is unfit for use in a special situation because of unpleasant connotations rising from the hearer's personal experience. The following tale from C. E. Pancoast's *A Quaker Forty-Niner* well illustrates biographical conditioning:

On one occasion we were together on Seventh Street below Race, where there was a Toy Store kept by an old Frenchman, who had once been arrested for stealing Crabs from a Market Stand. He was eccentric and irritable, and Boys, to plague him, were in the habit of going to his door and asking him if he had Crabs for sale, keeping, however, a reasonable distance from him and a clear road behind them. My Companion, Archie, asked me if I was fond of Crabs, and

I said "Yes." (He had touched me in a sensitive place, for all Boys from the lower part of Jersey are fond of Crabs.) He said, "So am I. Here is a Fip (old name for a 6¼ cent piece), go in that Store and you can get four cooked ones for it." I took the money, entered the Frenchman's Store, and asked for a Fip's worth of Crabs. He did not answer me, but came rapidly around the counter and assaulted me over the Head with a Toy Wheel Barrow in a most brutal manner, and would perhaps have killed me if his Daughter had not interfered and taken the broken Wheel Barrow from him.[6]

Even such private taboos may spring from a social context, however, especially when they involve class distinctions and snobbery, as does this little vignette from Somerset Maugham:

They dwelt behind a mask of respectability. You never caught them in their shirt sleeves with their feet on the table. The ladies put on afternoon dresses and were not visible till then; they lived privately with rigid economy so that you could not drop in for a casual meal, but when they entertained their tables groaned with food. Though catastrophe overwhelmed the family, they held their heads high and ignored it. One of the sons might have married an actress, but they never referred to the calamity, and though the neighbours said it was dreadful, they took ostentatious care not to mention the theatre in the presence of the afflicted. We all knew that the wife of Major Greencourt who had taken the Three Gables was connected with trade, but neither she nor the major ever so much as hinted at the discreditable secret; and though we sniffed at them behind their backs, we were too polite even to mention crockery (the source of Mrs. Greencourt's adequate income) in their presence.[7]

In other cases, the prohibition arises from the fact that the injudicious use of a word might be interpreted as an attempt to establish the superiority of the speaker over the hearer. In this light, the following literary situation becomes clear. A young girl has an interview with a man who has cheated her

---

[6] Charles Edward Pancoast, *A Quaker Forty-Niner* (Philadelphia: University of Pennsylvania Press, 1930), p. 18. Reprinted by permission of the University of Pennsylvania Press, publishers.

[7] W. Somerset Maugham, *Cakes and Ale* (New York: Doubleday, Doran & Company, 1930), pp. 94–95. Reprinted by permission of W. Somerset Maugham and William Heinemann, Ltd.

out of her inheritance; she finds him extremely unhappy and willing to make amends:

> When Stephen Potter went into his library after bidding Draxy good-by, he found on the table a small envelope addressed to him. It held this note:—
>
> "Mr. Potter:—I would not take the paper (the word 'money' had been scratched out and the word 'paper' substituted) for myself; but I think I ought to for my father, because it was a true debt, and he is an old man now, and not strong.
>
> "I am very sorry for you, Mr. Potter, and I hope you will become happy again. *Draxy Miller."*
>
> Draxy had intended to write, "I hope you will be 'good' again," but her heart failed her. "Perhaps he will understand that 'happy' means good," she said, and so wrote the gentler phrase.[8]

It is clear that the use of the word *good* would imply that Draxy wanted to assume the attitude of a moral adviser, a presumption which the addressee might resent.

The memoirs of Prince Bismarck contain a curious passage which seems to suggest that sensitivities aroused by the injudicious use of a presumptuous word may have serious political consequences:

> The emperor Wilhelm II does not feel the need of collaborators with opinions of their own, who might oppose him in their fields with the authority of factual knowledge and experience. The word *experience* in my mouth put him out of humor and brought forth the words, "Experience? Well, I certainly don't have that." [9]

One wonders what the history of our own time might have been if Bismarck's "experience" had taught him the wisdom of avoiding too frequent use of a word to which the Kaiser had shown himself allergic. It is not surprising that the ambitious young monarch resented the implication of Bismarck's superiority. Because similar cases arise constantly in everyday con-

---

[8] Helen Hunt Jackson, "Draxy Miller's Dowry," *Saxe Holm's Stories* (New York: Scribner, Armstrong & Co., 1874), p. 43.

[9] Otto von Bismarck, *Die gesammelten Werke,* ed. by G. Ritter and R. Stadelmann (Berlin: 1932), XV, 479. The translation is our own.

versation, we are tempted to formulate a rule of taboo: any word suggesting that the speaker considers himself on a higher level than his audience should be used with the utmost precaution.

The words *I* and *my* rarely fail to make an unpleasant impression if used too frequently or with too much stress. Both private and public careers can be damaged by the injudicious use of these pronouns. Among the attacks upon President Andrew Johnson that quickly followed his inauguration we find as early as September 5, 1866, the Cleveland *Leader* reporting a speech made in Albany by the President, as follows:

The President read the following poem to the Albanians.

I, I, I, I, I, I, I,
Me, me, me, me, me, me, me,
I, me, I, me, I, me, I,
Me, I, Me, I, Me, I, Me.

The newspapers of that year abound in examples where the phrase "my policy," which the President had used in more than one conspicuous place, is quoted without regard to context or to normal syntax. Even so dignified a critic as James Russell Lowell attacked it:

If it be a part of that inconsistent mixture of purely personal motives and more than legitimate executive action which Mr. Johnson is pleased to call his "policy," . . .[10]

And Petroleum V. Nasby, with that deadly criticism which can be delivered under the guise of friendship (see our chapter on humor), remarked: ". . . ef I shood have twins born to me this nite, I shood name em both Policy." [11]

Swedish newspapers of 1914 offer a very close parallel, both to the public reaction to the inappropriate use of a possessive pronoun and to the interesting technique of making that pronoun stand out by introducing a fragment of direct speech

---

[10] J. R. Lowell, "The Seward-Johnson Reaction," *Political Essays* (Boston: Houghton Mifflin Company, 1890), p. 306.

[11] Petroleum V. Nasby [David Ross Locke], *Swingin round the Cirkle* (Boston: Lee and Shepard, 1867), p. 106, under date of March 30, 1866.

into a third-person sentence. In addressing a political meeting the king had used the expression "my navy." In a country jealous of its democratic institutions, these words—implying that the king considered the country's fleet his personal property—could not fail to produce resentment. A favorite means of giving expression to this feeling was the use of "min flotta" as a tag phrase, out of grammatical context.

Chapter Five

SPEECH COMMUNITIES

We have now to familiarize ourselves with the concept of the speech community, i.e., a group of persons speaking a language perceptibly different from that of other groups. The number of persons forming such a unit is of only secondary importance. All English-speaking people form a speech community, but so also do two schoolboys who for their private use have invented a secret language not intelligible to their classmates. It follows that every individual belongs not to one but to many speech communities. An American college student, for instance, is a member of the English speech community. Since his language offers a considerable number of deviations from the English spoken in England or in Australia, while it is similar to the speech habits of other Americans, he belongs also to a narrower speech community, the American variety of English; also, of course, to some subdivision of the latter, say, the Southern dialect. As a college student, he is likely to use slang expressions not current in other circles. As a student of engineering he will acquire the technical vocabulary of this profession. If he is a football player, another set of technical words will be introduced into his speech. Each of these peculiarities will make him a member of a different speech community. In other words, the language of every individual presents itself as an intricate combination of influences from all the different groups of which he is a member.

From our definition it becomes clear that the term *speech community* is by no means synonymous with dialect, since by this latter word we mean a speech community contained within geographical boundaries; wherefore it should not be applied to speech units of a social, professional, or, in general, non-geographical character.

An idiom spoken by a speech community may owe its characteristics to a spontaneous development, based on two facts: (1) that not only the inhabitants of a geographic area but also the members of a profession or of a social class are in closer linguistic contact with each other than with persons outside their unit; and (2) that language is, to a large extent, an integral part of all organized human activity, which means that specialized activities such as professional work cannot fail to produce a specialized vocabulary, necessary to the members of the craft, but generally without meaning or interest to the outsider. We have already seen specimens of such specialization in the language of hunters, fishermen, and so on. In other cases, the speech habits of a community may give the impression of being due not to a natural development but to purposeful invention.

This is certainly true with regard to all sorts of secret languages, constructed for the exchange of information among the members of a limited group, in such a way that it remains unintelligible to persons not initiated.

The best-known example of an artificial idiom of this sort is the "cant" of thieves and rogues. The following passage, written in the days of King James I, still gives a good description of it.

It was necessary, that a people (so fast increasing, & so daily practising new and strange *Villanies*), should borrow to themselues a speech, which (so neere as they could) none but themselues should vnderstand: & for that cause was this Language, (which some call *Pedlers French,*) Invented, to th' intent that (albeit any Spies should secretly steale into their companies to discouer them) they might freely vtter their mindes one to another, yet auoide ye danger. The Language therefore of *canting,* they study euen from their Infancy, that is to say, from the very first houre, that they take vpon them the names of *Kinchin Coes,* [i.e., apprentices in crime] till they are grown *Rufflers,* or *Vpright men,* which are the highest in degree amongst them.[1]

To judge from the specimens given by Dekker and others, the result is a language that is conventional English only insofar as functional words (pronouns, prepositions, conjunctions, and the like) are concerned, while most words expressing a distinct meaning, such as nouns, adjectives, and verbs, are replaced by cant terms:

Stowe you, beene cofe: hold your peace good fellow.
And cut benar whiddes: and speake better words.
And bing we to Rome vile: and goe we to London.
To nip a boung: to cut a purse.
So shall we haue lowre: so shall we haue mony.
For the bowsing Ken: for the Ale-house.[2]

Another variation of rogues' slang, resting not on a special vocabulary but on systematic distortion of generally known words, is easy to learn but for that very reason less likely to evade the understanding of an outsider. Here is a specimen translated from seventeenth-century German:

A syllable that begins with a consonant and ends with a vowel is spoken twice in such a way that the repeated syllable loses its initial consonant and in its place is always put a "p," so that if I want to say *Du, geh, wie, da, wo, I have to say, Dupu, gehpeh, wiepie, dapa, wopo.*[3]

---

[1] Thomas Dekker, *Lanthorne and Candle-light,* Grosart Edition (London: 1885), p. 194. For modern underworld argot, the works of H. L. Mencken already cited are, as usual, rich, entertaining, and provocative. There is copious material in the collections of Eric Partridge and of J. S. Farmer and W. E. Henley. David W. Maurer's *The Big Con* (Indianapolis: The Bobbs-Merrill Company, 1940) is particularly useful, for Professor Maurer places all his data in their social and psychological contexts. Chapter IX is specifically devoted to "The Con Man and His Lingo," but the book is throughout filled with linguistic observation.

[2] Dekker, *op. cit.,* p. 198.

[3] Eine Silb so von einem Mitlauter sich anfähet, und auf einen Selblauter sich endigt, wird zweymahl also ausgesprochen, dass die wiederholte Silb ihren vornstehenden Mitlauter verliere, und an dessen stat allezeit gesetzt werde ein *p* . . . , als wen ich sagen wil: *Du, geh, wie, da, wo,*

The interesting thing about this particular lingo is that it is still alive among German school children, while we have no evidence of its still being in use among criminals. Some fifteen years ago, when visiting a boys' camp in Austria, one of the authors heard two boys conversing in a similar language, the "Elef-Sprache." Having practiced this idiom in his own boyhood, he joined their conversation with the unexpected result that he was made an honorary member of their secret society—on condition that he promised not to reveal the mysteries of "Elef" to any boy outside the brotherhood.

Still another variety of *Rotwelsch* (thieves' cant) is described by Schottelius in the following way:

> Each syllable that begins with a consonant throws the consonant to the end of the syllable and adds the letter *e* . . . *gib* becomes *ibge,* . . . *Haus, aushe.*[4]

Adepts in the American school language known as "pig Latin" will be surprised and no doubt gratified that this idiom, though of disreputable origin, is at least as venerable as years can make it.

Here the reader must use his imagination in order to understand fully the implications of the fact that the thieves' slang of centuries ago has become an idiom used by schoolboys. It is not the fact itself that matters but the psychology behind it. Try to imagine the pride of the first schoolboy who found himself in a position to instruct his mates in the use of the genuine language of the underworld, and imagine the eagerness with which they must have adopted that language—and you will feel that it would be a poor representation of the facts if all we had to say were: "Here we have an interesting example of the well-known experience that group speech occasionally spreads to

---

spricht man auf Rohtwelsch: *Dupu, gehpeh, wiepie, dapa, wopo.*—Justus George Schottelius, *Ausführliche Arbeit von der teutschen Haubt-Sprache* (Braunschweig; 1663), pp. 1265–1266.

[4] *Ibid.*, p. 1267. Eine jede Silb so von einem Mitlauter anfängt, wirft solchen Mitlauter hinten an die Silbe, und setzet dabey den Buchstab *e,* . . . als *gib* heisset *ibge,* . . . *Haus, aushe.*

other speech communities than those that invented it." To add a few generalities about the importance of imitation in language would be equally inadequate. What must be recognized is what we will call the theatrical component of linguistic behavior. The schoolboy who imitates the speech of criminals does not do so under the influence of some general imitative instinct; he wants to play the part of a robber or a pirate, and his speech is only one feature among many that help him to make himself and his friends believe in this role. Secret meeting places, terrible threats against any violator of the secret, masquerading, minor acts of violence, and other transgressions all contribute to make the performance more convincing. In short, read the first chapters of *Huckleberry Finn* and you will know what we mean.

It would be quite wrong to suppose that the use of language as part of a theatrical performance outside the theater is restricted to adolescents. We have already found some indications, and we will find many more, that many things in language can be explained in a similar way, and that imitation of other people's speech habits is very frequently nothing else but posing in a character that is not the speaker's own.

On the other hand, it would be imprudent to assume that the presence of this theatrical tendency must necessarily exclude other concurring motives. It cannot be stated with too much emphasis that language is an extremely complicated phenomenon, and that nothing is more common than the concurrence of different causes in the creation of one form of speech. Double motivation is evident in the following passages from Dickens:

[The situation: Pursuit of a criminal; on entering a tavern, the police inspector warns his helpers not to disclose their purpose but to pose as lime merchants.]

"You can't do better than be interested in some lime works anywhere down about Northfleet, and doubtful whether some of your lime don't get into bad company, as it comes up in barges."

"You hear, Eugene?" said Lightwood, over his shoulder. "You are deeply interested in lime."

"Without lime," returned that unmoved barrister-at-law, "my existence would be unilluminated by a ray of hope."

. . . . .

[Arrived at the inn, they use the word *lime* as a covering word, as often as their real purpose is alluded to.]

"It's a certain fact," said Mr. Inspector, "that this man we have received our information from," indicating Riderhood with his thumb over his shoulder, "has for some time past given the other man a bad name arising out of your lime barges. . . ."

. . . . .

[Understand a certain dark traffic going on on the river.]

"Speaking as a shipper of lime—" began Eugene.

"Which no man has a better right to do than yourself, you know," said Mr. Inspector.

"I hope not," said Eugene; "my father having been a shipper of lime before me, and my grandfather before him—in fact we have been a family immersed to the crowns of our heads in lime during several generations—I beg to observe that if this missing lime [i.e., the criminal] could be got hold of without any young female relative of any distinguished gentleman engaged in the lime trade [i.e., crime] . . . being present, I think it might be a more agreeable proceeding to the assisting bystanders, that is to say, lime-burners [representatives of the law]."

. . . . .

[The waiter, having served them, waits for a sign of approval.]

It was bestowed. (Mr. Inspector having proposed as an appropriate sentiment "The lime trade!"), and Bob withdrew. . . . It may be here in confidence admitted that, the room being close shut in his absence, there had not appeared to be the slightest reason for the elaborate maintenance of this same lime fiction. Only it had been regarded by Mr. Inspector as so uncommonly satisfactory, and so fraught with mysterious virtues, that neither of his clients had presumed to question it.[5]

Here is a very clear case of the concurrence of two different motives: a manner of speech invented for the sake of secrecy

[5] Charles Dickens, *Our Mutual Friend,* Book I, Chaps. XII and XIII, *passim.*

is kept up even after the circumstances have made all precaution unnecessary—merely because the actors enjoy their little comedy. Neither tendency is solely responsible for the speech act.

We conclude this discussion with another quotation which shows a connection between language used for masquerading purposes and one of the most interesting problems of linguistics: meaning and change of meaning. Whoever imitates the speech of a class to which he does not belong will occasionally be confronted with words he does not fully understand. But this lack of comprehension is no reason for excluding such unfamiliar words from the imitative performance; on the contrary, they may be even more impressive than words that are within anybody's grasp. What will happen in this case is that in the mouth of the imitator such words will assume a meaning different from the one they have within the circle to which they originally belonged.

[Tom Sawyer and his friends, planning to organize a robber band]:

"Must we always kill the people?"

"Oh, certainly. It's best. Some authorities think different, but mostly it's considered best to kill them—except some that you bring to the cave here, and keep them till they're ransomed."

"Ransomed? What's that?"

. . . . .

"Well, I don't know. But per'aps if we keep them till they're ransomed, it means that we keep them till they're dead."

"Now, that's something *like*. That'll answer. Why couldn't you said that before? We'll keep them till they're ransomed to death. . . ."

. . . . .

"I think that's foolishness. Why can't a body take a club and ransom them as soon as they get here?"

"Because it ain't in the books so—that's why. Now, Ben Rogers, do you want to do things regular, or don't you? . . . "No, sir, we'll just go on and ransom them in the regular way." [6]

[6] Mark Twain, *Huckleberry Finn*, Chap. 2.

Apart from belonging to speech communities, the individual is subject to many highly personal speech influences and tendencies, which, if not in accord with the pattern of his community, may involve him in all kinds of difficulty. Here is the true story of a boy who refused to accept the speech etiquette of his community:

Under spur of the ascetic religious teaching he had received from the pulpit utterances of men whose oratorical exaggerations he took in their literal sense, Edward had become positively morbid in his conscientiousness, during his early youth. . . . I challenged him to tell me why he had suddenly become so restrained in speech. For answer he opened the New Testament and showed me the passage which reads:

"But I say unto you, That every idle word that men shall speak, they shall give account thereof in the day of judgment."

After the fashion of that time he had taken that passage literally, as he took, and as the preachers insisted upon taking every other passage of the Scriptures. And by "idle words" he understood the text to mean all unnecessary words.

In those days well-ordered young persons were carefully taught to say "yes, ma'am" and "no, ma'am" "yes, sir" and "no, sir"; but Edward's spiritual eye was fixed upon "the day of judgment," and in fear of that he resolutely dropped the "ma'am" and "sir," as "idle words" for which, if he spoke them, he must give an account at that dread time.[7]

In this episode, the struggle between the individual and his community ends in what may be considered the natural way, in a victory for the unified majority as represented by a teacher and a respected older friend. In the biography of Edward Eggleston it remains an episode; in the history of the speech community it is of no importance at all.

Two centuries earlier, a very similar reform was launched by George Fox with an entirely different result. The decision of one man to accept the tradition of literal obedience to the Biblical injunction against superfluous words became the core around which a new speech community was formed.

[7] George Cary Eggleston, *The First of the Hoosiers* (Philadelphia: Drexel Biddle, 1903), pp. 169–172.

Chapter Six

RELIGIOUS AND POLITICAL SPEECH COMMUNITIES

RELIGIOUS group speech, exemplified in the following pages by a short study of the speech habits of the Religious Society of Friends, more commonly called "Quakers," is singularly instructive. It offers advantages not often within the reach of the linguist. Our sources for the study of many speech communities are not complete enough to provide an answer to all our questions. But religions, like doctrines and ideologies in general, require explanation and justification. Religious leaders have generally been prolific writers and apologists. Therefore, we can base an investigation of such a speech community on solid documentary proof.

Furthermore, the material offered by the history of such a group brings out some facts as important to all study of linguistic development and history as they are to the study of group speech. Here as elsewhere in human cultural behavior we find leaders and followers. A powerful and dominant personality can impose its will upon the group, in speech as definitely as in belief and practice. But, here as elsewhere, the leader himself is the product of his environment, and the rules he imposes are patterned on ways for which he is indebted to earlier tradition. His contribution has rarely the character of absolute creation. Much of his task is merely to turn earlier, and perhaps scattered, usage into a consistent "law." Even a mystical revelation will be found to give authority and meaning to previously considered habits. The ease, finally, with which the leader's will dominates his followers depends upon the degree to which his system gives shape and coherence and meaning to ideas or practices which they are already conditioned to receive because they also have been at least exposed to the same creative forces.

All this and more can be shown by a study of the Plain Speech of the Friends. Each of its peculiarities was part of the habitual personal speech of George Fox, the founder of the sect, before they were imposed by him upon the group. But nearly all can be shown to have existed in the speech of one or more of the many quietist and separatist sects popular in the England in which Fox grew up.

Naturally, Fox did not say so; it did not matter to him whether they were old or new. He was determined to preserve Biblical simplicity in speech as well as in manner and to avoid all the misuses of language of which he believed not only the worldly but the members of the official church to be guilty. Indeed, he thought he had a precise injunction from the Lord in Matthew 5:33–37 and James 5:12, verses which he referred to frequently and with emphasis. The commandment given in the Sermon on the Mount reads:

> Again, ye have heard that it hath been said by them of old time, Thou shalt not forswear thyself, but shalt perform unto the Lord thine oaths:
>
> But I say unto you, Swear not at all; neither by heaven; for it is God's throne:
>
> Nor by the earth; for it is his footstool: neither by Jerusalem; for it is the city of the great King.
>
> Neither shalt thou swear by thy head, because thou canst not make one hair white or black.
>
> But let your communication be, Yea, yea; Nay, nay: for whatsoever is more than these cometh of evil.

James condenses and repeats the same rule:

But above all things, my brethren, swear not, neither by heaven, neither by the earth, neither by any other oath; but let your yea be yea; and your nay, nay; lest ye fall into condemnation.

From Fox's effort to model his speech upon these and a few other passages in the Bible arose a number of deviations not unknown, of course, prior to Fox, for others had earlier read the same meanings into the same passages.

The first of these, reflecting a principle of such importance that adherence to it caused probably more persecution of the Quakers than any other practice they followed, was the absolute avoidance of all oaths, whether profane or required by law or government:

Then said the Judge to me "Will you take the oath of allegiance, George Fox?" I said, "I never took any oath in my life, nor any covenant or engagement." "Well," said he, "will you swear or no?" I answered, "I am a Christian, and Christ commands me not to swear; so does the apostle James; and whether I should obey God or man, do thou judge."

"I ask you again," said he, "whether you will swear or no." I answered again, "I am neither Turk, Jew, nor heathen, but a Christian, and should show forth Christianity. . . . My allegiance doth not lie in swearing, but in truth and faithfulness, for I honour all men, much more the King. But Christ, who is the Great Prophet, the King of kings, the Saviour and Judge of the whole world, saith I must not swear. Now, must I obey Christ or thee?" [1]

The points most interesting for the linguist in the drama here enacted are, first, that it was played hundreds of times all over England by Fox's followers in the years after 1662 (Quakerism accepted absolutely Fox's position on swearing); and, second, that the principles the man here enunciated were explicitly established in him, according to his own testimony, in his childhood:

When I came to eleven years of age I knew pureness and righteousness; for while a child I was taught how to walk to be kept pure.

---

[1] *George Fox: An Autobiography,* ed. by Rufus M. Jones (Philadelphia: Ferris & Leach, 1903), II, 414. Reprinted by permission of Elizabeth B. Jones.

The Lord taught me to be faithful in all things, and to act faithfully two ways, viz., inwardly, to God, and outwardly, to man; and to keep to Yea and Nay in all things. For the Lord showed me that, though the people of the world have mouths full of deceit, and changeable words, yet I was to keep to Yea and Nay in all things; and that my words should be few and savoury, seasoned with grace. . . .[2]

The child's habit and conviction continued in the young man. While he was still an apprentice, long before he was called to minister, he was notable for the fact that, as he said, "I used in my dealings the word Verily, and it was a common saying among those that knew me, 'If George says verily, there is no altering him.' " [3] Linguistic expression had not yet hardened into a final formula, but the psychological pattern was fixed. It comes as no surprise to learn that this young man's father was so pious that his neighbors called him "Righteous Christer" and that his mother was "an upright woman . . . of the stock of the martyrs." Nor is it surprising to learn that of the many pietistic sects flourishing in the England of Fox's youth, at least two that had a direct influence upon him and his movement, the Familists (or "Family of Love" or "House of Love") and the Baptists, rejected oaths.[4] Finally we are quite prepared to learn that Fox had a Baptist uncle with whom he was intimate enough to visit, and that he began his formal ministry among a group of "separated" Baptists in Mansfield. When we add to these details of the personal history of Fox the fact that among the earliest converts to Quakerism were many Baptists and Familists, the picture is complete: out of an elaborate context a man has found one detail in speech, which he has been used to since early childhood, to be a significant expression of principle. Once his thinking makes it part of a body of doctrine, it almost inevitably becomes an essential part of the speech habits of himself and of all those who follow him. And

---

[2] *Ibid.*, I, 66.

[3] *Ibid.*, I, 67.

[4] See William C. Braithwaite, *The Beginnings of Quakerism* (London: Macmillan & Co., 1912), p. 23; and Rufus Jones's Introduction to Fox's *Autobiography*, pp. 18 ff.

the converts will follow it the more easily because they are already prepared for it in their own antecedent speech and thought.

As the rationale for another deviation from common speech, his unwillingness to give the days of the week (and the months of the year) their common names, Fox referred to the first chapter of Genesis, taking care, however, not to let his audience forget that the rule is but an extension of the *yea and nay* principle:

My dear brethren in the covenant of life, keep to Yea and Nay, and call the days first-day, second-day . . . as they were given forth and called by God in the beginning.[5]

His objection to the "heathen" practice was not original. Both Separatists and Baptists had previously had the same scruple.[6]

To the same category belongs his use of "steeple-house" for any "church" or cathedral and the final choice by the Quakers of "meetinghouse" as the name for their own place of worship. To Fox "church" meant just what it means in the Bible, the community of believers, and could not be used in any material sense, as, for instance, to mean "a building consecrated to divine service." The following passage gives a very impressive account of his ideas:

At last one woman asked a question out of Peter, What that birth was, viz., a being born again of incorruptible seed, by the Word of God, that liveth and abideth for ever? And the priest said to her, "I permit not a woman to speak in the church"; though he had before given liberty for any to speak. Whereupon I was wrapped up, as in a rapture, in the Lord's power; and I stepped up and asked the priest, "Dost thou call this (the steeple-house) a church? Or dost thou call this mixed multitude a church?" For the woman asking a question, he ought to have answered it, having given liberty for any to speak.

But, instead of answering me, he asked me what a church was? I told him the church was the pillar and ground of truth, made up of

---

[5] *Epistles,* No. 48. Quoted from Braithwaite, *op. cit.,* pp. 139–140.

[6] Braithwaite, *loc. cit.* and Jones's Introduction to the *Autobiography,* I, 72, note 10.

living stones, living members, a spiritual household, which Christ was the head of; but he was not the head of a mixed multitude, or of an old house made up of lime, stones and wood.[7]

Again neither the conviction nor the scruple is original with Fox. The Baptists and the Familists had already reacted in the same way and with the same reasoning.

The most widely known peculiarity of Quaker speech, its refusal to use "you" as an address to a single person and its rejection of titles and compliments, seems to be different in origin. While the rejection of titles was not uncommon among other pietist sects, we have not been able to discover that limiting the second person singular to *thou* and *thee* was elsewhere prescribed. Fox himself explained it as the result of a direct order from God:

> Moreover, when the Lord sent me forth into the world, He forbade me to put off my hat to any, high or low; and I was required to Thee and Thou all men and women, without any respect to rich or poor, great or small. And as I travelled up and down I was not to bid people Good morrow, or Good evening; neither might I bow or scrape with my leg to any one; and this made the sects and professions to rage.[8]

But whatever the direct source, Fox serenely admitted in the same passage from which we have quoted that since "I was in that Spirit by which they [the Scriptures] were given forth . . . what the Lord opened in me I afterwards found was agreeable to them." Furthermore both he and his followers have generally based the justification of their habit, along with their rejection of "hat honor," titles, and all "bowings and scrapings with the leg," not upon "openings" alone but upon John 5:44:

> How can ye believe, which receive honour one of another, and seek not the honour that cometh from God only?

---

[7] Fox, *op. cit.*, I, 92–93. *Priest,* by the way, in Fox's use usually means Anglican minister and carries a derogatory connotation. Fox was violently opposed to any man's receiving pay for doing God's work. His use here echoes the note of social rebellion which runs through all of early Quakerism.

[8] *Ibid.*, I, 105–106.

And twelve or thirteen years later when, with the help of some learned friends, he published *A Battle-Door for Teachers and Professors to learn Singular & Plural: You to Many, and Thou to One* . . . ,[9] he contended that the "plural of honor" was contrary alike to the customary use of the Bible and the rules of grammar.

We can, however, cut deeper into this problem. The history of the non-Calvinist and non-Episcopalian religious movements of the seventeenth century and the history of manners both throw much light on it. These groups, which rejected predestination as they rejected ritual, believed that Grace was freely given to all men and that all men had the capacity to experience the Inner Light, that indeed there was something of God in all men.[10] They accepted the practical ethics of their positions and applied it to manners and the social structure. They tended toward democracy, sometimes even toward some variety of communism, and they necessarily rejected those customary forms of behavior which were to them denials of their principles. The whole complex of habits, of which *thou* and *thee* are but a part, has a unified ideological background shared by many.

In addition, we cannot recognize the full meaning of Quaker usage, the significance of its motivation, its radical quality, and the element of social rebellion it contained, unless we see it against the common practice of the seventeenth century in more orthodox circles. Braithwaite thus summarizes two of the conventions Quakers rejected:

> In that ceremonious age Quaker plainness seemed not only ill-bred but deliberately offensive. The hat was at this time commonly worn in the house and in church, but not during prayer nor in the presence of superiors. Lord Clarendon says that in his younger days he never kept on his hat before those older than himself (except at dinner), nor when grace was said at meals. To be uncovered before any one

---

[9] London: 1660.

[10] See Rufus M. Jones, *Studies in Mystical Religion* (London: Macmillan & Co., 1909); and his *Spiritual Reformers in the 16th & 17th Centuries* (London: Macmillan & Co., 1914).

was, accordingly, a distinctive mark of deference. It was the same with the plain language. When Lord Coke desired to anger Raleigh at his trial, he had addressed him with the insulting words, "All that Lord Cobham did was at thy instigation, thou viper: for I thou thee, thou traitor." But "thou" was the regular form of speech to inferiors, long after "you" had become customary between persons of equal rank. Fuller lays down the usage thus— "We maintain that 'thou' from superiors to inferiors is proper, as a sign of command; from equals to equals is passable as a note of familiarity; but from inferiors to superiors, if preceeding from ignorance, hath a smack of clownishness; if from affectation, a tone of contempt." For a servant to address his master with "thou," or a son his father, was therefore a gross affront and an act of insubordination, and we need not be surprised at the angry scenes which followed.[11]

So far we have been chiefly concerned with the leader, and with followers only to indicate their general preparation for becoming a speech community. But to understand how a group, held together by anything other than geography, comes into being is impossible until one sees something of the lives of the individuals that create it. Fortunately, the early Quakers were addicted to biography and autobiography. One of the most revealing is *The History of Thomas Ellwood,* a young gentleman of Oxfordshire, who in the winter of 1659–1660, at the age of twenty, turned Quaker. Soon after his conversion he was "required by . . . *Inward* and *Spiritual Law* . . . to *Cease to do Evil.*" The evils of which he stood convicted were pride in fine clothes, the use of titles of honor, the respect of persons implicit in uncovering the head and bowing, and, finally,

. . . *The Corrupt and Unsound Form of Speaking in the Plural Number to a Single Person* (YOU to *One,* instead of THOU;) contrary to the *Pure, Plain,* and *Single Language* of TRUTH (THOU to *One,* and YOU to more than *One*) which had always been used, by GOD to *Men,* and *Men* to GOD, as well as one to another, from the oldest Record of Time, till *Corrupt Men,* for *Corrupt Ends,* in later and *Corrupt Times,* to *Flatter, Fawn,* and *work* upon the *Cor-*

[11] William C. Braithwaite, *The Beginnings of Quakerism* (London: Macmillan & Co., 1912), pp. 493–494. Reprinted by permission of The Macmillan Company.

rupt Nature in *Men,* brought in that false and senseless Way of Speaking, YOU to *One;* which hath since corrupted the *Modern Languages,* and hath greatly debased the Spirits, and depraved the Manners of Men. This *Evil Custom* I had been as forward in as others; and this I was now called out of, and required to cease from.[12]

After a good deal of travail of spirit, he finally achieved the courage to announce his position to some of his old school friends, who looked "somewhat confusedly one upon another, [and] after a while took their Leave of me. . . ." His father, however, remained another matter:

. . . yet was not the Vail so done away, or fully rent, but that there still remained a Cloud upon my Understanding, with respect to my Carriage towards my Father. And that Notion, which the Enemy had brought into my Mind, That *I ought to put such a Difference between him and all others, as that, on the Account of Paternal Relation, I should still deport my self towards him, both in Gesture and Language, as I had always heretofore done;* did yet prevail with me. So that when I came home, I went to my Father bare-headed, as I used to do; and gave him a particular Account of the Business he had given me in Command, in such manner, that he, observing no Alteration in my Carriage towards him, found no Cause to take Offence at me.[13]

The inevitable hour could not be long postponed, however, and with the help of God and the encouragement received from a visit to Quaker friends, young Thomas was braced to act according to his convictions:

But when I came home, I understood my Father was from home. Wherefore I sate down, by the Fire, in the Kitchin; keeping my Mind retired to the Lord, the Breathings of Spirit to Him, that I might be preserved from Falling.

After some time I heard the Coach drive in, which put me into a little Fear, and a sort of Shivering came over me. But by that time he was alighted and come in, I had pretty well recovered my self; and as soon as I saw him, I rose up, and advanced a step or two

---

[12] *The History of the Life of Thomas Ellwood . . . Written by his own Hand* (London: 1714), p. 27.

[13] *Ibid.*, p. 37.

towards him, with my Head covered, said, *Isaac Penington* and his Wife remember their Loves to thee.

He made a Stop, to hear what I said, and observing that I did not stand bare, and that I used the word *Thee* to him; He, with a stern countenance, and Tone that spake high Displeasure, only said, *I shall talk with you, Sir, another time. . . .*[14]

From this time on, the struggle grew bitter. The boy was confined to the house. He was beaten each time he followed a Quaker habit. Each time he stood covered before his father he lost another hat until finally he had none, with the result that he caught a violent cold and was severely ill. And his speech annoyed his father as completely as his actions:

But whenever I had occasion to speak to my Father, though I had no Hat now to offend him; yet my Language did as much: for I durst not say YOU to him; but THOU, or THEE, as the Occasion required, and then would he be sure to fall on me with his Fists.

At one of these times, I remember, when he had beaten me in that Manner, he commanded me (as he commonly did at such times) to Go to my Chamber; which I did, and he followed me to the Bottom of the Stairs. Being come thither, he gave me a Parting-Blow; and in a very angry Tone, said, *Sirrah, if ever I hear you say* Thou *or* Thee *to me again, I'll strike your Teeth down your Throat.* I was greatly Grieved to hear him say so. And feeling a Word rise in my Heart unto him; I turned again, and calmly said unto him. Would it not be just, if GOD should serve thee so: when thou sayst *Thou* or *Thee* to Him? Though his Hand was up, I saw it sink, and his Countenance fall, and he turned away, and left me standing there.[15]

Not long afterward, the great Quaker family of the Peningtons rescued Thomas, took him home with them, and enabled him to become henceforth officially a Quaker. The Ellwood family broke up, and relations between father and son practically ceased. Clearly the freedom of a weaver's son like George Fox to choose his own way of life was a thing to be hard won by the heir of a county family. Yet Ellwood's experience is not exceptional. William Penn took his share of beating too, before,

---

[14] *Ibid.*, pp. 46–47.

[15] *Ibid.*, pp. 56–57.

at the age of twenty-three, he found his father trying to bargain with him to the effect that he might "thee and thou" whom he pleased if only he would promise not to use the impudent address to the King, the Duke of York, and himself.[16] Many a member of the upper middle class and aristocracy found the Society of Friends attractive. In the lives of all of them one can see the same pressures resulting from attaching themselves to a special and unpopular group, the same tendency for the larger social group to ostracize them, and the same cohesion within the group as a consequence of the ostracism.

The concentrated symbol of the antagonism against a new community is, of course, the name given to it. With what feelings the general seventeenth-century public reacted to the word *Quaker* is sharply brought out by our final quotation from Ellwood—when his elder sister discovered his conversion, she was, he says, "much troubled to find me a *Quaker,* a Name of Reproach and great Contempt then." The history of the name is as interesting as the linguistic habits of the people to whom it was applied. According to Fox[17] it was coined in 1650 by an enemy of the sect, "Justice Bennet, of Derby, who was the first that called us Quakers, because I bade them tremble at the word of the Lord." Barclay, however, and others do not take the word in the sense of "somebody who bids others tremble," but of "somebody who trembles":

> . . . sometimes the power of God will break forth into a whole meeting, and there will be such an inward travail, while each is seeking to overcome the evil in themselves, that by the strong contrary workings of these opposite powers, like the going of two contrary tides, every individual will be strongly exercised as in a day of battle, and thereby trembling and a motion of body will be upon most, if not upon all. . . . And from this the name of Quakers, i.e., Tremblers, was first reproachfully cast upon us; which though it be none of our choosing, yet in this respect we are not ashamed of it, but have rather reason to rejoice therefore, even that we are sensible of this

---

[16] William C. Braithwaite, *The Second Period of Quakerism* (London: Macmillan & Co., 1919), p. 60.

[17] Fox, *op. cit.,* I, 125.

power that hath oftentimes laid hold of our adversaries, and made them yield unto us, and join with us, and confess to the truth, before they had any distinct or discursive knowledge of our doctrines.[18]

It is clear from these quotations that already within the first generation of Quakers there existed two different views on the meaning of the word. This is by no means unnatural. Even a relatively small speech community like that of the first Friends is not absolutely uniform in its language, but consists of individuals who, having agreed on a few leading principles, still maintain a considerable variety of ideas and feelings not covered explicitly by these principles. The same words, used by different members of the group, may therefore carry different implications, none of which can be neglected by a linguist, since it is their sum that builds up the history of the word in question. As a matter of fact, neither Fox nor Barclay was wholly right. The Oxford English Dictionary quotes the word from private correspondence as in use in 1647 and as applied to others than Friends:

I heare of a sect of woemen (they are at Southworke) come from beyond Sea, called Quakers, and these swell, shiver, and shake, and when they come to themselves (for in all this fitt Mahomett's holy-ghost hath bin conversing with them) they begin to preache what hath bin delivered to them by the Spiritt.

Quaker was apparently a scornful name that could be applied to people seized with hysterical religious manifestations before either Justice Bennet used it, no doubt sarcastically, or George Fox wittily perverted it—whichever the case may have been. As applied to the Friends, its use came in rapidly. It was in print by 1652, appeared in the Journals of the House of Commons in 1654,[19] and, to judge from its occurrence in Ellwood, must have been the only popular name by the end of the decade. Once the Friends themselves adopted it, as they quickly did,

---

18 Robert Barclay, *An Apology for the True Chrisian Divinity* (Philadelphia: Friends' Book Association, n.d.), pp. 335–336.

19 See Braithwaite, *The Beginnings of Quakerism*, pp. 57–58, and Fox. *op. cit.*, I, 126, note.

using it as nearly interchangeable with Friend, the word lost its derogatory connotation, in proportion as the sect it named grew respectable in the eyes of the world.

Until now we have considered the existence of group language as a natural, but secondary, consequence of the existence of social bodies constituted by a common profession, common religious or political tenets, and so forth. The reverse can also be true. If a number of persons share conspicuous peculiarities of speech, then this very fact can solidify them into an even more unified and coherent group. That every Quaker was required to use certain distinctive forms of speech is not the whole story; the acceptance of these peculiarities drew a sharp line between this speech community and others, thereby helping to constitute and maintain the community as a unique organization. We have seen that by refusing to give others the forms of honor and polite address to which they felt themselves entitled, the early Friends suffered social ostracism and often severe punishment. Yet this separation from the outside world could not fail to strengthen the cohesive spirit of the group. The story of how the Peningtons gave young Ellwood their powerful aid could be repeated hundreds of times from the documents of the seventeenth-century Quakers. Whenever one of them found himself cast out by his previous group, he found a new place to rest and a new source of strength among his new fellows. Language, as we have pointed out before, is not solely a by-product of behavior, but also an element creating new forms of behavior.

There is a long way between the sufferings of the early Friends and the comfortable use of the no-longer dangerous words among their descendants. The belligerent atmosphere which *thou* created in the seventeenth century is in sharp contrast to the peaceful mood of which it is a symbol today. Expressions in their beginnings fraught with emotional life may, by frequent and thoughtless repetition, deteriorate into mechanized formulas. In this connection the following passage deserves careful consideration:

> Have you read a little pamphlet called "George Fox and his First Disciples"? I was charmed with it. Don't you remember I told you I was sure that the *thou* and *thee* of the Friends originated in a principle of Christian equality? This pamphlet confirms my conjecture. In the English language of George Fox's time, and in most European languages now, *thou* was used only to familiars and equals. . . . It was this distinction of language addressed to superiors, and to inferiors and equals, that the early Friends resisted. The custom had life in it then, for it was merely the outward expression of form of a vital principle. What is it now? An inherited formality, of which few stop to inquire the meaning. Thus have all human forms the seed of death within them; but luckily when the body becomes dead, the inward soul or principle seeks a new form and lives again.[20]

Lydia Child's comment may exaggerate the importance of the democratic theory beyond what the documents warrant. But the observation that, while speech habits reflecting a principle may deteriorate, the principle may live on and create new speech habits is suggestive. *Citoyen* as the general address of the French Revolution, *Comrade* as used by the Communist party and the American Legion, and *Genosse,* common among German socialists, are all speech forms based on the ideal of equality (although, to be sure, not Christian equality) and therefore in a manner of speaking a resurrection of the old Quaker principle—at least, as understood by Mrs. Child.

These party words remind us of how closely some of the linguistic developments of the French Revolution parallel developments in Quaker speech, though the motivation is essentially different.[21] The Quakers, as we have noted, changed the names of the weekdays into *first day, second day,* and so on. In 1793 in France a similar attack on the names of the days occurred, when they were replaced by *primidi, duodi, tridi,*

---

[20] *Letters of Lydia Maria Child* (Boston: Houghton Mifflin Company, 1883), pp. 27–28.

[21] We must here stress the importance of judging every development in language on its own merits and of avoiding the fallacy of assuming that similar development in different places and at different periods must necessarily be of similar origin.

and so on. The Quakers acted on the authority of the Bible and also from the objections of many pious Christians to the fact that words like *Wednesday* and *Saturday* contain the names of heathen gods. The French action, however, was based on anything but respect for the Bible and the sensibilities of Christian etymologists. In fact, the French regulation formed part of a general calendar reform directed chiefly against religion and aiming at the abolition of Sundays and holy days.[22]

Another striking parallel is the rejection of *vous* when speaking to one person only. The reasons given for this procedure in documents of the Revolution are, to a certain extent, similar to those used by the Quakers, but naturally the argument from Biblical usage has been abandoned in favor of political theory:

"Citoyens représentants, les principes de notre langue doivent nous être aussi chers que les lois de notre République. Nous distinguons trois personnes pour le singulier et trois pour le pluriel, et, au mépris de cette règle, l'esprit de fanatisme, d'orgueil et de féodalité, nous a fait contracter l'habitude de nous servir de la seconde personne du pluriel lorsque nous parlons à un seul. Beaucoup de maux résultent encore de cet abus; il oppose une barrière à l'intelligence des sans-culottes; il entretient la morgue du pervers et de l'adulation; sous le prétexte du respect, éloigne les principes des vertus fraternelles. . . .

"Je demande, au nom de tous mes commettants, un décret portant que tous les républicains françois seront tenus a l'avenir, pour se conformer aux principes de leur langage en ce qui concerne la distinction du singulier au pluriel, de tutoyer sans distinction ceux ou celles à qui ils parleront en seul, à peine d'être déclarés suspects, comme adulateurs, en se prêtant, par ce moyen, au soutien de la morgue qui sert de prétexte a l'inégalité entre nous." [23]

Do not allow yourself to be deceived by the logical façade of this argument. The whole question was one of burning political passions. Its reasoning may seem not far from that of the

---

[22] Ferdinand Brunot, *Histoire de la langue française* (Paris: Librairie Armand Colin, 1937), IX, 904 ff.

[23] Parliamentary speech by Malbec, October 31, 1793, quoted from Brunot, *op. cit.*, IX, 691.

early Friends, but its results were as different as the differences in spirit between the two. The hotheads of the Revolution were amply prepared to use violence even toward those who only from old habit retained the earlier use of *vous:*

Au café Procope, deux citoyens eurent querelle avec un des garçons du café, à cause que ce garçon ne les avait point tutoyés; ils l'appelèrent esclave, et l'injurièrent même d'un façon révoltante, d'autant que ce garçon est tres vieux et qu'il s'excusa, en se reprenant du mot *vous,* en disant toi.[24]

George Fox and his followers were equally prepared to suffer any amount of abuse and violence to preserve intact the righteousness of which saying *thou* was a symbol:

It was in the month called July, of this present year [1656], when Mary Fisher and Ann Austin arrived in the road before Boston, before ever a law was made there against the Quakers; and yet they were very ill treated. . . . The deputy-governor had them brought on shore, and committed them by a mittimus to prison as Quakers, upon this proof only, that one of them, speaking to him, had said *thee* instead of *you;* whereupon he said he needed no more, for now he saw they were Quakers.[25]

In England and America in Fox's day you could be imprisoned, beaten, and starved if you said *thou.* In France, little more than a century later, you might be injured *même d'une façon révoltante* if you did not. The moral seems to be that if you wish to depart from the speech of your contemporaries, you had better be prepared to stand what only a Quaker could describe with the mild word "exercises."

It is one of history's fine ironies to find, in the generation following the French Revolution, so democratic a society as a labor union forbidding the use of *tu* among its members. In his interesting biography, *Mémoires d'un Compagnon,* Agricol

---

[24] Rapports des Agents secrets du Ministre de l'Intérieur, December 25, 1793, quoted from Brunot, *op. cit.,* IX, 693.

[25] William Sewel, *The History . . . of the Christian People Called Quakers* (Philadelphia: Friends' Book Store, n.d.), I, 210.

Perdiguier summarizes the official rules of an organization of journeymen he joined at Avignon in 1822 or 1823:

Ce règlement portait que chacun devait participer aux frais de la Société; qu'il fallait être polis les uns pour les autres, ne point se tutoyer, ne point se donner de sobriquets; qu'on devait être respettueux envers la mère, envers le père, envers les soeurs et les frères, envers tous les membres de la Société, compagnons et affiliés; qu'on devait étre propre, rangé; que, dans la semaine, il ne fallait pas se présenter chez le mère en bras de chemise, ou avec son tablier, et, le dimanche, sans être cravaté et sans avoir des bas ou guêtres aux pieds.[26]

Evidently refraining from using the familiar address is meant to give a respectable tone to the union by bringing its speech habits into accordance with what are regarded to be those of the higher classes. Again we find forms of speech a part of non-linguistic general etiquette. Rejecting the custom of *tutoyment* is paralleled by prohibiting appearance in shirt sleeves (and without a cravat on Sundays), just as the Quakers' habit of using *thou* goes hand in hand with their refusal to remove their hats.

---

[26] Agricol Perdiguier, *Mémoires d'un Compagnon* (Moulins: Edition des Cahiers du Centre, 1914), p. 62.

Chapter Seven

PHONETIC CHANGE

SINCE the study of speech sounds is based on the anatomic and physiological study of the speech organs, it may seem rather remote from the humanistic view which underlies this book. The task of this chapter, then, is simply to show that it is not. Let us examine a very commonplace situation.

If you are a bridge player, you will probably have heard something like the following conversation:

"I bid a spade."

"How many spades?"

"*Ā* spade."

In the phrase "I bid a spade," the article will be pronounced with the reduced vowel it usually gets when unstressed [ə]; in the second instance, when repeated for the sake of verification, the "a" gets the protracted sound it has in *name* or *hate* [e].

Or, listen to a speaker whose nasal passages are obstructed in consequence of a head cold. His *n* and *m* will differ from his normal pronunciation. In extreme cases, you will hear, not *n* and *m,* but *d* and *b*.

Once your attention is directed toward everyday occurrences of this sort, you will find ample evidence of the fact that our speech sounds are subject to frequent alterations, resulting from the conditions under which a certain utterance is made. The range of possible reasons for occasional changes of this sort is unlimited. Excitement, or embarrassment, or the realization that your audience does not readily understand you will be certain to produce temporary deviations from your ordinary articulation; so will a hot potato in your mouth.

In view of the frequency with which phonetic changes occur in the speech of every individual, it is only natural that the history of language reveals phonetic changes on a larger scale. Since sound changes occur constantly in the speech of one person, we can be sure to discover massive group changes when we count the time by centuries and the speakers by the million. In fact, an ever so slight acquaintance with Anglo-Saxon and Old High German is sufficient to show that the phonetic structure of these languages has undergone considerable alteration, even though the spelling of our documents in these languages gives only a vague idea of how they really sounded. The remarkable thing is not that changes occur, but that, wherever they happen, they appear to be governed by surprisingly strict rules.

Here, instead of a lengthy explanation, is an example: Some very ancient runic inscriptions prove that primitive Germanic —the uniform dialect which later split into English, German, Scandinavian, and so on—possessed a word *staina* (accusative), "stone." It is quite possible, and indeed very likely, that already at that time, i.e., during the first Christian centuries, the spelling *ai* covered a number of phonetic variations; for instance, in the pronunciation of some speakers the first part of the diphthong may have varied in regard to length, tenseness, raising of the tongue, and the like. But it is highly improbable that the permissible variations can have had anything like the range we find in later Germanic languages. It is *stone* in English, *Stein* in standard German, *sten* in Danish and Swedish as well as in many German dialects; others have *Sta(n)*, *Stoa(n)* or *Stoi(n)*, and each of these spellings stands for a number of minor variations that are easily discernible to the ear, although their rendering in print would necessitate the use of an elaborate phonetic alphabet. Likewise, standard English *stone* varies in dialect to include such pronunciations as Scottish *stane* and New England *stun*.

Thus we find that, during the centuries that separate us

from the primitive Germanic period, a number of new variations have developed, which is only what was to be expected. However, a study of other words containing the Germanic diphthong *ai* reveals that the variations appearing in the development of *staina* form part of a very regular pattern. The relation connecting English *stone,* German *Stein,* Swedish *sten* is exactly the same as we find in the various forms of *bone* or of *alone:* English *bone, alone;* German *Bein, allein;* Swedish *ben, allena.* This regularity holds good not only for the standard languages but also for minor regional units. The statement that a certain Bavarian dialect uses the form *Stoa*(*n*) is practically equivalent to the more comprehensive assertion that it has *Stoa*(*n*) for *stone, Boa*(*n*) for *bone,* and *alloa*(*n*) for *alone.* A general statement of this type, "The Germanic diphthong *ei* has in such and such dialect changed to *oa,*" is called a phonetic law (*Lautgesetz*). Here are some other examples of phonetic laws: Primitive Germanic possessed the fricative sound represented by English *th;* in German this sound has been changed to *d* (e.g., English *thorn,* German *Dorn; thunder, Donner; think, denken*). Or, Latin *k* (spelled *c*), if followed by *a,* has been replaced in standard French by the sound *sh* (spelled *ch*), as, for instance, in *champ* from Latin *campus, chanter* from Latin *cantare, château* from Latin *castello.*

The discovery of phonetic laws—or rather of the fact that the history of language, insofar as phonetic changes are concerned, is not an accumulation of haphazard details but of tendencies so regular in their effect that the term *law* appears applicable—has had an enormous influence upon the development of linguistics. Before this discovery, the derivation of words was based on the observation of obvious similarities, plus a large amount of loose combination and mere guesswork. Now, however, linguistic investigation has become much more methodical; our knowledge of phonetic laws enables the scholar to see that frequently an inviting combination, say of a French word and a Latin one, has to be rejected as not being in accord with these laws, while possibilities apparently remote may become certainties. Thus, we can no longer believe that English *day* has anything to do with Latin *dies,* in spite of the identity of meaning and the strong similarity of form; to assume such a connection would mean that, in this particular case, well-established sound laws would have failed to function. On the other hand, nobody doubts that the French word for *thimble, dé,* is a derivative of Latin *digitale* (from *digitus,* "finger"); it is true that the difference in sound is much greater than that between *day* and *dies,* but it can be shown that every one of the steps that finally reduced the long Latin word to a monosyllable is in keeping with the phonetic laws of the French language.

There is a wide gap, however, between the admission that phonetic laws exist and a thorough understanding of this remarkable feature of linguistic development. Nobody has as yet succeeded in tracing a phonetic law from its earliest beginning to the accomplished fact. As long as our knowledge of earlier sound development rests on the study of written records, the task is hopeless, since no spelling system can adequately reproduce all the finer shades of spoken language. A few centuries from now, when a large number of phonographic records will have accumulated, it will perhaps be possible to undertake it with at least a fair chance of success. The following examples and remarks can certainly not furnish an exhaustive answer to the question of why and how the innumerable and frequently diverging sound variations of our daily speech should develop into phonetic laws. All we can hope to give are a few hints that must stand for what they may be worth.

> "You, Bull!" said the old man to the dog, which was showing more and more a disposition to make a meal of the incipient pedagogue, "you, Bull! git aout, you pup!" [1]

Eggleston, from whose novel *A Hoosier Schoolmaster* this passage is taken, gives the following explanation of the form *aout* in the Hoosier dialect (which to him means "the folk-speech of the southern part of Ohio, Indiana, and Illinois of

[1] Edward Eggleston, *A Hoosier Schoolmaster,* Chap. I.

forty years ago," [2] i.e., around 1850): "*Aout* is not the common form of *out,* as it is in certain rustic New England regions. The vowel is here drawn in this way for imperative emphasis, and it occurs as a consequence of drawling speech." [3]

The meaning of the last remark is not quite clear. If we understand it correctly, what Eggleston means to say is that, in this particular instance, the spelling is intended to suggest the emphasis normally connected with imperatives but that it can also occur elsewhere—for instance, in the lengthened forms of slow and apathetic speech. Be that as it may, there can be no doubt that in Eggleston's opinion the pronunciation of the word "out" may be changed into something like "aout," if it carries a stronger than normal stress.

With this observation in mind, we will certainly not suspect that the spelling "mouut" instead of "mout" (dialect form for *might*) in the following passage is due to a misprint:

> He entered the room as Seth Davis, frightened but furious, lifted himself from before the master's desk which he had just broken open. He had barely time to conceal something in his pocket and close the lid again before Uncle Ben approached him.
>
> "What mouut ye be doin' here, Seth Davis?" he asked with the slow deliberation which in that locality meant mischief.
>
> "And what mouut *you* be doin' here, Mister Ben Dabney?" said Seth, resuming his effrontery.[4]

In other instances, Bret Harte writes "mout": "It moutn't hev bin so long," [5] or "Ye mout hev noticed." [6] From this, it becomes evident that the lengthened form "mouut" is used with the intention of quiet emphasis, implying something like a hidden threat.

From these examples we learn that in various dialects the words *out* and *mout,* if used in emphatic speech, may be sub-

[2] *Ibid.,* Preface, Library Edition, p. 7.

[3] *Ibid.,* p. 39.

[4] Bret Harte, *Cressy,* Argonaut Edition, XXIV, 224.

[5] *Ibid.,* p. 34.

[6] *Ibid.,* p. 284.

ject to a phonetic change characterized as a trend toward "triphthongization." This, on the other hand, is only a continuation of a much older process, since both English *out* and its German cognate *aus* have achieved their present forms by a similar development. The Anglo-Saxon form is *ut,* the Old High German one *uz,* both with a long *u* as in *moon.* The question now is whether we may not assume that, in this instance as well as in many others, the diphthongized pronunciation began in the same way that the form *aout* indicates, that is, in cases where the word was produced under an emotional stress. Parallels in German dialects appear to favor this explanation. Both in the north and in the south of Germany (this term here being taken to mean the territory in which German is spoken), there are dialects that normally preserve the old monophthongs. This is true in Switzerland, as well as in a large part of the Lowlands adjoining the coast. In both districts, however, we find cases in which a higher than average stress produced diphthongized forms. In Cologne, for instance, the normal form of German *heraus* is *russ;* but an angry invitation to leave the premises ("Get out!") is regularly given the pronunciation *Raus!* In the Swiss dialect of Basel, the equivalent of German *tausend* is ordinarily *tusig;* but if used as an oath (curtailed from *tausend Teufel*) it is replaced by *tausig.* While these instances show that in some cases the change from monophthong to diphthong *may* be due to emphasis, it is doubtful, to say the least, whether all cases of diphthongization in modern English or German can be explained in this manner. It is hard to see how this explanation can apply to words like English *house,* German *Haus,* that likewise go back to older forms with *u* (Anglo-Saxon and Old High German *hūs*). Still, we find it a fact that in other fields of language, mainly in the domain of changes of meaning, originally emphatic speech forms show a strong tendency to supplant less emphatic ones.

If a comprehensive theory of phonetic change can be developed along these lines—and this we regard as by no means certain—the development would supposedly be that first a number of words acquired double forms, say normal *hūs* and emphatic *house,* and that the competition between these pairs was generally decided in favor of the emphatic, so that finally, after elimination of the unemphatic forms, the whole process attained the characteristic aspect of a phonetic law.

The question has been raised, and answered in the affirmative by some scholars, whether the imitation of individual peculiarities in the pronunciation of prominent persons can change the phonetic habits of whole speech communities. If this be true, then our chances of discovering the primary causes of this or that phonetic law are necessarily slender. Only in rare cases do our sources mention anything about the individual speech habits of political or cultural leaders.

There are exceptions, however. In discussing the dominating place of Melanchthon in the history of the Protestant church, a German writer makes the following statement:

> With many the superstitious evaluation of man had increased to such a degree that they actually made an idol of Philip and his artificial theology. His friend [Camerarius] admits that his students aped him in everything. For example: because he lisped a little, many lisped the same way; he jerked his shoulders a little in walking, gestured with his hands, moved his eyebrows, and so forth. All this many copied after him.[7]

Since this statement is based on information furnished by a personal friend of Melanchthon (his biographer Camerarius), we may consider it reliable. And the question arises whether there is any connection between Melanchthon's lisping and a widespread affectation among the German ladies in later times:

> The Saxon ladies resemble the Austrian no more than the Chinese those of London; they are very genteelly dressed after the French and English modes, and have generally pretty faces, but they are the most determined *minaudières* in the whole world. They would think it a mortal sin against good-breeding, if they either spoke or moved in a natural manner. They all affect a little soft lisp, and a pretty

[7] Translated from Gottfried Arnold, *Kirchen-und Ketzer-geschichte* (Frankfurt am Main: 1699), II, 96.

pitty-pat step; which female frailties ought, however, to be forgiven them, in favour of their civility and good-nature to strangers, which I have a great deal of reason to praise.[8]

On the surface, this appears to furnish a very good example of what we were looking for: a phonetic development beginning with one man's individual habits of pronunciation and ending in the acceptance of these habits by a large part of the speech community. It seems to be in three stages: (1) Melanchthon's lisping; (2) imitation of this peculiarity by a minor group, his students, many of whom must, moreover, have become preachers and thereby acquired an influence of their own; (3) acceptance by the ladies (probably more easily influenced by their ministers than the male part of the congregation). But we must remember that we have sufficient evidence for only the first two steps of this process. The connection between the second and third stages is hypothetical, for we cannot prove that the lisping fashion among the Saxon ladies originated in their imitation of what they might have heard from the pulpits. And, whatever the origin of this fashion may have been, it is evident that, in spreading, it must have met with older tendencies of speech based on different motives. We may trust Lady Mary's statement that, at her time, lisping had become part of a pattern of behavior characterized by her as *minauderie,* i.e., coquettish affectation, cuteness. And this aspect of the lisping fashion cannot possibly be derived from Melanchthon's deficient articulation, since we have positive evidence that lisping as a form of coquetry existed long before the Reformation. Some of our readers may find it amusing to test their philological abilities by trying to understand the following quotation from a Middle High German poem of about 1300:

> Swelhe meide und jungiu wîp sich flîzen
> Daz si den munt einhalp ûf rîzen
> Als ein ros an krummem zoume,
> Die gênt in einem tummen troume.

[8] Lady Mary Wortley Montagu, in a letter to the Countess of Mar, dated Leipzig, November 21, 1716.

Man hœrt ir genuoc lispen und zarten
Durch daz die jungen man ir warten.[9]

A similar phenomenon is traceable in medieval England. Here is a detail from Chaucer's description of his socially very adept Friar:

Somwhat he lipsed, for his wantownesse,
To make his Englissh sweete upon his tonge. . . .[10]

Other alleged instances of phonetic changes induced by mannerisms of prominent persons are still less able to stand the test of a thorough investigation. It has been claimed, for instance, that the pronunciation of "either" with a diphthong (as in *wine*) instead of the long vowel (as in *see*) is due to imitation by the English courtiers of the pronunciation used by King George I, who, being German-born, gave the spelling "ei" the sound value it has in his native tongue. This theory, however, has been successfully refuted by Louise Pound, who points out that the pronunciation has been recorded as in use at least thirteen years before the Hanoverian kings came to the English throne.[11]

Thus, while the theory that the personal example of a few leaders has played a major part in changing the phonetic habits of large speech communities is not, in itself, unlikely, it must be acknowledged that the evidence offered is, up to now, entirely insufficient.

Much more can be said in favor of a variation of this theory, namely, that certain class mannerisms have, by way of imitation, become the property of much wider circles than those in which they originated.

It is an established fact, for instance, that the so-called "nasal twang" was, in the seventeenth century and later, considered characteristic of the speech of Puritans and other religious sects. In *Hudibras,* Butler speaks of certain persons of an inquisitorial

[9] Hugo von Trimberg, *Der Renner* (Tübingen: 1909), lines 12109–12114.

[10] Chaucer, *Canterbury Tales,* Prologue, lines 264–265.

[11] Louise Pound, "On the Pronunciation of 'Either' and 'Neither,'" *American Speech,* VII (June, 1932), 371–376.

turn of mind who think themselves able to judge of a man's religious attitude from the details of his outward appearance and behavior:

To find, in lines of beard and face,
The physiognomy of grace;
And by the sound and twang of nose,
If all be sound within disclose,
Free from a crack, or flaw of sinning,
As men try pipkins by the ringing.[12]

Cowper, speaking of the essential qualities of a preacher:

I seek divine simplicity in him
Who handles things divine; and all besides,
Tho' learn'd with labour, and tho' much admir'd
By curious eyes and judgments ill-inform'd,
To me is odious as the nasal twang
Heard at conventicle, where worthy men,
Misled by custom, strain celestial themes
Through the prest nostril, spectacle-bestrid.[13]

Has this peculiarity of sectarian speech anything to do with the widespread tendency of nasal pronunciation that has, by foreign observers, been described as characteristic of American English, while American writers frequently attribute it not to United States speech in general but to certain regions only—usually New England?

That nasalization is a Puritan inheritance is commonly assumed. So careful a student as George Philip Krapp agrees that it finds its parallel and possible source in English Puritanism.[14] If the assumption is true, the following passage from F. H. Underwood's *Quabbin, The Story of a Small Town, with Outlooks upon Puritan Life* comes closer than anything we have found to describe how it came about:

---

[12] Samuel Butler, *Hudibras,* Part I, Canto III, lines 1155–1160.

[13] William Cowper, *The Task,* Book II, lines 432–439.

[14] George Philip Krapp, *The English Language in America* (New York: The Century Company, 1925), II, 23–24. Professor Krapp also suggests that it may owe something to an inheritance from the dialect of the English county of Essex.

The New England drawl and the nasal tone were probably derived originally from the meeting-house and the prayer-meetings. . . .

The virtue constantly insisted upon in the old times by parents and religious teachers was humility, self-abnegation. In repeating passages of Scripture, or of the Catechism, the tone was subdued. The religious spirit was manifested in awe and reverence, seldom in cheerfulness, and never in exaltation—except in such exaltation as was accompanied with moistened eyes and "tears in the voice." . . . The *noise,* no less than the manner, of a burly fox-hunter and athlete, would be abhorrent to one whose soul was melted in penitence, and who in his daily devotions *intoned* in dragging minor intervals the prayers that he dared not address to the Dread Majesty of Heaven with steady eyes and manly voice. There was a good deacon in Quabbin whose words, when he prayed, were joined, as by a singer's *portamento,* with *ah* and *er,* and with indescribable sounds, like the final hum of a nasal *m* and *n.* The words were hyphenated, and each sentence was a close-linked, long-drawn chain. Let such usages of speech go on for generations, and the infection will pervade the community. The child will be soothed by a nasal lullaby, and will drawl from the time he leaves his cradle. He will drawl at his lessons, and make catarrhal yells in the playground. As a lover he will drawl to his mistress, and repeat love's litany through the nose. When his duet with her is finished, and his snuffy voice extinct, he will be drawn (slowly) to his grave, to drawl no more.

It appears to be certain that the nasal and drawling tone is in a large measure the result of two and a half centuries of Puritan training. . . .[15]

A linguist, of course, will not undertake to answer questions of this sort as confidently as the author of a witty descriptive sketch. To us, however, the theory proposed by Underwood appears more plausible than the other commonest theory —the one we quote here from Mencken:

The causes of that twang have long engaged phonologists, and there is respectable opinion in favor of the theory that our generally dry climate and rapid changes of temperature produce an actual change in the membranes concerned in the production of sound. Perhaps

[15] Quoted in B. A. Botkin, *A Treasury of New England Folklore* (New York: Crown Publishers, 1947), pp. 768–769.

some such impediment to free and easy utterance is responsible both for the levelness of tone of American speech, and for the American tendency to pronounce the separate syllables of a word with much more care than an Englishman bestows upon them.[16]

It has been maintained, not without a strong a priori probability, that many linguistic features now in common use reflect the speech habits of the privileged classes of centuries ago. This of course applies to phonetics as well as to other provinces of speech. An amusing example of this sort has been pointed out by Ernest Weekley, who claims that the curious idiom spoken by Mrs. Gamp in Dickens' *Martin Chuzzlewit* preserves certain features of fashionable English as it was spoken in the seventeenth century. It is possible that the prevailing pronunciation of short *o* in General American English (*bond* pronounced with a vowel very similar to the one in German *Band*) is another instance of this tendency. The speech of Lord Foppington in Vanbrugh's *The Relapse,* evidently intended to portray a certain snobbish class idiom of the author's day, is full of forms like "Tam" for "Tom" where the *a* seems to stand for a sound similar to the General American variety of short *o* [ɑ], in contrast to the British pronunciation [ɔ].

That I'm afraid mayn't be so praper; far the lards I commonly eat with, are people of a nice conversation; and you know, Tam . . .[17]

If Weekley is right in his theory that Mrs. Gamp speaks the fashionable English of George I's days and if there actually is a connection between the unrounded *o* in Lord Foppington's lingo and that in modern American speech, then we are dealing with the same sort of linguistic mimicry of which we speak elsewhere: imitation based on a person's wish to become a member of a class not originally his own, or, at least, to make himself and others believe that he "belongs." And here, finally, we have reached a point where we can understand why this linguistic masquerade should lead to a regularity in phonetic

---

[16] Mencken, *The American Language, ed. cit.*, pp. 323–324.

[17] Sir John Vanbrugh, *The Relapse,* Act I, scene 3, lines 177–179.

habits that is not far remote from what we term phonetic law. The following passage is a good illustration:

In Lady Clonbrony's address there was a mixture of constraint, affectation, and indecision, unusual in a person of her birth, rank, and knowledge of the world. A natural and unnatural manner seemed struggling in all her gestures, and in every syllable that she articulated—a naturally free, familiar, good-natured, precipitate, Irish manner, had been schooled, and schooled late in life, into a sober, cold, still, stiff deportment, which she mistook for English. A strong Hibernian accent she had, with infinite difficulty, changed into an English tone. Mistaking reverse of wrong for right, she caricatured the English pronunciation; and the extraordinary precision of her London phraseology betrayed her not to be a Londoner, as the man who strove to pass for an Athenian was detected by his Attic dialect. Not aware of her real danger, Lady Clonbrony was, on the opposite side, in continual apprehension every time she opened her lips, lest some treacherous *a* or *e*, some strong *r*, some puzzling aspirate or non-aspirate, some unguarded note, interrogative, or expostulatory, should betray her to be an Irishwoman.[18]

The result of these endeavors is depicted, parodistically, by a native English lady:

". . . you *cawnt* conceive the *peens* she *teekes* to talk of the *teebles* and *cheers*, . . . and with so much *teeste* to speak pure English. . . ." [19]

The background of these contortions is, as far as the *ee*'s are concerned, the fact that there are many cases in which the Anglo-Irish dialect replaces an English *ee*-sound by *ā;* knowing that her natural *lave* and *aise* are *leave* and *ease* in English, Lady Clonbrony thinks herself on the safe side in replacing every long *a* of her dialect by *ee,* even though this procedure occasionally leads to impossible forms like *teebles* and *cheers.*

What this contributes to our understanding of phonetic law is that there are certain speech situations in which there is no longer a free choice between two or more phonetic varia-

[18] Maria Edgeworth, *The Absentee,* Chap. 1.
[19] *Ibid.*

tions, but where the consistent use of just one pronunciation and the avoidance of any deviation become a matter of great importance to the speaker. Such situations are highly favorable to the development of a rigid phonetic standard and, consequently, to the development of phonetic laws. That Lady Clonbrony carries the tendency too far is helpful to us here, whatever it may have done to her social pretensions in London. We cannot say just how, in specific cases, a given phonetic variation has started, but there obviously comes a time when every person who belongs to a group is constrained to adopt it wherever it occurs. And then it becomes a phonetic law, applied universally in a certain dialect unless it is interfered with by some other influence, even stronger.

Here, then, is your phonetic law. It is true that Maria Edgeworth represents it as applying to the speech of one person. But, since that person is typical of a class, we may assume that Lady Clonbrony's solecisms were shared by a whole speech community, namely, the whole group of Irish people whose ambition it was to pass for London socialites. The main point is that the language of such people is under constant social pressure—in other words, under the influence of a force that makes it imperative to be consistent in regard to certain phonetic habits. Even a single "by your lave" would give the speaker away and frustrate all her endeavors to conceal her Irish antecedents.

Although we know that Edgeworth's comments are based on observation, we have to admit that she has manipulated her linguistic facts for artistic purposes. It is particularly useful, therefore, to have a factual scientific study of similar data combining accurate analysis of speech sounds with keen understanding of their sociological background. Dr. Raven L. McDavid, Jr., has shown in a recent article that despite popular notions to the contrary there is a considerable tendency throughout much of South Carolina to pronounce the *r* in such words as *thirty, Thursday, worm, barn, beard,* and *father.*[20] With the help of

[20] Raven L. McDavid, Jr., "Postvocalic /-r/ in South Carolina: A Social Analysis," *American Speech,* XXIII (October–December, 1948), 194–

the field records collected for the *Linguistic Atlas of the Southern Atlantic States* McDavid has established a distribution of the areas in which such *r*'s are pronounced. By comparing the linguistic map thus established with one showing the spread of the plantation system, he makes it evident that the *r* is kept mainly in those regions where small-scale farming prevailed, whereas the plantation area is *r*-less. What agricultural systems have to do with the spread of a pronunciation pattern may not be immediately apparent, but the explanation given by Dr. McDavid is convincing. The *r*-less speech was originally at home along the sea coast in the region and among the people who maintained close cultural contacts with London. Its center was Charleston, and it spread from there just as far as the social influence and other prestige factors of the planter class (for whom Charleston was the center of gravity) themselves carried. But what is perhaps the most interesting feature of McDavid's brilliant article is the way he illustrates the social meaning of linguistic geography: a phonetic feature fully studied is found to be an index of sociological patterns and values.

In the meantime, since practical applications of scientific information are always sought, there are some ways in which this analysis of the social distribution of postvocalic /–r/ in South Carolina might be put to use by other social scientists. Just as in South Carolina, so probably in most of the other states of the Deep South, constriction is a linguistically peripheral feature found in culturally peripheral communities, generally on poor land among people who were driven on to that land—or, as with the textile workers, into their occupation —by the pressure of competition from the plantation system and Negro labor. It is among those people, whose cultural situation was originally brought about by Negro competition, that the fear of continuing Negro competition is keenest, and is most easily exploited by demagogues. It is from those people that the Ku Klux Klan, the Bleases and Talmadges and Bilbos, and the lynching mobs have tended to draw their strength. Consequently, a Southern official whose job dealt with interracial problems might screen with a little extra care those native applicants for, say, police jobs whose speech showed

203. Excerpts from this article are reprinted by permission of the author and *American Speech*.

strong constriction. And those interested in changing the racial attitudes of the whites might well concentrate their efforts on those areas where constriction has survived in greatest strength. Perhaps this suggestion is extreme, but it shows the possibilities. For language is primarily a vehicle of social intercommunication, and linguistic phenomena must always be examined for their correlation with other cultural phenomena—as for the correlation between the spread of the unconstricted postvocalic /–r/ in South Carolina and the rise of the plantation system.[21]

Both the complexity and the urgency of this view find expression in McDavid's concluding footnote:

It is not necessarily true, of course, that only those persons in the Deep South lacking post vocalic constriction of /–r/ would be likely not to mistreat Negroes. Many of the plantation caste would resent the notion of equality, much as they would resist anti-Negro mob violence by poor whites. But since the revision of racial attitudes is largely a matter of education, it can hardly be without significance that in South Carolina the postvocalic /–r/ loses constriction among the group with the greater amount of education. It is also worthy of note that almost every lynching in South Carolina in the last twenty-five years occurred in countries where the field work for the *South Atlantic Atlas* has disclosed strong constriction of postvocalic /–r/.[22]

Another case of regular sound change will necessarily result whenever an individual (or a group) abandons an original language in favor of a foreign one. In this instance, the novice will naturally substitute whatever likely sounds he has at his command for such sounds in the newly acquired language as he cannot produce satisfactorily. The result will, of course, be phonetic laws, if the correct sounds are altogether beyond the imitative capacity of the speaker. In the following passage, there is no exception from the rule that *w* is replaced by *v* (*vindows,* of course, does not count, since the second *w* is mute):

Hans Breitmann gife a barty,
I vent dere you'll pe pound.

---

[21] *Ibid.*, p. 203.
[22] *Ibid.*, p. 203, note 30.

I valtzet mit Matilda Yane
Und vent shpinnen round and round.
De pootiest Fraeulein in de House,
She vayed 'pout dwo hoondred pound,
And efery dime she gife a shoomp
She make de vindows sound.[23]

There is more in this language than just a laugh. Think of the conditions that must have prevailed in England during the centuries after the Norman conquest. The country must have been full of French barons who spoke very bad Saxon and Saxon commoners who murdered the French language. The French phonetic system apparently left no traces on the English; yet, if you want to understand the conditions under which the phonetic system of English was developed, a thorough knowledge of the Hans Breitmann variation of English may prove useful—if for no other reason, at least because the presence of so large and influential a foreign group would tend to weaken the conservative forces opposed to the change of speech forms. Abundant material illustrating the conditions produced by the collision of different languages is to be found in Mencken, *The American Language,* especially in the appendix, "Non-English Dialects in American." [24]

It is often hard to evaluate the importance of prestige variations, but in some cases, at least, they rise to the rank of symbols of important historical developments. One of the most perspicacious observations of Nietzsche takes such variations as both symbol and, in a profound sense, as cause:

The Tone of the German Language.—We know whence the German originated which for several centuries has been the universal literary language of Germany. Germans, with their reverence for everything that came from the *court,* intentionally took the chancery style as their pattern in all that they had to *write,* especially in their letters, records, wills, &c. To write in the chancery style, that was to write in court and government style,—that was regarded

[23] Charles G. Leland, *Hans Breitmann's Party* (Philadelphia: T. B. Peterson & Brothers, 1869), p. 5.

[24] Mencken, *op. cit.,* pp. 616–697.

as something select, compared with the language of the city in which a person lived. People gradually drew this inference, and spoke also as they wrote,—they thus became still more select in the forms of their words, in the choice of their terms and modes of expression, and finally also in their tones: they affected a court tone when they spoke, and the affectation at last became natural. . . . Now I notice that at present a similar striving after selectness of tone is spreading among the former admirers of the chancery style, and that the Germans are beginning to accommodate themselves to a peculiar "witchery of sound," which might in the long run become an actual danger to the German language,—for one may seek in vain for more execrable sounds in Europe. Something mocking, cold, indifferent and careless in the voice: that is what at present sounds "noble" to the Germans —and I hear the approval of this nobleness in the voices of young officials, teachers, women, and trades-people; indeed, even the little girls already imitate this German of the officers. For the officer, and in fact the Prussian officer is the inventor of these tones: this same officer, who as soldier and professional man possesses that admirable tact for modesty which the Germans as a whole might well imitate (German professors and musicians included!). But as soon as he speaks and moves he is the most immodest and inelegant figure in old Europe —no doubt unconsciously to himself! And unconsciously also to the good Germans, who gaze at him as the man of the foremost and most select society, and willingly let him "give them his tone." And indeed he gives it to them!—in the first place it is the sergeant-majors and non-commissioned officers that imitate his tone and coarsen it. . . . It is certain that the Germans martialise themselves at present in the tone of their language: it is probable that, being exercised to speak martially, they will finally write martially also. For habituation to definite tones extends deeply into the character:—people soon have the words and modes of expression, and finally also the thoughts which just suit these tones! [25]

Some of these statements cannot be accepted without reservation. The influence of the chancellery, for instance, quite indisputably an important factor in the history of the German language, is just one influence among many. But nobody can

---

[25] F. Nietzsche, *The Joyful Wisdom*, trans. by Thomas Common, New York: The Macmillan Company, 1924), pp. 141–143. Reprinted by permission of The Macmillan Company, publishers.

fail to be impressed by the fact that Nietzsche, in 1882, was able to predict from linguistic symptoms a general development that became manifest only in our own day. Let nobody think that the science of sounds, or for that matter any province of linguistics, is, as someone has said, the knowledge of things not worth knowing. It is true that it is a science based on the observation and collection of infinitesimal particles of knowledge; it is no less true that many linguists allow themselves to be buried in the abundance of minutiae, the significance of which they fail to understand. But it is also true that language is a most sensitive recorder of human development, and that we could profitably pay more and, above all, more intelligent attention to the oscillations of this instrument.

We have omitted many things from this book, sometimes because we had little to add to existing studies, sometimes because we wished to avoid technicalities easily understandable only to specialists in linguistic science. However, we now have to make an exception in favor of that technical simplification of the modern phonetician, the phoneme.

Since we are not writing for linguists exclusively, we must explain that about twenty-five years ago "phoneme" was a term meaning "something connected with sounds." After considerable initial confusion, the word, thanks to the clarifying influence of such scholars as Bloomfield and Twaddell, is now generally accepted as signifying the minimum sound element capable of carrying a meaning.[26]

Among the innumerable sound variations that are to be found in any language, very many are irrelevant to meaning. The vowel in *tin* can be pronounced more or less open, with more or less tension of the muscles regulating the speech apparatus, without any change in the meaning of the word, so long as it does not come too close to the vowel of *ten*. Similarly, the *t* is capable of many variations that do not influence the meaning of a word. But if, in producing the initial consonant

---

26 Leonard Bloomfield, *Language* (New York: Henry Holt and Company, 1933), Chaps. 5–7; W. F. Twaddell, *On Defining the Phoneme,* Linguistic Society of America: Language Monographs, No. XVI, 1935.

the vocal chords are in action, then we get a sound identical with the one used in *tin,* except in one respect: it becomes voiced instead of voiceless, and this variation is no longer without significance. In other words, we get *din,* a sound mass with a meaning entirely different from that of *tin.* Sound variations by which the meaning of a word is altered clearly have a right to be considered as a class by themselves, more important than the difference between a strongly articulated *t* and one produced with less air pressure, or between a high-pitched and a low-pitched *i.* Following Bloomfield, we reserve the term "phoneme" for such significant variations, while variations that have no influence on meaning are called "allophones."

When faced with the task of describing the sound system of a language, the student of phonetics finds this distinction most useful, since it enables him to concentrate on essential features only. Such a selection has great value also in the practical task of learning a language, as was proved during World War II, when it became necessary to train large numbers of students speedily in the use of foreign languages.

But valuable to both science and practice as phonemic analysis is, we cannot overlook the fact that nonphonemic variations may be of great importance in everything that touches the social aspects of language. To illustrate: in some parts of the United States the diphthong *ow* becomes a thriphthong, *eow* (*keow* for *cow*). No phonemes are involved: *cow* is cow, even if you call it a *keow.* But the allophone *eow* may expose the man who uses it to unfavorable reactions. How significant nonphonemic differences can be is well illustrated by this traditionally New England variant. One of the earliest secessionists, Nathaniel Beverley Tucker, in 1820, at the Missouri Constitutional Convention urged the exclusion of all Yankees from the state:

> When asked how he could make such a plan feasible, he replied that every one ferried across the Mississippi should be required to pronounce the word "cow." Those who said "keow" were to be debarred.[27]

[27] Carl Bridenbaugh, Introduction to his edition of Nathaniel Beverley

In all probability Tucker's suggestion is an adaptation of the well-known passage in Judges 12:5–6 from which the word *shibboleth* has passed into all modern languages:

> And the Gileadites took the passages of Jordan before the Ephraimites: and it was so, that when those Ephraimites which were escaped said, Let me go over; that the men of Gilead said unto him, Art thou an Ephraimite? If he said, Nay;
>
> Then said they unto him, Say now Shibboleth: and he said Sibboleth: for he could not frame to pronounce it right. Then they took him, and slew him at the passages of Jordan: and there fell at that time of the Ephraimites forty and two thousand.

Whether the difference in pronunciation was phonemic or not we do not know, but it is sure that the distinction was normally of no difference at all either to the Ephraimites or to their enemies.

The reaction to "objectionable" phonetic variation is not always as violent as in the two examples given above. But such variation often carries symbolic and connotative value. And very often in the relations of man to man, it may be a barrier to understanding. Augustus Thomas records how Richard Harding Davis was sometimes personally misunderstood for a nonphonemic variation:

> One spring afternoon in 1889 a member brought into the Lambs Club house—then on Twenty-sixth Street—as a guest Mr. Richard Harding Davis. I had not clearly caught the careless introduction, and, answering my question, Mr. Davis repeated the surname. He did not pronounce it as would a Middle Westerner like myself, but more as a citizen of London might. To spell his pronunciation *Dyvis* is to burlesque it slightly, but that is as near as it can be given phonetically. Several other words containing a long *a* were sounded by him in the sameway, and to my ear the rest of his speech had a related eccentricity. I am told that other men educated in certain Philadelphia schools have a similar diction, but at that time many of Mr. Davis's new acquaintances thought the manner was an affectation. I mention the peculiarity, which after years convinced me was

---

Tucker, *The Partisan Leader* (New York: Alfred A. Knopf, 1933), pp. xii–xiii.

as native to him as was the color of his eyes, because I am sure that it was a barrier between him and some persons who met him only casually.[28]

Such illustrations could be indefinitely multiplied. Obviously nonphonemic variations can be of the utmost importance in defining the status of a man, either as an individual or as a member of a class. Perhaps linguists should add to the concept of the phoneme as it is now understood, a concept which might be called "social phonemes"—that is, phonetic variations that do not affect the meaning of a word but may influence the social relations of the person who uses them.

---

[28] Augustus Thomas, Introduction to Richard Harding Davis, *Soldiers of Fortune* (New York: Charles Scribner's Sons, 1919). Reprinted by permission of Charles Scribner's Sons, publishers.

Chapter Eight

MAKING NEW WORDS

ALL normal children reach the stage when they ask incessantly "What's that?" and repeat with a monotony that exasperates all but the fondest parents, "What? What?" This is a natural and important period in the history of the child's mastery of language. Earlier he has been aware of and concerned about only a few names of toys, people, and physiological processes. Names seem necessary only for the most obvious facts of his existence. Suddenly he needs names for everything that comes into his ken, and he acquires a profound conviction that everything has a name. He has reached a turning point in his development. His vocabulary is multiplied within a few weeks, and the pace of his mental growth is rapidly accelerated.

In supposing that language has universality, that it covers the whole of one's world, the child is, of course, partially wrong. He is wrong insofar as language is limited and the universe is not, but right insofar as language is able to create expression for everything that becomes important enough to make a name necessary or desirable.

In the course of cultural change, nothing is more common than that the universe gets out of balance with language. New things are invented, and new ideas create a new way of looking at the world, or some segment of it. Whenever this occurs, there will be a temporary vacuum in the vocabulary. The fact lacks the word to express itself. There are two chief ways of bridging this gap.[1] One can take an old word and, by transfer of mean-

[1] A third way, actual word creation, although we are familiar with

ing, impose on it the task of designating the new meaning. Or one can combine two or more existing words or word elements so as to form a word, new as a combination but not new in the material from which it is formed. The invention of radio, for instance, enriched our vocabulary by both methods. *Antenna* illustrates the process of naming by word transfer, its zoological use dating, according to the *Oxford Dictionary,* from the fifteenth century. An example of word combination is *loudspeaker*. Since the transfer type of word origin involves change of meaning, it will be discussed under that heading. We especially refer the reader to our treatment of the word *torpedo* (Chapter XII), a word used to fill a linguistic vacuum created by a new invention. The present chapter is limited to a study of the way language develops its resources by its powers of combination.

Combination, which includes everything usually understood by word formation, works by several methods. These methods are not in themselves of very great significance, but, because different languages tend sometimes to use one more commonly than another, they do indicate characteristic features of a language. To mention a few of them may help to make clear how combination itself operates. For instance, the Germanic languages like English have almost unlimited power of simple compounding (mere placing of two words together), as illustrated by the vast number of our characteristic nouns like *jellyfish, baseball, railroad, bookworm,* and so on. In addition, syntactic combinations (joining words by the same means we use to create sentences) like *bull's-eye* (genitival), *already* (adverbial), *gainsay* (adverbial), *bluebell* (adjectival), *sergeant at arms* [2] (prepositional) are also integral parts of our linguistic

it in modern advertising, is still comparatively rare. We quote one instance —*googol*—taken from Edward Kasner and James Newman, *Mathematics and the Imagination* (New York: Simon and Schuster, 1940), p. 23. "The name 'googol' was invented by a child (Dr. Kasner's nine-year-old nephew) who was asked to think up a name for a very big number, namely, 1 with a hundred zeros after it."

[2] The fact that the Merriam-Webster dictionaries print *sergeant at arms* as three words while the Oxford dictionaries hyphenate it as one

structure and may even be so complex as *ne'er-do-well* and *whodunit.* French, on the other hand, shows a decided preference for the syntactic phrase over the simple compound. A vast number of nominal compounds in English or German have, for French equivalents, a pair of words linked into a phrase by *de* or some other preposition. A glance at any ordinary English-French dictionary makes the point immediately apparent. Here for illustration are a few listed under the head word *life* in the *Heath Dictionary:*

life-belt: *ceinture de sauvetage*
life-boat: *bateau de sauvetage*
life buoy: *bouée de sauvetage*
lifeguard: *garde du corps*
life-insurance: *assurance sur la vie*
life-policy: *police d'assurance sur la vie*
life-preserver: *appareil de sauvetage*
lifelessness: *absence de vie*

The list of French phrases could be extended as far as the parallel lists of compound words in German or English.

Both the Romance and Germanic languages, however, in the creation of new words employ with great frequency prefixes and suffixes added to an independent word stem. However, the distinction between compounds and words made with affixes becomes less sharp if viewed in the light of history. Even in modern examples it is sometimes doubtful whether we should call a compound one word or a number of words, while if we trace many affixes back to earlier stages of the language, the differences between them and independent words become blurred indeed. In eighth-century Latin (from Bede's *Ecclesiastical History*) occurs the sentence, *Scio, quod me haec insana mente*

is perhaps amusing but certainly irrelevant. Semantically it is one word with its own peculiar and distinct meaning. Absurdly enough the same dictionaries that list *sergeant at arms* as three words print *sergeant-at-law* as one. The unsystematic character of English typography, especially its often irreconcilable rules for hyphenation, make it a completely unreliable guide to the nature of compounds.

loqui arbitramini [3] ("I know you think that I speak that out of an insane mind"). Exactly the same combination *insanamente* is still used in Italian, only there it is no longer a coupling of two independent and meaningful words but a unified adverb *insanely*. *Mente* has been reduced to a mere suffix. French and Spanish have done exactly the same thing in the creation of their adverbial suffixes, *-ment* and *-mente*, respectively. Some of the commonest English suffixes are derived in a similar way from independent words. One of the clearest examples is *-dom* (*kingdom, wisdom,* and the like) from Anglo-Saxon *dōm*.

To take another quotation from Bede, in one manuscript of the Anglo-Saxon translation of his history, we read concerning a pair of offenders against church discipline, *Syn hi begen ðæs bisceopdomes wyrðe and scyldige* ("Let them be deserving of and guilty of the bishopdom").[4] It is clear that *bishopdom* cannot be taken with a modern meaning. What it actually signifies is shown by the wording of the Latin original, *excommunicationi subiacebit,* and of another Anglo-Saxon MS, which in place of *bisceopdomes* reads *biscopes dome*. The correct translation is, "Let them be guilty of the bishop's doom," that is, of his judgment—in this case, excommunication. The suffix *-dom* is obviously identical with the Anglo-Saxon noun *dōm* meaning judgment, the direct source of the modern English noun *doom*.[5]

From *bishopdom,* with its meaning of bishop's judgment and sentence, it is but a small step to *bishopdom,* with the mean-

---

[3] Jacob Schipper, "König Alfreds Übersetzung von Bedas Kirchengeschichte," *Bibliothek der Angelsächsischen Prosa* (Leipzig: 1899), p. 391.

[4] *Ibid.*, p. 377 (Ms. B).

[5] In Anglo-Saxon the phonetic form of the noun and the suffix is the same, and the difference today is simply due to the principle that the second part of compound nouns is, as a rule, less vigorously stressed than the first, and, accordingly, tends to undergo phonetic reduction. Compare the development of Anglo-Saxon *tun* in place names like *Taunton,* and notice the same thing happening centuries later when *Trent's Town* becomes *Trenton* (N.J.) and *Charlestown* becomes *Charleston* (S.C.). For these last two see George R. Stewart, *Names on the Land* (New York: Random House, 1945), pp. 122 and 196.

ing of the bishop's full dominion or power and of the geographical area in which it is exercised. So we read in the Anglo-Saxon Chronicle *Wine heold ðone biscepdom iii gear* ("Wine held the bishopric three years").[6] *Kingdom, earldom,* and so on, are clearly of the same pattern. We do not know how far the connection with *doom* was felt in all instances, but if *bishopdom* was felt to include the judiciary of the bishop, then *kingdom* and *earldom* are to be explained in the same way. *Christendom* carries us one step further. Used as a geographical expression, the world of Christians, it is also an abstraction capable of indicating the beliefs of Christians: *Æghwylc cristen man gyme his cristendomes georne* [7] ("Let each Christian man cherish his Christian faith gladly"). Such abstraction leads us into the same semantic pattern as *wisdom, freedom,* and the like. How far the process has gone is shown by *ðeowdom,* "serfdom," for the word means not the world in which the *ðeow* lives but the condition of being a serf. Apart, then, from the rare instances in which the suffix means judgment, we see that *-dom* has three areas of meaning: (1) dominion and area of dominion, (2) condition or state of being, and (3) the abstraction of an idea from a concrete noun or adjective.

Thanks to a fine collection by Professor Harold Wentworth, we are in a position to speak more fully than usual about the later history of the suffix.[8] Up to the third decade of the nineteenth century, its traditional functions stand out very clearly. New formations are not frequent but do occur from time to time, and those like *cuckoldom* (seventeenth century) and *puzzledom, awaredom* (eighteenth century) indicate that the suffix was capable of extension into new ranges of meaning, though hardly enough to disturb the traditional patterns. The picture developing in the early nineteenth century and persisting into our own time is entirely different. Wentworth

---

6 Bosworth-Toller, *Anglo-Saxon Dictionary,* under *bisceop-dom.*

7 *Ibid.,* under *Cristen-dom.*

8 Harold Wentworth, "The Allegedly Dead Suffix *-dom* in Modern English," *Publications of the Modern Language Association,* LVI (March, 1941), 280 ff.

lists close to three hundred formations found, for the first time, between 1810 and 1940. The list cannot be considered complete. Every reader of current magazines and newspapers may at any time find himself confronted with new coinages of this type.

While Wentworth has proved what he set out to prove, namely, that the suffix is still very much alive, many problems remain unanswered. The one we are here interested in is: Why this sudden outburst of vitality? What makes so many authors of the nineteenth and twentieth centuries create so many new words in *-dom,* when prior to about 1830 few seem to have felt much need to add to the limited stock of such words?

A full explanation of a linguistic process must consider two phases: the starting of the process by one or a few conspicuous individuals, and its adoption by a speech community, or at least by a considerable portion of it. And it is clear that this pattern of investigation must be followed in problems of word formation as well as in semantics. Wentworth makes it very easy to follow such a method because his material clearly brings out the fact that in the first forty years of the nineteenth century more than half the coinages in *-dom* are the work of Thomas Carlyle. Indeed, Carlyle's more than fifty per cent of these coinages was achieved in only eleven years (1829–1840) as against the forty years of all the rest of the English writers studied.

With all due respect to the author of a careful study, we would like to object to one of the implications of Wentworth's paper. If Wentworth is to be believed, Carlyle did with the suffix exactly what other people did—only a little more frequently. It is very clear, however, that the problem is not one of statistics but of Carlyle's peculiar needs as an interpreter of history, and an interpreter with his own highly individual point of view. Therefore it becomes more than a theoretical necessity to begin the investigation with a consideration of individual style; the very nature of the material requires it.

Having listed a number of Carlyle's coinages in *-dom,* Wentworth adds, "Excepting *philosophedom,* none of these Carlylean neoterisms are Carlylese, none are more eccentric or fanciful than those of his contemporaries—and ours." [9] Whether or not one agrees with the amount of eccentricity required to make Carlyle's prose Carlylese, certainly the bilingual *philosophedom* is a most striking formation and our investigation may well begin with it. In 1833, in his essay on Diderot, Carlyle attempted a characterization of Diderot's philosophic colleagues not just as individuals but as a group, thinking, acting, and living according to its own beliefs and laws, and thereby different from any other group, not only in the France of about 1750 but also in any other time and place. This characterization is central to Carlyle's understanding of the whole world through which Diderot moved. It is against that background that Diderot is illuminated, seen, and comprehended. Therefore, at the time Diderot emerges as an author in his own right, Carlyle pauses in his review of the man's career to sketch in this background:

First he uses a negative—he denies the legend of formal (and diabolical) organization:

That fable, indeed, first set afloat by some Trevoux Journalist of the period, and which has floated foolishly enough into every European ear since then, of there being an Association specially organized for the destruction of government, religion, society, civility (not to speak of tithes, rents, life and property), all over the world; which hell-serving Association met at the Baron d'Holbach's, there had its blue-light sederunts, and published Transactions legible to all,—was and remains nothing but a fable. Minute-books, president's-hammer, ballot-box, punch-bowl of such Pandemonium have not been produced to the world. The sect of Philosophes existed at Paris, but as other sects do. . . .[10]

Then, still emphasizing the unity of the group, Carlyle shifts his figures of speech to the metaphor of a band of actors:

A strange theatre that of French Philosophism; a strange dramatic corps! Such another corps for brilliancy and levity, for gifts and vices,

[9] *Ibid.*, p. 287.

[10] Thomas Carlyle, "Diderot," *Critical and Miscellaneous Essays*, Centenary Edition, III, 204.

and all manner of sparkling inconsistencies, the world is not like to see again.[11]

After this he devotes a paragraph each to the major figures—Voltaire, D'Alembert, Rousseau, Grimm, Helvétius, the Baron d'Holbach, and so forth. He concludes with a brief mention of the famous *salonnières* of the period, in which, for the sake of re-emphasizing this unity based on common philosophic attitudes, he ignores all differences between such ladies as Julie de Lespinasse and Madame du Deffand. They are all merely "philosophesses." Still concentrating on the idea of a group, he continues with paragraphs around these topic sentences:

> In a world so wide and multifarious, this little band of Philosophes, acting and speaking as they did, had a most various reception to expect. . . .
>
> Nor is Literature itself wholly Philosophe: apart from the Jesuit regulars, in their Trevoux Journals, Sermons, Episcopal Charges, and other camps or casemates, a considerable Guerilla or Reviewer force (consisting, as usual, of smugglers, unemployed destitute persons, deserters who have been refused promotion, and other the like broken characters) has organized itself, and maintains a harassing bush-warfare. . . .[12]

Finally all is pulled together into an authentic climax and epitomized with the word *philosophedom:*

> Among its more notable anomalies may be reckoned the relations of French Philosophism to Foreign Crowned Heads. In Prussia there is a Philosophe King; in Russia a Philosophe Empress: the whole North swarms with kinglets and queenlets of the like temper. Nay, as we have seen, they entertain their special ambassador in Philosophedom, their lion's-provider to furnish spiritual Philosophe-provender; and pay him well.[13]

Carlyle's rhetoric demands our attention. It is very meaningful. Nowhere is the peculiarity, the uniqueness of the group so apparent as here where Carlyle hammers at the word *philosophe*

---

[11] *Ibid.*, p. 206.
[12] *Ibid.*, pp. 212–213.
[13] *Ibid.*, p. 213.

with *Philosophism, Philosophe King, Philosophe Empress,* and *Philosophe-provender,* all in support of *Philosophedom.* Evidently *Philosophedom* does more than merely label the group. It is a hallmark, a title, a definition. By the introduction of the new name the group has been raised to the position of an independent power, endowed with a province of its own, the equal of kings and empresses, because it is as sovereign as they. That this is done with a certain irony in no way changes the fact that it is done.[14]

This brings us to the essential character of word formation. The creation of a new word does more than raise the number of words in a language from x to $x + 1$. A new idea or set of ideas or pattern of thought has been concentrated into one conspicuous and easily learned symbol. The study of this process goes far beyond the task of establishing the statistics of a word group and the dates of first appearance. The main question always remains: What state of ideas made the creation of a new word necessary?

Only rarely, as with *philosophedom,* is one lucky enough to find the process of creation developing in full view until it culminates in the coining of a new word. With *rascaldom,* another of Carlyle's early and favorite coinages, the case is slightly different but equally instructive. Studying it, we may see even more clearly the state of ideas that made a new creation necessary. It also appears first in the essay on Diderot:

> It seems probable that Denis, during these ten years of probation, walked chiefly in the subterranean shades of Rascaldom; now swilling from full Circe-goblets, now snuffing with haggard expectancy the hungry wind; always "sorely flamed-on from the neighbouring hell." In some of his fictitious writings, a most intimate acquaintance with

---

14 From the uniqueness of the human type described, it becomes apparent why Carlyle could not adapt the native word *philosopher*. Although *philosophe* is as capable in French of generalization as *philosopher* in English, the French word had special restricted meaning in the age of the *Encyclopédie*. *Philosopher* has never been so restricted in English. A mechanical application of the English word to the French thinkers would have distorted the idea.

the nether world of Polissons, Escrocs, Filles de Joie, Maroufles, Maquerelles, and their ways of doing, comes to light. . . .[15]

The idea of an underground sovereignty whose denizens are Polissons, Escrocs, Filles de Joie, Maroufles, and Maquerelles is not developed, as was the idea of Philosophedom, in plain view of the reader. Yet the process of creating the word *Rascaldom* is essentially the same. The idea of an organized Parisian rascality as an independent power is there, and an appropriate word for it has to be found.[16] Once created, the word is repeated in the essay, with the result that it is well established not only in the reader's but in the writer's consciousness. It is further reinforced by its repetition in context—for example, when he "walked chiefly in the subterranean shades of Rascaldom." A process of stereotyping occurs here as Carlyle repeats himself, fully aware of the fact that the word connotes an entire province of human behavior.

"Diderot" is one of several short studies on subjects related to the French Revolution which preceded Carlyle's famous history. Two others intimately connected by characters and narrative, which treat of minor but extravagantly dishonest persons, are "Count Cagliostro" and "The Diamond Necklace." Quackery and scoundrelism (to use Carlyle's own words) flourish. Rascaldom is everywhere. From peddling the "cantharidic wine of Egypt" to the stealing of fabulous jewels, there is no phase of crookedness omitted from the underworld described in these papers. Naturally, then, "Count Cagliostro" elaborates the underworld elements barely touched upon in "Diderot." And as Carlyle writes, the word *Rascaldom,* in full context as a region, comes once more into his mind:

This only is clear: That Beppo dived deep down into the lugubrious-obscure regions of Rascaldom; like a Knight to the palace of his

[15] "Diderot," *ed. cit.,* p. 194.

[16] Whether Carlyle's concept was in any way induced by Victor Hugo's *Notre Dame de Paris,* with its description of a subterranean beggars' kingdom in Paris, is outside our province. The dates, however, are suggestive; *Notre Dame* in 1831; "Diderot" in 1833. But pictures of organized Parisian rascality go back in French literature at least as far as Villon.

Fairy; remained unseen there, and returned thence armed at all points.[17]

But it is when Carlyle returns to this favorite field in "The Diamond Necklace" that he finds the idea first expressed in "Diderot" thematically most useful. The process of stereotyping becomes complete when, early in the essay, he deliberately (the deliberation being made evident by his use of quotation marks) quotes himself. Having introduced two of his most suspect characters, he describes one of their many crises by saying:

> As to Lamotte the husband, he, for shelter against much, decisively dives down to the "subterranean shades of Rascaldom"; gambles, swindles; can hope to live, miscellaneously, if not by the Grace of God, yet by the Oversight of the Devil,—for a time. Lamotte the wife also makes her packages: and waving the unseductive Count Boulainvilliers Save-all a disdainful farewell, removes to the *Belle Image* in Versailles. . . .[18]

In subsequent pages, Carlyle uses *Rascaldom* seven more times. The process of familiarization with the word is too conspicuous for him to have been any more unaware of his rhetorical device than he was of the repetition pointed out above. When he is through, the reader is conditioned to one pattern of thinking about *rascaldom* whenever the word crops up. Step by step the development is as follows: At first, Carlyle quotes the word from himself. *Subterranean* and *shades* help to fix the connotation that the author wishes to leave in the reader's mind—connotations of a province having its own inhabitants, behavior, and place coexistent with the provinces of the court and of such worlds as *philosophedom.* This is further emphasized by the parallel action of Mme Lamotte, who also seeks a *place* for her future base of operations. In the second stage, as illustrated by the phrase, "a certain Villette-de-Retaux . . . denizen of Rascaldom," a slight reminder is enough to make

---

[17] Carlyle, "Count Cagliostro," *Essays, ed. cit.,* III, 276.
[18] Carlyle, "The Diamond Necklace," *ibid.,* p. 357.

the reader think along the prescribed lines: the word *denizen* is sufficient. Subsequently, almost all the rest of the occurrences are made up of the phrase *of Rascaldom* added to a name and used as some sort of parodistic title. There is a Villette of Rascaldom just as there is a Phillipe, Duc d'Orleans. Villette becomes, along with the "Count" Cagliostro and the Comte and Comtesse de Lamotte, the equal of the Prince Cardinal Louis de Rohan, premier peer of France (the process is exactly that whereby, earlier, Carlyle had enobled the *Philosophes* and given *Philosophedom* a place in the world by supplying it with ambassadors). Finally we reach a third stage where *Rascaldom* is understood without the help of context: "Ill-gotten wealth endures not; Rascaldom has no strong-box." [19] *Rascaldom* is now a state, an institution, and a condition. It no more needs an identification with a place or personality than does the centuries-older compound *Christendom.*

With still greater force and concentration, the idea implied in *Rascaldom* is brought out in the conclusion of "The Diamond Necklace," separately entitled:

> Occasional Discourse, by Count Alessandro Cagliostro, Thaumaturgist, Prophet and Arch-Quack; delivered in the Bastille: Year of Lucifer, 5789; of the Mahometan Hegira from Mecca, 1201; of the Cagliostric Hegira from Palermo, 24; of the Vulgar Era, 1785.[20]

The leitmotiv in this mock discourse, however, is no longer rascaldom but its double, *scoundreldom.* The latter fulfills all the functions of the former.

Through a long preamble that constantly plays on the word *scoundrel,* the author works his way to a eulogy of *Scoundreldom,* in which the geographical and political aspect is strongly stressed. All the ideas connoted by *Rascaldom* are here, but sarcastically raised to a still higher level. *Scoundreldom* is no longer a mere province—it is an empire with a state religion and a sacred image (the gallows). We quote a few key sentences:

---

[19] *Ibid.,* p. 386.
[20] *Ibid.,* p. 392.

"Let the eye of the mind . . . astound itself with the magnificent extent of Scoundreldom; the deep, I may say unfathomable, significance of Scoundrelism."

"Yes, brethren, wide as the Sun's range is our Empire; wider than old Rome's in its palmiest era. I have in my time been far; in frozen Muscovy, in hot Calabria, east, west, wheresoever the sky overarches civilised man: and never hitherto saw I myself an alien; out of Scoundreldom I never was.

. . . . .

"But neither are we, my Fellow Scoundrels, without our Religion, our Worship; which, like the oldest, and all true Worships, is one of Fear. The Christians have their Cross, the Moslem their Crescent: but have not we too our—Gallows? . . . No Manicheans are we; our God is One. Great, exceeding great, I say, is the Gallows. . . . Fellow Scoundrels, fear the Gallows, and have no other fear! *This* is the Law and the Prophets."

"Such, so wide in compass, high, gallows-high in dignity, is the Scoundrel Empire; and for depth, it is deeper than the Foundations of the World." [21]

Taken as interpretations of the preliminary stages of the French Revolution all three words, *Philosophedom, Rascaldom,* and *Scoundreldom,* further the idea of a totalitarian kingdom doomed to annihilation because it is no longer totalitarian. It is surrounded and penetrated by powers which it cannot control. The independent kingdoms of the philosophe, the rascal, and, as Carlyle suggests in passing, of the *Jesuit* and the *valet,* become stronger than the kingdom of France.

This example should make it clear that studies like Professor Wentworth's, necessary as they are, are rather a beginning than a consummation. The facts needed collection and statistical treatment. But the knowledge that a new word is found for the first time in this or that author is comparatively less important in understanding the word than the reason why the creation of the word became a necessity. It is not possible to investigate every new word even as far as we have here done with two of Carlyle's, yet in the history of language the defini-

[21] *Ibid.*, pp. 393–395.

tion holds which Carlyle himself announced for the study of history in general: "History is the essence of innumerable biographies." In the same way, the history of language is nothing but the sum of innumerable biographies of words and word elements. The more thorough our knowledge of details of this sort, the firmer our grasp on the history of any language, or of language itself.

Anticipating a problem that will be discussed in the chapter on style, we may point out that freedom in handling the structural elements of the word, such as affixes, and creative inventiveness in making use of these elements are most important characteristics of both personal and period style. Much of the peculiar quality of Carlyle's style depends on his ability to form new words for new ideas. He was as creatively free in his use of *-ism, -ity, -anity,* and *-hood* as in his use of *-dom.* Not only his books but his private letters as well are generously sprinkled with such words as *Montagudom, illustrified, anities* ("Christianity . . . Paganity . . . and all manner of other *anities*"), *demirepdom, Cockneydom,* and so on. Clearly word coinage was a necessity to his self-expression.

Carlyle's general attitude toward language, as it appears in his innovations, is a problem in itself. It is by no means a foregone conclusion that a writer of his period should feel that language was something to be worked on rather than to be worked with. Writers of rank and acknowledged authorities on usage took exactly the opposite view. William Hazlitt, for instance, an essayist only seventeen years older than Carlyle, declared

> that words are like money . . . it is the stamp of custom alone that gives them circulation or value. I am fastidious in this respect, and would almost as soon coin the currency of the realm as counterfeit the King's English. I never invented or gave a new and unauthorised meaning to any word but one single one (the term *impersonal* applied to feelings) and that was in an abstruse metaphysical discussion to express a very difficult distinction. . . . As an author, I endeavour to employ plain words and popular modes of construction, as

were I a chapman and dealer, I should common weights and measures.[22]

How sensitive some of Carlyle's contemporaries were is shown by Landor's objection to Southey's use of *rewrite:* "I had thought it, and *reread,* the spawn infecting a muddier and shallower water. Properly *re* should precede none but words of Latin origin, though there are a few exceptions of some date and authority." And Macaulay objected to *gentlemanly:* "I never could break Sheridan of saying 'gentlemanly' though he allowed it was wrong." [23]

Why one author should insist on respecting whatever is traditional in language, while another would go to the limit in the use of daring innovation, is, in any final analysis, a matter of personal psychology. Any of the forces that conditioned him—home, training, personal contacts, acceptance or rejection of current modes of thinking, the not always understood forces of his psychic experience, in short, any one of the influences which create the man—have their place in forming his way of expressing himself. Carlyle's biographer has claimed, on Carlyle's own authority, that the roots of his style are to be found in the speech habits of his earliest surroundings:

This style, which has been such a stone of stumbling, originated, he has often said to myself, in the old farmhouse at Annandale. The humour of it came from his mother. The form was his father's common mode of speech, and had been adopted by himself for its brevity and emphasis. He was aware of its singularity and feared that it might be mistaken for affectation, but it was a natural growth. . . .[24]

---

[22] William Hazlitt, "On Familiar Style," *Table Talk,* Everyman's Edition, p. 244.

[23] Both the Landor and Macaulay quotations are taken from George H. McKnight, *Modern English in the Making* (New York: D. Appleton and Company, 1928), p. 510. McKnight's chapter on "The Nineteenth Century" contains an excellent review of the struggles between purism and freedom in language during this period.

[24] J. A. Froude, *Thomas Carlyle* (London: Longmans, Green and Co., 1885), I, 40.

This may be true in more than one sense. The proverbial terseness of Scottish colloquialism may very well have given the pattern for many a Carlylean phrase. On the other hand, it is equally possible that much of his boldness is the result of a reaction against an extremely conservative school tradition. The following anecdote, told to James M. Barrie by Carlyle's brother James, of the school the Carlyles attended, seems to suggest a degree of linguistic orthodoxy little short of despotism:

"You make a terrible to-do nowadays about education by what was the case in my young days. One day at the school when I was a nine-year-old my teacher was hearing me say my catechers (catechism), and I said 'he believes' instead of 'he believeth.' He knocked me down and pulled my lugs and banged me on the desks; and I ran out and lay at the foot of a hedge among dockens and nettles for three whole days." Three whole days seems a long time for a nine-year-old, but they were queer ones, the Carlyles.[25]

Small wonder if a boy who grew up among such taboos enjoyed breaking a few later! The compelling neurosis that drove Carlyle into savage fits of unhappiness and despair may also have forced its way into expression by means of his volcanic style. And, on a very different level, his genuine antipathy for the "logical," utilitarian doctrines of Bentham and the Mills, father and son, may likewise have influenced him to adopt an expression as sharply in contrast to theirs as was his emotional thinking. Froude's biography is full of material amply supporting both views.

The main point which must be made, however, is the simple truth that new ideas called for new words. It was largely with this argument that Carlyle defended himself from the criticisms of his friend John Sterling:

Know thy thought—believe it—front heaven and earth with it, in whatsoever words nature and art have made readiest for thee. If one

[25] J. M. Barrie, *The Greenwood Hat* (New York: Charles Scribner's Sons, 1938), pp. 36–37.

has thoughts not hitherto uttered in English books, I see nothing for it but you must use words *not* found there, must *make* words, with moderation and discretion of course.[26]

The words come out sometimes even in spite of the self-criticism of the author. Carlyle acknowledged in the same letter that "the objections to phraseology and style have good grounds to stand on." But such considerations could only be nodded to "as one passed."

The whole question of *-dom* as a characteristically Carlylean form is of importance for the history of its further development because of Carlyle's enormous influence upon nineteenth-century writing and thinking. To some authors, the taking up of such a suffix would be simply a matter of imitation. We are probably not far from right in supposing that when Carlyle's influence was at its height, many a young and serious-minded author tried to place himself among the elect by creating a new word in *-dom*. But there is another and more serious side to the question. The result of Carlyle's use of various words in *-dom* is evidently the fact that to the formative elements of English there has been added, and popularized, a suffix with the special task of describing a state within a state—a province perhaps more or less geographical, but largely ideological or social, that follows its own laws in disregard of or even in opposition to those regulating the established government or established social custom.

Whether such an element will remain the exclusive property of its author or of a small group—say, historians—or whether it will be put to use among a wider circle will depend on general conditions that have nothing to do with the personality and the influence of its creator. Suppose that this suffix in its Carlylean interpretation is made available to a country which is on the verge of being broken up into geographical sections, each with its own ideology, customs, and social and economic structure. Would it not be a natural linguistic de-

---

[26] Carlyle in letter to John Sterling, quoted in Froude, *op. cit.*, p. 41.

velopment to find new words in *-dom* for the purpose of characterizing such semi-independent and conflicting political organisms? This was exactly the condition of the United States in the decades before the Civil War. Sectionalism, to use a common tag of the period and of the Reconstruction immediately following, is one of the dominating problems of the country. And in the language of the time we find just what we should expect.

A number of forms in *-dom* from this period are listed by Wentworth—*Yankeedom, negrodom, rebeldom, cottondom, planterdom,* and *abolitiondom.* We can ourselves add to Wentworth's entries several more that come directly from the conflict of North and South:

chatteldom (1857): Although I am a "small fisted farmer" I feel as if I occupy a much higher and more independent position than the most wealthy slave-holder that can be found in all "chatteldom," . . .[27]

niggerdom (1862): . . . the burning sin of shrouding the light of such an intellect in the mists of niggerdom, . . .[28]

secessiondom (1862): . . . in the very heart of secessiondom, . . .[29]

Hunkerdom (1862): For the last ten years, yea, eleven, next seventeenth of March, the Hunkerdom of the North has been engaged in a constant effort to save the Union.[30]

Davisdom (1866): . . . thwarting Secretary Chase in his laudable efforts to prevent arms from passing through *any* custom house, en route to Davisdom.[31]

The Reconstruction naturally added more such words. We give two samples not hitherto listed:

carpet-baggerdom (1868): Do they want to know what carpet-baggers can do? Let them look at that towering monument, that crowning

---

[27] Ashland [Ohio] *Times,* January 1, 1857.

[28] James Robert Gilmore (Edmund Kirke, pseud.) *Among the Pines* (1862), p. 57.

[29] *Ibid.,* p. 63, and see also p. 166.

[30] David Christy, *Pulpit Politics* (1862), p. 544.

[31] R. M. Devens (Frazer Kirkland, pseud.) *The Pictorial Book of Anecdotes and Incidents of the War of the Rebellion* (1866), p. 405.

glory of progressive and enterprising carpet-baggerdom—the city of Chicago.[32]

Bulldozerdom (1884): Democracy in Bulldozerdom.[33]

Naturally, with the pattern of creation so well established, we find other political words in *-dom,* which do not immediately reveal their sources in the slavery conflict but come from the same camp. We give one of each:

fogydom (1855): The nomination of this true man [Chase] has struck terror into the ranks of fogydom. . . . To universal fogydom and all its venerable "Grandfather grey beards" it is a bitter dose.[34]

Cossackdom (1852): Let the Russian Czar erect his rule upon the ruins of the Republic, and the servile Hunkers [Conservative Democrats] would name Cossackdom a foundation on which to "go on and build." [35]

It is equally inevitable that conspicuous movements other than the struggle of North and South should receive their labels stamped in this same pattern. It is natural, for instance, to expect *Tammany Ringdom;* [36] and a group so involved in controversy and bitterness as the Latter-day Saints were bound to be categorized under the tag of *Mormondom* (listed by Wentworth) and *Brighamdom* (1874): "I see nothing in Utah so sacred, that we should not give Brighamdom the bayonet, the same as we did Jeffdom." [37]

Few aspects of a man's use of a word can be harder to ascertain and describe accurately than the tone he has given it, but most readers will probably agree that Carlyle's use of *philosophedom, rascaldom,* and *scoundreldom* is not without humor. The quality of that humor varies, from the pleasant irony of *philosophedom,* through the scorn implicit in *Villette of Ras-*

---

[32] *Speeches, Correspondence and Political Papers of Carl Schurz,* ed. by Frederic Bancroft (New York: G. P. Putnam's Sons, 1913), I, 455.

[33] *Ohio State Journal,* June 19, 1884.

[34] Ravenna [Ohio] *Campaign Democrat,* August 20, 1855.

[35] *Scott Battery,* July 27, 1852. Report of speech in Cincinnati by Karl Heinzen.

[36] *Harper's Weekly,* October 29, 1870, p. 697.

[37] Rusling, *Across America,* p. 204. Note also *Jeffdom.*

caldom, to brutal sarcasm in the uses of *scoundreldom* (the smile provided by Cagliostro's mock address is grim). All these words are touched also with contempt, only a little in the first but with a heavy load in the last.

In employing *-dom* for purposes of humor and satire, Carlyle is quite in line with a traditional use of the word, modern but much older than he, and very common among his contemporaries and successors. The words may vary in their connotations from the gay and lighthearted to the savage, yet a touch of some kind of humor and an element of satire are frequent in new coinages from the seventeenth century to our own day. The *Oxford Dictionary* quotes from 1650 under *squiredom:* "The utmost title we must now expect, is a Gentleman; it may be if we straine hard, we may hap to vent a few Squiredomes." The edged humor is evident. So also is the satirical and witty contempt in Dryden's use of *cuckoldom* (1678): "He takes Pains enough o' conscience for his cuckoldom; and, by my Troth, has earn'd it fairly." To skip a century, Wentworth's earliest entry after 1800 is Sydney Smith's *Noodledom* (1810). It is used in his review, "Female Education," to describe the source of the more banal masculine clichés about women:

> . . . there is nothing which requires more vigilance than the current phrases of the day, of which there are always some resorted to in every dispute, and from the sovereign authority of which it is often vain to make any appeal. "The true theatre for a woman is the sick-chamber"; —"Nothing so honourable to a woman as not to be spoken of at all." These two phrases, the delight of *Noodledom*. . . .[38]

Light satire and fun are characteristically present in the coinages in *-dom* of the author who after Carlyle, according to Wentworth, created more such words than any other British writer of the period. Thackeray's famous *swelldom,* and his *Turkeydom* and *Doctordom,* all occur in contexts full of the tolerant irony so often (and so easily) employed by middle-aged gentlemen contemplating the love affairs of youth. Thackeray

[38] Sydney Smith, *Essays* (London: Longmans, Green and Co., 1876), p. 201.

uses *swelldom* (1855) in a passage which not only jests at the woes of young Clive Newcome in his inability to win the beautiful Ethel but also makes fun of Tennyson's grotesquely sentimental ballad *The Lord of Burleigh:*

"This isn't the moment, when all Swelldom is at her feet, for me to come forward and say, 'Maiden, I have watched thee daily, and I think thou lovest me well.' I read that ballad to her at Baden, sir. I drew a picture of the Lord of Burleigh wooing the maiden, and asked what she would have done?" [39]

Doctordom (1849) appears in a scene, very similar in tone, in which young Pendennis (aged eighteen) has to defend for the first time his passion for an actress: "Pen thought himself a man, and a match for all the Doctors in Doctordom." [40] *Turkeydom,* also from Pendennis, is very obvious:

. . . and does anyone dare to suppose that the writer would incite the women to revolt? Never, by the whiskers of the Prophet, again he says. He wears a beard, and he likes his women to be slaves. What man doesn't? What man would be henpecked, I say? We will cut off all the heads in Christendom or Turkeydom rather than that.[41]

Whenever major authors adopt a device, they are sure to be followed by a vast number of imitators, who make the trick fashionable, at least for a time. A contemporary of Carlyle and Thackeray, the American journalist N. P. Willis, like them, found *-dom* useful. He was an indefatigable word coiner, and much after their fashion. A cursory reading of his *Hurry-graphs; or Sketches of Scenery, Celebrities, and Society* turns up many such verbal stunts as an "unerringly *comme il faut* lady" (p. 202), "overcome-itude" (p. 222), "Jenny-Lind-ism" (p. 233), "woman-esquely" in contrast to "man-ishly" (p. 238), and so on.[42] There are half a dozen coinages in *-dom: Listen-to-reason-dom* (p. 176), the world of a typical New York audience for

---

[39] William M. Thackeray, *The Newcomes,* Chap. XLIII.

[40] William M. Thackeray, *Pendennis,* Chap. VI.

[41] *Ibid.,* Chap. LIII.

[42] N. Parker Willis, *Hurry-graphs; or Sketches of Scenery, Celebrities and Society, Taken from Life* (New York: Charles Scribner, 1851).

Emerson's lectures; *Slate-and-pencil-dom* (p. 204), "which is bounded South by the Lehigh and North by the Penobscot"; *Dickens-dom* (p. 226), "a moveable Dickens-dom, bounded by every four walls that contained him and his friends"; *October-dom* (pp. 301–302), fashionable out-of-town visitors to New York; *Conversation-dom* and *Boys-and-girls-dom* (p. 329), "the definite separation . . . between Conversation-dom and Boys-and-girls-dom."

Even so brief a vocabulary list makes Willis' preoccupations evident. He was the columnist and critic of fashionable New York society in the forties and fifties of the last century. In this world the camellia—or japonica, to give it the name Willis used regularly—was very much the fashionable flower.[43]

When Willis categorized society, he found the japonica as significant a symbol as jewels:

> What we want is what they have in Paris—a society separate from fashion—the admission to which would be a compliment to the quality of a man—which would give its entertainments with humbler surroundings, but with wit, sparkle and zest unknown to the japonicas and diamonds—a freer society as to etiquette and dress—and a circle of which the power to contribute to its pleasure and brilliancy would be the otherwise un-catechised pass.[44]

To a man of Willis' verbal fluency, it is not far from this to the creation of *japonica-dom,* a single-word description of "the class uptown who usually wear in their hair the expensive exotic commonly called a japonica." [45] As with *swelldom,* the province

[43] Marguerite Gautier's red and white camellias first made their appearance in 1848. Dramatized in 1849, *La dame aux camellias* was first acted in Paris in February, 1852. In 1855, *Camille,* acted by the great French actress Rachel, took New York utterly by storm. It is worth noting in connection with the vogue of the flower that, in the play, the frail Marguerite's naughty symbolism is ignored.

[44] Willis, *op. cit.,* p. 266.

[45] Quoted from F. L. Pattee, *The Feminine Fifties* (New York: D. Appleton–Century Company, 1940), p. 250. Since Mr. Pattee apparently did not care for documentation, we can do no better than join the series of authors and books (including the *Oxford English Dictionary* and the *Amer-*

of *japonica-dom* is synonymous with a class well defined in social and financial terms—the "five-dollar-billers." And the word, like Willis' *uppertendom,* helped to push a little farther the usefulness of the suffix.

Considering to what extent the English-speaking world has, in the last few generations, become conscious of social and economic classes, it is to be expected that a suffix as useful as *-dom* in revealing the existence of groups within an area would be popular. There are few things that modern society is as self-conscious of as it is of the existence of separate classes. The strife between North and South produced coinages no more accurately reflecting the thinking of the time than do these (we quote from Wentworth): *serfdom* (1850), *uppertendom* (1854), *lowertwentydom* (1855), *lower ten-thousand-dom* (1870), *pauperdom* (1870), *villadom* (1880), *wagedom* (1885), *millionairedom* (1890), *yachtdom* (1901), *suburbandom* (1902), *middleclassdom* (1908), *slumdom* (1927), *bourgeoisdom* (1933), *Biddledom* (1939). Similiarly, other recognizable groups are labeled by such new words as these latest ones from Wentworth's list: *Nazidom* (1933), *gangsterdom* (1934), *Civil Servicedom* (1937), *sportsdom* (1939), *dictatordom* (1939), *Amishdom* (1940).

Word elements, like independent words, have a social and intellectual status of their own—that is, they may be used by people of one class and not by another, or they may be used creatively in writing and only rarely in speech. New words in *-dom,* for example, seem common only in writing. As frequent a device as it has become in journalism, and commonly as it has been employed by essayists and novelists, it is not an ordinary formative element in oral speech. In fact, most of the coinages of the last hundred years are merely nonce words, or barely more than that. Few have become part of the established vocabulary. A test by one of the authors with a group of students over the use of the recent words in Wentworth's list, indicated that

---

ican English Dictionary) who quote the word, without telling where in Willis it may be found. Whoever has tried to read a few of Willis' once admired sketches will not be too hard on us when we declare that we read as much of the stuff as we could stand.

only *Nazidom* had ever even been heard in oral use by the students. We ourselves would add *gangsterdom* but, even so, the fact that the words belong to written not oral use is evident. The point will be made more emphatic by the contrast offered in Lincoln's use of *unbeknownst-like* and Eggleston's use of *shuck up like* (see Chapter XV). These anecdotes exhibit the suffix *-like* in free use as a formative word element in oral speech. They also show clearly the cultural level at which the suffix is freely used. Lincoln and Eggleston alike recognize it as belonging to the lower levels of literacy. The social differences between *-dom* and *-like* are as great as the differences in their oral utility.

For reasons that should by now be obvious, we cannot here attempt anything like a full and systematic presentation of the wide field of word formation. Suffice it to state that such a work not only would grow to much larger bulk than this entire book, but that the task cannot be done until a large number of formative elements have been given extended treatment.

It is important, however, to understand how intimate are the connections between this language problem and all the other fields of linguistic investigation. The development of *-dom,* for instance, is phonetic as well as semantic. The psychology of word taboos also enters into word formation. We have seen that unwillingness to pronounce an "unpleasant" word or a word offensive to a large number of people creates a tendency to disguise it phonetically or otherwise. And in some cases it will be enough to add a new suffix in order to supply the concealing "make-up" which will permit the outlawed word to enter good society—or, at least, a particular society. The reader will remember that the word *abolition* had a hateful sound not only in the South but also to many people in the North. With this in mind, we will not consider Lincoln's use of *abolishment* in his message to Congress recommending compensated emancipation (March 6, 1862) a mere coincidence:

Resolved, That the United States ought to cooperate with any State which may adopt a gradual abolishment of slavery, giving to such

State in its discretion to compensate for the inconveniences, public and private, produced by such change of system.[46]

It is hard to be sure that one does not read into such a text something that is not there, but we believe we are right in thinking that the word *abolishment* was deliberately substituted for *abolition* because of the strong contemporary feeling about the latter. In his sermon "The Beginning of Freedom," preached March 9, 1862, Henry Ward Beecher called particular attention to Lincoln's choice of the word:

. . . a document initiating emancipation, or the *abolishment* of slavery, as President Lincoln peculiarly styles it. . . .[47]

Among the many things we omit is a thorough discussion of negative word formation, that is, the creation of new words by the curtailing of old ones. One usually views these forms, like *canter* from *Canterbury trot, spat* from *spatterdash,* and *tarp* from *tarpaulin,* as products of a laziness or an economy of language (occurring in one of the many milieus which develop their own slang and trade or professional argot). But abbreviations of that sort may contain euphemistic elements as well. *T.B.* has certainly a less ominous sound than *tuberculosis.* Whether the same thing applies to *con* for *consumption* in the following is hard to say:

The warden was a kindly enough man in the ordinary relations of life, but nine years as a tamer of man-beasts in a great stone cage had overlaid his sympathies with a thickening callus.

"One of our lifers that we won't have with us much longer," he said casually, noting that the governor's eyes followed the sick convict. "When the con gets one of these hill billies he goes mighty fast." [48]

---

[46] *The Writings of Abraham Lincoln* (New York: G. P. Putnam's Sons, 1923), V, 440.

[47] Henry Ward Beecher, *Freedom and War* (Boston: Ticknor & Fields, 1863), p. 227.

[48] Irvin S. Cobb, "Exit of Anse Dugmore," *The Escape of Mr. Trimm* (New York: Review of Reviews Corporation, 1918), pp. 187–188.

If the warden's choice of words is not due to a kindly man's softening and avoidance of a harsher term, it is probably professional slang.

The following quotations not only illustrate the social level which have, in some times and places, been implied in short forms, but show also how completely the social attitude toward utterly commonplace things can change. If today the father of a boy commonly called *Tom* addresses him as *Thomas,* then probably the boy feels that this deviation from familiar style forecasts the rising of a wind that will blow him no good. But a century ago at least some people considered the shortened form in a light hardly less unpleasant than a social evil:

"Tom," said I—let me stop and moralize a little upon this name. I would never call a child, Tom. There is something fatal in the word. I have known more drunken Toms than of all other names. It is a low-bred name. Bill, Jim, Joe, Sam, Ike, are all bad, but none equal to Tom. "Two of my drunkenest companions," said Reagan, "afterwards, my best friends, were Toms—now Thomas Elting and Thomas Nolan." Parents, don't nickname your children, it is a step down that may carry them to the bottom of the ladder.

Give your children good names; names they will not be ashamed of in after life, and never cut them short. Never call, William, Bill; or, Catherine, Kate; or Mary, that most beautiful of all names, a name I love, Moll; it will, perhaps, be the direct cause of their ruin as they grow up.

If the reader can stand it, we would like to quote one further remarkable passage from the same source:

"No; that won't do. I shall get to thinking what a poor, dirty miserable wretch I am, and how I am living with this woman, who is not a bad woman by nature; and then I will drink, and then she will drink—oh, cursed rum!—and what is to prevent us? But if we were married, my wife, yes, Mr. Pease, my wife, would say, 'Thomas'—she would not say, 'Tom, you dirty brute,'—don't be tempted'. . . ." [49]

---

[49] Solon Robinson, *Hot Corn: Life Scenes in New York Illustrated. Including the Story of Little Katy, Madalina, the Rag-Picker's Daughter, Wild Maggie, &c.* (New York: De Witt and Davenport, 1854), pp. 78 and 95. The book, dedicated by the author to his friend Horace Greeley, was very

To pull us back to the clipped forms of today, we note that just as the word *Tom* might have once apparently robbed a man of his self-respect, so now a name like *Lancelot* might be equally destructive to the personality and position of one who as *Lance* can hold up his head bravely among his fellows. Our authority, in case any mid-twentieth-century American needs one, is Damon Runyon:

> . . . the reason I know this story is because Lance McGowan tells most of it to me, as Lance knows that I know his real name is Lancelot, and he feels under great obligation to me because I never mention the matter publicly.[50]

---

popular. The stories in it first appeared in the pages of Greeley's paper, the *Tribune*. The title words have reference neither to swing nor to vaudeville, nor, despite the fact that they were written for "all who would promote temperance," have they any connection with any kind of liquor.

[50] "The Old Doll's House," *The Best of Damon Runyon,* Pocket Books Edition (n.d.), p. 73.

Chapter Nine

MEANING

LANGUAGE is largely a system of signals which the speaker uses in order to make the people addressed by him react in a certain way. This is evident in all cases in which orders are given or wishes expressed. But the many instances in which the use of language is calculated to impart information, apparently with no intention of provoking an immediate action by the hearer, are not essentially different. The teacher who informs his pupils of what he means by the expression "square root" does not expect an immediate reaction on their part. But the information thus given prepares his audience for future action; they will now be able to react in accordance with the teacher's wishes should he, on a later occasion, use the sentence: "Give the square root of four."

The successful use of language in order to make others react in accordance with the speaker's intentions is, then, impossible unless the signals are properly understood. This understanding can be secured by definitions and explanations. We do not make use of these helps, however, except in cases where we realize or anticipate difficulty. To define every word we utter is a manifest impossibility since the explanation has to be given in words which, in their turn, would have to be defined if we wanted to be sure that no misunderstanding could occur. Instead we work on the theory that our listeners, as members of our own speech community, will on the basis of earlier experiences be able to interpret our verbal signals in conformity with our intentions.

It is clear that this reliance on the hearer's ability to understand our signals is justified only insofar as his knowledge of the language used in a special case is approximately the same as the speaker's. Not even then is there an absolute guarantee against misunderstanding, since many word signals are traditionally used for two or more different purposes. From our discussion of euphemistic expressions we know that language is not always meant to express the speaker's ideas in an unambiguous way. In order to express the idea that a person is dead we can use any number of phrases that might just as well have a less ominous meaning. Compare the two following passages:

Third Ser.
Where's the knight?—
O sir, the gentleman you wounded is
Newly departed!
Sir Wal. Dead? . . .[1]

In this case the word *departed* is understood correctly, i.e., in the way it is meant by the speaker. Nevertheless it might, in Middleton's language, just as well mean that the person in question has left. In the same scene occurs the line, "I pray, depart, sirs, and take your murderer along with you . . . ." Evidently the correct understanding is helped along by the nature of the situation: in the former passage the speaker knows that the inflicted wound is grave enough to preclude the idea that the victim has just walked off.

Whenever the situation is of a nature to make developments in different directions equally possible, the danger of a misunderstanding is increased. Here is an instance in which a young man has made an unsuccessful attempt to kill his rival, and has fled; the woman in the case is informed of the occurrence by her father:

"Elsie, my dear, your cousin Richard has left us."
She grew still paler, as she asked,—
"Is he dead?"

---

[1] Thomas Middleton, *A Chaste Maid in Cheapside,* Act V, scene 1.

Dudley Venner started to see the expression with which Elsie put this question.

"He is living,—but dead to us from this day forward," said her father.[2]

The following *quid pro quo* is likewise based on a traditional euphemism, the use of "spirits" for intoxicating beverages:

"Why, you look as fresh as a new-blown rose."

Mrs. Bird held down her head, and actually appeared confused. Soon she gathered courage to speak. "Why, Mr. Turtle, how can you think so—I'm an old woman."

"Not so old arter all," said Ike, "you've taken good care of your sperits and complexion."

"Why, Mrs. Bird don't use *sperits!*" exclaimed Mrs. Brown, looking down over her spectacles, at Ike, with horror.

"Not them kind," said Ike—"but her nat'ral sperits, I mean. Now," continued Ike, "here's Squire Longbow, past fifty, hearty as a buck, full-er fire, and can kick up his heels as high as his head—all owin' to his sperits. . . ." [3]

Euphemism, of course, is by no means the only factor unfavorable to complete understanding. The speaker and the hearer may belong to different speech communities, in which case the latter may be familiar with the sound of the former's words but not with the finer shades of their meaning. In 1943, a misunderstanding of this sort caused a great deal of excitement in American political and military circles. Mr. William J. Jeffers had expressed the opinion that the Army and Navy factory expediters were "loafers," who made off with materials he could have used better. He explained afterwards, as a result of the difficulties his remark had plunged him into, that "on the railroad we speak of a loafing job as a job that isn't necessary. Therefore, a fellow holding down such a job is a loafer." [4]

---

[2] Oliver Wendell Holmes, *Elsie Venner,* Chap. XXVI.

[3] H. H. Riley, *The Puddleford Papers* (New York: Derby & Jackson, 1857), Chap. IX.

[4] New York *Times,* January 30, 1943, p. 1. See also *Time,* February 15, 1943, p. 16.

From this last example it becomes clear that some misunderstandings of this sort are by no means harmless. In common life they may be easily corrected by a subsequent explanation, but if they occur in public utterances, the damage can rarely be completely repaired by such expedients. Even supposing that every single man who had heard or read about Mr. Jeffers' "loafers" was reached by his later explanation, there can hardly be any doubt that the first unfavorable impression created by his words must have lingered, at least in some quarters.

Language as a means of communication becomes still less satisfactory when misunderstandings are deliberately employed to evade a command or to gain an advantage in debate. Here are two examples of such "misunderstanding," the first translated from German, the second from American politics:

> There was elected to the Diet Schaffranek, who demonstrated to us in Polish as a parliamentary orator the proverbial impossibility of fraternizing between Germans and Poles. Such a thing was possible in Silesia only on the basis of the official authority of the Catholic interests. Upon the complaint of the Prince-Bishop, Schaffranek when reelected was forbidden to "sit" on the left [auf der Linken zu "sitzen"]. In consequence, this sturdily built priest stood for five and six hours a day, and ten hours during double sessions, before the benches of the left, straight as a sentinel, and did not need to arise whenever he took the floor for an anti-German speech.[5]

The misunderstanding in this case is caused, or rather feigned, by the double meaning of "to sit on the left." The spiritual authorities intended this to mean: to declare one's sympathy with the "Left," the opposition party, by taking a seat among its members. Father Schaffranek took advantage of the fact that the literal meaning of the phrase did not prevent his standing where he was forbidden to sit.

Our second example is from the Cleveland *Leader* of August 29, 1866:

> In President Johnson's recent revolutionary speech to the dele-

[5] Translated from Otto von Bismarck, *Die gesammelten Werke,* ed. by G. Ritter and R. Stadelmann (Berlin: 1932), XV, 333.

gation from the Philadelphia Convention, he denounces Congress as a "Congress of part of the states hanging on the verge of government." The use of the word "verge" is significant. In the sense in which it is known to the English law, it is defined to be "a privileged space around or immediately adjoining the king's residence."

When the "humble individual" from Tennessee dons the imperial purple, the dignity of his office will require that he keep his "verge" free from intrusion. None but those basking in the radiant smiles of the dictator will be permitted to hang upon the verge or to enter the sacred precincts of the king's palace.

From what we know of President Johnson's education it appears highly improbable that he was aware of the technical meaning of *verge* in English law. To him, the word simply meant "on the edge or outskirts" of government. But in the bitterness of the struggle between the President and Congress, the paper found the technical meaning much too useful as propaganda to forgo employing it.

An incident of a similar sort but of much greater importance is connected with the history of the Revolutionary War. In 1766, an English Act of Parliament (the repeal of the Stamp Act) had stated

That the King's Majesty, by and with the consent of the lords spiritual and temporal, and Commons of Great Britain in Parliament assembled, had, hath, and of right ought to have full power and authority to make laws and statutes of sufficient force and validity to bind the colonies and people of America, subjects of the Crown of Great Britain, in all cases what so ever.[6]

It appears evident that the word "to bind" was not intended to suggest any debasing treatment of the colonists, but was used in the technical sense it has within the speech community of jurists: "to oblige or constrain with legal authority." Whether the people of America actually did not understand this, or did not choose to understand it, the expression must have had a hateful sound to them, and ten years later enough of their in-

[6] Declaratory Act of Parliament, February 24, 1766, quoted in "The American Crisis," *The Life and Works of Thomas Paine,* ed. by William H. Van der Weyde (New Rochelle, N.Y.: Tom Paine National Historical Association, 1925), II, 313, note.

dignation must have been still alive to offer Tom Paine a theme with which to raise that indignation to a new emotional pitch. In *The American Crisis* he uses the phrase not once but repeatedly. He makes it the theme of a symphony based on the motif of chains and slavery:

Britain, with an army to enforce her tyranny, has declared that she has a right (*not only to* TAX) but *"to* BIND *us in* ALL CASES WHATSOEVER" and if being *bound in that manner,* is not slavery, then is there not such a thing as slavery upon earth. Even the expression is impious; for so unlimited a power can belong only to God.[7]

. . . if a thief breaks into my house, burns and destroys my property, and kills or threatens to kill me, or those that are in it, and to *"bind me in all cases whatsoever"* to his absolute will, am I to suffer it? [8]

One of the greatest degrees of sentimental union which America ever knew, was in denying the right of the British Parliament *"to bind the colonies in all cases whatsoever.*[9]

A person, to use a trite phrase, must be a Whig or a Tory in a lump. . . . If he says he is against the united independence of the continent, he is to all intents and purposes against her in all the rest; because *this last* comprehends the whole. And he may just as well say, that Britain was right in declaring us rebels; right in taxing us; and right in declaring her *"right to bind the colonies in all cases whatsoever."* [10]

This case shows what many other examples will confirm, that the misunderstanding is based not so much on the definable meaning of a word but on certain less distinct elements that are usually called connotations. We can hardly assume that the word "to bind" meant something logically different to the authors of the Parliamentary Act and to the American public, such as would have been true if the colonists had taken the word to be synonymous with "to fetter" instead of "to constrain legally." It was not the logical significance of the word

---

7 *Ibid.*, II, 264.
8 *Ibid.*, p. 274.
9 *Ibid.*, p. 313.
10 *Ibid.*, pp. 314–315.

that was misunderstood and propagandized but its emotional value. To Parliament, it was a precise word referring to recognized relations between a legal authority and the persons governed by it and without any intention of offending those so bound; to the colonists, it was a word so closely connected with the ideas of imprisonment and slavery that they considered it an attack on their personal rights and political dignity.

It is the fact that a word not only "means" what its logical definition makes it mean but can call to life all sorts of associative ideas and emotions which makes language such an excellent material for poetry and, at the same time, such an imperfect and even dangerous instrument for any sort of discussion of a scientific or political nature. In poetry, the word *moonlight* is a highly effective word because, apart from meaning "the light of the moon," it also calls up visions of stillness, mystery, beauty, and perhaps love. That these visions are not absolutely the same for each reader of a poem to the moon is no disadvantage to the poet. On the contrary, the more varied the associative values of the word, the greater the number of readers to whom it may appeal in one way or another. In logical discussion, on the other hand, the peripheral elements of meaning represent a constant danger. Even if we tried, we could not keep our language free from words whose emotional value is strong enough to blunt our own mental functions and those of our listeners. As long as words express ideas and conditions about which we are concerned, the word can arouse exactly all the emotion of the thing of which it is the symbol. If, as is often the case, the two parties in a discussion use the same words with different connotations it becomes difficult to reach an agreement. Many scientific discussions have been prolonged and many political conflicts embittered by this insufficiency of language.

A prominent author of the post-Civil War Reconstruction period, Albion W. Tourgée, offers a keen analysis of the misunderstandings which resulted from the fact that in the two sections of the United States the same words were used with radically different connotations of meaning. The word *aboli-*

tionist, according to Tourgée, meant two widely different things:

AT THE NORTH

Abolitionist.—One who favors the emancipation of slaves.

AT THE SOUTH

Abolitionist.—One who favors emancipation + infidel + murderer + thief + ravisher + incendiary + all hell's accumulated horrors, "not otherwise appropriated." [11]

Carpet-bagger offered a similar pattern of meanings:

"Carpet-bagger," which was in some sense the lineal descendant of "abolitionist," was, as was very proper for a second edition, a considerable improvement on its immediate predecessor. It was undefined and undefinable. To the Southern mind it meant a scion of the North, a son of an "abolitionist," a creature of the conqueror, a witness of their defeat, a mark of their degradation: to them he was hateful because he recalled all of evil or shame which they had ever known. They hissed the name through lips hot with hate, *because* his presence was hateful to that dear, dead Confederacy which they held in tender memory, and mourned for in widow's weeds, as was but natural that they should do. They hated the Northern man, who came among them as the representative and embodiment of that selfish, malign, and envious North, which had sent forth the "abolitionist" in *ante bellum* days, had crushed the fair South in her heroic struggle. . . .

To the Northern mind, however, the word had no vicarious significance. To their apprehension, the hatred it embodied was purely personal, and without regard to race or nativity. They *thought* (foolish creatures!) that it was meant to apply solely to those, who without any visible means of support, lingering in the wake of a victorious army, preyed upon the conquered people.

So these formulated significations prevailed:—

AT THE NORTH

Carpet-bagger.—A man without means, character, or occupation, an adventurer, a camp-follower, a "bummer."

---

[11] Albion W. Tourgée, *A Fool's Errand* (New York: Fords, Howard, & Hulbert, 1879), p. 159.

AT THE SOUTH

Carpet-bagger.—A man of Northern birth + an abolitionist (according to the Southern definition) + an incarnation of Northern hate, envy, spleen, greed, hypocrisy, and all uncleanness.[12]

The hindrances to correct understanding that appear to be inseparable even from carefully worded language are so obvious that they could not fail to provoke more or less serious attempts to reach or at least approach an ideal language in which each word should have a single unmistakable meaning and each idea should be expressed by just one significant word, not as is often true in natural language by a number of nearly equivalent synonyms. The mere fact that from Locke to Korzybski attempts have had to be repeated again and again seems to show that a really foolproof language is beyond human possibilities. It could be reached only if we could rid language of one of its basic tasks, its function to give vent to emotions. This does not mean that the endeavors to remove or at least neutralize the hindrances that language sometimes raises to our understanding have been altogether in vain. They have at least served to make some of us aware of the pitfalls concealed in others' speech and in our own, and to immunize us against linguistic trickery of the grosser kind.

---

[12] *Ibid.*, pp. 160–161. It is with regret that we refrain from quoting more of Tourgée's remarks on these and similar matters. They are equally interesting to the linguist and to the historian. A passage (p. 121) about the confusion of ideas resulting from the various connotations of the word "slavery" in the North and in the South, before and after the Civil War, is particularly worth reading.

Chapter Ten

CHANGE OF MEANING

MEANING, as well as every other feature of language, is subject to constant fluctuations. The same meaning never occurs twice. Even a commonplace phrase like "my daughter" has not the identical significance today that it had yesterday. The short intervening space of time has brought with it certain changes in her growth, in her knowledge, in her attitude toward persons and things, as well as in my attitude toward her. Accordingly, the meaning of today's "my daughter" can be defined as "my daughter as she was yesterday plus all the changes that have occurred during the last twenty-four hours."

However, in speaking of changes of meaning, we do not, in general, think of these minor fluctuations but, rather, of certain phenomena on a larger scale that become apparent if we confront modern vocabularies with earlier stages of the same language. Discounting certain phonetic changes, we consider our "meat" to be the same word as Middle-English *mete,* which means "food"; we identify "cheek" with Anglo-Saxon *ceace* "jaw"; and "starve" with Anglo-Saxon *steorfan,* which means "to die." On the basis of these identifications, we pronounce these words to have undergone not mere occasional fluctuations of meaning but established and general changes of meaning. It is the task of the linguist, of course, to attempt an explanation of these changes.

In view of the frequent occurrence of misunderstandings, some authors have advanced the opinion that change of meaning, as we observe it in comparing the different periods of language, is largely due to misapprehension.

It must be admitted that several cases on record appear to support this theory. If the following report is trustworthy, the word *yegg* has come by its present meaning, "a burglar or safebreaker," by way of a misunderstanding:

In speaking of the cook ovens [in the Chinatown of San Francisco] I may say that it was there the word "yegg" originated. It has not yet been locked in the dictionary, but it has a place in our language and it's about time its derivation was settled once and for all. It is a corruption of "yekk," a word from one of the many dialects spoken in Chinatown, and it means beggar. When a hypo or beggar approached a Chinaman to ask for something to eat, he was greeted with the exclamation, "yekk man, yekk man."

The underworld is quick to seize upon strange words, and the bums and hypos in Chinatown were calling themselves yeggmen years before the term was taken out on the road and given currency by eastbound beggars. In no time it had a verb hung on it, and to yegg meant to beg.

The late William A. Pinkerton was responsible for its changed meaning. His business consisted largely of asking questions and necessarily he acquired much misinformation. A burglar with some humor fell into Pinkerton's hands and when asked who was breaking open the country "jugs" he whispered to the detective that it was the yeggs. Investigation convinced Pinkerton that there were a lot of men drifting about the country who called themselves yeggs. The word went into a series of magazine articles Pinkerton was writing at the time and was fastened upon the "box" men. Its meaning has since widened until now the term "yegg" includes all criminals whose work is "heavy." [1]

Derring-do, now used as an archaic word for reckless courage, is a well-attested example of change of meaning due to misunderstanding. The history of the change begins with *Troilus and Criseyde,* where Chaucer says:

---

[1] Jack Black, *You Can't Win* (New York: The Macmillan Company, 1927), p. 172. *Yegg* is not listed in the *American English Dictionary.* The *Oxford English Dictionary,* clearly as an unsupported hypothesis, remarks that it is "said to be the surname of an American burglar and safebreaker."

And certeynly in storye it is yfounde,
That Troilus was nevere unto no wight,
As in his tyme, in no degree secounde
In durryng don that longeth to a knight.[2]

Here *durryng don* (of which *derring-do* is only a spelling variation) is no noun but a verbal combination: "He was second to none in daring to do what belongs to a knight." Spenser, however, who frequently borrowed from Chaucer in order to give an old-time coloring to his style, did not understand the grammatical structure of this passage, even though Chaucer in this same stanza repeats the phrase in the infinitive—*to durre don,* "to dare to do"—in a way which might have enlightened his follower. Spenser derived a noun from it, which in its turn was taken up by others:

So from immortall race he does proceede,
That mortall hands may not withstand his might,
Drad for his derring doe and bloudy deed;
For all in blood and spoile is his delight.[3]

That in this case the change of meaning is complicated by a change of grammatical function does not materially alter its character.

The classical example of semantic change caused by misunderstanding is offered by the history of *weird.* Holinshed, to whom Shakespeare is indebted for the plot of *Macbeth,* says of the witches who prophesied Macbeth's future greatness that

. . . the common opinion was, that these women were either the weird sisters, that is (as ye would say) the goddesses of destinie, or else some nymphs or feiries, indued with knowledge of prophesie by their necromanticall science, because euerie thing came to passe as they had spoken.[4]

Holinshed's explanation that the weird sisters are the goddesses of fate is quite correct. *Weird* is a Northern form of Old

[2] Chaucer, *Troilus and Criseyde,* Book V, lines 834–837.

[3] Spenser, *The Faerie Queene,* Book II, canto iv, stanza 42.

[4] *Holinshed's Chronicle As Used in Shakespeare's Plays,* Everyman's Library, p. 211.

English *wyrd,* fate, destiny. Shakespeare took over the word as it was. He probably understood it correctly, for he also speaks of the "weird women" as giving promises. To judge from the citations in the *Oxford English Dictionary,* later generations were either vague about the meaning of the word and hence did what we regularly do when confronted with an unfamiliar word—guessed at its sense from the character of the persons and situations involved; or else the suggestive connotations of *weird* extended themselves even over its known primary meaning. At any rate, as a result apparently of its use by such romantic poets as Shelley the word came to be an equivalent of *uncanny, strange,* even *odd* and *unusual.*

In acknowledging that some words have, and others may have, developed new meanings by way of faulty understanding, however, we have not admitted that this is the normal way in which new meanings come into existence. It is easy to see that all three examples have one thing in common: the men from whom the words were learned and those who, by insufficient understanding, altered their meanings belong to entirely different speech communities. One might almost say that we are dealing with incorrect translations from a foreign language. This is certainly not an exaggeration in the case of "yegg," borrowed from English-speaking Chinese, although willful deception appears to have been added to the normal difficulties of understanding. But it is also true in a certain sense of our relation to earlier writers in our own language, many of whose words are as unfamiliar to us as foreign idioms.

Since all our examples are of an exceptional character, it would be extremely hasty to conclude from them that changes of meaning under more normal circumstances, i.e., if the speaker or writer belongs to essentially the same speech community as the listener or reader, must necessarily follow the same pattern. In many a case, semantic change has taken place in which lack of understanding has played no part at all. We follow our usual method of discussing one or two examples of which we have detailed knowledge before attempting to establish a theory.

Until October 29, 1835, the word *Loco-foco* meant just one thing: a friction match. The word was an artificial trade name given to a certain brand of matches and probably designed to suggest something easily set afire, with Latin *locus,* "place," "spot," and Italian *fuoco,* "fire," furnishing the material for the coinage.

On this very day, however, something happened which caused the word to develop a new meaning that finally superseded the original one. At a Democratic party meeting in New York the assembly was presented with a prepared list of candidates for political offices which its sponsors, the group known as the Tammany Society, expected to pass in a hurry before any opposition could be voiced. The left-wing faction of the party, a group known as the Equal Rights Democrats, had been warned of the planned maneuver and prepared a countermove. All at once they unfurled banners inscribed with the names of opposition candidates, and the tumult that ensued grew so violent that the Tammany men found it wise to attempt to break off the meeting—in vain—by turning off the gas. Loco-foco matches and candles were lit, the meeting was continued, and the Equal Rights ticket was passed:

The morning of the 30th of October, 1835, was a joyous one to the readers of the Whig press in the city. Descriptions, both grave and ridiculous, were given of the scene of the previous evening in Tammany Hall, and great were the exultations over the divisions in the ranks of the Democracy. The Courier and Enquirer took the lead in this labor of love, and bedubbed the anti-monopolists with the name of Loco-Focos. But the Whig press, true to its natural dislike of real democracy, took sides with the monopolists; at least so far as to abuse the friends of Equal Rights without stint or conscience. On the other side, the New York Times, the cherished organ of the oldest and wisest of the monopoly Democracy, lifts up its voice in mingled tones of shame, chagrin, and denunciation. . . . But this was not all; for it undertook the Herculean task of castigating the whole of the Equal Rights democracy. That the reader may be enabled to form some idea of the glorious feats of this protégé of the "thirty-six fathers," its epithets are extracted, leaving the imagination to supply the context which was equally classic, moral and instructive. *"Disor-*

ganizers"—"Intruders"—"Revolters"—"Agrarians"—"Working Men's faction"—"Rowdies"—"Odds and Ends of extinct party"—"Eleventh hour Democrats"—"Sweepings and remnants of all recent factions"—"Renegade anti-Masons"—"Pests of party"—"Bad factionists"—"Fanny Wright men"—"Noisy brawlers"—"Political nuisances"—"Loco-Foco party" — "Carbonari" — "Infidels" — "Pledge spouters" —"Resolution mongers"—"Small fry of small politicians"—"Small lights"—"Fire flies of faction"—"Unclean birds"—"Jack o'Lanterns who shine in an unhealthy atmosphere"—"Noisy discontented politicians"—"Scum of politics"—"Knaves"—"Political cheats and swindlers"—"The Guy Fawkes of politics"!!! [5]

It becomes clear at once that this overnight change of *Loco-foco* from the name of a match to that of a political party is not based on a misunderstanding. It would be absurd to think that some people, in speaking of the meeting, refer to the matches as "Loco-focos," while others, unfamiliar with this trade name, made the wrong guess that the word referred to the Equal Rights party. Even without Byrdsall's express statement, it would be impossible to doubt that the first persons to use the new meaning intended to create a new nickname for political opponents. The mechanism of this process is, of course, entirely different from that of a misunderstanding. A change of meaning based on misunderstanding takes place if *A* uses a word in its traditional ("correct") meaning while *B*, unfamiliar with the word, has to guess at its sense from the context and guesses wrong. In the case of *Loco-foco* the persons who gave it its new meaning used it intentionally in an untraditional sense but were nevertheless understood correctly, i.e., as they had intended to be understood. Everyone of their readers knew at once that the Equal Rights party, not safety matches, was alluded to.

Changes of this type are extremely frequent. While it would take much labor to collect as many as a dozen examples in which the new meaning is clearly due to misunderstanding, any number of occurrences could be cited that were inaugurated by a speaker's voluntary decision to deviate from the traditional meaning of a word and were completed by the hearer's ability

---

[5] F. Byrdsall, *The History of the Loco-Foco or Equal Rights Party* (New York: Clement & Packard, 1842), pp. 28–29.

to understand the new meaning although, up to the critical moment, the word meant to him something different. This, then, is a type of semantic change that can be considered normal, while changes based on misunderstanding are decidedly exceptional.

From here on, our discussion must proceed along lines similar to those we followed in investigating the nature of phonetic changes and speech communities. To begin with, the innovation is a merely individual act: it consists simply in the fact that some person decides to use an old expression in a context in which it has not been used before, thereby transferring it into a new sphere of vocabulary, say from technology into politics. However, if this personal speech act is to result in a generally accepted change of meaning, it is necessary not only that the speaker be understood according to his intentions but also that a large number of other persons be prepared to take their cue from him and to incorporate the new meaning in their own speech. If the second step is not taken, the innovation remains a matter of personal style, a characteristic of language as used by a certain individual; as such it may be interesting enough, but it can hardly be considered a concern of the linguist in his dealings with the general development of language. If, on the other hand, the new expression is adopted by a sufficient number of imitators, then each imitation helps to establish the new meaning until what has started as a personal deviation from general speech habits becomes a new element in the common vocabulary. The completion of such semantic changes will necessarily go hand in hand with a decrease in the frequency of the word or words which, before the new expression was introduced, had the exclusive privilege of designating the idea, now partially (sometimes exclusively) annexed by the newcomer. Every case in which an Equal Rights Democrat was called a "Loco-foco" must evidently have reduced the number of occurrences of the former expression. Thus there exists an intimate connection between the problem of new meanings and the question of why well-known and apparently necessary words can become extinct.

It is now clear that two things are essential in order fully to understand a change of meaning. (1) If we know the originator of the change, then there is sense in the question: What caused him to deviate from common usage and what made him choose just this one word as the object and the means of his innovation? If he is a writer, we will study his works with a view of finding other new words and meanings introduced by him and of establishing certain tendencies of his linguistic productivity, thereby trying to contribute to the knowledge of his individual psychology (see discussions of Carlyle's use of *-dom* and Chapter XIII on personal style). It is true that in most cases the originator of a semantic change is unknown, but even so, we can often define the group of persons within which a certain change of meaning must have begun. It is, then, just as likely to prove a valuable guide to an understanding of the speaking and thinking habits of the groups from which it emanates, as the individual changes introduced by an author are a guide to his personality.

(2) As soon as the origin of a new meaning has been established, we must try to answer the question: By what qualities of the word and needs of the community was it raised from the status of an individual peculiarity of speech to an acknowledged element of the vocabulary of a whole speech community? That a new word or meaning has made its appearance in a certain language is not, of course, proof of its having ever been generally accepted. Speech innovations of every sort are constantly cropping up, but in most cases they do not influence the formation of the common vocabulary. We hear them and forget about them almost immediately. Even if they are striking enough to force themselves upon our attention, we may not be prepared to incorporate them with our own stock of words and phrases. Everything that is new in language has to overcome a large measure of inertia, if not of hostility, before it can be accepted, and we must not forget that the introduction of a new word into the speech of a large community presupposes its acceptance by millions of individual speakers. If, therefore, in opposition to the generally conservative attitude of the large

majority, a considerable number of persons not only notice a new expression but decide to make active use of it, then the individual reactions of all persons participating in this process of acceptance must be directed by some unifying influence that makes the millions all take the same favorable attitude toward the innovation. In other words, the attitude of the speech community must be one of collective preparedness—*kollektive Bereitschaft,* as a Swiss scholar, Gustav Bally, has aptly termed it.[6] To explain the success of a new word is, therefore, equivalent to showing up the factors that created this collective preparedness.

The case of *Loco-foco* is very revealing even in this respect. A community in a state of high political tension gets the news of the dramatic meeting in which the Loco-foco matches played such an important part. Every newspaper not only gives the factual report but expresses its opinion about what has happened. Thousands of citizens discuss it in their private conversation. In view of all this, the official name of Equal Rights party becomes insufficient. Even if the discussion were carried on in cold blood and in a spirit of impartiality, it would become a tedious thing to repeat that name every time the party has to be mentioned, and any newly invented name would probably be gratefully accepted as alleviating the necessity for endless repetitions. As it is, the discussion is far from being dispassionate. The enemies of the party in particular are full of excitement and anger over the successful trick, and a veritable flood of abusive terms directed against the Equal Rights party is the result. Byrdsall has done us the service of collecting a list of these terms from one of the contemporary papers. Had he failed to do so, we would still have guessed that just such an orgy of abuse must have followed the incident, and it would have been the duty of the investigating linguist to verify this suspicion.

After the first excitement has subsided, the need for a multitude of expressions for the same thing is of course reduced.

[6] Gustav Bally, "Psychologische Phänomene im Bedeutungswandel," *Sprache und Dichtung,* XXX (Bern: 1924), 8 ff.

But while it lasts, everybody has heard them, and some of them may have become so familiar to all of the speech community that they will survive; not, however, wholly unchanged, because the more they are used the weaker will become their derogatory power. From terms of abuse they will, very likely, change into comparatively neutral everyday words.

In this process a secondary change of meaning will frequently develop. Once on the march, a new word is not likely to stop at the exact boundary line of the meaning it was originally intended to express. *Loco-foco* was intended as a nickname for the Equal Rights Democrats only. Very soon, however, it became used against Democrats in general, no matter what wing of the party they adhered to. The following passage is from a late but very vivid account of the campaign of William Henry Harrison:

> They [the Whigs] peremptorily refused to designate their opponents any longer by their ancient title of "Democrats." They said it was too sober, too grave—the very sound made them melancholy; and they never applied the word "democrat" to their adversaries again. They called them *"Loco-focos"*—said there was something light as well as sulphurous about that name which pleased them; and ever afterwards they refused to recognize their adversaries by any other title. Their coat of arms was a log cabin, with the string of the door-latch upon the outside, a jug of hard cider, a 'coon *rampant,* regarding with a sardonic grin a "loco-foco" *couchant.*[7]

The reasons the word showed such power of expansion, not only over *Democrat* but over all the competitors listed by Byrdsall, are probably only in part recognized by Williams. In addition, it is strongly abusive only during the first period of its existence and later, therefore, had better chances of adoption by neutral persons and even by the members of the party. Still, it was closely associated with the idea of fire and therefore recommended itself to the enemy parties who, by a slight twist of meaning accomplished by a few well-chosen adjectives, could easily make it suggest that the persons so designated were

[7] James Williams, *The Rise and Fall of "The Model Republic"* (London: R. Bentley, 1863), pp. 278–279.

dangerous political incendiaries. Notice that accusations of "incendiarism" are extremely common in the political debates of those days and that other epithets in Byrdsall's list likewise allude to various fiery phenomena: "Fire flies of faction," "Jack o'Lanterns who shine in an unhealthy atmosphere," "The Guy Fawkes of politics." Not the least important reason for the success of *Loco-foco* is probably the sound effect of the word, originally calculated by the inventors of the matches so designated to arrest the attention of the public, but no less useful to those who wanted to make the term serve their political intentions. And, of course, we must remember that, among all its competitors, *Loco-foco* stood out as the one word having the closest relation to the event that had caused all the emotion.

Very probably, this analysis is far from complete, but it will suffice to bring out a few important things. Here are some of the most obvious inferences:

There exist changes of meaning in which misunderstanding has no, or no appreciable, part.

The phenomenon is closely connected, on the one hand, with that of competition between words of similar function; on the other, with the fact that important ideas are likely to develop an abundance of synonyms.

Emotional elements are of supreme importance to the whole process.

Some time during the year 1861, at the height of the remarkable vogue of name-calling that preceded, accompanied, and followed the Civil War, the abusive vocabulary of the Unionists was enriched by the introduction of the name *copperhead* for such Northern Democrats as were in sympathy with the South. Until then the word had been the name of a venomous snake, and like other words of its group, as for instance, *snake, reptile, adder,* it had occasionally been applied with derogatory meaning to human beings. From the examples listed in the *Dictionary of American English,* it appears that it had been used to describe, in turn, Indians, Dutch settlers in New York, Presbyterians, and red-headed persons, this last use being perhaps a reflection of the old prejudice that ascribed red hair to Judas—or perhaps merely a slighting metaphor based on the color of copper. None of these applications appears to have survived the Civil War; whoever first used the word in its new political sense may, therefore, be said to have originated a permanent change of meaning. The new phase in the history of the word seems to begin with its use in the *Detroit Free Press* of May 5, 1861:

> These neutral papers are always deceptive. In some parts of the country they go by the name of rattlesnake papers; but a friend suggests to us that they ought to be called Copperheads—because the first named reptile always gives notice before he bites, whereas the neutral papers never show their colors before they apply their fangs.[8]

It is not surprising that the name of this "friend," if, indeed, he is anything more than a fiction of the writer, is forgotten. What he did is really very little; finding a new use for an old word is certainly no achievement deserving immortality. Not what the innovator did but what his contemporaries did with his innovation is what really matters. Thanks to the painstaking investigations of Albert Matthews [9] and of Paul S. Smith,[10] we know that the new expression met with success—not, it seems, immediately, but as soon as the approaching elections of 1862 intensified the political struggle in the North and consequently the search for new emotional words. At first the word appears to have been limited to the Middle West. The Cincinnati *Gazette* has it on July 30, 1862, the Chicago *Tribune* on August 3 and 5, the Cincinnati *Commercial* on August 21. The Columbus *Crisis* of October 22 quotes it from the Ashland

[8] Detroit *Free Press,* May 5, 1861, quoted in *Journalism Quarterly,* XVI, 345. We wish to record one use prior to the Civil War in which *copperhead* clearly refers to the Democratic party. The Ohio State *Journal* of February 4, 1857, in speaking of the Cadiz [Ohio] *Sentinel* says, "This paper is locofocoish of the most intensified copper-head stripe." It seems to us now that this use is isolated. In any case, it does not change the fact that a new epoch in the history of the word starts with the use of the Detroit *Free Press.*

[9] *Publications of the Colonial Society of Massachusetts,* XX, 205 ff.

[10] *American Historical Review,* XXXII, 799 ff.

Union. By January, 1863, the word is in almost daily use in the Chicago *Tribune*. Matthews gives quotations from this paper of January 6, 7, 8, 9, 10, 15, 22, and so on. During the same month, if not earlier, it invaded the East. A cartoon in *Harper's Weekly* shows Vallandigham and other Peace Democrats applying for admission to Jefferson Davis' residence in Richmond and being refused by a colored servant with the words, "He [Davis] haven't got no friends at the Norf; and when he wants any, he won't choose'em among de Peace Sneeks." If the pun is not obvious, the title of the cartoon "Reception of the Copperheads at Richmond" makes it so. On February 13, the New York *Times* has an editorial called "The Western Copperheads." The following day, the New York *Tribune* writes about the "Copperhead Conspiracy." From then on, the word is in universal use.

The best proof that a political catchword is taking effect is usually found in the reactions of the persons against whom it is directed. As long as a new slogan produces no large-scale repercussions, it can safely be ignored. Not before its sting is felt will the attacked party be compelled to take countermeasures. A common one consists in a ready acceptance of the abusive term, for, if used by a speaker about himself, it loses much of its poison. As early as February 14, 1863, in a speech delivered in Newark, New Jersey, one of the leading Northern Democrats, Vallandigham, tried this method: "There are others here from the Northwest, all 'Butternuts,' [11] 'Copperheads' like myself. (Cheers)"

Somewhat later a more subtle attempt was made to neutralize the aggressive force of *Copperhead*. A certain type of copper penny with a feminine head representing the Goddess of Liberty was adopted as a party badge—a visible expression of the idea that the Copperheads were the real champions of freedom. Surely a clever countermove and, by its very failure, a stringent proof of the power of the new slogan.

Thus it appears that both friend and enemy contributed

11 "Butternut" is another nickname for the Northern Democrats. Its history is treated in Matthews' paper.

to the rapid spread of the new word. The reason that we found it necessary to illustrate this process by so many quotations and references follows from what we have already said: the invention of a new word or meaning of a word is only a first impulse. As far as the history of a language, as distinct from individual style, is concerned, the second stage is by far the more important. It consists in the acceptance of the new mode of speech by all, or at least by a large part, of the speech community. It is in the description of this second stage that so many otherwise valuable studies in word history fail. Therefore we have preferred to brave the common charge that philologists habitually delight in the accumulation of trifling detail rather than stint the description of an essential process. Only by presenting a large number of instances could we show the existence of that "collective preparedness" which explains why a word invented by one man became, within scarcely more than one year, the common property of millions. Why that preparedness existed is evident from the state of public feeling during this period. The attitude of a Northern majority against such persons in their midst as sympathized with secession had become increasingly bitter. Terms like *Northern Democrat* or *Peace Democrat,* although describing the minority in a logically adequate way, were incapable of expressing the hostility of which this group was the object. Thus there had arisen a discrepancy between the traditional vocabulary as it was before *Copperhead* was put into circulation, and the need of expression existing in a group numerically and politically dominant. This linguistic vacuum was bound to be filled by any new word offered by some creative person, provided it characterized the dissenting party in an adequately unpleasant way.

We have already pointed out that the emotional connotations of a word form part of its biography. Passages like the following provide useful evidence:

> The Copperhead is described by naturalists as "An American venomous serpent, the most dangerous after the rattlesnake. . . ." The rattlesnake, with all its venom, has one virtue—it never strikes without warning. . . . Your copperhead is no such chivalrous foe; for

> he hides in the grass, silent and treacherous, springs upon you unawares. . . . No rattle, no hiss, but a lurking watchfulness and a leap at your throat. . . . There is a remarkable fitness in the name—let the traitors be called "Copperheads." [12]

Now this is the same idea as that expressed in the passage quoted above from the Detroit *Free Press,* but nobody can fail to see the increased virulence of this second version. A still higher note of indignation is struck in Bret Harte's poem *The Copperhead* (1864). We quote all of it in order not to spoil its effect of abusive contempt:

> There is peace in the swamp where the Copperhead sleeps,
> Where the waters are stagnant, the white vapor creeps,
> Where the musk of Magnolia hangs thick in the air,
> And the lilies' phylacteries broaden in prayer.
> There is peace in the swamp, though the quiet is death,
> Though the mist is miasma, the upas-tree's breath,
> Though no echo awakes to the cooing of doves,—
> There is peace: yes, the peace that the Copperhead loves.
>
> Go seek him: he coils in the ooze and the drip,
> Like a thong idly flung from the slave-driver's whip;
> But beware the false footstep,—the stumble that brings
> A deadlier lash than the overseer swings.
> Never arrow so true, never bullet so dread,
> As the straight steady stroke of that hammer-shaped head;
> Whether slave or proud planter, who braves that dull crest,
> Woe to him who shall trouble the Copperhead's rest!
>
> Then why waste your labors, brave hearts and strong men,
> In tracking a trail to the Copperhead's den?
> Lay your axe to the cypress, hew open the shade
> To the free sky and sunshine Jehovah has made;
> Let the breeze of the North sweep the vapors away,
> Till the stagnant lake ripples, the freed waters play;
> And then to your heel can you righteously doom
> The Copperhead born of its shadow and gloom!

---

[12] New York *Tribune,* February 16, 1863, quoted in Matthews, *op. cit.,* p. 231.

An attempt to trace the history of *Copperhead* from the time of the Civil War to the First World War, when it had a sporadic revival as a synonym of *pro-German,* would involve too complex a study. All we wish to point out here is that during the Reconstruction period the word underwent a secondary change of meaning to the extent that it became more and more a synonym of Democrat, used, of course, only abusively. Both the derogatory character of the word and the expansion of its meaning become clear from an episode in Congress (1870), when Blaine discussed the consequences of admitting a congressman from Tennessee accused of having supported the Confederate Constitution.

> [Mr. Blaine] . . . If the Committee of Election shall report that he is ineligible on that account, why of course then this copperhead competitor by this construction comes immediately in.
>
> Eldridge.—I rise to a question of order. I insist that the term copperhead is not parliamentary.
>
> Mr. Blaine.—I recall the word. I never used it before in a debate here. I will say his Democratic competitor.
>
> The Speaker overruled the point of order on the ground that he was not speaking of any gentleman in the House, but Mr. Blaine refused to be thus upheld: "I did not withdraw the word as a question of order. I should have told the gentleman that he had made no point of order. As a question of taste I confess that I have transgressed, and as a question of taste I change the word. It was in bad taste, as it always is, to use offensive political epithets in debate." [13]

This same change is further documented by the following quotation which we cannot date exactly but which probably comes from Cleveland's first term:

> Rev. N. W. Cleveland, brother of the President, complains in the papers that his parishioners call him a "copperhead," and even insinuate that a man cannot be both a Democrat and a consistent Christian.[14]

---

[13] Gail Hamilton (Mary Abigail Dodge), *Biography of James G. Blaine* (Norwich, Conn.: Henry Bill Publishing Co., 1895), p. 198.

[14] *The Complete Works of Brann the Iconoclast* (New York: The Brann Publishers, Inc., 1919), V, 51.

In every language there are certain words which can be said to have a periodic existence. They lie dormant for long periods, only to be revived whenever special circumstances make them useful to fill what we have called a "vacuum" in the vocabulary. The word *draft* in the limited sense of "induction into an army" was an extremely frequent word during the Civil War, the First World War, and the Second World War. During the intervening periods it can hardly be said to have been an active part of the vocabulary. The same holds for *contraband* which, since the sixteenth century, has meant forbidden traffic, smuggling, and, in particular, goods subjected to confiscation by a belligerent on account of their possible usefulness to the enemy. The word drops out of use in peacetimes but regains its importance whenever war is declared.

During the Civil War, however, a change of meaning took place, which we shall now study fully because it is another of those rare examples which can be dated to the very day.

In the early days of the Civil War the treatment of fugitive slaves was an intricate problem to the Northern armies. Law, as it then still existed, prescribed that such slaves should be returned to their masters, a course which the majority of the North deeply resented. How the difficulty was finally solved is described in the autobiography of General Benjamin F. Butler. On May 24, 1861, a Southern officer presented himself under a a flag of truce, and between him and Butler the following conversation took place:

> "I am informed," said Major Carey, "that three negroes belonging to Colonel Mallory have escaped within your lines. I am Colonel Mallory's agent and have charge of his property. What do you mean to do with those negroes?"
>
> "I intend to hold them," said I.
>
> "Do you mean, then, to set aside your constitutional obligation to return them?"
>
> "I mean to take Virginia at her word, as declared in the ordinance of secession passed yesterday. I am under no constitutional obligations to a foreign country, which Virginia now claims to be."

"But you say we cannot secede," he answered, "and so you cannot consistently detain the negroes."

"But you say you have seceded, so you cannot consistently claim them. I shall hold these negroes as contraband of war, since they are engaged in the construction of your battery and are claimed as your property. The question is simply whether they shall be used for or against the Government of the United States." [15]

It is hardly necessary to give examples of the frequency with which this word, in its legal meaning and as applied to the special problem of the escaped slave, occurs from then on. Its rapidly achieved popularity is partly due to the same motives we discussed under *Copperhead*—the uniformity of thought and feeling caused by the war—but also to the more practical motive that it helped to solve a legal difficulty. Together, these forces were strong enough to outweigh certain disadvantages of the word arising from juridical doubts as to whether Butler's legal reasoning was correct (". . . as a lawyer I was never very proud of it. . . ."),[16] and from the unwillingness of the Northern abolitionists to speak of Negroes as if they were ordinary chattels. The reaction of one of the leading abolitionists is very characteristic in both ways:

. . . Butler pronounced that magic word "contraband," and summoned the negro into the arena. . . . It was a poor word. Some doubt —I do not—whether it is sound law. . . . Contraband is a bad word, and may be bad law, but just then it was worth all the Constitution. . . .[17]

As we have seen in the cases of *Loco-foco* and *Copperhead,* the primary change of meaning was quickly followed by a secondary extension. As a word used to settle a legal question, it had originally a strictly defined sense. Entering the common vocabulary, it was quickly stripped of the technical elements of its meaning, until finally it came very close to being a synonym

[15] *Autobiography and Personal Reminiscences of Major-General Benj. F. Butler; Butler's Book* (Boston: A. M. Thayer and Co., 1892), p. 257.

[16] *Ibid.*, p. 259.

[17] Wendell Phillips, *Speeches, Lectures, and Letters* (Boston: James Redpath, 1863), pp. 529–530.

of *Negro.* It was, in fact, so used by Mark Twain less than a year after Butler's decisive action. In a letter dated May 11, 1862, from Esmeralda, California, and discussing office arrangements with his brother, Mark Twain wrote, ". . . the whole to be kept in parlor order by two likely contrabands at big wages. . . ."[18] On March 9, 1863, a drawing in *Harper's Weekly* entitled "Contrabands Coming into Our Lines under the Proclamation" shows a motley crowd of Negroes, including women and babies, who could not by any stretch of the imagination be considered contraband in Butler's sense. According to Edmund N. Hatcher, the Negro troops of the Union Army were themselves using the word by the end of the war. He records that in Petersburg, Virginia, on April 3, 1865, they were singing the popular "In the Year of Jubilo:"

He six foot one way, two foot tudder,
An' he weigh t'ree hundred pound,
His coat so big, he couldn't pay de tailor,
An' it won't go half way round.
He drill so much, dey call him Cap'an,
An' he get so drefful tanned!
I spec' he try an' fool dem Yankees,
For to tink he's contraband.
De massa run, ha! ha!
De darkey stay, ho! ho!
It must be now de kingdom comin',
An' de yar ob Jubilo.[19]

A final example of the shift comes from the *Atlantic Monthly,* November, 1867 (quoted in the *Dictionary of American English*). In an article about how the actor T. D. Rice created the character, Jim Crow, we find: "After the play, Rice having shaded his own countenance to the 'contraband' hue, ordered Cuff to disrobe, and proceeded to invest himself in the cast-off apparel."

---

[18] *Mark Twain's Letters,* Paine Edition (New York: Gabriel Wells, 1923), I, 75.

[19] Edmund N. Hatcher, *The Last Four Weeks of the War* (Columbus, Ohio: 1892), p. 132.

These secondary expansions of meaning are as regular as they are important. A word cannot be confined within rigid limits of meaning under the impact of sudden popularity. A word in fashion is constantly used by people without regard to its original limitations.[20] *Loco-foco,* originally an Equal Rights Democrat, soon became any Democrat; the same meaning awaited *Copperhead,* although originally it meant a Northern Democrat favoring the South. And *contraband,* originally a fugitive Negro held by the North to prevent his being used in the Southern war effort, almost at once became a name for any Negro.

Carpetbagger (already discussed in Chapter IX) is another word subjected to the same tendency. Before going into details, we must dwell for a moment on the interesting and controversial question of its origin. Tourgée, whose lively interest in questions of language makes him a witness not easily to be discounted, offers the following explanation:

> The origin of this new vehicle of malignity is said to have been this. In one of the North-western States, during the early days of "wildcat money" as it was termed, a plan was devised for preventing the solvency of the State banks from being too readily tested. An organization was formed which secured its issues by the mortgage of land, which mortgage the State had power to enforce as upon forfeiture, on behalf of the creditors, whenever the notes of the organization (they called it a bank) "should go to protest." To avoid this contingency was then the prime object. As the law had neglected to provide that banks organized under it should have a permanent place of business, this object was for a considerable time attained by neglecting to open any office, or having any permanent place of doing business, and putting their notes in circulation by means of agents, who carried the bill about the country in *carpet-bags,* and were hence denominated, "Carpet-baggers." It is said that one of these veritable carpetbaggers, an editor, who during the war had exhausted all the expletives of which he was master, in denunciation of Lincoln and the officers and men of the Federal army, and had, in return, been branded

[20] For the record, on August 8, 1945, two days after the first use of an atomic bomb, a bridge player was overheard saying, in spreading his hand, "I have two atomic bombs," meaning two aces.

with that term of ineffaceable shame "Copperhead," was therefore at a loss for some fresh epithet to bestow upon the new class whom he had honored with his hate, and suddenly bethought himself of his own nickname. Whereupon he shouted, "Carpet-baggers!" Instantly it spread through the press of the South; and, with its usual subserviency, that of the North followed in its lead, and re-echoed its maledictions.[21]

In apparent contrast to this is a statement by Oliver P. Temple:

Mr. [Andrew J.] Fletcher was one of the first, if not the very first, in the State to denounce the hordes of greedy office-seekers who came from the North in the rear of the army in the closing days of the War. He was ready to welcome the genuine settler, but for the adventurer who came to prey on the people of the South he had an undisguised contempt and hatred. In a speech in Nashville he had the boldness to use an expression that has since become national, in reference to this class of men. He said:

"No one more gladly welcomes the Northern man who comes in all sincerity to make a home here, and to become one of our people, than I, but for the adventurer and the office-seeker who comes among us with one dirty shirt and and a pair of dirty socks, in an old rusty carpet bag, and before his washing is done becomes a candidate for office, I have no welcome."

This was the origin of the term "carpet bag," and out of it grew the well known term "carpet-bag government." [22]

This digression is intended as food for thought for etymologists. The discrepancy betweeen Tourgée's and Temple's histories may be an entirely superficial one. It is quite possible, and indeed likely, that both authors are correct. Much unnecessary controversy about word origins has been caused by a tendency among scholars to consider such problems in the light of an "either . . . or" where an "as well as" would be more appropriate (compare the previously given etymology of *Quaker*).

---

[21] Tourgée, *A Fool's Errand, ed. cit.*, p. 158.

[22] Oliver P. Temple, *Notable Men of Tennessee* (New York: Cosmopolitan Press, 1912), p. 126.

Returning to the question of secondary shifts of meaning, we note that the original sense of *carpetbagger,* a Northern man arriving in the South poor and rapidly gaining riches and influence, is soon subject to fluctuations. A Congressional Report of 1872 contains this testimony given by General James H. Clanton of Alabama:

> *Question.* How is the epithet carpet-bagger, which is so odious, applied, and to whom do you apply it?
>
> *Answer.* If a man should come there and invest $100,000, and in the next year should seek the highest offices, by appealing to the basest prejudices of an ignorant race, we would call him a political carpet-bagger. . . .
>
> *Question.* Does the term carpet-bagger apply to a man coming from Georgia to Alabama?
>
> *Answer.* Yes, he would be a Georgia carpet-bagger, if he came in the same way. We set down our own people who act that way as the meanest.[23]

It appears from this that neither the idea of poverty nor that of Northern origin is any longer an indispensable element of the meaning. Thus its use has been extended to cases to which a few years earlier it could not have been applied.

In later Northern usage, the range of meaning is further extended. In the following quotation it means a politician running for office outside his home district, even if it is only a question of wards and city blocks:

> We were told at the meeting that Mr. Croker, leader of Tammany Hall, had sent word to Timothy D. Sullivan, leader of the district and known as Big Tim, that Mr. Miner was to supplant Tim Campbell as representative from that district. Tim's friends were incensed over what they called carpet-bagging and the violation of home rule by the attempt to impose a resident of Madison Avenue on the people of Grand Street and East Broadway.[24]

The incident referred to occurred in 1894.

---

[23] Forty-second Cong., 2d Sess., H.R. No. 22, Pt. 1, pp. 296–297.

[24] Alfred E. Smith, *Up to Now* (New York: The Viking Press, 1929), p. 54.

Chapter Eleven

TYPES OF SEMANTIC CHANGE

FROM the examples already given, the reader should by now be aware that as far as meaning is concerned every word is an individual case. The history of the word *contraband* can never be repeated. A word history is actually a biography. Each word of a given group will show typical characteristics, just as the biography of a man will show those characteristics which he has in common with the other men of his class and profession. But for each the most striking features will not be those based on group distinctions but those which create or derive from his unique personality.

Under these conditions it is easy to understand why changes of meaning do not readily lend themselves to classification or systematic description. Many attempts at classification have been made, however, more perhaps to facilitate the practical handling of the material than from a hope of arriving at a better theoretical understanding. Perhaps the commonest scheme is that developed many years ago by Hermann Paul in his *Prinzipien der Sprachgeschichte*. With minor variations it recurs in many discussions of semantics. The formulation of it given here is borrowed, as are the examples, from Leonard Bloomfield's *Language:*

Narrowing:
Old English *mete* "food" > *meat* "edible flesh"

Old English *dēor* "beast" > *deer* "wild ruminant of a particular species"

Old English *hund* "dog" > *hound* "hunting-dog of a particular breed"

Widening:

Middle English *bridde* "young birdling" > *bird*

Middle English *dogge* "dog of a particular (ancient) breed" > *dog*

Latin *virtūs* "quality of a man (*vir*), manliness" > French *vertu* (> English *virtue*) "good quality"

Metaphor:

Primitive Germanic *['bitraz] "biting" (derivative of *['bi:to:] "I bite") > *bitter* "harsh of taste"

Metonymy—the meanings are near each other in space or time:

Old English *cēace* "jaw" > *cheek*

Old French *joue* "cheek" > *jaw*

Synecdoche—the meanings are related as whole and part:

Primitive Germanic *['tu:naz] "fence" (so still German *Zaun*) > *town*

pre-English *['stobo:] "heated room" (compare German *Stube,* formerly "heated room," now "living room") > *stove*

Hyperbole—from stronger to weaker meaning:

pre-French **ex-tonāre* "to strike with thunder" > French *étonner* "to astonish" (from Old French, English borrowed *astound, astonish*)

Litotes—from weaker to stronger meaning:

pre-English *['kwalljan] "to torment" (so still German *quälen*) > Old English *cwellan* "to kill"

Degeneration:

Old English *cnafa* "boy, servant" > *knave*

Elevation:

Old English *cniht* "boy, servant" (compare German *Knecht* "servant") > *knight.*[1]

---

[1] Leonard Bloomfield, *Language* (New York: Henry Holt and Company, 1933), pp. 426–427. Reprinted by permission of Henry Holt and Company, publishers. Following common practice among linguists, Bloomfield uses a star to indicate a hypothetical form, encloses phonetic transcriptions within square brackets, and marks long vowels within the transcriptions

This classification has been frequently criticized. It is obviously not ideal. Take the group *Mister, Monsieur, Herr,* all of them words which were originally titles of honor, but which in our present use do not confer any social distinction. They would naturally, therefore, be considered examples of Paul's degeneration, but they could just as well be used as samples of widening of meaning. Middle High German *Herre* meant a nobleman; now *Herr* may be applied to any masculine adult not belonging to the lowest social classes. Such classifications are scientifically unsatisfactory because they are not mutually exclusive.

What makes the value of such classification more than doubtful, however, is not the excusable (perhaps, at the present stage of our knowledge, unavoidable) imperfection of the scheme. The real danger lies in the illusion that the giving of labels can take the place of explanation based upon understanding of the material. One puts a certain change of meaning into the pigeonhole labeled "deterioration" or "hyperbole" and feels that one has disposed of it satisfactorily. But this way of treating semantic change is nothing but an exercise in the gentle art of fooling oneself. We are going to take up the points of classification one by one to show that the labels hide more than they reveal about the psychology which creates the changes.

The category called "widening of meaning" can be treated briefly. Almost every example discussed in our general remarks about semantic change is relevant here. *Loco-foco* widens its meaning to become a synonym for *Democrat. Contraband* becomes a word for *Negro.* And so on. In these cases, semantic expansion is a consequence of strong emotional connotations which do not permit the word to remain confined within its narrow original meaning. Since we have the full histories of comparatively few words, it would not be safe to call this the only, or even the main, source of extension of meaning. But whoever wishes to explain historically such changes of meaning

---

with a colon and stress accent with a vertical stroke before the syllable accented.

should watch for any indications of feeling which the word in its earlier stages was capable of arousing.

Narrowing of meaning seems a more complicated matter. Many forces may restrict the area of meaning covered by a word. Among several we might mention taboo (for example, *the Lord*), and the emphatic use of words which, within one word, concentrate the meaning of a group of words, as, for instance, a noun plus adjectives ("He was a *man!*"). The word *abolition,* already treated, is a sample of this type. But most important is probably the extension of another word. What, in the result, looks like a contraction of the field of word *A* is often an expansion of word *B,* which has been stopped before it succeeded in exterminating *A* altogether. The "narrowing of meaning" in *hund* to *hound* is more instructive as a warning than as an addition to factual knowledge. If, instead of comparing the final narrowed result, we analyze the act by which this result has been reached, we discover that we are dealing not with narrowing but with widening of meaning. The driving force is not the narrowing in the word *hound* but the fact that, for one reason or another, the original narrow field of *dog* entered on its career of expansion during the Middle English period. The result is that almost the whole field of *hound* has been annexed by *dog,* except the rather limited area which *hound* still possesses in modern English. Evidently a case like this requires answers to two distinct questions. First, why did *dog* expand? The reason for that expansion is not wholly clear, but in our present context it is sufficient simply to admit it as a fact. If *dog* originally meant a large dog of mastiff type, as it certainly does in French and German, then the process may be considered a case of exaggeration. But there are other possibilities. Second, how do we account for the resistance of *hound* within a certain narrow field, and only there? This question, difficult in many similar cases, can be answered here, with a fair degree of confidence, from material studied in an earlier chapter. *Hound* could not be displaced in that part of its original field which was protected by the strong, conservative character of traditional hunting speech. Because of the peculiar technical pride of the adept in, and the snob appeal of, this group language, it is simply impossible for a huntsman to refer to his hounds as *dogs* without degrading himself in the eyes of his fellow sportsmen. This becomes very clear from the following dialogue. An American in England is taking part in a fox hunt. The huntsman dares to presume upon his supposed unfamiliarity with English hunting terms:

> He was roused from his dream by hearing the huntsman say in a quizzical voice:
>
> "How do you like the dogs, sir?"
>
> To his last day Lugley, the huntsman, remembered the slow look of cold surprise, of masterful malice, scathing him from head to foot. The words that followed the look, simple as they were, drove home the naked reproof:
>
> "What is your name, my man?"
>
> "Lugley, sir."
>
> "Lugley! Lugley! H'm! Well, Lugley, I like the *hounds* better than I like you. Who is Master of the Hounds, Lugley?"
>
> "Captain Maudsley, sir."
>
> "Just so. You are satisfied with your place, Lugley?"
>
> "Yes, sir," said the man in a humble voice, now cowed.[2]

From what we have learned in previous chapters the mechanism of litotes should be clear enough. It simply will not do to state things in accurately descriptive terms whenever there is a danger that a blunt statement might cause resentment either in our human interlocutors or in gods, ghosts, or demons. For this reason we speak of lunatics as *deranged* or *eccentric,* of a fat woman as *plump* or *stout,* and of an intoxicated man as *exhilarated, happy, lit up*—or any of dozens of other terms which the reader can no doubt supply in ample quantity. Whenever such understatements become customary, a change "from weaker to stronger meaning" is the result. Compare what is said about *lunatic* in Chapter IV.

The mechanism of hyperbole is nothing but that of litotes put in reverse. Just as it may sometimes be desirable to express unpleasant things by understatement, so at other times we may

---

[2] Gilbert Parker, *The Trespasser,* Chap. IV.

give pleasure to our listeners and advantage to ourselves by stressing pleasant things as strongly as possible. "I am delighted" for "I am pleased"; "I am proud of you" for "I approve of you"; "brilliant work" for "a job well done." If phrases like these become customary, they will lose their exaggerative power and move "from stronger to weaker meaning." The history of the word *adore* (see Chapter III) has already illustrated this change. A similar mechanism is at work whenever a man uses words which may be a subjectively appropriate way of giving vent to his feelings, while to others they may appear to be plain exaggerations: *a killing headache, mortally afraid, scared to death, paralyzed with fear.*

From the hints given about the nature of understatement and hyperbole, it will by now have become clear how strongly these phenomena are influenced by social forces. Such influences are still clearer in many cases of degeneration. To illustrate our point, we will treat one group of words subject to deterioration—titles of honor—at some length. One expects titles of honor and similar words to show only limited tendencies to change. To begin with, their meaning is usually well defined. Unless an Englishman is the oldest in the male line of descent in a noble family, for instance, or is awarded the privilege of adding a word like *baronet* or *viscount* to his name by a special act of the Crown, he will never have a right to these titles.[3] Furthermore, the titles of nobility, as a whole, form a graded and well-classified system, within which words are not interchangeable. A baronet cannot, at will, exchange his baronetcy for an earldom or vice versa, and this legal protection has pretty well preserved the value of some English titles, but by no means of all. Yet readers of Proust's *A la recherche du temps perdu* will recall that in a country which does not offer such legal protection, titles shift with amusing irony and are to be had easily enough by anyone with a sufficiently thick skin.

In practice, the use and meaning of titles is anything but

[3] Even courtesy titles are elaborately codified in customary use, and titles in the female line have the same protections as others.

stable. An important feature in the psychology of their varying value is revealed by the following passage:

> [Some people, in praying, speak to God] as the crafty Beggars use those they address to, when they are ignorant of their Quality. The Novices amongst 'em may innocently come out, perhaps, with a *Good Sir,* or a *Good Forsooth!* But with the old Stagers, no matter whom they meet in a Coach, 'tis always *Good your Honour!* or *Good your Lordship!* or *your Ladyship!*. For if there shou'd be really a *Lord* in the case, we shou'd be undone (say they) for want of giving the Title: but if the Party shou'd be no *Lord,* there wou'd be no Offence; it wou'd not be ill taken.[4]

If this form of *captatio benevolentiae* were limited to beggars and other persons of low social standing, we should hardly find it a factor of influence in the development of language. It is, however, a fact that very respectable persons do not find it below their dignity to use this very device:

> The question of how to address a certain person being under discussion he [James Russell Lowell] said to a friend of mine: "I make it a rule to address a man by the highest title to which by the utmost stretch of courtesy he may be supposed to be entitled." [5]

It cannot be denied that in many cases the trick produces favorable results—not only with adolescents, as in the following fictional example:

> She gratified me by calling me Mr. Ashenden. I think she was the first person who had ever done so and it made me feel grown up. I resented it vastly when people called me Master Willie. I thought it a ridiculous name for anyone to have. In fact I did not like either of my names and spent much time inventing others that would have suited me better. The ones I preferred were Roderic Ravensworth and I covered sheets of writing paper with this signature in a suitably dashing hand. I did not mind Ludovic Montgomery either.[6]

---

[4] Anthony, Earl of Shaftesbury, *Characteristicks,* 4th ed. (1727), I, 35–36.

[5] Robert U. Johnson, *Remembered Yesterdays* (Boston: Little, Brown and Company, 1923), p. 330.

[6] Maugham, *Cakes and Ale,* Chap. VII. Reprinted by permission of W. Somerset Maugham and William Heinemann, Ltd.

This widespread habit of giving persons a higher title than they can justly claim is, of course, the very opposite of the strictly regulated official usage. The example of Lowell shows that this form of flattery is by no means restricted to countries in which aristocracy is still an important social factor. Many instances could be adduced to show that similar tendencies existed, and still exist, in our own country:

> Colonel Wheeler was the standard-bearer of the flag of independence in the Hissawachee bottom. He had been a Captain in the Revolution; but Revolutionary titles showed a marked tendency to grow during the quarter of a century that followed the close of the war. An ex-officer's neighbors carried him forward with his advancing age; a sort of ideal promotion by brevet gauged the appreciation of military titles as the Revolution passed into history and heroes became scarcer. And emigration always advanced a man several degrees—new neighbors, in their uncertainty about his rank, being prone to give him the benefit of all doubts, and exalt as far as possible the lustre which the new-comer conferred upon the settlement. Thus Captain Wheeler in Maryland was Major Wheeler in Western Pennsylvania, and a full-blown Colonel by the time he had made his second move, into the settlement on Hissawachee Creek. And yet I may be wrong. Perhaps it was not the transplanting that did it. Even had he remained on the "Eastern Shore," he might have passed through a process of canonization as he advanced in life that would have brought him to a colonelcy: other men did. For what is a Colonel but a Captain gone to seed? [7]

The people who have a genuine claim to titles will, of course, try to counteract their misuse, but without much success, since they naturally are a minority:

---

[7] Edward Eggleston, *Circuit Rider,* Chap. IX. It may not be out of the way to take this survival from an undemocratic organization of society as an indication of the fact that matters of language cannot be effectively regulated by law. The Constitution provides, as is well known, for the abolition of all titles of nobility. The public, however, unwilling to give up long-established habits of speech, finds a substitute for the outlawed words in military and legal titles used with the same latitude as was customary with the old titles of nobility, and frequently from the same motives of flattery.

You may be sure the ladies are not wanting, on their side, in cherishing and improving these important *piques,* which divide the town [of Ratisbon] almost into as many parties as there are families, and they choose rather to suffer the mortification of sitting almost alone on their assembly nights, than to recede one jot from their pretensions. . . . The foundation of these everlasting disputes turns entirely upon place, and the title of Excellency, which they all pretend to; and, what is very hard, will give it to nobody. For my part, I could not forbear advising them (for the public good) to give the title of Excellency to every body, which would include receiving it from every body; but the very mention of such a dishonourable peace was received with as much indignation as Mrs. Blackacre did the notion of a reference. . . .[8]

This amusing vignette of German social life in the eighteenth century shows, among other things, that, whenever social ambitions and jealousies are concerned, there is a definite countercurrent to the lavish use of titles in the tendency to ignore and dispute even well-established claims. Conditions of this sort in the legal profession in England, with its strictly defined castes, caused Trollope to observe shrewdly and, no doubt correctly, that "ladies belonging to the families of solicitors always talk about lawyers, and never about attorneys or barristers." [9]

Degeneration of titles, of course, can be caused by claims like those ridiculed by Lady Mary Montague as well as by flattering misuse. European conditions of this sort have an exact counterpart in American reluctance to apply words like *servant* to persons in menial position. It is, moreover, characteristically American that this reluctance is frequently shared by the employer as being inconsistent with a democratic society. The following comment by Oliver Wendell Holmes puts the situation admirably:

Abel was Dr. Kittredge's hired man. . . . Abel Stebbins was a good specimen of that extraordinary hybrid or mule between democ-

[8] Lady Mary Wortley Montagu in a letter to Mrs. Thistlethwayte, August 30, 1716.

[9] Anthony Trollope, *Last Chronicle of Barsetshire,* Chap. LXXI.

racy and chrysocracy, a native-born New England serving-man. The Old World has nothing at all like him. He is at once an Emperor and a subordinate. In one hand he holds one five-millionth part (be the same more or less) of the power that sways the destinies of the Great Republic. His other hand is in your boot, which he is about to polish.

. . . . .

Abel Stebbins, the Doctor's man, took the true American view of his difficult position. He sold his time to the Doctor, and, having sold it, he took care to fulfil his half of the bargain. The Doctor, on his part, treated him, not like a gentleman, because one does not order a gentleman to bring up his horse or run his errands, but he treated him like a man. Every order was given in courteous terms. . . . Abel had Revolutionary blood in his veins, and though he saw fit to "hire out," he could never stand the word "servant," or consider himself the inferior one of the two high contracting parties.[10]

Tourgée, with his usual sensitivity to the connotations of American usage, also observed it:

"I beg, madam, that you will not leave me out of the arrangements made necessary by my carelessness. I have a servant who is a most experienced nurse, as well as a most capable manager of a household. I insist, madam, on placing him at your service."

. . . . .

Still the feeling of independence that is innate with the class to which she belonged withheld the woman from a frank acceptance of the proffered aid. Perhaps this feeling arose in part from the manner in which he spoke of the one he desired to send, as—"a servant." Somehow, the word was very repulsive to the ears of the great masses of the North, and every possible paraphrasis was employed to avoid its use.[11]

A final quotation, from Bayard Taylor's account of the California Gold Rush, explains the habit as a reflection of the instability of classes in American life:

---

[10] Oliver Wendell Holmes, *Elsie Venner,* Chap. IX.

[11] Albion W. Tourgée, *Hot Plowshares* (New York: Fords, Howard, & Hulbert, 1883), Chap. IV.

There are cries of "steward!" from all parts of the room—the word "waiter" is not considered sufficiently respectful, seeing that the waiter may have been a lawyer or merchant's clerk a few months before.[12]

In discussing litotes and hyperbole we found that, apart from the fact that they move in opposite directions, their mechanisms are essentially the same. One would expect that since degeneration and elevation are logically a pair of opposites, they would supplement and balance each other in a similar way. This, however, is only partially true. A more fruitful way of looking at the problem is expressed in the rule that semantic change is not an affair of isolated words but of word groups held together by social or emotional patterns of behavior. The elevation of the word *boss* was a product of the same social situation that brought about substitutions for the word *servant*. We quote a couple of illustrations from the early uses of the word listed in the *Dictionary of American English:*

Master is not a word in the vocabulary of hired people. *Bos,* a Dutch one of similar import, is substituted. (James Flint, *Letters from America,* 9, 1818).

No one, in this republican country, will use the term master or mistress; "employers," and the Dutch word "boss," are used instead.—Isaac Holmes, *An Account of the United States of America* (1823), p. 342.

Only a little later the American critic and novelist James Fenimore Cooper made the same observation:

In consequence of the domestic servants of America having once been negro-slaves, a prejudice has arisen among the laboring classes of the whites, who not only dislike the term servant, but have also rejected that of master. So far has this prejudice gone, that in lieu of the latter, they have resorted to the use of the word *boss,* which has precisely the same meaning in Dutch! How far a subterfuge of this nature is worthy of a manly and common sense people, will admit of question.[13]

---

12 Bayard Taylor, *Eldorado,* Chap. XII.

13 James Fenimore Cooper, *The American Democrat* (reprinted, New York: Alfred A. Knopf, 1931), p. 114.

It is interesting to note that Cooper is aware of the linguistic and social forces linking *boss* and *help.* He goes on to say:

> A similar objection may be made to the use of the word "help," which is not only an innovation on a just and established term, but which does not properly convey the meaning intended. . . . Nothing is . . . gained, while something is lost in simplicity and clearness by the substitution of new and imperfect terms, for the long established words of the language. In all cases in which the people of America have retained the *things* of their ancestors, they should not be ashamed to keep the *names.*[14]

The point on which a linguist cannot agree with Cooper is his idea that *boss* "has precisely the same meaning in Dutch" that *master* has in English. From the treatment of *baas* in Vries and Te Winkel, *Woordenbock der Nederlandsche Taal,* it is clear that it belongs to an entirely different social milieu. For the word's first meaning, the Dutch dictionary gives *paterfamilias,* head of the household. It is by no means impossible to use the word in Dutch for the master-servant relationship, but primarily it is a term of respectful endearment, rather than one of social distinction. If the Dutch settlers of America used it as did their European cousins, it is not difficult to understand how it fitted into an American social scheme at once democratic and patriarchal. On the other hand, we also see that this first American use of *boss* contained the elements of a change of meaning. No matter what you call the man who pays you for your services, the title you give him will sooner or later tend to mean just master. In present American usage the word *boss* has not always completed this full change of meaning, especially perhaps in rural speech and in small businesses. Some elements of the familiar, even sometimes of the affectionate, still cling to it. But how nearly it has become a synonym for *master* is evident from the verb *to boss,* which cannot mean anything but to assume full, and even dictatorial, authority. Thus the word may be considered an example of elevation. It has moved from con-

---

[14] *Ibid.,* pp. 114–115.

noting authority based on affection and mutual consideration to the less limited connotations of authority based upon power.

The three groups distinguished as *metaphor, metonymy,* and *synecdoche* form perhaps the most doubtful part of the conventional classification. The objection raised to Paul's categories in general, that they are not mutually exclusive, applies to them with still greater force. The very assignment of a particular case of transferred meaning to one of these three may easily depend on one's point of view. In British parliamentary use the word *Crown* can mean the king acting in his official character. Should this be classified as a metonymy or as a synecdoche? If you think of the king as a person sometimes wearing a crown, then it is a metonymy (connection "in space or time"); [15] if you think of him in full regalia, of which the crown is a part, then it becomes a synecdoche ("meanings related as whole and part"). To use an example which we have employed in other contexts, since *Loco-foco* in politics originally meant people who, on a certain occasion, had used Loco-focos, the change of meaning may be called a metonymy; on the other hand, our material indicates that at least some of those who used the new meaning intended to characterize the party so designated as incendiaries. From this point of view, the word is clearly a metaphor.

Not only within the group of three is it hard to make clear distinctions; it is equally hard to draw distinctions between this group and the other classes already discussed. *Brass hat* (or, according to the preferred recent version, simply *brass*) can no doubt be classified as either a metonymy or a synecdoche. Since the word in both its clipped and full forms may or may not be used in a derogatory sense, it sometimes means merely a high-ranking officer. In this way the term shows a tendency to lose its derogatory character, thereby undergoing *elevation.* Furthermore, since nowadays even civilians in high administrative positions can be spoken of as *brass hats,* undoubtedly a

[15] The reader will notice that Bloomfield's definition of metonymy is not identical with that of many rhetoricians. We use the word in this discussion solely as Bloomfield defines it.

widening of meaning is under way. Examples of similar difficulties in classification could be given indefinitely.

In view of these conditions, we shall use the term "transferred speech" to stand for the entire group of three in the traditional classification—metaphor, metonymy, and synecdoche, usually substituting metaphor as a brief, though loosely applied, synonym.

Metaphor is usually considered a specific device of poetry, and rightfully so, for it often has the power of presenting an idea in more concentrated form than nonmetaphorical speech. To illustrate with a prosaic little story, Judge Allen G. Thurman of Ohio, Cleveland's running mate in the presidential election of 1888, no doubt had ample claim as a man and as a politician to the esteem of his country, but notice how one metaphor can remove all his good qualities from the range of our consideration, to concentrate it upon a weakness:

> . . . he was now advanced in years, feeble in health, and belonged wholly to the past. The average voter knew little about him except that he was in the habit of carrying and frequently brandishing a large red bandanna—a fact which gave point to a remark made by Senator Riddleberger of Virginia soon after the Convention. Some one asked the Senator what he thought of the nomination for the Vice-Presidency.
>
> "Think?" said he. "Why, I think that you've simply nominated a pocket-handkerchief." [16]

The tendency of the senator's remark was to reduce Thurman to a symbol of limp ineffectuality, a rag to be carried in someone else's pocket and probably to do someone else's dirty work. We would not claim poetry for the senator's remark, but one of the requirements of poetry is to present experience with the same vivid concentration upon the essential. Few devices achieve this end as well as metaphor.

If we analyze common conversation, we are frequently aware of an element of compromise in it. Academic life, for instance, frequently forces professors into discussion of their

[16] Harry Thurston Peck, *Twenty Years of the Republic* (New York: Dodd, Mead & Company, 1913), p. 156.

common problems. To some of them, the topic discussed may be of dominating interest, but one or two of the group, if the subject were not forced upon them, might prefer to talk about their latest fishing trip. In such a situation courtesy will probably keep the bored rebel from saying, "To hell with your deans! I want to talk about the trout I caught last week." In the actual conversation on which we base these observations, the unhappy professor listened politely and even offered an occasional remark connected with the subject under discussion. The possibility of using metaphorical speech enabled him to bring in isolated elements of what would have been the subject of his own choice—fishing. He used expressions like, "Do you think the Dean will rise to such bait?" and "They are just trying to fish in troubled waters." We do not want to suggest that the introduction of such fishing phrases was an intentional attempt to slant the conversation. It is much more likely that it resulted from the workings of what we have now become accustomed to call the subconscious mind. In other words, he had fishing "on his mind" and, in one way or another, it forced itself into his conversation. Every reader is in a position to observe cases of this sort. They will convince him that, viewed as a social function, metaphor enables us to condense into one verbal expression our personal interests and the subjects forced upon us by a social situation.

In literature the situation is somewhat different but not fundamentally so. Similar conflicts arise from the author's choice of a main subject and the unconnected, often irrelevant, ideas that may cross his mind. The conflict does not arise from outside interference, but it is nonetheless there. How intimately a man's preoccupations can influence his expression is well illustrated by the following case. In 1843 Lincoln was a member of a Whig committee for which he wrote a circular on taxation (March 4, 1843). A few weeks later (March 26) he wrote a letter to a friend giving the reasons for his failure to be reelected to the Illinois legislature. Evidently tax problems were still on his mind and managed to insert themselves into this discussion of an unrelated topic by way of metaphor:

There was, too, the strangest combination of church influence against me. Baker is a Campbellite; and therefore, as I suppose, with few exceptions, got all that church. My wife has some relations in the Presbyterian churches, and some with the Episcopal churches; and therefore, wherever it would tell, I was set down as either the one or the other, while it was everywhere contended that no Christian ought to go for me, because I belonged to no church, was suspected of being a deist, and had talked about fighting a duel. With all these things, Baker, of course, had nothing to do. Nor do I complain of them. As to his own church going for him, I think that was right enough, and as to the influences I have spoken of in the other, though they were very strong, it would be grossly untrue and unjust to charge that they acted upon them in a body, or were very near so. I only mean that those influences levied a tax of a considerable per cent. upon my strength throughout the religious controversy.[17]

It is already evident from our examples that metaphors are likely to reveal something of the speaker's or writer's personal character or interests. We are not surprised, then, to observe that writers of fiction and drama have long used them as a device for characterization. Often, indeed, we know practically nothing about a figure in a novel save what we can infer from the fact that his talk is rooted in, for example, sailor's or gambler's language. Smollett's creation Captain Crowe, in *The Adventures of Sir Launcelot Greaves,* is a perfect example of the novelist's use of the device. It is the essential element in his technique of characterization. In the conversation which leads into the speech we quote, a subject has been given—the captain's loss of an inheritance. How Crowe tells his story, however, is shaped by the major interest of his life, seafaring:

"Belay, Tom, belay; pr'ythee, don't veer out such a deal of jaw. Clap a stopper on thy cable and bring thyself up, my lad—what a deal of stuff thou hast pumped up concerning bursting and starting, and pulling ships; Laud have mercy upon us!—look ye here, brother—look ye here—mind these poor crippled joints; two fingers on the starboard, and three on the larboard hand; crooked, d'ye see, like the knees of a bilander. I'll tell you what, brother, you seem to be a

[17] *Speeches and Letters of Abraham Lincoln,* Everyman Edition, pp. 18–19.

—ship deep laden—rich cargo—current setting into the bay—hard gale—lee shore—all hands in the boat—tow round the headland—self pulling for dear blood, against the whole crew—snap go the finger-braces—crack went the eye-blocks. Bounce daylight—flash starlight—down I foundered, dark as hell—whiz went my ears, and my head spun like a whirligig. That don't signify—I'm a Yorkshire boy, as the saying is—all my life at sea, brother, by reason of an old grandmother and maiden aunt, a couple of old stinking—kept me these forty years out of my grandfather's estate. Hearing as how they had taken their departure, came ashore, hired horses, and clapped on all my canvas, steering to the northward, to take possession of my— But it don't signify talking—these two old piratical—had held a palaver with a lawyer—an attorney, Tom, d'ye mind me, an attorney—and by his assistance hove me out of my inheritance. That is all, brother—hove me out of five hundred pounds a year—that's all—what signifies—but such windfalls we don't every day pick up along shore. Fill about, brother—yes, by the Lord! those two smuggling harridans, with the assistance of an attorney—an attorney, Tom—hove me out of five hundred a year." [18]

One may doubt that real people are ever as consistent in their speech as Captain Crowe. Certainly art has here perfected life. On the other hand we do not care to doubt that an anecdote like the following account of Old Ben Winnie, "who first introduced draw poker in these upper regions [Arkansas]," is based on factual observation, as it purports to be:

We remember the fact that a venerable and world-wide known Bishop, travelling from Tennessee to Louisiana, stopped over night at Uncle Winnie's. The old man had great respect for the Bishop, and after supper he sat himself down and highly gratified "his old woman" by listening to a long talk about "the necessity of being saved," Uncle Winnie every now and then chiming in with a commentary, as follows:

"That's right, Bishop; the devil goes about as you say with a pack of marked cards in his pocket, and will cheat whoever plays with him."

"That's right, Bishop; an honest life, when you are played out, is a braggin' hand, all aces—nothing can beat it."

---

[18] Tobias G. Smollett, *The Adventures of Sir Launcelot Greaves,* Chap. I.

"That's right, Bishop; I never know'd a man that cheated that didn't get caught at last, and perhaps lynched, or at least put off the boat at the first wood-yard."

"That's right, Bishop; the Bible is a trump—there's no mistake about that."[19]

Until now we have considered metaphor a means of enabling a participant in a conversation to do justice to his own interests while accepting a topic thrust upon him by somebody else. Common as this situation is, it is probably not as productive of metaphoric speech as its opposite: the speaker who, having chosen his subject and at the same time suspecting that his interlocutor is only moderately interested, shapes his language to make it more palatable. Metaphor is a most efficient way of achieving this aim, but naturally the metaphors used will be determined not by the interests of the speaker but by what he knows, or hopes, to be the interests of his audience. The most typical situation of this sort is the one in which the teacher finds himself. On the most elementary level of teaching—teaching counting or similar skills—the instructor is likely to introduce elements of a metaphorical character in order to attract the learner. There is probably no father who would say that if you have one and add two you get three. It is always and everywhere if you have one apple and John gives you two apples, you have three apples. We dare say that in Burma parents deal in mangoes. Granted that this is not a metaphor in the exact meaning of the word, it is evidently the same sort of working on the hearer's interests that we meet in textbooks for more mature students where there can be no doubt that we are dealing with metaphor. Here from a library catalogue is a little sampling of several dozen textbooks all of which call themselves *adventures:*

Adventures in Bird Protection
Adventures in Education
Adventures in Homemaking
Adventures in Reading

---

[19] *Spirit of the Times,* March 2, 1861, p. 1, col. 3.

Adventures in Respiration
Adventures in Teacher Education
Adventures in Thrift

The same process is equally useful in the instruction of the sophisticated intellect. So Ruth Benedict, seeking to describe a conflict of cultures and something of the tragic consequence for the loser, borrowed a metaphor from a chief of the Digger Indians:

"In the beginning," he said, "God gave to every people a cup, a cup of clay, and from this cup they drank their life. . . . They all dipped in the water . . . but their cups were different. Our cup is broken now. It has passed away."

Our cup is broken. Those things that had given significance to the life of his people, the domestic rituals of eating, the obligations of the economic system, the succession of ceremonials in the villages, possession in the bear dance, their standards of right and wrong—these were gone, and with them the shape and meaning of their life. He did not mean that there was any question of the extinction of his people. But he had in mind the loss of something that had value equal to that of life itself, the whole fabric of his people's standards and beliefs. There were other cups of living left, and they held perhaps the same water, but the loss was irreparable. It was no matter of tinkering with an addition here, lopping off something there. The modelling had been fundamental, it was somehow all of a piece. It had been their own.[20]

What holds true for teachers is equally true for preachers or for any other persons whose duties demand that they make a public appeal. How completely a metaphor can command an audience is made absurdly evident in the following account of an antislavery speech in 1834:

Mr. Thompson then went on to give us a graphic glowing account of the long and fierce conflict they had had in England for the abolition of slavery in the British West Indies. His eloquence rose to a still higher order. His narrative became a *continuous metaphor,* ad-

[20] Ruth Benedict, *Patterns of Culture* (Boston: Houghton Mifflin Company, 1934), p. 22. Reprinted by permission of Houghton Mifflin Company, publishers.

mirably sustained. He represented the antislavery enterprise in which he had been so long engaged as a stout, well-built ship, manned by a noble-hearted crew, launched upon a stormy ocean, bound to carry inestimable relief to 80,000 sufferers in a far-distant land. He clothed all the kinds of opposition they had met, all the difficulties they had contended with, in imagery suggested by the observation and experience of the voyager across the Atlantic in the most tempestuous season of the year. In the height of his descriptions, my attention was withdrawn from the emotions enkindled in my own bosom sufficiently to observe the effect of his eloquence upon half a dozen boys, of twelve or fourteen years of age, sitting together not far from the platform. They were completely possessed by it. When the ship reeled or plunged or staggered in the storms, they unconsciously went through the same motions. When the enemy attacked her, the boys took the liveliest part in battle,—manning the guns, or handing shot and shell, or pressing forward to repulse the boarders. When the ship struck upon an iceberg, the boys almost fell from their seats in the recoil. When the sails and topmasts were well-nigh carried away by the gale, they seemed to be straining themselves to prevent the damage; and when at length the ship triumphantly sailed into her destined port with colors flying and signals of glad tidings floating from her topmast, and the shout of welcome rose from thousands of expectant freedmen on the shore, the boys gave three loud cheers, "Hurrah! Hurrah!! Hurrah!!!" This irrepressible explosion of their feelings brought them at once to themselves. They blushed, covered their faces, sank down on their seats, one of them upon the floor.[21]

There seems to be a considerable difference, however, between the way in which Thompson is reported to have used his seafaring metaphor, as a kind of rhetorical concession to his audience, and another use which we illustrate from the famous sermon of Father Mapple in *Moby Dick*. The reader observes Mapple's sailor's dress, the ladder replacing the pulpit stairs, the decoration of pulpit and wall, and the minister's opening command, "Starboard gangway, there! side away to larboard—larboard gangway, to starboard! Midships! midships!" The sermon begins:

---

[21] Samuel J. May, *Some Recollections of Our Antislavery Conflict* (Boston: Fields, Osgood & Co., 1869), pp. 118–119.

"Beloved shipmates, clinch the last verse of the first chapter of Jonah—'And God had prepared a great fish to swallow up Jonah'

"Shipmates, this book, containing only four chapters—four yarns—is one of the smallest strands in the mighty cable of the Scriptures. Yet what depths of the soul does Jonah's deep sea-line sound!—"

From this beginning to its conclusions the sermon is a complex of seafaring metaphor. Even the climactic end uses such figures as

"Delight,—top-gallant delight is to him, who acknowledges no law or lord, but the Lord his God, and is only a patriot to heaven. Delight is to him, whom all the waves of the billows of the seas of the boisterous mob can never shake from this sure Keel of the Ages." [22]

These metaphors are not designed to bridge a gap between the speaker and his audience. They, like his dress and the *décor* of the chapel, stress the fact that no such gap exists. Father Mapple's audience is not supposed to feel that he is a preacher giving advice about spiritual things but rather that he is as good a seaman as they—that he is, in fact, one of them.

We have now stated three different but not mutually exclusive social functions of metaphor: (1) to enable a speaker to introduce his personal interests into a speech situation not of his own choosing, (2) to enable a speaker to awaken an interest in a topic about which his audience may not be originally concerned, (3) to establish an intellectual or emotional speech community by exploiting common interests.

To consider a speech act as an individual act is entirely inadequate. Language is a matter of give-and-take, of constant influence back and forth between the people who use it. Any word uttered is likely to become a stimulus creating a further speech response. A metaphor, for instance, may be successful and immediately, therefore, may not only be adopted into current speech by people who want to show themselves as belonging to the group for whom it was intended, but may also be given a much richer development by them with further applications. New metaphors emerge from the same area. The original speaker

[22] Herman Melville, *Moby Dick,* Chap. IX.

has touched a real source of community interest and inspired a community reaction.

For example, *Time* magazine, reporting a matter of diplomatic maneuvering, seized upon one of President Franklin D. Roosevelt's figures of speech for elaborate development:

> *Base on Balls.* Franklin Roosevelt, who dearly loves a baseball metaphor, came up with one of his choicest. In Martinique, pro-Vichy Admiral Georges Robert had given way to anti-Vichy Henri-Etienne Hoppenot. . . . Said the President: We waited it out and we got a base on balls.
>
> But many a pop bottle was still coming Pitcher Roosevelt's way as a result of the Administration refusal to recognize the French Committee of Liberation in Algiers. . . . At his press conference, the President went on the defensive: the Administration was the victim of vicious propaganda. It sided neither with Giraud nor with De Gaulle, it was not trying to interfere in internal French affairs. And there the contest settled into the early-inning doldrums, with no one quite sure what Pitcher Roosevelt had up his sleeve.[23]

The nation at large seems to have been willing to allow *Time* its play and to forget about it. In the rush of events of 1943 there was not leisure enough to dwell either on the affairs of Martinique or the passing cleverness of a news magazine. But longer enduring crises have left their mark, by just such means, upon a community vocabulary. While many important historical words remain to be investigated, we are fortunate in having information about how, prior to the Civil War, the organization for helping escaped slaves came by its name, the *Underground Railroad.* Levi Coffin, one of the most prominent organizers of the institution, tells the story in his *Reminiscences.* A group of Southerners was trying to trace escaped slaves in Southern Ohio and Indiana:

> The hunters, who had gone northward toward the lakes, returned without having obtained any clue to their valuable missing property. They remained at Richmond a few days, then the whole party returned South. But before going, they conferred upon me a high

[23] *Time,* XLII (July 26, 1943), 20. Courtesy of *Time,* Copyright Time, Inc., 1943.

honor. They said that they could never get the slightest intelligence of their slaves after they reached my house, and declared that there must be an Underground Railroad, of which I was president. They repeated this several times in Richmond, and I heard of it when next I went to attend the board of bank directors at that place.

Some of my friends asked me if I had heard of my promotion to office, and when I said I had not, they told me what the Kentuckians had said. I replied that I would accept that position or any other they were disposed to give me on that road—conductor, engineer, fireman or brakeman. This was the first time I ever heard of the Underground Railroad.

The saying of the Kentuckians soon became widely circulated, and I frequently received letters addressed to "Levi Coffin, President of the Underground Railroad." I had the honor of wearing that title for more than thirty years, and it was not until the great celebration of the Fifteenth Amendment to the Constitution, by the colored people at Cincinnati, that I resigned the office, and laid aside the name conferred on me by Southern slave-hunters. On that occasion I said that our underground work was done, and that as we had no more use for the road, I would suggest that the rails be taken up and disposed of, and the proceeds appropriated for the education of the freed slaves.[24]

The way in which the introduction of the word immediately acted as a stimulus is no more striking than it is characteristic. The slave hunters who made the wisecrack were first to react to their own stimulus by bestowing the title of *president* on Coffin. The next stage is Coffin's own reaction when he introduces *conductor, engineer, fireman,* and *brakeman*—all used metaphorically. The last paragraph of our quotation shows how, from these beginnings, a group slang developed. It made abundant—in fact, nearly exhaustive—use of the possibilities of the master metaphor. The organization is called by its initials, the U.G.R.R.; [25] the wagon in which the Negroes were carried became the *car,* and Coffin's horse the *locomotive.*

The whole book is full of examples of this sort. One of

---

[24] *Reminiscences of Levi Coffin, the Reputed President of the Underground Railroad,* 3d ed. (Cincinnati: Robert Clarke Company, 1898), pp. 189–190.

[25] *Ibid.,* p. 107.

them can be taken as a sample of the typical conversation of the Coffin group:

She [Mrs. Coffin] spoke to these conductors, and asked: "What have you got there?"

One of them replied: "All Kentucky."

"Well, bring all Kentucky in," she answered, then stepped back to our room and told me to get up, for all Kentucky had come. I sprang up and dressed quickly, and when I went out, I found the fugitives all seated in the room, my wife having welcomed them and invited them to take chairs and sit down. I said to one of the conductors:

"The train has brought some valuable looking passengers this time. How many have you?"

"Only seventeen this load," he replied.

"Well," I said, "seventeen full-grown darkies and two able-bodied Hoosiers are about as many as the cars can bear at one time. Now you may switch off and put your locomotives in my stable and let them blow off steam, and we will water and feed them." [26]

How intimate a part of the life and group style of Coffin's circle this body of metaphor became is evident from the familiar quality of the jest in the following anecdote. The metaphors show themselves as part of the casual repartee of social communication among friends and neighbors who are, at the moment, not the least concerned with slaves. When the Prince of Wales visited Cincinnati a few years before the Civil War, his tour of the city took him past the Coffin house:

The Prince, who was riding in an open carriage, took off his hat and made a graceful bow as he passed our house. Some of our company wondered why he should be brought through our quiet locality, for it was quite unusual for public guests to be conducted through that neighborhood of family dwelling-houses.

Others replied: "It is not at all strange; the Prince has been to Canada and seen the terminus of the Underground Railroad, and of course he wished to see this end of it, and as this house is the principal depot, he wished to take a fair view of the premises so that he could make a correct report to the Queen."

---

[26] *Ibid.*, p. 183.

This explanation seemed satisfactory to the company, and caused a hearty laugh among us.[27]

Finally, the fact that these metaphors achieved something like national use is shown not only by Coffin's remark that he received letters addressed to him as President of the Underground Railroad, but also by the fact that they are not yet entirely dead. To the personal knowledge of the writers, people in Oberlin and Wellington, Ohio, interested in the history of their communities, still refer to the towns as *stations* on the Underground Railroad.

It is common knowledge that an enormous number of the words we use are faded metaphors. Jean Paul's statement that language is a herbary of withered metaphors may be more a captivating aphorism than a literal truth, but nobody doubts that words as varied and as common as *brood, tulip, grenade, front,* and any number of others are metaphors which, having lost their earlier meaning, have therefore lost their metaphoric value. Taken as elements of the dictionary, words of this kind look like isolated cases of metaphorical creation. But we suspect that some, if not all of them, may have come into use as parts of a metaphorical system, that is, parts of a coherent mass of metaphors developed from a master metaphor acting as a stimulus, with secondary metaphors as reactions to that stimulus. We do not know who was first to compare a presidential election to a horse race, but we can be fairly sure that the man who first called an election a *presidential race,* or a *race to the White House* was indirectly responsible for a number of other metaphors, like *to run for the presidency, a stalking horse, a dark horse, a party hack, to have the inside track*—all phrases which are still felt to be metaphors from the race track. With others, *walk over,* for instance, the connection is now obscured but can still be made apparent from earlier sources. On September 21, 1836, the Louisville *Journal* noticed: "In Maryland on the 6th inst., the Whig nag walked round the course. The Van Buren pony ran at the top of his speed, and was beaten by two whole

[27] *Ibid.,* pp. 595–596.

lengths after all. Let him be used hereafter for a dray-horse." [28] Although the idiom here is walk *round,* not *over,* the rich context makes the appearance of *walk over* a few years later only to be expected: ". . . Clay will have only to walk over the course." [29]

We have discussed earlier the intimate connection between culture and language. This group of metaphors cannot be adequately understood without a knowledge of its specifically American background. True, there are race tracks in other countries, and no law in France or Spain forbids applying metaphors from the sport to politics. But nowhere, not even in England, where both horse racing and politics have been the special interest of the privileged classes, are we likely to find the combination of three decisive elements: widespread interest in racing, universal interest in politics, and a tendency to represent politicians as animals of a lower order.[30]

It is not the static conditions of culture alone, but also the impact of those important events which penetrate a nation's consciousness, that shape its speech. Here is the way a contemporary saw the gold rush in California:

> No wonder the world . . . ran wild when golden plains and silver mountains outspread themselves before its famished eyes. All Christendom felt the throb of an insatiable greed. The lust of sudden wealth thrilled peer and pauper. . . . A grain of yellow dust inflamed a hundred hearts. A single nugget fired a thousand souls to new exertion. Men who would have died clods lived to be envied of princes through the lust born of a gold-streaked lump of snowy quartz shown in a shop window. Thousands failed. Thousands died. The highways to the land of promise became endless charnels. Dead men's bones pointed the way to those who came after. The sharks of the

---

[28] Louisville *Journal,* September 21, 1836.

[29] *National Intelligencer,* 1844. Quoted in Meade Minnigerode, *Presidential Years, 1787–1860* (New York: G. P. Putnam's Sons, 1928), p. 236.

[30] The probability that these track metaphors were originally derogatory is sustained by the contemporary cartoons based on the equation of presidential election with a horse race. See Albert Shaw, *Cartoon History of Abraham Lincoln: His Path to the Presidency* (New York: Review of Reviews Corporation, 1929), pp. 68, 85, 100, 101, and *passim.*

southern seas grew fat on frequent corpses; yet over the dead all the more greedily pressed the living. For every one that fell there were a thousand that sprang up. For every one that went there were ten thousand that sought to go. For every one that came back laden there were a million who dreamed that they might some time know a like good fortune, and, because of this dream, wrought more earnestly, saved more persistently, and so achieved more richly than they otherwise would have done. Thus Science and Greed stirred the world into new life.

Wherever trade went, the fever flew. Gold flowed through the world like water, in comparison with the dearth that had been. Half a decade yielded more than half a century had given before. "Dust" and "nuggets" grew familiar to all eyes. The slang of the mining camp crept into the world's speech.[31]

The truth of Tourgée's concluding remark lies in such metaphors, now mostly faded, as *pan out, wash out, bedrock, rock bottom, make a strike, strike it rich, stake out a claim, worked out, pay dirt, bonanza, slumgullion, slug* (a coin). They are not, like our previous examples, the result of a master metaphor, but their creation was psychologically akin. They were all shaped by one force, one social and professional group, one historical community—the Forty-niners.

The question has often been asked whether meaning changes can be formulated into laws similar to those characteristic of phonetic changes. Scholars have often tried to find groups of synonyms which show the same patterns of change, developing the same secondary meanings. *Brilliant* and its synonyms are an instance, not only in English but in many languages. We have *clear, brilliant, coruscating, illustrious, sparkling, glittering, bright, splendid, resplendent, dazzling, glowing.* All of them primarily describe an optical impression, but the metaphorical meanings of them all indicate some degree of excellence, or attempt at excellence, in character or achievement. But no matter how many groups of this sort can be found, it can hardly be supposed that they could ever help us to discover a pattern of change as regular as the consistent action of

---

31 Tourgée, *Hot Plowshares*, pp. 217–218.

phonetic laws. If you take a group like *throw, chuck, hurl, sling, cast,* you see at once that their metaphorical possibilities do not run on parallel lines and that they do not lead to the same secondary results. Their meaning is identical only insofar as they all describe the action of throwing. They are so different in their emotional and social connotations that each is adaptable to only limited situations. And their usefulness clearly depends on just these connotations. The metaphoric possibilities of any two of these words, therefore, would be widely dissimilar. The same man who would speak of *throwing* a party would possibly be inclined to *sling* a party, but would not *cast* a party, and would *chuck* a party only when he was trying to escape it rather than give it.

On the other hand, the very difficulty which arises from the fact that language is a means of expressing emotions as well as things and ideas, may point the way to a solution. Many years ago one of the authors of this book attempted to state a pattern for changes of meaning:

> If at a certain time a complex of ideas becomes so strongly loaded with feeling that it pulls a word out of the limits of its original meaning and causes it to take on a new meaning, then we may expect that the same complex will force other words belonging to this sphere out of the area in which they have been used. They too will thereby develop new meanings.[32]

As at the time of its first formulation, this "law of semantic change" stands as a mere suggestion: it has not been disproved by adverse criticism, but it is equally hard to prove that there are no exceptions. Ample illustration, however, is easy. In the first chapter of Louisa M. Alcott's account of her experience as a nurse in the Civil War, she shows perfectly the pull through one word of such an emotional complex. Because of pre-existing circumstances and emotions, the word *enlisted* in the following quotation sets off an outburst of metaphor:

---

[32] Hans Sperber, *Zeitschrift für deutsches Altertum,* LIX (N.F., Vol. XLVII), 55–56.

"I've enlisted!"

. . . . .

As boys going to sea immediately become nautical in speech, walk as if they already had their "sea legs" on, and shiver their timbers on all possible occasions, so I turned military at once, called my dinner my rations, saluted all new comers, and ordered a dress parade that very afternoon. Having reviewed every rag I possessed, I detailed some for picket duty while airing over the fence; some to the sanitary influences of the wash-tub; others to mount guard in the trunk; while the weak and wounded went to the Workbasket Hospital, to be made ready for active service again. To this squad I devoted myself for a week. . . .[33]

It is true that Miss Alcott's description of herself is on the level of individual psychology only (in fact, it illustrates so well the impact of personal experience upon personal style that we must ask the reader to remember it when we come to a later chapter). But the machinery by which it operates parallels exactly the development of community metaphors already recorded in the history of the *Underground Railroad.* Finally, whether or not the "law" can be made to stand as a law, it is a most useful working hypothesis. Whoever approaches a vocabulary problem without striving to find connections and contexts, instead of isolated occurrences, will find himself hopelessly lost in innumerable and insignificant details. If, on the other hand, he has his eye fixed on the emotional values of words and on the fact that these values are common to many words grouped around a center of interest, the chances are that he will find himself rewarded by the discovery that many seemingly unrelated things in language form an interrelated and meaningful whole. He will be in no danger of overlooking the dominating fact that whatever linguistic material he discovers is rooted in the community of interests and feelings prevailing at the time and in the place of their creation.

Before we conclude this chapter, we must set down one important limitation to our statement that there are no ex-

[33] Louisa M. Alcott, *Hospital Sketches,* Chap. I.

ceptions to our law of semantic change. As formulated, it applies only to the cases where the fate of a metaphor is determined by the common interests of a speech community, not by the arbitrary action of a single person. There are, however, conditions that permit an individual to fix the name of a thing once and for all. If that name happens to be a metaphor, it may become common property of the speech community, even without the support of common interest. The typical case is that of the inventor who gives his invention a name that the community accepts along with the thing itself. But the special problem of the relation of words and things, even though it also is usually in part a problem of metaphor, we leave to a separate chapter.

Chapter Twelve

WORDS AND THINGS: CULTURAL CHANGE AND MEANING CHANGE

EVERY American understands the meaning of *stump* in sentences like "he was unrivalled by any stump orator of the day" [1] and "this year things were not going very well for him on the stump." [2] But the majority—at least if our students are representative—do not know how the word acquired the meaning of political speaking. The peculiar exigencies of public life in early America developed, even before the Revolution, certain recognized forms of public address. Things which would now be discussed in a hall were then discussed in open-air meetings. The speaker, who had to compete not only with the noise of a more or less undisciplined crowd but also with the sounds of what we wrongly call silent nature, would naturally try to find a vantage point where he could be seen and heard. In some places a rock might be handy or a barrel brought up, but almost everywhere in the clearings a tree stump would offer itself as a primitive platform. As early as 1775 such a scene is described in a Tory ballad:

---

[1] James A. Farley, *Behind the Ballots* (New York: Harcourt, Brace and Company, 1939), p. 25.

[2] Wilbur L. Cross, *Connecticut Yankee* (New Haven: Yale University Press, 1943), p. 235.

When Congress sent great Washington
All clothed in power and breeches,
To meet old Britain's warlike sons
And make some rebel speeches;

. . . . .

Upon a stump, he placed himself,
Great Washington did he,
And through the nose of lawyer Close
Proclaimed great Liberty.[3]

Wirt's *Life of Patrick Henry* provides an even earlier example: an anecdote from the French and Indian wars describes the stump as "the common *rostrum,* you know, of the field-orator of Virginia." [4] In the 1820's when the Eastern cities like Boston and New York had their indoor meeting places and even rural communities had reached the point at which the erection of a platform added dignity to the occasion, the stump was still in common use in the South. David Crockett's campaigns were carried on in the old fashion. His autobiography records a story of his first campaign for Congress in 1827 when, at a political gathering in a crossroads clearing, he "mounted the stump that had been cut down for the occasion, and began to bushwhack in the most approved style." [5]

The linguist has now to ask why, when the stump rostrum disappeared even in the remote parts of the country, did not the word *stump* disappear from the political vocabulary? The answer is that by this time the word had acquired connotations which suggested not so much the actual presence of a stump as a certain style ("bushwhacking") favored by those who had used the stump as a platform. The process—and its symptomatic value as an indication of the lowering of the tone of political address in the second quarter of the nineteenth century—is clearly illustrated in Garnett Andrews' *Reminiscences of an Old Georgia Lawyer:*

---

[3] Frank Moore, ed., *Songs and Ballads of the American Revolution* (New York: D. Appleton & Company, 1856), pp. 99–101.

[4] William Wirt, *The Life and Character of Patrick Henry* (Philadelphia: Porter & Coates, n.d.), p. 21.

[5] *Life of David Crockett . . . an Autobiography* (New York: Perkins Book Co., 1903), p. 240.

The lawyers of that day differed from those of the present in not practicing popular oratory "from the stump." I do not remember to have heard or to have heard of, any one canvassing from that forum prior to the advent of nullification. With that doctrine came popular oratory as a means of winning the "sweet voices" of the people. Though I recollect the barbecue, the grocery-treats and such like convivial entertainments, at which candidates "most did congregate," and in which they participated, I have no recollection of "the gift of the gab" being called into requisition. It was not thought a necessary accomplishment for our early Presidents and Governors, nor important, even, for members of Congress, to be "gifted" in that way. Our people did not then, as now, graduate a man's talents by his tongue only. Men of worth, learning and station had a fair chance for office, though not winning of speech. Now, if Washington were living, with all his prestige, I don't know but he might be turned down, by the popular vote of a county, where all the voters could be addressed by a second-rate lawyer who might "get the grin against him from the stump." [6]

What the stump style was like can be gathered from anecdotes like the following successful impertinence of Crockett's. He was being completely ignored by one of his competitors, General William Arnold, at an open-air political rally. Arnold

had been speaking for a considerable time, when a large flock of guinea-fowls came very near to where he was, and set up the most unmerciful chattering that ever was heard. They so confused the general that he made a stop, and requested that they might be driven away. I let him finish his speech, and then walking up to him, said aloud, "Well, colonel, you are the first man I ever saw that understood the language of fowls." I told him that he had not had the politeness to name me in his speech, and that when my little friends, the guinea-fowls, had come up and began to holler, "Crockett, Crockett, Crockett," he had been ungenerous enough to stop, and drive *them* all away. This raised a universal shout among the people for me, and the general seemed mighty bad plagued.[7]

Perhaps even more revealing is this one vouched for by Garnett Andrews:

[6] Garnett Andrews, *Reminiscences of an Old Georgia Lawyer* (Atlanta, Georgia: Franklin Steam Printing House, 1870), p. 22.

[7] Crockett, *op. cit.*, p. 159.

Now, the Democratic orator, coming from the literary and wealthy town of Athens, was dressed as became a gentleman from such a place—from such a city, I should say, for there are neither towns nor villages now. And our Colonel, the Whig, coming from the back-woods, was dressed like a back-woodsman. The Democrat happening to speak of himself as one of the "wool-hat boys," his adversary replied to that part of his speech, after the following manner:

"The gentleman spoke of himself as one of the 'wool-hat boys.' Now, look at this picture and then look on that. Here I am with my short homespun-jacket, cotton-shirt, copperas-pants, red-shoes, tanned and made by my old friend, Dick Spooner, and there lies my wool-hat, made by my other neighbor, Tom Hasklet. And there sits your 'wool-hat boy' with his broad-cloth coat, linen-shirt, white-vest, so fine that I don't know what to call it, cassimere-pants, shining, polished boots, and there lies his fine beaver, too stuck-up and proud to come near my old wool-hat."

Here the Democrat rose and said, "If I do wear fine clothes they are not paid for." [8]

Before attempting to draw our conclusions, we cannot resist quoting one more of Andrews' anecdotes about this same orator. We can justify including it here because in a book which tries to illustrate the social point of view about language, this story is necessary to make complete the picture of the milieu from which came "stump speaking." And we should also like to pass on to our reader some of the fun we have had in collecting our material.

Delivering a fourth of July speech, after the usual denunciations of the mother country and laudations of the United States, he led off in this style:

"Whose afeared? whose scared, though she does call herself mistress of the seas? for if she is mistress we will be masters. And, my fellow citizens, by rights they are our seas anyhow, for if there had been no Mississippi they would have had no seas no how. And if we were to turn that river into the lakes or the big cave of Kentucky, we would leave her ships in a puddle-hole at the bottom, surrounded by fluttering fish, turtles, snakes and alligators." Great applause.[9]

---

[8] Andrews, *op. cit.*, pp. 82–83.

[9] *Ibid.*, p. 82.

Such examples of chauvinism and of how "to get the grin" against an opponent make us see how effective this stump style was in winning an unsophisticated audience. But to make permanent the place of the word in American political life the disapproval of the upper classes of the mode it characterized was also important, probably in exact proportion to its popular appeal. Pejorative connotations can entrench a word as firmly as any other. And the upper classes did disapprove of stump speaking. By 1880 Justin McCarthy could speak of "a series of enterprises which in the homely and undignified language of American politics would probably be called 'stumping the country.'"[10] The fact that McCarthy was British had something to do, of course, with the harshness of his remark, but it is certainly not the whole explanation. Few American authors have given more convincing evidence of their sympathetic understanding of popular American points of view and customs than James Russell Lowell. Still even to him the use of stump language meant bad taste, and, if resorted to by a President of the United States, it was more than offensive—it was unforgivable. As the first point in his essay, "The President on the Stump," he declared that "Mr. Johnson is the first of our Presidents who has descended to the stump, and spoken to the people as if they were a mob."

To try now to state in linguistic terms the problem we have been tracing, evidently *stump* and the many phrases containing the word have undergone a change of meaning. But, at least in one respect, the process is different from the processes analyzed in the last chapter. Semantic changes based on metaphor and similar devices are regularly achieved by the conscious and purposeful action of transferring a word from its original sphere to some area of meaning—say from the race track into politics. Nothing of such an aimed action can be the cause of the change of meaning in *stump*—at any rate, as far as these earlier uses are concerned. Here the change of meaning is evidently caused by facts outside language. Tree stumps were used by public

[10] Justin McCarthy, *History of Our Own Times* (New York: Harper & Brothers, n.d.), I, 48.

speakers. This custom became more or less obsolete. But before the stump had disappeared as the political stage, the word *stump* had acquired a usefulness not limited to situations where speaking from a real stump was alluded to. The word could therefore survive even after its origin was no longer evident in the thing it described. When Lowell said that the President *descended* to the stump, instead of *mounted,* the original meaning was not present in his mind. Thus a change of meaning was completed that cannot be explained by any conscious action on the part of the speakers, but resulted from the natural wear and tear of an often used word.

The validity of our sketch in general cannot be weakened by pointing to cases where an occasional use of *stump* indicates deliberate metaphor. The editorial writer of the Richmond *Whig* may have had a feeling of deliberate metaphor when he spoke of

> . . . an innovation in New York electioneering, which we hail with the greatest satisfaction, as promising auspicious results to the American character and institutions. We mean the introduction of the good old Virginia mode of taking the stump—of going before the People, and discussing in their presence the great affairs of State. . . .[11]

The general change, nevertheless, was clearly the combined result of the action of a large number of individual speakers. It would be absurd to assume that each individual contributing to the result acted from the same motive or with the same understanding, either in shifting meaning or in shifting the grammatical function of the word from noun to verb or adjective. What most people are unaware of may appear to others a slight and unessential inaccuracy, and to the few others whose linguistic awareness is constantly alert, a metaphor.

What we learn from the history of *stump* is that many word problems cannot be fully understood unless we know something of the history of the thing which the words designate. This seems a self-evident truism, but to the great damage of etymology and word history its importance was not realized until the late 1890's, when Rudolf Meringer and Hugo Schu-

[11] Richmond *Whig,* September, 1840.

chardt launched their *Wörter-und-Sachen* investigations—studies combining word history with culture history.[12]

The type of semantic change that *stump* represents is by no means rare. In modern use there exists a large number of words whose meanings cannot be explained on the basis of modern conditions but become clear if we study the history of the things involved. A *ring* in general is something round, and therefore the place where a boxing contest is fought could never have been called a *ring* if from the very beginning it had been what it is today, a roped-in square. But before boxing became a well-regulated sport, the battleground was not limited by ropes but by the spectators themselves, who formed a circle around the contestants. This is the situation implied by the earliest (1659) quotation in the *Oxford English Dictionary:* "The soldyers generally say they will not fight, but will make a ring for their officers to fight in." It takes very little knowledge of human nature to see that as soon as a fistic brawl was in the offing the cry, "Form a ring," would call spectators. Here are the natural-sounding preliminaries to a ruckus in Cincinnati in 1856:

> "What!" exclaimed Hoss Head, drawing himself out to his full length and giving the diminutives before him rather a scornful look. "What! you want to fight, do you? Just clar a ring, boys, and stan' back, if you want to see me eat them two critters in half a minit. I can do it by any watch in this crowd. Just clar the ring." [13]

We do not know at what date a staked, roped, square ring became mandatory. The earliest rules of prize fighting, Jack Broughton's in 1743, do not mention it but do refer to "being parted from the rails," which suggests that the stage in his amphitheater was somehow enclosed. But not until the London Prize-Ring Rules of 1838 do we find a defined square required—in contests where rules could be enforced: "The ring shall be made on the turf, and shall be four-and-twenty feet square, formed of eight stakes and ropes. . . ." [14] However, Wignall

[12] The magazine *Wörter und Sachen* was not founded until 1909.

[13] *Green Peas, Picked from the Patch of Invisible Green, Esq.*, (Cincinnati: Moore, Wilstach, Keys & Overend, 1856), p. 23.

[14] Quoted in Trevor C. Wignall, *The Story of Boxing* (London: Hutchinson & Co., 1923), p. 312.

reproduces a print of Richard Humphries, a popular fighter of the 1780's, on the turf in a staked and roped "ring." Probably more important than the dates of the introduction of the square ring is the fact that its use was of slow growth. A distinction between a match and a brawl was for a long time very hard to make. What surprises the modern reader of a book like Wignall's is that down past the middle of the nineteenth century in both England and America the bruisers who fought even championship matches fought as many of their contests outside the ring as in it. The curious can find in Wignall, for instance, dozens of stories of more or less official matches fought with bare knuckles wherever it was handy in streets, in alleys, in fields, on docks, and in innyards. If the ring was used at all, it was likely to be a hastily staked-up affair, ready for moving at a moment's notice of the arrival of the police, and often broken down by the spectators, eager to see better or to aid in the mayhem if the fighter on whom the big money was placed was in danger of losing.

To take only one example, here is a characteristic fight in the career of the man who was from 1852 to 1858 the recognized champion of America, John Morrissey. Morrissey apparently fought only three of his fights under the formal conditions of the London Prize-Ring Rules. The rest were brawls, mostly the inevitable concomitant of gang warfare. This one was at least not casual, for a formal challenge had been made and accepted and a place and date set "to fight to a finish for a side bet of $100 and the glory of being the kingpin bruiser of New York:"

Numerous admirers . . . had cleared a place for the fight. . . . There was no ring, but by general consent the throng had kept a space open for the combat. . . . The fight began with some light sparring. . . . Then Morrissey made a rush. . . .

Clutching each other in grips of steel they butted and pounded their heads together, tearing at each other's face with their teeth and gouging for the eyes with talon-like fingers. . . . They never changed positions while the struggle went on, for the minute they were down the crowd closed in on them and the surging bodies of the combatants pressed against the feet and legs of the surrounding on lookers. The wonder is that the two on the ground were saved from being trampled to death.[15]

The most easily available picture of a typical early ring is the Currier and Ives print of 1860 showing *The Great Fight for the Championship between John C. Heenan "The Benicia Boy," & Tom Sayers "Champion of England."* It places the boxers in this, the most memorable boxing match of the nineteenth century, in a roped-off square similar to that in use today, save that it is not on a platform in an arena but staked into the ground outdoors.[16] Even here, however, in a great international match, carefully organized and well refereed, reported by journalists as famous as William Makepeace Thackeray, the distinguished audience before the end rushed the ring and

> scarcely left the combatants six square feet to fight in. Umpires, referees, and all were overwhelmed, and the whole thing became a mere close mob round the two fighting men. After this, four other rounds were fought, in the midst of this dense mass of partisans of either side, who, however, allowed the men to fight in the fairest way they could, consistent with their having hardly any room to fight at all.[17]

Obviously prize fighting in 1860 was not yet so far removed from the primitive that the ring was necessarily more than a mob of spectators encircling the boxers.

Pictures and antiques are of inestimable value to the linguist in this kind of research. But language itself can often supply the necessary detail. Even without pictures of a square ring, we should know what had occurred to the boxing place

---

15 This eyewitness account appeared in *The Police Gazette* in 1880, but we have excerpted a few lines from the quotations used by Herbert Asbury in *Sucker's Progress* (New York: Dodd, Mead & Company, 1938), pp. 366–367.

16 Harry T. Peters, *Currier and Ives* (New York: Doubleday, Doran & Company, 1942), plate 55.

17 From the report of the London *Times,* quoted by Wignall, *op. cit.,* p. 184.

as soon as we read in any writer of the past that a boxer retires to his corner.

The changes which turned a ring into a square were gradual, as is natural enough when a fight can be anything from a brawl to a duel or an exhibition, and when, as was true of John Morrissey, the same man could engage in all three in pursuit of his professional career. But frequently the word which depends on a thing or a situation for its meaning can have that meaning changed almost overnight. In 1931 Frederick Lewis Allen found it necessary in *Only Yesterday* to explain that the New York Curb Market had been in 1919 literally what its name implies, an open air exchange in the street:

> The Curb Market record referred to trading on a real curb—to that extraordinary outdoor market in Broad Street, New York, where boys with telephone receivers clamped to their heads hung out of windows high above the street and grimaced and wigwagged through the din to traders clustered on the pavement below.[18]

The Curb was housed in its present building on Trinity Place in 1921. Immediately thereupon the word, following the pattern of *stump,* was left with a meaning which referred only to the nature of its selling activities and its method of listing securities, not to its physical place of operation. With its change of place a change of meaning had been made complete, and a skilled journalist only a few years later found it wise to remind his readers of the facts.

The word *knot* as used in determining the progress of a ship has given rise to amateurish suggestions. It has even been explained as a wrong spelling of the abbreviation *naut.* for *nautical* (*mile*). It is nothing more, however, than the common word *knot,* and its technical meaning becomes clear from passages like the following early description of the method of logging a ship's progress:

> The English have another invention. They have a sandglass, which runs only a half a minute or the one hundred twentieth part of an

[18] Frederick Lewis Allen, *Only Yesterday* (New York: Harper & Brothers, 1931), p. 9.

hour in order to measure the way as exactly as possible. Furthermore they also have, around a revolving wheel or axis, a long line, which is divided into certain parts by several knots. To the end of this line they tie a little boat about one foot long and half as wide, to the back end of which they attach a plate of lead so that it may sink deeper than the front and so that the wind cannot carry it away. . . . It must remain steadily at the place where it is thrown in, while the ship sails on. It unwinds continuously as the ship progresses. Then how many knots are unreeled while the sand glass runs must be observed. If six appear within half a minute, one concludes that the ship is sailing two miles an hour. If more or fewer appear, one establishes the proportion.[19]

The knotted line is only part of a measuring apparatus consisting of a reel, the line itself, and a piece of wood (the "little boat"), which in English has the name *log*. The earliest form of the *log* which we have been able to find is the one pictured in the *Encyclopedia Britannica* and there described as "a wooden quadrant about ½ in. thick with a radius of about 5 or 6 in., its circumference being weighted with lead to keep it upright in the sea and to retard its passage through the water." Primitive as this looks compared to the developed modern patent or continuous log, it is probably a highly refined form of something still more primitive. The conjecture seems likely that the first log was only a sizable piece of wood attached to a measurable line; hence the name. "But some derive the naut. *log* from Arab. *lauh,* plank, tablet. Hence *log-book,* originally for recording rate of progress, and verb to *log,* enter in book." [20] We cannot now prove either etymology, but clearly the problem is to be settled by a study of the history of the thing as well as of the word.

These samples should have convinced the reader of how important it is in any philological investigation to be acquainted with cultural history and especially with its most commonplace facts—the history of tools, the habits of sportsmen, sailors,

[19] Translated from *"Fortsetzung des Geöffneten See-Hafens,"* pp. 74–75, *Der Geöffnete Ritter-Platz* (Hamburg; 1715).

[20] Ernest Weekley, *Concise Etymological Dictionary of Modern English* (New York: E. P. Dutton & Co., 1924), s.v. *log*.

businessmen, and what not. But it is no less important to be familiar with the ideas of the past, including its errors and superstitions. Not even the shrewdest guess can discover the relation between *barnacle,* the marine crustacean, and *barnacle goose.* What one must know, according to the evidence massed in the *Oxford English Dictionary,* is the folk belief that the goose, a winter visitor to the British Isles but nesting in the Arctic, was once supposed to be born from the shell fish. So strong was the belief that Trevisa is quoted as declaring that "men of relygyon eet barnacles upon fastynge dayes because they ben not engendred with flesshe." The first element of the name of the goose became the name of its supposed parent.

Another bit of forgotten folklore is preserved in the word *shrew.* Why a quarrelsome and ill-disposed woman should be called by a name originally belonging to the shrewmouse we can discover only by studying the reputation of that innocuous and even useful little animal. As late as 1776 Gilbert White records in a letter the superstition as still a matter of belief in his parish "that a shrew-mouse is of so baneful and deleterious a nature, that wherever it creeps over a beast, be it horse, cow, or sheep, the suffering animal is afflicted with cruel anguish, and threatened with the loss of the use of the limb." [21] This certainly explains how the word could be applied to an obnoxious person. But here as elsewhere we find a word history that involves more than one process. *Shrew* could also be treated as a narrowing of meaning, for the word was once applied to men as well as to women. It has been a common epithet of the Devil, and, before it was limited particularly to the turbulent scold, it carried the meanings of wickedness and malignancy and could be applied to things as well as to people of evil nature or influence.

We have yet to consider the type of meaning change which occurs when an inventor chooses to give his product a name already existing in the language. The word acquires a new meaning by the act of being fixed to the new invention. The

---

[21] Gilbert White, *The Natural History of Selborne* (London: George Routledge and Sons, 1880), p. 197.

acceptance and the subsequent development of the new meaning depend on the fate of the invention itself. If it is successful, then its name and the change of meaning involved in that name will automatically become successful.

The history of *torpedo* offers a good illustration. It was originally the name of a fish of the ray family (*torpedinidae*), capable of emitting electric discharges. The name is derived from Latin *torpere,* "to be numb or stiff." There existed Enlish names for this fish, as for instance, *cramp-fish, cramp-ray,* and *numb-fish,* which, however, were early superseded by the Latin term. The fish's curious electrical power provided an atmosphere of mystery to a people who knew nothing of electricity. Naturally they regarded it as venomous and thought of it with horror. The *Oxford Dictionary* illustrates the use of the word in the sixteenth century with the quotation (1589), "like the fish Torpedo, which being towchd sends her venime alongst line and angle rod, till it cease on the finger, and so mar a fisher for euer." The traditionally dangerous nature of the fish made it early a suitable source of metaphor. Christopher Marlowe applied it to a dangerous human being:

> Fair queen, forbear to angle for the fish
> Which, being caught, strikes him that takes it dead;
> I mean that vile torpedo, Gaveston,
> That now I hope floats on the Irish seas.[22]

Another metaphorical use is illustrated by Dr. Johnson's remark, "Tom Birch is as brisk as a bee in conversation; but no sooner does he take a pen in his hand, than it becomes a torpedo to him, and benumbs all his faculties." [23]

Torpedo was introduced into the terminology of naval warfare in connection with the invention of what can only be described as a mine-laying submarine, first tried out against the British fleet in New York Harbor in 1776. According to the *Military Journal* of James Thacher, "Mr. Bushnell gave to

---

[22] Christopher Marlowe, *Edward II,* Act I, scene 4.

[23] *Boswell's Life of Johnson,* Oxford Edition (London: Humphrey Milford, 1922), I, 109.

his machine the name of American Turtle or Torpedo."[24] Thacher further describes it thus:

The external appearance of the torpedo, bears some resemblance to two upper tortoise shells, of equal size, placed in contact, leaving at that part, which represents the head of the animal, a flue, or opening sufficiently capacious to contain the operator, and air to support him thirty minutes. At the bottom, opposite to the entrance, is placed a quantity of lead for ballast. The operator sits upright, and holds an oar for rowing forward or backward, and is furnished with a rudder for steering. An aperture at the bottom with its valve, admits water for the purpose of descending, and two brass forcing pumps serve to eject the water within, when necessary for ascending. The vessel is made completely water tight, furnished with glass windows for the admission of light, with ventilators and air pipes, and is so ballasted, with lead fixed at the bottom, as to render it solid, and obviate all danger of oversetting. Behind the submarine vessel, is a place above the rudder for carrying a large powder magazine; this is made of two pieces of oak timber, large enough when hollowed out, to contain one hundred and fifty pounds of powder, with the apparatus used for firing it, and is secured in its place, by a screw turned by the operator. It is lighter than water, that it may rise against the object to which it is intended to be fastened. Within the magazine, is an apparatus constructed to run any proposed length of time under twelve hours; when it has run out its time, it unpinions a strong lock, resembling a gun lock, which gives fire to the powder. This apparatus is so pinioned, that it cannot possibly move, till, by casting off the magazine from the vessel, it is set in motion. The skilful operator can swim so low on the surface of the water, as to approach very near a ship in the night, without fear of being discovered; and may if he choose, approach the stern or stem, above water, with very little danger. He can sink very quickly, keep at any necessary depth, and row a great distance in any direction he desires without coming to the surface. When he rises to the surface, he can soon obtain a fresh supply of air, and if necessary, he may then descend again and pursue his course. Mr. Bushnell found, that it required many trials and considerable instruction to make a man of common ingenuity a skilful operator.[25]

---

[24] James Thacher, *Military Journal* (Boston: Richardson and Lord, 1823), p. 75.

[25] *Ibid.*, pp. 146–147.

Bushnell's invention, though it deeply interested the American generals of the Revolution, had little practical success. We have no means of ascertaining how well known the word *torpedo* was in his time. At any rate, however, it was not applied to his explosive but to the machine which carried it. The later history of the word begins with the work of Robert Fulton.

Just how early Fulton used the word it is difficult to discover. According to H. W. Dickinson, he would seem to have used it to describe the explosive carried by his submarine, the *Nautilus,* as early as 1798, but Dickinson does not quote the direct evidence.[26] And if a letter quoted by Dickinson is as Fulton wrote it, then he used *torpedo* in English on November 7, 1800: "The success of this experiment has given me several new ideas which I hope will facilitate much the use of carcasses of powder or torpedoes." [27] Certainly, however, *torpedo* was not in common use, for throughout the voluminous correspondence and reports printed by Dickinson and by William Parsons,[28] the ordinary words used by Fulton and his acquaintances are *submarine bomb, carcass, coffer, explosion,* and *petard.* And we must bear in mind that all of Fulton's work prior to 1807 took place within a limited circle of experts, since in both France and England his experiments were treated as military secrets.

The public history of the invention began with Fulton's experiments in New York, July 20, 1807, and by that time he had evidently decided that, from among the many names previously used, his apparatus would be called a torpedo.[29] The

26 H. W. Dickinson, *Robert Fulton* (London: John Lane, 1913), p. 84.

27 *Ibid.,* p. 106 ff. Fulton's English spelling is usually so unstandardized that this letter must be a translation from French, editorially corrected, or the work of a secretary, and therefore not necessarily reliable.

28 William Parsons, *Robert Fulton and the Submarine* (New York: Columbia University Press, 1922).

29 His reasons for finally settling on this name are beyond our knowledge. It should be noted, however, that in calling his submarine a *nautilus,* he made use of another metaphor based on the name of a marine animal. The innovations introduced by a speaker or writer should be considered as a whole (see Chapters XIII and XIV).

following day he wrote a letter to "the Governor and Magistrates of the city of New York" containing the sentence, ". . . it is very easy to conceive that by organization and practice the application of the torpedoes will, like every other art, progress in perfection." [30] From this time on the name was established in American and, later on, in international use. Fulton himself used it constantly in his pamphlet, *Torpedo War, and Submarine Explosions* (1810),[31] and already in August, 1807, Washington Irving's *Salmagundi* contained a paper, "Plans for Defending Our Harbour," introduced by a sham quotation from Confucius:

> Long-fong teko buzz tor-pe-do,
> Fudge ——
> We'll blow the villains all sky high;
> But do it with econo—my.

Irving also used the word in the text itself:

> The society have, it seems, invented a cunning machine, shrewdly yclep'd a *Torpedo;* by which the stoutest line of battleship, even a *Santissima Trinidada,* may be caught napping and decomposed in a twinkling. . . .

Very soon the newspapers carried the word back to Europe, thus starting it on its international career. On September 7, 1807, one of Fulton's English associates, Commodore E. W. C. R. Owen, sent the Admiralty *A Description of the Machine invented by Mr. Robert Fulton for exploding under Ships' Bottoms and by him called the Torpedo.* He was prompted by a newspaper account of Fulton's letter to the magistrates of New York.

The further history of *torpedo* reveals a kind of meaning change essentially different from the types we have previously dealt with. When Bushnell first applied the name to his infernal machine, his mental picture was not the one the word

---

[30] Dickinson, *op. cit.*, p. 207

[31] Reprinted New York: W. Abbatt, 1914.

now evokes. He used the word to describe his submarine together with the explosive bomb it carried. This latter contrivance was shaped somewhat like a top. Today a *torpedo* means not only an explosive independent of its carrier but something shaped like a fish. The elaborate device that now speeds a torpedo toward its goal is similar to Bushnell's in motive power only insofar as he already used a propeller, though this was driven by a man who turned a crank. The explosive was not shot but stealthily screwed to the bottom of the vessel to be destroyed. The briefest comparison of Bushnell's torpedo with one of World War II shows how much the word has changed its meaning during the intervening years. The shift is second only to the radical change involved in the transference by metaphor of the name of the electric ray to a weapon of war.

What happened to Bushnell's word is that without leaving the general sphere of ideas into which it was introduced, its secondary meanings concerned with shape, function, and mechanism have changed. The process has not been primarily linguistic. The forces which made it lie totally outside language. The thing called *torpedo* has undergone various changes and the word has just trailed behind. The process differs essentially from the original act of metaphoric creation. A metaphor is a jump in meaning achieved by someone who knows what he is doing. This second type is gradual and unconscious, the result of the speech of generations who did not think they were saying anything new.

During the Civil War a torpedo was in use that still kept one of the main features of the Bushnell invention. The U. S. Torpedo-Boat *New Era,* as described in 1864 by *Harper's Weekly,* still carried an apparatus by which the torpedo itself was brought in close contact with the attacked vessel:

. . . a long iron arm carries the basket containing the torpedo out from the vessel, and, . . . by means of a rod within this arm, the torpedo is released from its receptacle and is deposited in the water in just such a position as allows it to float up against the bottom of the vessel intended to be destroyed. . . . At the moment fixed upon

. . . the cap is exploded, and the work is done. . . . The invention of this ingenious machine, by Chief-Engineer W. W. Wood, U.S.N., introduces a new era in submarine warfare.[32]

Surprising as it may now seem, in at least one famous instance this primitive contraption worked. In October, 1864, a young daredevil of the Federal Navy, Lieutenant William B. Cushing, blew up the Confederate ironclad, *Albemarle*—and of course his own ship—by just this device.

Other changes in the structure of the torpedo are regularly discussed and sometimes pictured in the press of the Civil War. In most cases the word means a contrivance of the type now called a *mine*—a mechanism in the nature of a trap or ambush, without motion of its own, and dangerous only when struck. Of that type certainly were the "torpedoes" in Mobile Bay that called forth Admiral Farragut's grandiosely scornful order, August 5, 1864, "Damn the torpedoes! Go ahead!" A third type of Civil War torpedo, also described in *Harper's Weekly* (February 8, 1862), was a river torpedo, set afloat in the current with the hope that it would strike something. In the same magazine on September 19, 1863, there is a sketch of a land torpedo to be buried in the earth.

The interesting point is that all these things and more are called *torpedoes,* and that the name finally was given also to the prototype of the modern torpedo—streamlined, fishlike, launched from a tube, and proceeding under its own power.

The story is not yet finished, however. Two further metaphorical developments of torpedo must still be mentioned. The first is probably not well known to the present generation of boys, for current regulations against an explosive Fourth of July have affected its vitality, but their fathers may recall much the same sort of torpedo as Louis R. Effler records in *My Memoirs of the Gay 90's:*

. . . George and I each had a cigar-box full of potash and sulphur torpedoes, wrapped in tinfoil. . . . These were our "home-grown" torpedoes: for making a lot of noise! . . . We used to throw these

[32] *Harper's Weekly,* VIII (October 1, 1864), 625.

tinfoil "torpedoes" at brick buildings and scare the inmates half to death! [33]

There was nothing new in the 1890's about either the gadget or the use of the word. More than half a century earlier the *American Journal of Science* described it under the heading of "Fulminating Silver":

Chemists are too well acquainted with the tremendous energy of this preparation, to make any comments upon its powers necessary. . . . It is true, it is put up in small quantities, in the little toys called torpedoes, and, if exploded one by one, they will ordinarily do no harm; but as they fall into the hands of children, we can never be sure that they will be discreetly used.[34]

Clearly these toys were not developments of the marine torpedo. The name is therefore a metaphor. The young nuisances who destroyed the peace of their elders with them called them *torpedoes* with the full knowledge that they were not. Equally interesting with this development of secondary metaphor is the point which the linguist has to learn: that he cannot trust his feeling about the age of a word use. We sometimes assume that old age accompanies only the venerable, and that the trivial cannot be old. This is probably generally wrong, but nowhere more wrong than in the history of toys, where we frequently find conservatism strong.

Another purely metaphorical extension of *torpedo* has developed in modern American underworld argot, where *torpedo* means hired assassin. We quote from the newspaper column of Victor Riesel, "Inside Labor":

A slashing job (knives) costs $50. Broken bones raise to $75 the ante of pennyante torpedoes hired in from outlying slum sections. . . .

Most of the goons who let themselves out for hire these days are very young toughs hired by the old-timers. . . .

. . . . .

[33] Toledo, Ohio: Privately printed, 1942, p. 293.

[34] I (1818–1819), 169.

From these new mobs come the muscle men used by the "respectable" racket combines. . . .

. . . . .

And a few days ago, a long-time idealist, young in years, old in crusades, husband of a tubercular wife, father of four kids being brought up in the heart of a New York district where life gets rough at times, was slashed to death by three goons.

They were the men of strange faces, the torpedoes-to-let, who probably were hired just to give the man a going over, but let their enthusiasm for their work carry them away. They were the hoods whom this idealist—an organizer for the ladies garment workers—feared. . . .

. . . . .

What are the police waiting for—more blood? If it comes, the stuff will be on their hands for not closing in before the torpedoes explode again.[35]

Now that we have finished our examples what conclusions emerge about the study of words and things? The *Wörter-und-Sachen* type of meaning and the metaphor type can be kept apart in conscious use. In individual segments the changes they bring about can be studied separately too. But in the total history of a word they cannot be divorced. Stages of conscious change and unconscious use (with semantic change occurring simply because the object changes) follow upon each other. Conscious metaphor becomes subject to unconscious change, and the altered meaning produces new metaphor.

A special aspect of the problem shows itself whenever the *Wörter-und-Sachen* method leads us to individual invention. Here the problem is different, for the inventor's power of name-giving is great. Out of whatever common fund of available names and under the influence of whatever personal experience he acts, he still chooses a word. The question then is not, as it so often is in language, one of existing terms competing with each other, some of which will be rejected, but of one name given and fixed and continued perhaps for the life of the thing.

[35] Columbus *Citizen,* May 16, 1949. Reprinted by permission of Victor Riesel.

Finally there is a moral for the student. The linguist is constantly forced to speak of things of which he can know only a little. He speaks of torpedoes with small technical knowledge, for the scholar cannot permit the traditional limits of specialization to forbid inquiry. Exposing oneself to the danger of error is less unscholarly than permitting oneself to be hampered by the fear of acknowledging one's ignorance. The greater danger lies in the sort of specialization which tempts the student into a feeling of infallibility in a limited area.

Chapter Thirteen

PERSONAL STYLE

ALL children know and few adults forget the parental cry, "Now where did you pick that up?" It is heard in all proper households when the children bring home for the first time a bit of profanity, obscenity, or a new polysyllable. The child has succumbed to the allurements of rough company. The gang is pursuing forbidden knowledge. Or the child, who but recently had to have "Li'l Abner" and "Dick Tracy" read aloud to him, has taken a sudden interest in mechanics. Some new outside force in his environment has taught him the new word and conditioned him in its use, perhaps with social correctness, perhaps with disastrous ineptitude. It is, for the moment at least, his individual speech, and his parents' assumption that it is a symptom of something is correct. The parent recognizes that the child has heretofore used a set pattern of expression—call it *style*—and that deviations from it reflect some sort of personal experience.

As we grow older and much of our vocabulary and idiom becomes conventionalized into the pattern of speech common in our community, we still recognize that our expression as individuals has its own special flavor. We have ways of saying things peculiar to ourselves. And when we read the writing of others, we recognize of each man that his style is in some measure not just characteristic of him as a member of a group—it is also original. If we read carefully we too are constantly wondering, "Now where did he pick that up?" What prompted him to think of this special way of expressing himself? What has made his style personal to him?

The parent pursuing his analysis is usually able to find out what he wishes to know. The child can say he heard it from so-and-so. But we are rarely able to get such direct answers from authors, however eager our interest in their language. Hence a common technique for the study of literature here becomes useful to the linguist. Examples of striking expression that can be traced to their sources are of real importance to all students of language as well as to those with a special interest in that aspect of language which we call literary style. Every such expression is a symptom. Rightly interpreted it will reveal something of the writer's personality and life, and, what is more important for us in this book, will reveal something of the way in which language is constantly adapted by the individual to satisfy his personal needs. No serious student can fail to be aware that when we speak of "language" in general we mean an abstraction of what is actually spoken by individuals. Whoever tries to understand this complicated abstract without understanding why he himself expresses himself in just this or that manner is trying to make bricks without straw.

Here then are some samples of the way in which specific people have chosen their words.

Ely Culbertson provides our first. In discussing the possible responses to an asking bid (if the reader is a bridge player we need not explain what that is, and if he isn't we can't) he uses a figure of speech so striking as to seem farfetched:

> The responding hand can do only one of five things: sign off, bid a new suit, raise the asked suit, respond with four or five no trump. *He cannot pass*—except under ether.[1]

One can hardly fail to ask what exceptional circumstance brought "except under ether" to Culbertson's mind, and no one could know had not Culbertson himself given the right answer in his autobiography. In *The Strange Lives of One Man*

---

[1] Ely Culbertson, *Contract Bridge Complete* (Philadelphia: The John C. Winston Company, 1936), p. 291.

he tells of an operation he had to undergo while deeply immersed in the writing of his *Contract Bridge Blue Book:*

> And then came disaster. I suddenly fell ill. Scarcely able to walk, I was taken to New York, where the doctor ordered an immediate operation. In the French Hospital, under ether, my subconscious kept on dictating the book, for my first words as I came out were, "After a forcing bid, never pass!" This was one of the slogans I had built for the system.[2]

What happened then is this: a personal experience of a very special sort had created in a man's mind a close association between the ideas of an operation under ether and a forcing bid in bridge. Six years later the connection between these normally widely separated ideas was still strong enough to influence his choice of words. It is possible that the word *pass* acted as the trigger to release the mechanism since it also forms part of the slang expression *to pass out* (as under ether). But without Culbertson's personal experience there would have been no such mechanism to release.

Our next sample comes from a man and a Congressional investigation now largely forgotten. A couple of generations ago, however, the name of Jim Fisk, Jr., indicated one of the most flamboyant personalities of the Gilded Age. He was a peddler, merchant, railroad magnate, patron of light opera and of the light ladies who sang in it, and finally the murdered victim of a famous and scandalous love affair. All the country knew Fisk after the gaudy catastrophe of Black Friday (September 24, 1869), on which day Fisk and Jay Gould barely failed in their fantastic attempt to corner the country's gold market and thereby precipitated both a crash that ruined half of Wall Street and the investigation of the Garfield Committee. It is interesting to watch the reckless Fisk in the formal situation of the witness stand avoiding a current bit of slang with careful propriety and later explaining his euphemistic image as a result of personal memories:

---

[2] Ely Culbertson, *The Strange Lives of One Man* (Philadelphia: The John C. Winston Company, 1940), p. 545.

"What do you mean, Colonel," said senator Cox to Fisk, "by the place where the woodbine twineth?" To which interrogatory Fisk responded: "You see, I was before that learned and dignified body, the Committee on Banking and Currency, and when Garfield asked me where the money got by Corbin went to, I could not make a vulgar reply and say 'up a spout,' but observing, while peddling through New England, that every spout of house or cottage had woodbine twining about it, I said, naturally enough, where the woodbine twineth."[3]

Culbertson's figure everyone will regard as highly individual. Fisk's, although it became proverbial and may actually have been so when he used it, Cox found so puzzling that he asked for an explanation. But our third illustration might not at first seem unusual to anyone. The metaphorical use of *picture* in the sense of a man's coordinated impressions and ideas of an event is by no means so rare that in itself it should call for comment. But if an author uses it page after page, then evidently we have a right to inquire into the reason for such preference. The book we have in mind is *Memoirs of a Murder Man,* the professional biography of Arthur A. Carey, former Chief of the Homicide Bureau of the New York City police. It was written by Carey in collaboration with Howard McLellan.[4] Carey's

---

[3] Willoughby Jones, *The Life of James Fisk, Jr.* (Philadelphia: Union Publishing Company, 1872), p. 455.

[4] Arthur A. Carey and Howard McLellan, *Memoirs of a Murder Man* (Garden City, N.Y.: Doubleday, Doran & Company, 1930). That two authors are here concerned—the man who lived the events described and the journalist who helped him compose the book about them—somewhat complicates our problem. The material the book provides is not philologically ideal because one cannot always be sure to which of the two men a certain expression rightfully belongs. As far as the use of *picture* is concerned, however, we are on safe ground. McLellan's Introduction states that the use of the word is characteristic of Carey: "Outside, on the man hunt in the field, he betrays another characteristic mark. He comes, for the first time, upon the scene where murder has been done. He looks about with an all-inclusive glance at the body of the victim, the setting, and invariably in a quiet voice remarks: 'Well, this is the picture I get.'" The excerpts from this work are reprinted by permission of Doubleday & Company, Inc., publisher.

fondness for the word *picture* is evident from such chapter titles as "Picture of a Thief," "In The Immortal's Picture-land," "My First Murder Picture," "Faulty Pictures by Feminine Hands." In the text itself the word is found incessantly. For instance, on pages 19 to 23 it occurs ten times. There are dozens of other uses scattered through the book.

Fortunately for the interpreter, Carey tells with great emphasis of two experiences in which the word figures and both of which impressed him deeply. The first occurred when he was a boy:

> The most impressive murder scene I ever looked upon was not an actuality but a picture. I don't recall how old I was, but I was old enough to be impressed. It was the first I had ever seen. It was a wash drawing from the brush of a newspaper artist. It was labeled "The Unsolved Murder." It depicted in graphic detail a bedchamber in a pretentious home and upon the floor in night attire was the body of a man. The room was in disorder. I was looking at it when a veteran precinct detective saw me.
>
> "Was this a real murder?" I asked.
>
> "Don't you know, my lad, what that is?" he said in surprise. "That was the biggest murder case this town ever had. The Nathan case. I worked on it. . . ."
>
> "That's a perfect picture of the scene," the detective went on.
>
> . . . . .
>
> The detective held me enthralled. There was a pause when he finished his story. Then he went on:
>
> "Now, if you've got the detective bee in your bonnet take a good long look at that picture. In this game everything is pictures, pictures, pictures."
>
> Long after he left me I was still looking at the picture unaware that destiny was cutting me out then to spend the rest of my life looking at pictures, real pictures of murder and its authors, and, from these pictures, develop whatever special talent I may have in the art, or trade, or profession of murder inquiry.[5]

The second was his experience as a young man working with and being trained by Thomas F. Byrnes, chief of the New

[5] *Ibid.*, pp. 11–13.

York police and certainly the most famous American police detective of his day. Of Byrnes Carey says:

> A thing about him that impressed me most deeply was his expression "Here's the picture I get" when he was discussing a crime, or "Now this is the picture I want you to get" when he was assigning a detective to a case. They are two expressions that cling to my tongue today.
>
> . . . . .
>
> He had a pat formula for detectives. . . . The greatest factors in detective success, he always said, were habitual close observation and great experience, ability to see the most insignificant things, and to fit them together and develop a perfect memory.
>
> They had to be picture builders. He summed this up as follows: "A good detective works like a good physician who sees at a glance the nature of his patient's illness. He gets a picture, compares it with other pictures, and then acts." [6]

Our examples thus far have not been taken from the high levels of poetry and fiction. Their authors are not supposed, at least, to have been creative. And the old theory that the true *furor poeticus* is of a very special sort peculiar to poets (or at least to poets of rank) and different from the speech mechanism of ordinary men has not lost all its influence. There are plenty of instances, nevertheless, in which passages which at first seem to be the work of the poet's unbridled fancy can be traced back to the homeliest and most immediate sort of experience—just as with the stylistic peculiarities of the most ordinary writer. Take as an example these lines from "The Conclusion to Part the First" of Coleridge's "Christabel," a poem of witchcraft, vampires, and otherworld diablerie:

> And see! the lady Christabel
> Gathers herself from out her trance;
> Her limbs relax, her countenance
> Grows sad and soft; the smooth thin lids
> Close o'er her eyes; and tears she sheds—
> Large tears that leave the lashes bright!

---

[6] *Ibid.*, pp. 30–31.

And oft the while she seems to smile
As infants at a sudden light!

The whole context of the poem places this detail of the tears and the simile of the smiling of infants in a world of the romantic imagination. We have no reasonable basis for assuming that Coleridge had ever watched a beautiful girl relax from the spells of a vampire, lamia, or witch. We might think of it, therefore, simply as the result of the poet's eye having rolled in a fine frenzy were it not that in another, earlier poem of Coleridge's the same detail appears in a more realistic setting. "The Nightingale," frankly called a conversation poem, works toward its conclusion with the following fatherly anecdote about "my dear babe":

. . . and once, when he awoke
In most distressful mood (some inward pain
Had made up that strange thing, an infant's dream),
I hurried with him to our orchard-plot,
And he beheld the moon, and, hushed at once,
Suspends his sobs, and laughs most silently,
While his fair eyes, that swam with undropped tears,
Did glitter in the yellow moonbeam!

Further data are available to show that the above passage is simply a transcript of reality, and that both it and the romantic scene in "Christabel" derive from an experience of the simplest domesticity—though of a poet's domesticity, to be sure. Coleridge's Notebook gives us the fragments of this little prose tale concerning a misadventure of his baby son Hartley.

—Hartley fell down and hurt himself— I caught him up crying and screaming—and ran out of doors with him.—The Moon caught his eye—he ceased crying immediately—and his eyes and the tears in them, how they glittered in the Moonlight! [7]

---

[7] Quoted in J. L. Lowes, *The Road to Xanadu,* new and enlarged ed. (Boston: Houghton Mifflin Company, 1930), p. 8. We owe the suggestion for this example to Lowes's note 24 of Chap. I. The exact date of the passage in the Notebook is uncertain, but obviously earlier than the date in April, 1798, of the composition of "The Nightingale." For a review of the history of "Christabel" we have used Arthur H. Nethercot, *The Road to*

Thinking back to "Christabel," now, we see three steps in the development of the imagery with which Coleridge chose to summarize how his heroine succumbed to the spells of the evil Geraldine. First there was the simple reality of his effort to quiet his small son. Then shortly after, in a poem designed to record the personal experience of an evening, and held together by the thread of the joyous beneficence of nature, he was reminded that his son is nature's playmate. The night, the moon, and the influence, "full of love and joyance," of nature, combine to remind him of the boy's tumble and of how a glimpse of the moon healed the fright and pain. Except that the fall has been changed to an infant's dream, the version is merely an exact record. Over two years later the third step occurred which took the experience forever out of reality. In a scene where he had already compared the methods of the witch to the ministrations of a mother, he had to describe how the girl Christabel sank into sleep, half frightened, half happy. The image of the earlier experience already twice put into words came back: the tears glittering on the lashes, the smile emerging from grief, and the moon now softened to a sudden light.

Our next sample illustrates the linguistic relations of literature and life from a somewhat different point of view. The following passage from Byron's *Manfred* is, as has long been recognized, little more than a versified repetition of an image which Byron used first in a diary kept during a trip through the Swiss Alps in 1816:

It is not noon; the sunbow's rays still arch
The torrent with the many hues of heaven,
And roll the sheeted silver's waving column
O'er the crag's headlong perpendicular,
And fling its lines of foaming light along,
And to and fro, like the pale courser's tail,
The Giant steed, to be bestrode by Death,
As told in the Apocalypse.[8]

Tryermaine (Chicago: The University of Chicago Press, 1939), Chap. I. See especially p. 12 for the date of October, 1800, for "The Conclusion to Part the First."

[8] *Manfred,* Act II, scene 2, lines 95–102.

Here under the date of September 22 is the relevant passage in the diary, which we quote from the edition of Thomas Moore, who first pointed out the parallel:

Landed at Newhause; passed Interlachen; entered upon a range of scenes beyond all description, or previous conception. Passed a rock; inscription—two brothers—one murdered the other; just the place for it. . . . Set out to see the valley; heard an avalanche fall, like thunder; glaciers enormous; storm came on, thunder, lightning, hail; all in perfection, and beautiful. I was on horseback; guide wanted to carry my cane; I was going to give it him, when I recollected that it was a sword-stick, and I thought the lightning might be attracted towards him; kept it myself. . . . The torrent is in shape curving over the rock, like the *tail* of a white horse streaming in the wind, such as it might be conceived would be that of the "pale horse" on which Death is mounted in the Apocalypse. It is neither mist nor water, but a something between both; its immense height (nine hundred feet) gives it a wave or curve, a spreading here, or condensation there, wonderful and indescribable.[9]

The first two acts of *Manfred* were written during this same time of Byron's residence in Switzerland. The description of the Alpine waterfall in the play is clearly a direct result of the experience recorded in the diary (in fact, *Manfred* is full of reminiscences of his excursion through the Alps). However our problem is not now the relation between the diary and *Manfred* but rather to trace the ultimate origin in the diary of the singular comparison of the waterfall to the tail of Death's horse. In all our previous examples an actual experience in life is behind a literary or colloquial expression; in this instance the experience upon which the metaphor is based is itself literary—the Book of Revelation.

It may be that as Byron wrote at the end of his day the memory of the grave of the two brothers brought to his mind the clauses in Revelation, Chapter 6, verses 4 and 11: "they should kill one another" and "their brethren, that should be killed." Certainly he echoed them. The remainder of the description might then naturally be composed under the influ-

[9] *Letters and Journals of Lord Byron* (Paris: 1833), I, 489–490.

ence of other lines from the same chapter. But it is more likely that he had already been thinking in the language and imagery of this section of Revelation as a result of the events of the day and hence unconsciously patterned his phrase about the brothers upon those quoted. What probably set him off was the total experience of being on horseback with a sword in his hand, hearing an avalanche fall, and riding through a thunderstorm with the possibility of death not remote in his mind. All of these details of actuality, as well as suggestive lines about the murder of brothers, are present in Chapter 6 of Revelation, especially as that is reinforced by two verses in the immediate vicinity: "out of the throne proceeded lightnings and thunderings and voices" [10] and "there were voices, and thunderings, and lightnings, and an earthquake." [11] The first verse of Chapter 6 gives us "as it were the noise of thunder." Verse 2 brings in the "white horse." In verse 4 a horseman is given "a great sword," while here also occurs the clause "that they should kill one another." Verse 8 supplies the climactic image that Byron himself labels as borrowed from the Apocalypse: "And I looked, and behold a pale horse: and his name that sat on him was Death." (That death was in Byron's mind is evident from his refusal to give the guide the sword-stick.) In verse 11 occurs "their brethren, that should be killed." In verse 12 begins the scene of the "great earthquake" which continues to the end of the chapter, and which might well suggest itself to one's mind during an avalanche even did it not include a couple of lines so immediately appropriate as "And said to the mountains and rocks, Fall on us." [12] In sum almost everything in the scenery

---

[10] Revelation 4:5.

[11] Revelation 8:5.

[12] Revelation 6:16. That the avalanches of Switzerland and this especial Biblical terror had a peculiar force and attractiveness for Byron is suggested by the fact that he uses them both in *Manfred* (Act I, scene 2, lines 335–337):

> Ye toppling crags of ice!
> Ye avalanches, whom a breath draws down
> In mountainous o'erwhelming, come and crush me!

See also lines 353–361.

and the events of Byron's ride emphasized the Apocalyptic atmosphere. It is entirely fitting that the climax of the whole description should be a metaphor directly referring to the Book of Revelation: "The torrent is in shape curving over the rock, like the *tail* of a white horse streaming in the wind, such as it might be conceived would be that of the 'pale horse' on which Death is mounted in the Apocalypse."

To the literate man the influences of literature and spoken language do not all run one way. They exist in an interrelationship. Here is one instance where literature is the fundamental experience behind a linguistic expression, and the actualities of the day serve only as the mechanism to release a metaphor. That the metaphor was vital enough to be later transplanted into a poem simply makes evident the power of the original literary impression as a means of conveying to others Byron's excited awareness of Alpine scenery.

The idea that a poet's imagery is derived from his experience is not new. Of late it has been very popular. And scholars have used it to study—sometimes absurdly—biography as well as style. Heinrich Mutschmann, for instance, in his work on Milton [13] was interested in just one point: finding many images in which light seemed to have a troubling or hostile character, he decided, no doubt wrongly, that Milton was probably an albino with the albino's peculiar sensitivity to light. Less confined in her interest, Caroline Spurgeon [14] thought that by cataloguing Shakespeare's images she could, among much else, discern such things as his reaction to the total environment of his youth in Stratford. The number of varying techniques employed by such investigators, and their varying results, make it pretty clear that no method is as yet firmly established. And the sharply adverse criticism many of these efforts have received is often soundly based.

We must here point out that the ambitions of the biographical students are entirely different from ours when we try

---

13 *The Secret of John Milton* (Dorpat: C. Mattiesen, 1925).

14 *Shakespeare's Imagery and What It Tells Us* (Cambridge: Cambridge University Press, 1935).

to see where certain speakers and writers got their images. What such scholars want to do is not to explain why one's language may be individualized by this or that experience; they want to use his whole vocabulary, or at least some important section of it, as a biographical source. They cannot, therefore, be satisfied to pick out a few metaphors here and there, because such a method is much more likely to indicate the personal interests of the investigator than the main characteristics of the poet. Instead they must present their whole material in something resembling a statistical analysis. And here trouble begins. Mere tabulation is not adequate. It only counts things and becomes misleading whenever the material has to be evaluated. Here, to illustrate, are two falconry metaphors from Shakespeare:

> This outward-sainted deputy,
> Whose settled visage and deliberate word
> Nips youth i' the head, *and follies doth emmew*
> *As falcon doth the fowl. . .*[15]

> *If I do prove her haggard,*
> *Though that her jesses were my dear heart-strings,*
> *I'd whistle her off and let her down the wind*
> *To prey at fortune.*[16]

The first sample contains only a simple comparison, which to Shakespeare's contemporaries probably sounded as commonplace as "red as a rose." In the second a sustained image not only shows intimate knowledge of the technical language of falconry; it also depicts admirably Othello's tragic effort to assume a cavalier attitude by making the loss of his wife's affection appear no more important than the loss of a hunting bird. To say that the two examples reveal equally the author's interest would be preposterous.

The dilemma, then, is this: a merely statistical method will confuse rather than illuminate because it gives the same value to the tritest and to the most individual expression. On the other hand, as soon as the investigator starts evaluating his ex-

---

[15] *Measure for Measure,* Act III, scene 1, lines 89–92.

[16] *Othello,* Act III, scene 3, lines 260–263.

amples from an artistic point of view he has deviated from the straight path of scientific objectivity. He is in danger of declaring one image of more weight than a dozen others taken together, merely because it appeals to his esthetic sense. Yet we have no means of evaluation other than the impression the image makes on the reader. You are damned if you do and damned if you don't.

There are still other traps to be avoided. How, for instance, should one classify Shakespeare's phrase *foul sin* in *Henry IV, Part II:*

> "The time will come, that foul sin, gathering head,
> Shall break into corruption:" . . .[17]

Is *foul* an image of smell as in *The Tempest,* "that the foul lake / O'er-stunk their feet"? [18] Or an image of sight like this from the same play, "With colors fairer painted their foul ends"? [19] Or should we think of it rather as an image from medicine, not concentrated upon any single sense? It is so used a few lines earlier in the same scene in *Henry IV:*

> KING HENRY. Then you perceive the body of our kingdom
> How foul it is; what rank diseases grow,
> And with what danger, near the heart of it.
> WARWICK. It is but as a body yet distemper'd,
> Which to his former strength may be restor'd
> With good advice and little medicine!
> My Lord Northumberland will soon be cool'd.[20]

The dominant image of the whole passage seems to be the comparison of England to a diseased body. No one sense alone is appealed to. In such cases it is likely that the author, however annoying to the classifier, prefers the word of multiple connotations because through it he multiplies his chances of touching a spot of high sensitivity in the minds of his audience.

---

[17] Act III, scene 1, lines 76–77.
[18] Act IV, scene 1, lines 183–184.
[19] Act I, scene 2, line 143.
[20] Act III, scene 1, lines 38–44.

Even more difficult are the problems presented by negative evidence. Does the insignificant part that fishing imagery plays in Shakespeare justify the conclusion that Shakespeare was uninterested in fishing? Miss Spurgeon took the affirmative. But Lillian Herlands Hornstein, to whose excellent article, "Analysis of Imagery: A Critique of Literary Method," [21] we are deeply indebted, supports the negative with a most impressive argument: if there ever was a man whose interest in fishing cannot be doubted, it is certainly the author of *The Compleat Angler*—yet an analysis of the metaphors in Walton's *Life of Dr. John Donne* shows not one fishing image. Does this not, as Mrs. Hornstein seems to imply, demolish analysis of imagery as a workable clue to an author's personality and life? In our opinion it does not. It shows only that the theorem that an author's language reflects his personality is not convertible. It would be safe to claim that a poet's frequent use of horse metaphors showed interest in horses. But we have no right to suppose that the lack of such metaphors shows him to be no horseman. A number of forces could prevent even a very genuine interest from finding its way into metaphorical language.

Let us look for a moment at the forces which might have influenced Walton's style. He wrote in a most serious mood. He was a devout man, and his subject, John Donne, was perhaps the most distinguished preacher of his time. Moreover the task had assumed the proportions of a solemn duty performed for a dead friend: Walton wrote the life because his friend Sir Henry Wotton, who had originally intended to do it, died "before he performed it." We can easily imagine a man in such circumstances feeling that to bring in the amusements of his idle hours would be trivial and irrelevant. He might well consciously and unconsciously seek to remove his mind utterly from them and from his ordinary pursuits until his dedicated task was done.

We need not and should not be satisfied, however, with saying that this theory necessarily explains how Walton wrote. Our ideas of why fishing imagery in Izaak Walton never came

---

21 *Publications of the Modern Language Association*, LVII (September, 1942), 638–653.

to play the part of King Charles's head [22] must be either substantiated or disproved by comparing the style of the *Life of Donne* with the rest of Walton's five short biographies. The examination shows that fishing metaphors are absent in all. There is but one bare reference to fishing, and that a remark by Sir Henry Wotton quoted directly by Walton in his *Life of Wotton*. Having got our facts now, we return to our theory and see that we need further explanation. We have to admit a number of possibilities. Walton's pattern for biography may, of course, have been settled for him by the first life he wrote—that of Donne. Or he may have been able to express so easily and fully his love of fishing by indulging in the sport itself and in writing about it directly that he had no need to express it in his other writing. There may have been some sort of psychological wall between his pastime and the work he undertook in more serious mood. The wall might even have been a real necessity. To allow his mind to dwell on fishing might have destroyed his writing economy.[23] Walton may have been writing in a prose tradition which did not seem to him to allow much imagery of any sort—the paucity of metaphors of any kind throughout all the lives is striking. Finally, any combination of these factors may have affected him.

Perhaps this example is a good illustration of the constant interaction of fact and theory in linguistic work. Unless a

---

[22] ". . . Did he say anything to you about King Charles the First, child?"

"Yes, aunt."

"Ah!" said my aunt, rubbing her nose as if she were a little vexed. "That's his allegorical way of expressing it. He connects his illness with great disturbance and agitation, naturally, and that's the figure, or the simile, or whatever it's called, which he chooses to use. And why shouldn't he, if he thinks proper?"

I said, "Certainly, aunt."—Charles Dickens, *David Copperfield,* Chap. XIV.

[23] We have failed to find any chess metaphors in several hundred pages of Henry Thomas Buckle's *History of Civilization in England,* yet Buckle was one of the strong players of his time—a fact that might be puzzling to a linguist but not to a chess player, who knows how even the passing thought of a chess problem can distract him from other business.

linguist belongs among those lucky people who are perfectly satisfied to pile up detail without bothering about its significance, or those equally fortunate who enjoy building up magnificent systems without caring about their factual basis, he will have to make facts support his theories and also use theoretical concepts as signposts to give his fact finding direction and purpose.

Here is a story picked up in the Rhineland where, as evil tongues would have it, adulteration of wine is as much at home as the making of wine. On his deathbed an old wine merchant called his sons together to give them a secret for unfailing success: "One can make wine out of grapes as well." The application of our parable is this: scholars have sometimes brought together imposing masses of valuable data without ever subjecting them to the pressure and fermentation of a theory. There are also plenty of scholars to concoct theories, and sometimes sell them, without using any grapes at all. The proper thing to do is evidently to make wine out of grapes—or, to drop the metaphor, to build from as rich a body of fact as one can collect that theory only which the facts can sustain. If this is one's working principle, then the theory will grow better as the stock of facts grows. Under the stimulus of the theory, furthermore, one's facts become more plentiful and richer in meaning, for it constantly requires us to take care of new problems. The value of Mrs. Hornstein's observation about Walton is not that she shows the method to be unreliable. Rather, she has made us aware of further complexities.

The people who have undertaken to discover from imagery the state of Milton's health and the quality of Shakespeare's physical agility have hitched their horses behind the carts. Linguistic methods will no doubt be perfected in time which will shed light on the unknown parts of an author's biography. But the methodical way to the solution of such problems lies not in a study of authors whose lives are only fragmentarily known. Science needs cases where both a rich linguistic material is available and the facts of the author's life can be studied with reasonable fullness and reliability.

To study a man like Oscar Wilde, as has been done by Professor Arthur N. Nethercot in a recent article,[24] may offer a step in the right direction. The paper shows that a consciousness of guilt pervades most of Wilde's work long before the scandal and trial took place which forced into the light data that would otherwise have remained at best a conjecture only. What makes the case interesting to the philologist is the use Nethercot makes of linguistic material—comparisons, metaphors, and the like. We also see how essential it is that evidence of this sort be brought in not in scraps but as a solid body. As for the specific fixation which was an ultimate source of Wilde's guilt, Professor Nethercot's conclusions rest on eight or ten images, references, and themes. Were it not for the evidence of the trial and the later biographies inspired by it, we could not accept it as proof of Wilde's homosexuality. A full analysis of Wilde's imagery, based on a complete and systematized collection, is needed. Wilde could be made a test case for linguistic-biographical method. And it would not be hard to find other writers whose lives we know fully and in whose choices of words we could see the results of the way they had lived.

Although many scholars have placed metaphor at the center of their investigations, we must not forget that it is only one element of personal style. Syntax, phonetic habits, word formation, speech inhibitions, and favored attitudes such as one's attitude toward literary models or established speech traditions may create just as distinctive characteristics of individual style as metaphor. All of them combine in a man's speech to give a unified and single impression, as we partially saw in examining Carlyle's contribution to the place of the suffix *-dom* in modern English.

The best method of estimating the importance of these elements would be to trace them in the style of a living speaker. But to get even a sketch of his speech personality, one would have to have notebook in hand whenever one talked with the object of study, whom, moreover, one would have to know well.

[24] "Wilde and the Devil's Advocate," *Publications of the Modern Language Association,* LIX (September, 1944), 833–850.

Since this is a bigger piece of work than we can undertake, we are choosing an example which, although taken from fiction, is sufficiently based on observation of reality to serve as a substitute. Billy Badger, from William Gilmore Simms's *Border Beagles*,[25] is the owner of Zion, a frontier plantation in Mississippi. Simms uses little direct description, and Badger's manners and character are largely revealed by his own speech and by what others say about him. As described by the youth who wishes to marry his daughter,

> Billy Badger's a crumpy, stiff sort of a person—a raal, true-believing methodist, that preaches himself, when the parson don't come, and, to my way of thinking, makes a deuced sight the best prayer of any among them.[26]

Young Rawlins' remark leads right to the center of Badger's speech personality. Only exceptionally gifted persons have a wide command of speech styles. Most of us are limited to one. Some are at their best (most characteristic) telling a funny story. Others in witty repartee, still others in logically constructed explanations, or in semilyrical description. Billy Badger's speech evidently derives its most characteristic quality from the sermon—though, to be sure, from a type not heard now in the well-to-do churches of a well-to-do suburb. When informed of an attempted highway robbery in the neighborhood of his home, Badger expresses concern that such things should happen in his otherwise peaceful vicinity and his resolution to bring the malefactors to justice. These two simple ideas, which might have been expressed in as many sentences, swell in his mouth into veritable preaching. We quote only a part:

---

[25] William Gilmore Simms, *Border Beagles,* new and rev. ed. (New York: Belford, Clarke & Co., 1885). While Simms's young heroes and heroines are apt to be as conventionally drawn as those of any prolific romancer, his minor characters are definitely intended to be realistic. They served to create what Simms was consciously trying to portray, the real life of the South in the first half of the nineteenth century. Perhaps Badger's grammar is more literate than exact realism would warrant but that does not affect the qualities we are analyzing.

[26] *Ibid.,* p. 170.

"Evil is abroad in the world . . . there is no place altogether secure from the dominion of Satan; but that here, so nigh unto Zion, where I have, for the space of two blessed years, striven to uphold the work and the worship of our heavenly Father—that sin should so boldly demean herself, seems to be as passing strange, as it is sad. But, marvel ye not, Walter Rawlins, at what I am about to say to you; and regard it not as unbecoming in one who preaches peace on earth and goodwill to all men, if I declare to you that we must all arise and put on the armor of strife, yea, the very armor of man, and gird upon our thighs the carnal weapons of human wrath. The traveller must not be stricken down upon the highway without summons of eternity, without warning to prepare for death in season. We must go forth in seeking for these bloody men; we must put them to defiance; and as they have not hearkened to our words of prayer and peace, neither have they given heed to the forbearance of our own example, then must we use against them the same weapons which they are so ready to use against the wayfaring man, and we must smite them hip and thigh to their utter undoing. If they will not hearken to the imploring angel; if they will not heed the promise of the forgiving angel; nor incline their hearts to the prayers of the righteous, God will commission the destroying angel, even as he has commissioned him against the Amalekite and the Assyrian of old, until there be none left to tell the story of their undeserving, and their heaped-up bones alone shall remain to declare their sudden punishment, in warning to the other tribes of evildoers which shall follow them. . . . My heart is full of shame within me, that I should have fought the good fight with so feeble an arm, and should have gone into the battle with a spirit waxing faint in the hour when there is most need of performance. Here, Mr. Wilson, . . . did I pitch my tent, at a time when the land around me was in possession of the heathen, though even then decreed for the heritage of the believing. . . ." [27]

This speech might seem to illustrate the man in a semi-official mood. In addressing strangers, and the injured parties to boot, Badger no doubt has the feeling of representing the respectable members of his community in a situation they all deplore. But that this is, after all, simply his habitual way of expressing himself, used in private conversation and to his

[27] *Ibid.*, pp. 193–194.

familiars as well as to strangers, is clear from the further description by young Walter Rawlins:

Though he's a gruff and grumpy sort of person, he's mighty fond of a confabulation, and so long as you'll listen, and even if you wont listen, he'll still talk on, exhorting, as it were, and mighty airnest. When he once gits hold of the flesh and the devil, there's no telling how long he'll hold on. It's no trifle that'll make him let go; and you'll see the blood git up into his face, and the veins grow big on his forehead, and the foam will come out and stand in his mouth-corners long before he'll think you've had enough. He never asks how you like the thing, for he always concludes that he knows best what's good for everybody; and as for disagreeing with him, when once you set eyes on him, you'll see for yourself that that's out of the question. I tell you, sir, Mr. Vernon, he looks like all the Laws and the Prophets; and he speaks as if he stood on a high place, and we were all put below to listen to him.[28]

One need not be very well versed in the Bible to recognize in Badger's speech a number of phrases almost exactly borrowed from it: "peace on earth and good will to all men" (Luke, 2:14), "smite them hip and thigh" (Judges 15:8), "incline their hearts" (Joshua 24:23, and elsewhere), "the destroying angel" (I Chronicles 21:12), "fought the good fight" (I Timothy 6:12), "pitch my tent" (Genesis 33:18).[29]

The single borrowed word or phrase, however, is only one element—although usually the first to attract the reader's attention—in the whole structure of the man's style. The Biblical pattern is easily recognized in details as small as the morphology of the single word and as large as the syntax and rhythm of the complete sentence. Morphologically one finds such archaisms as *ye,*[30] *thou seest, hath,* and other archaic forms are scat-

---

[28] *Ibid.*, p. 171.

[29] Observe, by the way, that the mere fact of using Biblical quotations in everyday speech situations is apt to cause a change of meaning. One cannot suppose that when Badger says, "Here, Mr. Wilson . . . did I pitch my tent," he is thinking of the very beginning of his settlement when he might conceivably have used a tent.

[30] Note the use of *ye* in the singular, which Badger seems to like as an emphatic form of the singular *you.*

tered throughout, such as "many . . . have had the fountains of life to spring," *nigh unto, marvel ye not,* and *yea.* The syntactic and rhetorical structure is largely determined by a Biblical fondness for repetition ("we must all arise and put on the armor of strife, yea, the very armor of man, and gird upon our thighs the carnal weapons of human wrath"; "without summons of eternity, without warning to prepare for death in season"), for parallelism ("as they have not hearkened to our words of prayer and peace, neither have they given heed to the forbearance of our example"), and for pleonasm ("my heart is full of shame within me"). Uncommon word order also helps to emphasize Biblical rhythm ("Here . . . did I pitch my tent"; "marvel ye not").

Rarely is stylistic imitation only the mechanical adaptation of one's speech to somebody else's speech pattern. There is, of course, a sort of schoolboy imitation which it would be hard to call anything but parrotlike. But even in this lowest form there is frequently present a profound motive—the desire to enhance one's humble self by coming closer to an ideal represented by the teacher or author one admiringly imitates. This element of identification by imitation seems to be unmistakable in Badger's style. By speaking as he does, he creates the fiction that he himself is one of those Old Testament characters who sat in judgment with appropriateness, who didn't raise a cabin but pitched a tent, who didn't just kill their enemies—gentile tribes—but smote them hip and thigh, and whose enemies, moreover, were not theirs alone but emphatically the enemies of God. So at the climax of his outburst Badger prophesies, drawing an exact analogy with Biblical story, that "God will commission the destroying angel even as he has commissioned him against the Amalekite and the Assyrian of old, until there be none left to tell the story of their undeserving. . . ." To Badger this is not a rhetorical device; he carries such imitation into his private life by calling his home Zion. And his niece Rachel and son Gideon were "names out of the Scriptures," thus bearing witness of his desire to appear as one of the chosen of the Lord.

What does not appear from the printed pages is the style of delivery of his speech. In passing we should note that by making Badger use the single form *ware* for *were* Simms hints that we should imagine his pronunciation as tinged with dialect. But that is less important for us here than the qualities that reinforce the Biblical pattern. Fortunately Simms has supplemented the direct discourse with an outright description:

. . . he never yet unbent a muscle of his hard countenance, nor modulated to softness the harsh accents of a voice, stern, cold, slow, emphatic, and measuredly monotonous. . . . his congratulations to the party on their escape, were uttered with very much like the manner which he employed when saying grace before the morning meal. . . .

William Badger had no sympathy with the enthusiasm that dilates readily at every impulse. His enthusiasm was all religious; his zeal, deep, earnest, and perpetually glowing, was restrained by that decorum alone, which is the fruit of intense veneration. To speak fast, seemed to his mind to indulge in levity; to utter promptly his feelings, might be to do injustice to his own judgment, to the governing providence of God, or to the rights and interests of others. . . .

"I have seen him in a roaring passion," said Rawlins to his companion, "when he didn't know what he said or did, and swore like a Mississippi boatman; and yet one word came out after another jist as slowly as if he was making his morning prayer." [31]

To complete the picture we have to point out that Badger possesses a very clear etiquette of speech—or perhaps two, one for himself, another for the less fortunate who are not in such close communion with God. When his son Gideon interrupts his invective by suggesting that the robbers are probably not local men and that the neighborhood should be absolved from blame,

The father, slowly and without a word, when he first heard the voice of the son, wheeled his chair about so that he might face the speaker. . . .

"And what know you, Gideon Badger, of the hearts of men, even though they be neighbors unto Zion's Hill? And what know you of these robbers, of whom you speak so readily, that you should venture

[31] Simms, *op. cit.*, pp. 191–192.

to hope—ay, sir, I say to hope—that all or even any of those who hearken to God's word in this place, are free from the damnable leprosy of sin? There is great presumption in thy thoughts, Gideon Badger, which should be chastened by prayer, by the prayer of an anguished spirit, that knows its own presumption. . . . When thou speakest so freely of the goodness of thy neighbors, I greatly fear thou speakest a vain thing. . . ." [32]

Once more we are clearly landed in the subject of speech inhibitions. They are to be seen even more sharply in the next quotation. Fond as he is himself of Biblical phraseology and comparison, Badger objects to it sternly when used thoughtlessly for emphasis or as part of colloquial idiom. When Walter Rawlins says that the report of a man's death is "true as gospel" the reproof is immediate and crushing:

"Make no irreverent comparisons, young man, between such truth which thou tellest, on the authority of thy mortal sight, and that wondrous truth of the gospel which comes of the sight of God." [33]

These inhibitions are more profound than merely a taboo against holy words in ordinary use. He is equally severe with Walter when that young man with vigorous masculine pride is explaining and justifying his bold action at the scene of the attempted robbery. Badger cuts him short with,

"It needs not that we should speak longer in this idle fashion: thou hast too great a vanity of thy speech, Walter Rawlins. It is a sin in youth to multiply words, having neither experience nor thinking to make them stable and of fitting effect. . . . I will speak more to thee of this subject on the way homeward." [34]

Simms has given a very consistent account of Badger's speech. There is no detail which one fails to understand as soon as one understands his attitude and personality. This, we think, is the fundamental problem of all analyses of personal style. It is not a question of amassing detail but of trying to discover the shaping forces at work through all the details. Tabulations

---

[32] *Ibid.*, p. 196.
[33] *Ibid.*, p. 197.
[34] *Ibid.*, p. 200.

of rhetorical devices, or statistics on sentence length, or even, for that matter, the tabulations of images, are meaningless unless one can discern the forces that have motivated such choices. It may be very difficult to discover these creative sources of style. Often, of course, they may lie in fairly obvious places—formal education, friendships in stimulating literary circles, direct literary models exerting their influence through a man's favorite reading—all of them forces which modern literary scholarship has excellent techniques for investigating and which the trained literary historian can handle with relative ease. Very often, however, these shaping forces are hidden in the deeper levels of an author's or a speaker's experience. He may well be largely unaware of them himself, and they may have their roots where only the most intimate biography can reveal them. Indeed they may never be adequately known. Yet only in their light can the really personal elements in a personal style be understood.

Chapter Fourteen

PERSONAL STYLE AND PERIOD STYLE: A VICTORIAN POET

THE old Methodist in the preceding chapter was presented by Simms as an individual, interesting both as a character and because of his fate, but Simms intended at the same time to depict a type. In the America of the later eighteenth and early nineteenth centuries there were many such, most of them gone to their graves anonymously, a few like Lorenzo Dow and Peter Cartwright still well known to us from their own writings. They supply ample proof that however individual Billy Badger may be as a character in *Border Beagles,* his speech is strongly traditional. It belongs to his kind and time. To many of his real-life contemporaries the Bible set a dominant speech pattern as definitely as their interpretations of it influenced their behavior.

The full understanding of a work of literature is a study of many elements, among which language and style, however important, are only one. The personality that decides an author's choice of his models, his plot, and his social and esthetic tendencies is the same that decides his choice of words, his sentence structures, and his rhythms. His total artistic personality has an essential unity as truly as Billy Badger's. And, like Billy Badger's, an author's style is the result of factors of which some are peculiar to him and others are shared by the men of his kind and time. To understand his work, then, is to see the constant interplay of literary concept and linguistic medium and to see it in both its personal and period aspects. Alfred Tennyson's once-admired "The Revenge: A Ballad of the Fleet" offers a concrete opportunity to test our theory of the complex unity of style.

Tennyson spent the winter of 1873 in London and on March 9 looked up the Secretary of the Hakluyt Society to talk about the Elizabethan seadog, Sir Richard Grenville. Tennyson had been interested in Grenville and his battle with the Spaniards ever since he had read the account of it by his friend James Anthony Froude in the essay "England's Forgotten Worthies." [1] After his talk he wrote enthusiastically to his wife: "Sir Richard Grenville in one ship, the *Revenge,* fought fifty-three Spanish ships of the line for fifteen hours: a tremendous story, out-rivalling Agincourt." When he came home, still fascinated by the story, he read aloud Froude's version to Mrs. Tennyson and shortly afterward composed one line:

> At Flores in the Azores Sir Richard Grenville lay.

And there it stopped.

Four years later, again in London, he ran across Edward Arber's reprint of the Elizabethan documents concerning the *Revenge* [2] and recognized that at last he had the material, more adequate than Froude's summary, to work with. He composed the poem during the rest of 1877 and published it in March of 1878.

Those are the facts as they are recorded by Tennyson's son Hallam,[3] and his grandson Sir Charles Tennyson.[4] They tell us

---

[1] First published in the *Westminster Review,* July 1, 1852; reprinted in *Short Studies on Great Subjects* (London: Longmans, Green and Co., 1867), 2 vols.

[2] Edward Arber, *English Reprints,* No. 29 (London: 1871).

[3] Hallam Tennyson, *Alfred Lord Tennyson, a Memoir* (New York: The Macmillan Company, 1898), 2 vols.

[4] Sir Charles Tennyson, *Alfred Tennyson* (New York: The Macmillan Company, 1949).

more than we often know about the genesis of a poem but are still not full enough to make psychological speculation unnecessary. Hallam calls the line quoted the "germ" of the poem; Sir Charles, its "key line." What exactly do they mean? Hardly something so commonplace as that the line was the first one composed. "Germ" must mean here the cell from which the poem grew. And "key line" suggests that it unlocked the whole poetic process. The two metaphors say much the same thing and must mean that the finding of this first rhyme marked the step between the receptive task of studying sources and the creative act by which the historical narrative became a poem.

For us the most significant aspect of Tennyson's behavior is the fact that the creative process—even suspended as it was for four years—began with an element of language; a sound pattern, a rhyme that happened to catch his ear. That, though it hung fire for a time, was the trigger which set off the poem. Are we justified, however, in saying it "happened"? One doubts it if one thinks of such other famous examples as "The Charge of the Light Brigade," in which, according to Tennyson's own account, the arresting phrase read in the London *Times,* "Some one had blundered," touched off the process that created a poem; or *Northern Farmer, New Style,* of which also the poet tells us that it was founded on the single sentence, "When I canters my 'erse along the ramper (highway) I 'ears 'proputty, proputty, proputty'." Hallam Tennyson says outright in his *Memoir* "My father's poems were generally based on some single phrase like 'Someone had blundered': and were rolled about, so to speak, in his head, before he wrote them down. . . ." [5] And we must add to these instances the numerous examples of nonverbal sound as a motivation to poetry in Tennyson, the most famous of which is no doubt the song from "The Princess," "The splendour falls on castle walls," the result of listening to the echoes of a bugle at Killarney. Thus at the beginning of our investigation we discover that to Tennyson sound was not only a tool that he used with great skill but also

[5] *Memoir,* I, 268.

an inspiration. His work is stamped with his power over sound and his dependence upon it.

Any reader of Hallam Tennyson's *Memoir* of his father is struck by the number of references to the poet's concern for the sound of verse, both his own and others':

"Browning," he said, "never greatly cares about the glory of words or beauty of form. . . . Sometimes I cannot read him. He seldom attempts the marriage of sense with sound, although he shows a spontaneous felicity in the adaptation of words to ideas and feelings. . . . He has plenty of music in him, but he cannot get it out." [6]

He felt what Cowper calls the "musical finesse" of Pope, and admired single lines and couplets very much; but he found the "regular da da, da da" of his heroic metre monotonous. He quoted

"What dire offence from amorous causes springs."

" 'Amrus causiz springs,' horrible! I would sooner die than write such a line!! Archbishop Trench (not then archbishop) was the only critic who said of my first volume, 'What a singular absence of the 's'!" [7]

[Of Goethe] "He could not quite overcome the harshnesses of the German language. 'Kennst du das Land?' is a perfect poem, but 'Beschützer ziehn' is a hideous sound in the middle." [8]

[Of Collins] ". . . what a bad, hissing line is that in the poem on the death of Thomson,

'The year's best sweets shall duteous rise.' " [9]

My father expressed the view that, "as the English language is much finer than the Italian for variety of sound, so Milton for sound is often finer than Dante." He quoted Milton, Virgil, Dante and Homer to illustrate his meaning; then said:

"What, for example, can be more monotonous than the first lines of the 'Inferno' with their *'a-s'*?

'Nel mezzo del cammin di nostr*a* vit*a*
Mi ritrov*a*i per un*a* selv*a* oscur*a*,
Chè l*a* diritt*a* vi*a* er*a* sm*a*rrit*a*—'

and so on." [10]

---

[6] *Ibid.*, II, 285.
[7] *Ibid.*, p. 286.
[8] *Ibid.*, p. 288.
[9] *Ibid.*, p. 289.
[10] *Ibid.*, p. 215.

[After receiving a French translation of some of his own lyrics] "What a poor language French is for translating English poetry, although it is the best language for delicate *nuances* of meaning. How absurd 'Ring out, wild bells' sounds in the translation 'Sonnez, Cloches, Sonnez,' and what a ridiculous rendering of 'He cometh not, she said' is 'Tom ne vient pas'!" [11]

That Tennyson was deliberate about the effects he sought to produce and likewise thought that he had achieved the "marriage of sense to sound" comes out often:

[Reading "The Revenge" aloud to the violinist Joachim], on reading the line

And the sun went down, and the stars came out far over the summer sea,

he asked Joachim, "Could you do that on your violin?"

—the peace of nature after the thunder of the battle.[12]

[While he was publishing the first installment of the *Idylls of the King*] He found out that the "E" in "Enid" was pronounced short (as if it were spelt "Ennid"), and so altered the phrase in the proofs "wedded Enid" to "married Enid." [13]

He insisted that in his line "Free will, foreknowledge absolute," *knowledge* be pronounced with a long O. " 'Fore-knowledge' would be horrible there." [14]

And the historian Lecky says, "He once rebuked me for pronouncing 'knowledge' in the way which is now usual, maintaining that the full sound of 'know' should be given. I defended myself by quoting Swift's lines on the Irish Parliament:

'Not a bow-shot from the college,
Half the world from sense and knowledge,'

but he only said he hoped I would never pronounce the word in this way in reading his poetry." [15]

---

[11] *Ibid.*, I, 385.
[12] *Ibid.*, II, 233.
[13] *Ibid.*, p. 125.
[14] *Ibid.*, p. 400.
[15] *Ibid.*, p. 203.

He criticized an accentual misreading of his own quantitative lines modelled upon Catullus. People "don't understand English scansion. In the line 'Dream not of where some sunny rose may linger' they said the first syllable of sunny was long, whereas it evidently is short. Doubling the *n* in English makes the vowel before short." [16]

Frequently he called special attention to the "vowel music" of lines like

> Come down, O maid, from yonder mountain height.

[Reading aloud to a friend he told her] "to listen to the sound of the sea in the line,

> The league-long roller thundering on the reef,

and to mark Miriam Lane's chatter in

> He ceased; and Miriam Lane
> Made such a voluble chatter promising all." [17]

He enjoyed experimenting with classical quantitative rhythms and once "confessed that he believed he knew the quantity of every word in the English language except perhaps 'scissors'." [18]

We give one final quotation to show not merely his concern for meter and its variation, but for many of the details of verse:

"The English public think that blank verse is the easiest thing in the world to write, mere prose cut up into five-foot lines; whereas it is one of the most difficult. In a blank verse you can have from three up to eight beats; but, if you vary the beats unusually, your ordinary newspaper critic sets up a howl. The varying of the beats, of the construction of the feet, of the emphasis, of the extra-metrical syllables and of the pauses, helps to make the greatness of blank verse. There are many other things besides, for instance a fine ear for vowel-sounds, and the kicking of the geese out of the boat (i.e. doing away with sibilations); but few educated men really understand the structure of blank verse. I never put two 'ss' together in any verse of mine. My line is not, as often quoted,

---

16 *Ibid.*, p. 400.

17 *Ibid.*, pp. 409–410.

18 *Ibid.*, p. 231.

And freedom broaden*s* *s*lowly down—

but

And freedom slowly broadens down.

People sometimes say how 'studiedly alliterative' Tennyson's verse is. Why, when I spout my lines first, they come out so alliteratively that I have sometimes no end of trouble to get rid of the alliteration." [19]

The above passages make it emphatically clear that to Tennyson what he regarded as beauty of sound was one of the governing principles of verse. In addition he was mindful of those elements of verse which we conventionally analyze as offering poetry the peculiar advantage of making sound contributory to meaning and emotion. Any consideration, then, of his personal style must discuss them.

The meaning—i.e., the psychological result on the reader—of such devices as rhyme, alliteration, assonance, and special patterns of vowels and consonants is very hard to determine. In regularly recurring rhymes or in rhythmically placed alliterations people find the same pleasure that makes all rhythm universally attractive. But beyond that, analysis has to be subjective to a degree which makes positive statement treacherous. It involves one's individual and community taste and experience, and all the intricate conditioning which goes to make them. If the student claims that this or that sound has special emotional or dramatic power, or that it suggests the thing in itself by sheer sound apart from meaning, he must be aware that any student with a different background of conditioning

---

[19] *Ibid.*, pp. 14–15. The reader will have noticed by now Tennyson's objection to the sound of *s*. Apparently his ear did not always function. Or perhaps he did not object to *sh,* which occurs twice in line 3 of "The Revenge"—a line, furthermore, which alliterates on *s*. In some contexts he could not have objected to it as much as he thought he did. His lyric *The Brook* is so full of the sound that it is difficult to choose the most conspicuous stanza:

I slip, I slide, I gloom, I glance,
Among my skimming swallows;
I make the netted sunbeam dance
Against the sandy shallows.

experience is privileged to disagree. Clever versifiers have long amused themselves with writing arrant nonsense in the "stateliest" rhythms of poetry; words like *undulant fever* and *malaria* have very "beautiful" sounds; English dogs onomatopoetically say *bow-wow,* while French dogs say, with no doubt equal onomatopoetic veracity, *gnaf-gnaf.*

Word meaning will have to be accepted as the basis for most of the special sound effects we have to analyze. The "crash of the cannonades" in Stanza XI of "The Revenge" may be strongly suggestive of actual battle, but, if so, it is not just because of sound. However onomatopoetic *crash* may be in battle contexts, it has no sound value at all as the name of a cotton or linen cloth; and *canon* with one *n* suggests nothing more militant than *Barchester Towers.*

Perhaps, however, our varied experiences do result in a certain consensus of opinion. Subjective as our individual reactions may be, literate people have been conditioned by centuries of the literary choices of poets and critics into accepting a reasonably common body of poetic device and reacting to it as they are expected to, whether or not there is a demonstrable physiological basis for it. Moreover, while the existence of convention by no means frees us from the danger of speculating about things which are not there, we are fortunate in dealing with Tennyson because he accepted this body of convention for his own work and that of others. And his readers have accepted it in his poems. To what extent it may have objective reality apart from our subjective highly conditioned response is immaterial. These things exist in Tennyson's work if for no other reason than that his readers, with varying degrees of consciousness, think they find them, and he thought he put them there.

To discover that "The Revenge" began with a sound pattern places us on firm ground, then, if we consider the basic facts of Tennyson's poetic personality, and we may expect that any analysis of the poem's language will require a good deal of attention to its sound.

Prior to any rhymes, however, prior even to the idea of

writing a poem about the *Revenge,* was Tennyson's interest in the narrative which Froude had acquainted him with. We can have no better way of seeing what forces of literary concern, of personal and period style shaped the poem than to see what Tennyson did with his sources, Froude's essay and the accounts reprinted by Arber. These latter are Sir Walter Raleigh's *A Report of the Trvth of the Fight about the Iles of Açores, this last Sommer. Betwixt the Reuenge, one of her Maiesties Shippes, and an Armada of the King of Spaine* (1591); and a fragment of Jan Huygen van Linschoten's *Discours of Voyages into ye Easte and West Indies* (1598).[20]

Both the original prose accounts seem like objective reporting, so far as the battle is concerned. Van Linschoten's is the more matter-of-fact. It is the version of a curious bystander, his feelings untouched by the event. Raleigh's, written to quiet a quarrel between the followers of Lord Thomas Howard and the friends of Sir Richard Grenville as to which conducted himself more creditably on the occasion, gives, however, a special effect of objectivity (it is not necessarily a matter of the truth, of course, but of giving the impression of the truth). We do not mean to imply that the whole paper is free from tendency: the beginning and the end are strongly anti-Spanish. But one feels that this is skillful propaganda, designed to focus contemporary attention on England's national antipathy toward Spain, and thereby to remove it from criticism of Howard and Grenville. Notwithstanding Raleigh's deliberate chauvinism, the account of the fight itself seems judicious and factual.

Raleigh's effort to defend the reputation of his cousin Grenville without offending the friends of Howard influenced his language as well as his selection of data. It is instructive to compare his phrasing with that of another contemporary, Monson. In his treatment of Grenville, Raleigh says that even though flight would have been better, "Notwithstanding out of the

[20] It seems likely that Gervase Markham's poem, *The Most Honorable Tragedie of Sir Richard Grinuile, Knight* (1595), also included by Arber, left a couple of faint traces on Tennyson's choice of words. But if so, the influence is so very slight that we can safely ignore it here.

greatnesse of his minde, he could not bee perswaded." But Monson, in place of attributing "greatness of mind" to Grenville, calls him "a stubborn man," "head-strong and rash," "wilful," and speaks of the "cross and perverse Fortune which happened by means of Sir *Richard Greenvile*."[21] Raleigh's account, however, with its carefully concealed balance of praise and blame, leaves us thinking of Grenville as the gallant commander of gallant men facing terrific odds.

Despite Tennyson's acquaintance with Raleigh and van Linschoten, it is not surprising to find that his reading and rereading of Froude left the strongest stamp on his mind. There is a period style of thinking as well as a period style of expression. Froude is the least objective of Tennyson's sources. Largely following Raleigh, he heightens Raleigh's anti-Catholic, anti-Spanish bias and especially he heightens every emotional and heroic aspect of the story. Tennyson accepts the offered lead. He dramatizes, idealizes, and sentimentalizes, not just because of the psychological weight of first impressions, but because he shares with Froude a common Victorian view of Elizabethan history.

Specifically this acceptance of Froude's interpretation offers Tennyson a chance to shorten his narrative and concentrate it far beyond any of his sources. His aim leads him toward the suppression of and deviation from historical truth, almost always following hints received from Froude.[22]

Tennyson like Froude omits all mention of the piratical intent of the English expedition, which was sent out to intercept a Spanish treasure fleet coming from the West Indies, and of the consequent fact that the catastrophe was the result of

[21] Arber, *op. cit.*, pp. 5–6.

[22] Froude's motivations and Tennyson's were probably much the same. What in a poet, however, is not only justifiable but shows, if it is successful, an artistic sureness which is the highest form of artistic integrity, is in a historian nothing of the kind. One may suggest that a greater poet than Tennyson might not have found conventional simplifications necessary. But one may not question either his skill or his integrity in allowing his ideal of the story to shape the structure of his narrative. The historian is rarely justified in succumbing to such tendencies.

meeting the protective Spanish convoy before the treasure ships arrived. He omits all description of the expedition's make-up and organization, including such significant facts as that Lord Thomas Howard was commander of the English fleet, therefore Grenville's superior officer, and that he gave orders for the whole fleet to avoid the Spanish. Tennyson describes the two men as nobly agreeing on the very point that caused their contemporaries to debate hotly which had betrayed the other.[23] Further, still following Froude, or perhaps motivated by the same impulse to amplify the heroics of the situation (caution has often seemed incompatible with heroism in idealized narrative), he does not indicate that the English were on the lookout for the Spanish armada which was covering the approach of the treature ships. He begins:

> At Flores in the Azores Sir Richard Grenville lay,
> And a pinnace, like a flutter'd bird, came flying from far away:
> "Spanish ships of war at sea! we have sighted fifty-three!"

In this rapid introduction we are not given the impression that the pinnace was an English reconnaissance boat which had been out following the Spanish for three days, yet so Raleigh tells us. Instead, we plunge at once into the direct statements of Howard that he cannot fight; of Grenville that he may not leave the scene immediately. Here we get Tennyson's sole motivation for the action—the heroic statement that

> ". . . I've ninety men and more that are lying sick ashore.
> I should count myself the coward if I left them, my Lord Howard,
> To these Inquisition dogs and the devildoms of Spain."

But Raleigh has something quite different to say about this situation. It was not just the *Revenge* but "manie of our shippes companies" that "were on shore in the Iland." Moreover neither

---

[23] Since the resulting quarrel is what prompted Raleigh's *Report* it is worth noting that he shrewdly never mentions it. Van Linschoten, however, whose version Tennyson also used, is specific on the point of Howard's order and Grenville's disobedience. Froude follows van Linschoten, but so inconspicuously that unless one already knows the story one cannot get the point.

Raleigh nor any other original source says that it was the sick who were ashore. Froude certainly drew this inference, but from Raleigh's statement that the shore party was foraging for "such thinges as they coulde either for money, or by force recouer," a bit of piracy seems as likely. Raleigh does make it clear that Grenville's ship "was the last waied, to recouer the men that were upon the Iland, which otherwise had beene lost." But so far as sickness among the crew was concerned, he also shows that the *Revenge* was not the worst off: the *Bonaventure* did not have enough sound men even to "handle her maine saile," and had to have twenty men taken from another ship to man her.

Tennyson's use of this sentimental motivation is significant because it places the responsibility for the tragic waste of the lives of men on the one thing the Victorian mind would, under the circumstances, find an acceptable excuse, the humanitarian desire of Sir Richard to rescue sick men. There is naturally no hint of such motivation in either Raleigh or van Linschoten. Tennyson owes it to Froude. Van Linschoten says only:

> But when they perceyued the kings Army to be strong, the Admirall being the Lorde *Thomas Howard,* commaunded his Fleete not to fall vpon them, nor any of them once to seperate their shippes from him, vnlesse he gaue commission so to doe: notwithstanding the Vice Admirall Sir Rychard Greenfield, being in the ship called the Reuenge went into the Spanish fleete, and shot among them, doing them great hurte, and thinking the rest of the company would haue followed: which they did not, but left him there, and sayled away: the cause why could not be knowne. . . .[24]

Raleigh's statement implies no more than that you cannot sail a ship without men. It also ignores the reaction of Grenville's men to their situation.[25] But Tennyson not only builds the heroics of the speech we have already quoted, he underscores

[24] Arber, *op. cit.,* p. 90.

[25] Moreover we learn from Sir Richard Hawkins, what neither Raleigh nor Tennyson suggests, that as vice-admiral it was Grenville's duty to be last in the fleet. The vice-admiral was the rear guard, to use a military phrase, and necessarily the last to leave the anchorage. See Arber, pp. 6–7.

it with what is clearly intended to be a noble pathos. A separate stanza is devoted to the gentle affection of strong men caring for sick comrades:

So Lord Howard past away with five ships of war that day,
Till he melted like a cloud in the silent summer heaven;
But Sir Richard bore in hand all his sick men from the land
Very carefully and slow,
Men of Bideford in Devon,
And we laid them on the ballast down below;
For we brought them all aboard,
And they blest him in their pain, that they were not left to Spain,
To the thumb-screw and the stake, for the glory of the Lord.[26]

This stanza demands attention. Tennyson's shrewd manipulation of fact is evident at the outset when he implies that Howard and the fleet were out of sight before Grenville had rescued his men. Absolutely to the contrary, Raleigh says:

The Foresight of the Queenes commanded by M. *Th. Vauisor,* performed a verie great fight, and stayd two houres as neere the *Reuenge* as the wether wold permit him, not forsaking the fight, till hee was like to be encompassed by the squadrons, and with great difficultie cleared himselfe. The rest gave diuers voleies of shot, and entred as far as the place permitted and their own necessities, to keep the weather gage of the enemy, vntill they were parted by night.[27]

Notice, then, in the detail added by the poet the concreteness of "bore in hand," with its suggestion of physical aid given men too ill to move unassisted. Notice too the repetition of *sick*—three times in fifteen lines. "Very carefully and slow" and the verb *laid* in "we laid them on the ballast down below" complete the picture of invalid helplessness and of the tenderness which it calls forth, and leave both firmly planted on the reader's mind. But perhaps the most skilled evocation of pathos in the stanza is the line "Men of Bideford in Devon." Tennyson's localization—it is solely Tennyson's—immediately calls up the charm of a small seaport town, the beauty of Devonshire, and

[26] Stanza III.
[27] Arber, *op. cit.,* pp. 25–26.

all that Victorian devotion could pack into the meaning of home. Once you know that these men are from a particular place they cease being lay figures and merely part of the *décor* of the drama. They become men. They have mothers and wives and children. And to the English reader, who might well know that Sir Richard was himself a Bideford man, the line could suggest that some of the sailors were bound to Sir Richard by years of acquaintance and by the almost patriarchal traditional loyalties of the county squire for the families of his estate and parish.

We do not know, as a matter of fact, where the *Revenge's* sailors came from. No Elizabethan source ever thought of indicating.

We are still not through with our stanza. "For we brought them all aboard" repeats what has already been once said ("bore . . . all his sick men from the land") with deliberate emphasis. The rhetorical device of repetition will not allow us to forget the strength of love in Sir Richard and his men, nor the pride of a strong man in his bravery. Then Tennyson sounds a double note: pathos again, in "they blest him in their pain" (the love of comrades is not one-sided), and, for the second time in the poem, the flamboyant anti-Spanish, anti-Catholic motive:

And they blest him in their pain, that they were not left to Spain,
To the thumb-screw and the stake, for the glory of the Lord.

"Left to Spain" implies, even without the final line, something threatening. But poets have always found the figure of speech, metonymy, effective, so Tennyson adds "the thumb-screw and the stake" to call to mind vividly and concretely some of the tortures of the Inquisition—and finishes the stanza with a final, savage sarcasm at the expense of Spanish Catholicism, "for the glory of the Lord."

It is worth attention that neither Raleigh nor van Linschoten expresses such a fear. Raleigh does include a violent attack on Spanish religion as a veil for hypocrisy, greed, and treachery, but only after he has recorded the fact that the

Spaniards offered jobs in the Spanish service to those Englishmen who survived the capture of the *Revenge*—a detail which again Tennyson carefully omits. Yet to include what he and Froude regarded as an essential part—and sound justification—of Elizabethan patriotism and, more important, the final and emotionally strongest justification of his hero's action, otherwise perhaps indefensible, he refers to the Spanish Inquisition in terms which remove the whole action from the field of intellectual consideration.

Undoubtedly the influence of his period is at work upon Tennyson here as obviously as it is in his sentimentalization. The bitter, long-continued debates over the complex problems of Irish government, religion, and education, together with the Oxford Movement and the conversion to Roman Catholicism of such prominent Anglican preachers as Newman and Manning, renewed for a generation or more much of the traditional anti-Catholic feeling of England. The horrors of the Inquisition became an especially potent symbol to Protestant Englishmen. Froude's *History of England . . .* (1856–1870) is strongly colored with it; the essay from which Tennyson here borrowed devotes pages to it. Charles Kingsley's popular historical novel *Westward Ho!* (1855), intensely propagandistic, anti-Catholic to the core, uses the Inquisition for some of its most melodramatic appeal. In 1870 England was particularly troubled by the Ecumenical Council, which met at Rome to decide, among other things, the question of Papal Infallibility. Tennyson's close friend Prime Minister Gladstone and his cabinet considered political action against the Vatican. And four years later Gladstone attacked the doctrine very energetically in a pamphlet, *The Vatican Decrees in their bearing on civil allegiance,* an attack renewed in the following year with *Vaticanism.*[28]

---

[28] We ask the reader to recall that Tennyson first became interested in the story of Grenville as a subject for poetry in 1873 and published the ballad in 1878. The extent to which the poet's own feelings were engaged by this mass reaction of his time is revealed in an anecdote told by his

It is also significant that in the last half of the nineteenth century the Inquisition was not entirely a thing of the past to the average English reader. Gladstone himself in another pamphlet in 1875 mentioned the case of an Italian priest who was condemned to life imprisonment by the Inquisition as late as 1863. It is true that he does not appear entirely convinced that the story was genuine; nonetheless he uses it in a propagandistic treatise.[29]

We have not the space to analyze all the poem fully, but a few further passages are too interesting to ignore. For instance, the poet suppresses entirely van Linschoten's harsh review of his hero's character:

> This sir *Richard Greenfield* . . . was a man very vnquiet in his minde, and greatly affected to warre . . . he had performed many valiant actes, and was greatlie feared in these Islands [the Azores],

---

friend Louisa E. Ward: "A large party was at their house one evening, and Tennyson was persuaded to read aloud, and chose the 'Revenge.' Something or other, I suppose the 'Inquisition Dogs' and the 'Devildoms of Spain,' excited him as he read, and by the time he had finished he had worked himself into a state, which I have occasionally, but seldom, seen at other times, of fury against the Catholic Church, as exemplified by the Inquisition, persecution of heretics, etc.; in fact, all the artillery of prejudice at which Catholics can afford to laugh. It happened, however, that my husband, one of my sisters, and myself were the only Catholics there, and were sitting together in the same part of the room. As he talked he turned towards us and addressed us personally in a violent tirade which loyalty to our convictions made it impossible for us not to answer, though our attempts at explanation and contradiction were drowned in his fierce and eloquent denunciations. Every one in the room looked very uncomfortable. I myself hardly knew whether to laugh or cry, and was never more relieved than, when his flow of words had exhausted itself, he began to read another poem."—Louisa E. Ward, *Tennyson and His Friends,* ed. by Hallam Tennyson (London: Macmillan & Co., 1912), pp. 316–317. Reprinted by permission of The Macmillan Company.

29 "Italy and Her Church," *Gleanings of Past Years* (New York: Charles Scribner's Sons, 1879), VI, 277. The philologist is in his full right in paying attention even to unwarranted stories of that sort. To him it may be more important to know what people say about an historical event than to learn the exact truth about it.

and knowne of euery man, but of nature very seuere, so that his owne people hated him for his fiercenes, and spake verie hardly of him. . . .[30]

Such a comment would have been disastrous to the effects of loving concern aimed at in the stanzas just analyzed.

Again in Stanzas XI and XII, at the climax of the poem, Tennyson entirely recasts the narrative, not only suppressing the true action, but even giving it a contrary meaning. Raleigh is our only factual source for what happened on the English ship after she had been rendered helpless, her powder exhausted, and many of her crew killed or wounded. Grenville himself was seriously injured. He commanded his master gunner to sink the ship rather than surrender, and an action developed, led by the principal officers on board, the captain and the master, which was little short of mutiny. It ended with the master and some of the men stealing away from the ship, despite Vice-Admiral Grenville, to arrange the surrender. Even to hint at such a mutinous clash between Grenville and his men would have destroyed Tennyson's sentimental values, especially when Froude had already shown the way with a much softened version.

But Sir Richard cried in his English pride:
"We have fought such a fight for a day and a night
As may never be fought again!
We have won great glory, my men!
And a day less or more
At sea or ashore,
We die—does it matter when?
Sink me the ship, Master Gunner—sink her, split her in twain!
Fall into the hands of God, not into the hands of Spain!"

And the gunner said, "Ay, ay," but the seamen made reply:
"We have children, we have wives,
And the Lord hath spared our lives.
We will make the Spaniard promise, if we yield, to let us go;
We shall live to fight again and to strike another blow."
And the lion there lay dying, and they yielded to the foe.

---

[30] Arber, *op. cit.*, pp. 91–92.

The effect of the poetical version is of a strong man defeated and preferring to die rather than surrender, but turned from his wish out of consideration for his men, who have moved him with a pathetic appeal. Once more Tennyson has rejected actuality for the traditional protective codes of the officer and the patriarchal gentry of England. There may be more of real drama in Raleigh's version, but it sadly lacks the display of ideal bravery and ideal comradeship needed to satisfy Tennyson.

The actual conclusion to this episode again wants the color of the ideal, for in Raleigh's account Sir Richard, as he is carried from his ship, faints and asks his men to pray for him —a fact touching enough in its quick insight into the physical and mental state of the man. But again it has no place in the ballad of the *Revenge*. Tennyson omits it and substitutes

And the lion there lay dying, and they yielded to the foe.
And the stately Spanish men to their flagship bore him then,
Where they laid him by the mast, old Sir Richard caught at last, . . .

The tone has been changed completely. The man has given place to the hero, and the eternal pathos of human weakness to the obvious metaphor of the dying lion, "caught at last."

In this same passage occurs another striking and typical suppression: Raleigh reports realistically at the time of Grenville's removal that the ship was "maruellous vnsauerie, filled with bloud and bodies of deade, and wounded men like a slaughter house." In omitting these details Tennyson is no doubt following the pattern of his age. Froude quotes only the phrase, "maruellous vnsauerie," either unwilling to shock the readers of the *Westminster Review* with the image of a bloody slaughterhouse, or afraid that the picture might somehow tarnish the luster of England's Forgotten Worthies. In Tennyson the detail is too ugly even to be hinted at. The gruesome is not heroic.

One more major manipulation of fact remains, Sir Richard's death. Raleigh tells us:

The Generall vsed Sir *Richard* with all humanitie, and left nothing vnattempted that tended to his recouerie, highly commending his valour and worthines, and greatly bewailed the daunger wherein he was. . . .

. . . . .

Syr *Richard* died as it is said, the second or third day aboard the Generall . . . the comfort that remaineth to his friends is, that he hath ended his life honourably in respect of the reputation wonne to his nation and country, and of the same to his posteritie, and that being dead, he hath not outliued his owne honour.[31]

This is distinguished praise, but again it does not fit the pattern of melodrama so clearly outlined in our poem. The proper end for a man whose most gallant heroism has led only to defeat is not to be nursed by his conquerors for two or three days. Art must correct the fumbling ineptitudes of life. So Tennyson ignores Raleigh and turns to van Linschoten, who conveniently does not say when Grenville died, and who, furthermore, gives Grenville some last words worthy of the occasion:

But feeling the hower of death to approach, hee spake these wordes in Spanish, and said: Here die I *Richard Greenfield,* with a joyfull and quiet mind, for that I haue ended my life as a true soldier ought to do, that hath fought for his countrey, Queene, religion, and honor, whereby my soule most ioyful departeth out of this bodie, and shall alwaies leaue behinde it an euerlasting fame of a valiant and true soldier, that hath done his dutie, as he was bound to doe. When he had finished these or such other like words, hee gave vp the Ghost, with great and stout courage, and no man could perceiue any true signe of heauinesse in him.[32]

Tennyson has done little more than cut and versify, though he has done that characteristically:

. . . they laid him by the mast, old Sir Richard caught at last,
And they praised him to his face with their courtly foreign grace;
But he rose upon their decks, and he cried:
"I have fought for Queen and Faith like a valiant man and true;

[31] *Ibid.,* pp. 24–25.
[32] *Ibid.,* p. 91.

> I have only done my duty as a man is bound to do.
> With a joyful spirit I Sir Richard Grenville die!"
> And he fell upon their decks, and he died.

One notices that in the poem the death is almost immediate upon Grenville's capture. One notices, too, that Tennyson, sensitively aware of that nineteenth-century conception of a gentleman which includes modesty as a prime virtue, discreetly omits Grenville's Elizabethan boast concerning his "everlasting fame of a valiant and true soldier." And finally one is aware that the poem omits the factual prose statement that Sir Richard spoke in Spanish and the doubting anticlimax, "When he had finished these or such other like words . . ." We must not be allowed to think of modifying detail. We move fast. We must not have our emotions dulled by a chronicler's conscientious doubts.

We need not examine all of Tennyson's suppressions and modifications, for they are all of a piece throughout the poem. They lead to a structural concentration upon the heroism of Grenville and his men, and they define that heroism in Victorian terms. For instance, Tennyson never lets us know that there were, besides the six battleships referred to by Howard ("We are six ships of the line; can we fight with fifty-three?"), nine or ten other ships in the English fleet; nor that two of the English ships gallantly stood by to do what they could to help Grenville, one staying on the scene all night. To have included such detail would have diffused the heroic force by making others share in it and by making the reader less conscious of the odds. Likewise the sentimentalizing of Grenville's relations with his men defines Tennyson's concept of the heroic, just as setting them against the Inquisition gives body to what could otherwise hardly be called pure-minded patriotism. Actually both reasons add up to the same thing: a correction of reality. This is the event and these are the characters not as they were, not even as they were supposed to be by a favorable propagandist, but as they ought to have been to provide a perfect epic episode. This need to remold fact into something more ideally heroic, or rather, something more near to the ideal of the heroic held by both the poet and his period, is the clue to our understanding of the poem.

We have thus far paid little attention to the purely verbal devices of the poem. In examining Tennyson's handling of his sources, however, our remarks have not been irrelevant to our subject of language and style. Why a poet has chosen one word rather than another, or used the metaphor that he has in a given place, or fashioned a certain rhyme scheme or pattern of assonance or alliteration, it is profitless to inquire until one is fully aware of what he seeks to do. We have been designing the only background against which the discussion of verbal detail can have any point in the consideration of art. We hope now to make it clear that Tennyson's tendency in choosing his words is exactly the same as his tendency to shape his facts into something more noble than reality.

The same negative and positive attitudes which govern the one govern the other. We have already seen the positive principle operate in Stanza III with the significant addition of "carefully and slow," and "Men of Bideford in Devon." The negative emerges as strongly in Stanza X and again in XIII. In X when Tennyson describes Sir Richard's being doubly wounded, he says, "But a bullet struck him that was dressing it suddenly dead." In place of the vague "him," Raleigh says, "his chirurgion." Did Tennyson object to the connotations of pain, ugly sight, and smell in his heroic scene? He has carefully bracketed it in a fourfold repetition of "Fight on!" so that the reader can think only of the heroism and not of the disgusting spectacle of a man wounded in his torso. (He has also substituted *side* for *body* as the place of the wound.) Or did he feel that heroism is more heroic and pathetic if wounds are dressed without the care of a skilled physician? Probably the former, since we find only the pleasant and gracious ". . . the stately Spanish men to their flagship bore him then," in place of Raleigh's comparison, already quoted, to the slaughterhouse. The omission has almost the character of taboo avoidance such as we saw in the earlier chapters of this book. Much as more recent poets and readers might disagree, Tennyson clearly felt (along with the majority of his contemporaries) that the physically repellent was as much at variance with a picture of a heroic ideal as the detail that Sir Richard's men were afraid of him.[33]

The positive principle shows up strikingly in a set of additions which run throughout the poem. In four places Raleigh refers to the Spanish ships as large: "the great *San Philip*," "so huge and high carged," "the great *San Philip*," "two mightie Gallions." He does not refer to the size of the *Revenge*.[34] Tennyson unobtrusively, by the use of single words and epithets, creates a feeling of overwhelming size on the one hand and pitiable, but gallant, littleness on the other, again reinforcing the emotional pattern of the poem. He directly refers to the *Revenge* six times. All but one of these references (and the exception will be given special analysis) is dominated by the word *little:* "the little Revenge" (33), "the little Revenge (36),

[33] That such handling of detail is neither casual nor accidental—that behind it stands a definite artistic personality with conscious theories about esthetics—is made clear again and again in Hallam Tennyson's *Memoir*. For example, "There were talks with Millais 'as to the limits of realism in painting.' My father hated the modern realism in painting and literature, notably as shown by the French schools. With regard to certain English pictures he said to Millais that from his point of view, 'if you have human beings before a wall, the wall ought to be picturesquely painted, and in harmony with the idea pervading the picture, but must not be made obtrusive by the bricks being *too* minutely drawn, since it is the human beings that ought to have the real interest for us in a dramatic picture.' "—I, 380–381.

Equally emphatic is this comment: "I agree with Wordsworth that Art is selection. Look at Zola for instance: he shows the evils of the world without the ideal. His Art becomes monstrous therefore, because he does not practise selection. In the noblest genius there is need of self-restraint." —II, 337.

[34] According to Arber, p. 8, however, she was "the crack ship of her class in the British navy," although that was the second, not the first class. Drake chose her as his vice-admiral's ship in the great channel action in 1588. She was selected as a model "by the first seamen of the time as the best type for future ships." She was only five hundred tons, but clearly not in any sense an inferior ship. The English ships were regularly much smaller than the Spanish galleons, to which they were in action often superior because of their greater maneuverability.

"mad little craft" (38), "one little ship" (107), "the little Revenge" (118). Against these are balanced the following references to the Spanish ships, in which subject, modifiers, and verbs are all made to suggest bigness. When first they appear in the action they are *"huge sea-castles heaving* upon the weather bow" (24). The participle as well as the epithet helps in the connotation. The next is more complicated, for number is used along with connotative verbs, and an action is presented in which the Goliath-like attitude of the Spaniards is brought directly into contrast with the insouciance of the David-*Revenge:*

Thousands of their soldiers *look'd down* from their decks and laugh'd,
Thousands of their seamen *made mock* at the mad little craft.

Size is further emphasized by rhetorical balance with repetition of "thousands" as the required enumeration of both soldiers and seamen.

In the third reference the italicized epithet as well as the participle phrases were added by Tennyson to Raleigh to make the lines: "Their *mountain-like* San Philip . . . of fifteen hundred tons . . . *up-shadowing high above* us with her *yawning tiers* of guns."

Line 43 continues the intensified description by taking Raleigh's "great" and heightening it with a significant verb plus a simile:

> . . . the *great* San Philip *hung above us like a cloud*
> *Whence the thunderbolt will fall*
> *Long and loud.*

Line 50 repeats "the great San Philip"—but this time with an irony that makes it serve a double purpose:

But anon the great San Philip, she bethought herself and went,
Having that within her womb that had left her ill content.

The "high-built galleons" of line 58, together with the surrounding passage, removes the concentration upon the *San*

Philip alone, and reminds us of the vast number of the powerful Spanish ships.

The total effect of these groups is heightened also by contrasting the "thousands" mentioned in lines 37 and 38 with the *Revenge's* "hundred" of 22 and 34, and the "poor hundred" of 76. In sum, the entire poem is colored by these contrasts of size.

Although Tennyson does not use many formal similes and metaphors, two force themselves upon our attention. One, "and the lion there lay dying," applied to Grenville after defeat, we have already noted. The other occurs near the beginning of the fight:

> And a dozen times we shook 'em off as a dog that shakes his ears
> When he leaps from the water to the land.

Both similes imply qualities of stalwart strength and fidelity in the English. Against them Tennyson has balanced a characterization of the Spanish also highly figurative:

> "To these Inquisition dogs and the devildoms of Spain."
>
> . . . . .
>
> And Sir Richard said again: "We be all good English men.
> Let us bang these dogs of Seville, the children of the devil,
> For I never turn'd my back upon Don or devil yet."

Evidently the connotative meanings of the word *dog* depend entirely upon context: *dog-hero* and *dog-devil* are two different dogs. But more important for us at the moment is the antithesis between the two characterizations and the consequent weighting of the reader's attitude. Tennyson allows the Spanish only one dignified description. It would be unfair to think that a concession only to the exigencies of history. For while it is true that Raleigh and van Linschoten make much of the courtesy with which the Spanish treated Grenville, it is also true that heroic poetry has allowed courtesy between greathearted foes ever since the time when Achilles entertained Priam in his tent. Therefore Tennyson can, after the climax of his poem, drop all suggestion of the violence of Grenville's feeling about his enemies;[35] and he can, in his own right as narrator, speak of "the stately Spanish men" and admit that "they praised him to his face with their courtly foreign grace." But one must note even here that the phrase "to his face" and the adjective "foreign" suggest a courtesy not in keeping with the reticence and reserve of "good English men." And Sir Richard spurns it by dying promptly.

In the next and last stanza Tennyson concentrates a powerful rhetorical device upon the captured "little Revenge." The detail of how she was sunk in a great storm along with the greater part of her Spanish captors is historical and is recorded in the various contemporary prose accounts, including Raleigh's and van Linschoten's. Tennyson's treatment is his own, and centers upon the figure of personification (this is the exception mentioned earlier in our discussion of the direct references to the ship):

And they mann'd the Revenge with a swarthier alien crew,
And away she sail'd with her loss and long'd for her own;
When a wind from the lands they had ruin'd awoke from sleep,
And the water began to heave and the weather to moan,
And or ever that evening ended a great gale blew,
And a wave like the wave that is raised by an earthquake grew,
Till it smote on their hulls and their sails and their masts and their
flags,
And the whole sea plunged and fell on the shot-shatter'd navy of Spain,
And the little Revenge herself went down by the island crags
To be lost evermore in the main.

After the concrete "swarthier," a word rarely used in English fiction and poetry to describe desirable brunette per-

[35] For instance, van Linschoten's account of Grenville's behavior while he was a captive: ". . . as he continued among the Spanish Captaines while they were at dinner or supper with him, he would carouse three or foure glasses of wine, and in a brauerie take the glasses betweene his teeth and crash them in peeces and swallow them downe, so that often times the blood ran out of his mouth without any harme at all vnto him, and this was told me by diuers credible persons that many times stoode and behelde him."—Arber, *op. cit.*, p. 92. Tennyson's private comment about this anecdote when he told it to Carlyle differed from his public literary attitude: "There's a man for you," he said. See *Memoir*, II, 234.

sons, and the meaningful abstract, "alien," Tennyson turns to personification for the pathos of the next lines. The ship herself mourns. And she longs for "her own." The line has the same quality of pathos possessed by "Very carefully and slow,/ Men of Bideford in Devon." The verbal device of personification produces it. And repetition in the next to the last line of the poem maintains its emotional spell.

An element of style which we have not yet discussed, somewhat different from period style, is the relation between the poet's individual manner and the stock of idiom—fixed patterns of diction and grammar, ideas already put into words—which he finds ready for him in his mother tongue. This figure of speech by which a ship has become a sentient woman, grieving for her dead as she goes to her own doom, achieves its ease, naturalness, and force by the peculiarity of English grammar which enables Tennyson to use the pronoun "she," "her," and "herself." Although English no longer usually exhibits grammatical gender, we commonly use it with a few nouns, of which *ship* is one. Even the greatest poet cannot shape a language of his own independently of the linguistic inheritance left by his ancestors; the easy strength of this thoroughly poetic figure is a slight but perceptive elaboration of an English habit of speech.

But Tennyson is still not through with the heroic justification of his action. Personification continues. The west wind *awakes from sleep*—a wind from the lands the Spaniards had ruined. With this localization divine vengeance is evoked, not, of course, for the capture of the *Revenge*—that might become absurd—but for the evil done in the New World by the Spanish in their greed for gold, a much more subtle shift since it places Grenville and his men squarely on the side of God. With powerful sound effects, with the prodigious simile of "a wave like the wave that is raised by an earthquake," with order of climax as that wave smites first hulls, then sails, and finally masts and flags, and at the end with hyperbole as the "*whole sea* plunged and fell," the Spanish fleet goes down.

The last descriptive word we get of it, however, is the adjective "shot-shattered." It was not the storm which ripped open the hulls of Spain: God and Sir Richard together have won the day. And the little *Revenge* sinks with the solemnity of perfect anapests in the final line.

Lest we seem to exaggerate the meaning of "a wind from the lands they had ruin'd," we quote Raleigh on this storm:

> Thus it hath pleased God to fight for us, and to defend the iustice of our cause, against the ambicious and bloudy pretenses of the Spaniard, who seeking to deuour all nations, are themselves deuoured. A manifest testimonie how iniust and displeasing, their attempts are in the sight of God, who hath pleased to witnes by the successe of their affaires, his mislike of their bloudy and iniurious designes. . . .[36]

And as evidence of a poet's tact in suppression as well as creation we also quote van Linschoten on the same point:

> . . . some of them openly said in the Isle of *Tercera,* that they beleeued verily God would consume them, and that hee tooke part with Lutheranes and Heretickes: saying further that so soone as they had throwne the dead bodie of the Viceadmirall Sir *Richard Greenfield* over borde, they verily thought that as he had a deuilish faith and religion, and therefore ye deuils loued him, so hee presently sunke into the bottome of the sea, and downe into Hell, where he raysed up all the deuilles to the revenge of his death: and that they brought so great stormes and torments vpon the Spaniardes, because they onely maintained the Catholike and Romish religion. . . .[37]

In making Spanish colonial administration the motive for divine vengeance Tennyson probably is indebted to Froude, who makes Spanish colonial brutality in the Americas a major theme of his essay. Raleigh mentions it only very briefly [38] and not in connection with the storm; van Linschoten, not at all. It is also interesting to note that Froude with the scepticism of his class and time here pointedly disavows any belief in divine intervention (although he allows himself to make a comparison, strongly loaded with the implication of God's aid in destroying enemies, with Samson in Gaza). Tennyson also was too much

---

36 Arber, *op. cit.,* p. 26.

37 *Ibid.,* p. 95.

38 *Ibid.,* p. 29.

affected by the thinking of his period to claim outright what Raleigh claims; he dares only to suggest it by subtle juxtaposition of ideas.

Two other verbal devices also assist at the creation of special dramatic and poetic effects. The first is Tennyson's infrequent but recurrent use of archaic grammatical forms: "Then *sware* Lord Thomas Howard" (4), "Then *spake* Sir Richard Grenville" (8), "We *be* all good English men" (29), "And the Lord *hath* spared our lives" (93), "And had *holden* the power and glory" (106), "*And or* ever that evening ended" (114). These six archaisms appearing at intervals from the first to the last stanza are just enough to give the poem a slight flavor of the past—to suggest the time when a battleship of fifteen hundred tons was mountainlike. To the literary romanticist they add dignity, too, echoing faintly the grave diction of the Bible and the great poetry of the Renaissance, contemporary to Sir Richard. They add to rather than detract from the effect of reality, for we have always found it easier to believe in the authenticity of romantic heroism in the past or far away. Tennyson's artistic deftness, furthermore, is apparent: to have used more, to have used Raleigh's grammar, for instance, as Chatterton tried to use Middle English, would have created an effect of quaint artificiality and literary affectation destructive of the illusion of the poem.

The second device is equally unobtrusive, equally effective. The poem begins and ends from the point of view of the omniscient author, which enables the poet to swing at once into swift action, without the need to identify a narrator. It also allows him to conclude with a description by one who can even see into the minds of the Spaniards, the soul of the *Revenge,* and the intentions of God. Then in the exciting main section he shifts us to the point of view of one of Grenville's men, a participant in the fight, by the use of the first person plural pronoun. The first use,

> And *we* laid them on the ballast down below;
> For *we* brought them all aboard,

heightens the pathos of a significant stanza. The reader shares the emotion of a man who has helped carry his sick comrades. As soon as one's thought has been captured by the consequent awareness that Grenville's men know their leader cares for his own (a good deal of which is dependent on the two *we*'s), one is quite prepared to believe that after Grenville's flamboyant, "Let us bang those dogs of Seville,"

> . . . *we* roar'd a hurrah, and so
> The little Revenge ran on sheer into the heart of the foe.

Even though the reader may know that, according to van Linschoten, Sir Richard "threatned both him [the Master], and all the rest that were in the ship, that if any man laid hand vppon it [the main sail], he would cause him to be hanged, and so by that occasion they were compelled to fight . . . ," [39] he still accepts the Tennysonian version, so vivid is the sense of unity provided by the participating *we*'s. *We, us,* and *our* then recur through the rest of the description of the fight: lines 41, 42, 52, 54, 62, 71, 72, 74, 75, 76, 77. The last group occurs in the summarizing picture of the results of the fight, concentrating the effects of the disaster upon the people who experienced it. Then suddenly they cease. The poem reverts to the third person, broken only by dramatic speech. So to the end.

Thus far our verbal analysis has dealt chiefly with the direct meanings or with the connotations of words. As with actual narrative detail, Tennyson's guiding principle has been the exaltation of romantic heroism in a tale from his country's past. Now however we come to a third factor. The pattern of the poem apart from its exclusion or inclusion of fact, its verse architecture, and, inseparable from its structure, the sound effects gained from its meter and rhythm, its rhyme, and its alliterations, dissonances, or alternations of vowels, all the many devices of word manipulation of which Tennyson was a master—these are of equal importance with the problems already discussed. Therefore we must now make specific some of

[39] *Ibid.*, p. 92.

the generalizations about sound symbolism and values with which we began our analysis, recalling always that verse structure and sound must be treated together. They interact upon each other too intimately to be divorced. And if poetry is not merely a mannered way of saying something which can be said just as well (or better) in prose, then the peculiar resources of poetry must be explored.

Tennyson calls his poem a ballad. But just as he has slightly flavored his diction with archaism, so in verse form he has only suggested the traditional ballad stanza and rhythm. The typical ballad (though there are many exceptions) has a four-line stanza of alternating iambic tetrameter and trimeter, a regular pattern, which suggests a recurring melody or tune. One of Tennyson's stanzas (verse paragraphs might almost be a better word) has twenty-one lines; the shortest has five. In meter the lines vary from two feet (dimeter) to seven (heptameter). And the rhythm is so fluid and variable that the safest name for it is simply duple-triple; dactyls and trochees occur so frequently that even iambic-anapestic is hardly accurate. Nevertheless he manages to suggest the ballad form, for most of the long lines (and some short ones) employ a heavy caesural pause, which tends to break the line in two and thereby approximates the common ballad swing. The device of internal rhyme, occurring intermittently but in nearly every stanza, further heightens the ballad effect.

For an audience which has long kept alive in its history ballads like *Chevy Chase* and *Sir Patrick Spens* it is easy to see why Tennyson would try to leave a balladlike impression. Why then did he not just write a ballad and have done with it? One may not be dogmatic about a poet's preferences, of course, but one may judge finished results: and what appears in the poem is that the duple-triple rhythm, variable meter, and irregular stanza lengths enable Tennyson to achieve effects which no fixed form would. Duple-triple rhythm is the most flexible and free of all rhythms, short of free verse. It permits a great deal of variation in the placing of accent and follows more closely than any other the natural rhythms of

English speech. It permits practically any phrasal pattern normal to English.[40] Moreover it is capable of a flowing movement which need never become monotonous to the ear. It can adapt itself to the colloquial freedom of "For I never turned my back," or the melodious swing of "Till he melted like a cloud in the silent summer heaven," with equal ease. It easily permits, in skilled hands, blocks of accented syllables and is therefore useful for onomatopoetic effects like "In the crash of the cánnónádes and the desperate strife." Combined with such varying meters and stanza lengths as Tennyson creates here, it can move from the urgency of, "For he said, 'Fight on! fight on!' " to the grave solemnity of the whole concluding stanza.

It is easy to understand why Tennyson, seeking to invoke the help of tradition as well as to preserve freedom for a variety of dramatic and descriptive effects, wrote a ballad, but wrote it in this form, suggestive rather than closely imitative of the traditional type.

Now let us examine some specific modifications of rhythm and meter.[41] Line 3 shifts suddenly into trochees: "Spanish ships of war at sea! we have sighted fifty-three!" [24] This is an obvious example of what Tennyson does throughout the poem: he varies the rhythm so constantly that it never has a chance to settle into the steady beat of anapests and iambs, which would have a tendency either toward monotony and an excessive, almost soporific, melodiousness, or toward jingling, which are the greatest dangers of the rhythm. But the change

---

[40] The greatest triumphs of poetry are achieved when this flexibility is reached in spite of the restraints of fixed form and self-imposed laws. Many a fastidious reader of verse prefers the fine balance between art and natural speech forced upon the poet by the requirements of iambic rhythm. The greatest poetry in English is rarely in duple-triple rhythm.

[41] Even though one may think the amount of variety to be so great as to render the name anapestic-iambic hexameters inaccurate there are still more of such lines than of any other one type. For convenience' sake, then, we can label a few of the many metrical and rhythmical peculiarities of the poem as variations from that pattern.

[42] The last half-line can be read either as trochees or as an anapest followed by iambs.

has a function perhaps even more important. The direct attack on the accented syllable is in this context dramatic. It gives the abrupt effect of a call, an urgent and unexpected warning. A rhythmical variation has become part of the dramatic and heroic structure of the poem.

The same device is used for much the same purpose in the line, "We have children, we have wives," from Stanza XII. The lines already discussed,

> Very carefully and slow,
> Men of Bideford in Devon,

get some of their sentimental meaning from the introductory trochees.

Other more subtle rhythmic modifications are equally significant, among them Tennyson's shifting the caesura or even omitting it altogether. The commonest line of the poem is one like

> And the stately Spanish men // to their flagship bore him then.

The caesura occurs exactly midway in a line which repeats for each half the pattern of anapest, plus two iambs.[43] Now compare

> And they stared at the dead that had been so valiant and true,
> And had holden the power and glory of Spain so cheap
> That he dared her with one little ship and his English few.

Each of these is pentameter. In the first only the fourth foot is iambic. In the next two the last foot of each breaks the anapestic beat. And the caesura is so light that the lines may even be read without it, though probably most readers would mark it briefly after *dead, Spain,* and *ship,* that is, after the second, the fourth, and the third feet respectively. Notice how the device throws emphasis on *dead,* on *so cheap,* and distributes it between *one little ship* and *English few.* And how the suspension of pause where you expect it forces the words *power and glory of Spain* into weighty place. Each accented word in these three

[43] The line may be read as trochaic octameter, if one chooses, but the caesura is unchanged.

lines is important. The thought must flow solemnly through them, for each contributes to Tennyson's exalted interpretation of the event. The careful lightening and shifting of the pauses until there is almost none save at the ends of the lines ensures the result.

But Tennyson is not yet through with his skilled manipulations. The next line breaks the pattern startlingly with the short, full-stopped half-line, intended to be climactic and sharp: "Was he devil or man?" Then it swings on in the familiar rhythm, "He was devil for aught they knew," for there is still a little narrative to be unfolded.

At least once the caesura was omitted entirely. The line, "Till it smote on their hulls and their sails and their masts and their flags," gets its force not only from the verb, in which both denotative and connotative meanings are strong, and from the order of its nouns, but also from the unbroken sweep of its perfect anapests in a stanza that has no other line like it. The next line, equally forceful, changes the pattern completely. The three stresses placed together on *whole, sea,* and *plunged,* followed by the iamb *and fell,* seem to suggest an accumulation of force and the climax of its being hurled against the ships:

And the whole sea plunged and fell on the shot-shatter'd navy of
Spain.[44]

Tennyson has also combined variation in rhythm and meter with the rhetorical device of repetition in a way that reinforces the structural pattern of the poem, as well as adds a vivid sense of the heroic continuation of the fight. The actual

---

[44] Here we are in the very difficult topic of sound symbolism, where students disagree. Tennyson specifically believed that he could and did represent physical movement by poetic rhythm:

"Warren asked him about his blank verse, and my father told him that it was very various, but variations in the metre were disliked by ordinary readers, such as

Dust, and the points of lances bicker in it—

the short syllables expressing the movement of the light."—*Memoir,* II, 403–414.

battle is the heart of the poem. It begins in Stanza VII to end in XI. Repetition runs through the entire account. The irony of Spanish defeat is developed by the repetition of the phrase "the great San Philip" in the beginning lines of Stanzas VII and VIII. Again in VIII repetition and clause-parallelism help to convey the sense of tense and spirited action:

> For a dozen times they came with their pikes and musqueteers,
> And a dozen times we shook 'em off as a dog that shakes his ears.

But the most striking is the framing device that brackets the action of the night with repetition and contrast. Stanza IX begins:

> And the sun went down, and the stars came out far over the summer sea,
> But never a moment ceased the fight of the one and the fifty-three.

Stanza XI adapts the lines to the dawn and the end of the fight:

> And the night went down, and the sun smiled out far over the summer sea,
> And the Spanish fleet with broken sides lay round us all in a ring.[45]

In between these two passages Tennyson twice repeats for emphasis. The rhythmically unique "For he said, 'Fight on! fight on!' " which begins X, also concludes it. Midway in IX occur three lines built on parallelism and made particularly emphatic by trochaic variation and by two pauses instead of the usual caesura:

> Ship after ship, the whole night long, their high-built galleons came,
> Ship after ship, the whole night long, with her battle thunder and flame;
> Ship after ship, the whole night long, drew back with her dead and her shame.

---

[45] Note the failure in the expected rhyme. It would be an irritating blemish, were it not picked up in line 73. As it is, it creates a neat suspension of sound to parallel the suspended statement Tennyson has to make about the Spanish attitude toward the *Revenge*.

The total effect of all these repetitions is to frame the structural climax of the poem. Such treatment not only gives the ballad special emphasis on its single most thrilling section; it also helps to impose an almost classic structure of introduction, mounting action, climax, resolving action, and denouement. It gives a sharpness of outline, a clarity and firmness of movement, which even Raleigh's expertly told version lacks.

The special sound effects which poetry uses more consistently than any other form of speech we can expect Tennyson to use conspicuously. To analyze them fully in a poem the length of "The Revenge" would expand the chapter forbiddingly—and unnecessarily, for the reader can find plenty of examples. We content ourselves with pointing out a few in the first stanza, which seem to us characteristic. The varying number of accents in the lines (the variation depending in part on the reader) and the heavy caesuras, accentuated in four verses by internal rhyme, reinforce the intended and significant ballad effect. The identical rhyme, "fifty-three," emphasizes at the beginning an essential thematic contrast and provides an interlocking device, giving auditory unity to an irregular stanzaic structure (Tennyson does not consistently use identical rhyme; he also uses in other stanzas widely spaced rhyme in addition to internal rhyme and couplet alternations for this same purpose). The suspension of internal rhyme in line 7, where one is led to expect it by the scheme of the preceding four lines, still further emphasizes the contrast between *six* and *fifty-three*. It also serves to break what would otherwise get to be an obvious and monotonous pattern. A number of other devices give oral texture to the stanza and occur throughout the poem: extra rhyme, *Flores—Azores;* alliteration, *flutter'd—flying—far, Spanish—ships—sea—sighted.* To the same end subtle differences exist between the vowel and consonant patterns of such lines as

Then sware Lord Thomas Howard: " 'Fore God I am no coward;
But I cannot meet them here, for my ships are out of gear,
And the half my men are sick. I must fly, but follow quick."

The first with its prevailing low back vowels, *r*-sounds,[46] and resonant voiced *d*'s, contrasts sharply with the prevailingly higher front vowels of the lines following, especially as these are reinforced with the less resonant, voiceless consonants *t, p,* and *k*. The impression made on two readers, at least, is that Tennyson, seeking to establish a dominant tone, intended to emphasize the gravity of an oath by giving it a resounding vocal effect, and to contrast it with the urgent speed of the rest by use of lighter sounds. Of course such variation also provides the shifting oral texture necessary to keep verse interesting to the ear in a poem of 119 lines.

Such material gives a fair estimate of one side of Tennyson's poetic personality: it shows something about him as an acoustic organism. But the psychological characteristics of a poet are bound to come out in his work just as definitely as the physiological and, like them, will continually influence his language in ways that are peculiar to him. One poem does not reveal the total poet of course, and we do not care to attempt an analysis of the secret places of Tennyson's heart. Still one cannot fail to see that "The Revenge" reveals attitudes habitual with him. Themes apparent here are over many years present in his other work: his admiration for the idealized heroic ("The Charge of the Light Brigade," "The Defense of Lucknow," "The Charge of the Heavy Brigade," "Epitaph on General Gordon," "Sir Galahad," *Idylls of the King*); his concern for the idea of British national greatness ("To the Queen," "On the Jubilee of Queen Victoria," "The Fleet," "Ode on the Death of the Duke of Wellington," most of the poems mentioned above); his liking for the English yeoman (*The Northern Farmer* poems, "Enoch Arden," "The Northern Cobbler"); his pleasure in themes from British history (the plays *Harold, Becket,* and *Queen Mary*); and his taste for obvious pathos ("Rispah," "Dora," "In the Children's Hospital").

Negative traits are equally apparent. Tennyson's bias toward softening the brutal and getting away from the ugly

[46] Spoken in a dialect which does not pronounce *r* in such locations, these would tend to lengthen the vowels they follow.

shows itself as clearly here as it did in the years of his concentration upon the *Idylls of the King* in place of writing about the nineteenth-century problems some of his contemporaries wished him to choose; or in his avoidance of the rude details of hopeless poverty in his poems of humble life. Carlyle recognized the tendency and summarized it when he said about "The Revenge": "I knew that Alfred would treat that episode in a masterful manner, and he'd not allude to Elizabeth's starving the poor sailors." [47]

While there is nothing in the poem that we cannot recognize as a part of Tennyson's poetic personality, we must be careful not to confuse the personality of the poet as artist with that exhibited in the ordinary circumstances of day-by-day living. The artist Tennyson refused to admit even of an Elizabethan sea dog that his reason for being in the Azores was to pirate Spanish gold, but the man could fret about the amount of cash he got for this very poem: Charles Tennyson reports that one time when the poet was reading "The Revenge" aloud to an audience "in the impressive chaunt which was so characteristic of him" he ended, with no change in attitude or expression, "and the scoundrels only gave me £300 for that. It was worth £500!" [48] The man Tennyson might admire a hero who like Grenville chewed up wineglasses, but the artist had no use for such a type. To the poet a word like *slaughterhouse,* or even possibly so innocent a word as *surgeon,* might be objectionable while the man could admire the Duke of Wellington for calling a fellow mortal a *damned fool.* Indeed the man Tennyson was himself not a stranger in the forbidden provinces of language. E. F. Benson tells the tale of the unfortunate composer who was listening to Tennyson read his own verse aloud:

> . . . at a pause in the reading, he said, "That's an awfully jolly stanza." Tennyson eyed him. "Don't say 'awfully,'" he said. "What shall I say then?" asked the composer. "Say 'bloody,'" said Tennyson.[49]

---

[47] Hallam Tennyson, *op. cit.,* II, 234.

[48] Charles Tennyson, *op. cit.,* p. 442.

[49] E. F. Benson, *As We Were,* p. 102. Copyright 1930 by E. F. Benson. Reprinted by permission of Longmans, Green and Company, publishers.

Another of Benson's stories illustrates one problem of personality still further:

A pleasant link between the author of so much noble verse and the lover of less exalted rhymes was his affection for the form known as the "Limerick." He liked its terseness, he also, it is idle to deny, took a sort of school-boy pleasure in the hectic situations which it sometimes disclosed. Little tales of the same sort pleased him: he could tell them himself with considerable gusto. In this connection I cannot forebear to recount a story which though I will not vouch for its authenticity, I give on the authority of Sir Edmund Gosse. He and my father [the Archbishop of Canterbury] were talking about Tennyson: they were contrasting him with Dickens; Dickens they agreed was not very markedly Puritanical in his life, whereas Tennyson was Galahad. But Dickens abhorred any sort of coarseness in conversation, whereas Tennyson had no great objection to it. Then said my father:

"Yes, that's quite true. I went out for a walk with him the last time I ever saw him, and he suddenly said to me, 'Shall I tell you a bawdy story?' Of course I said, 'No, certainly not.' "[50]

However the two personalities are not wholly separate. The one helps to shape the other. The artist's language has a way of reflecting the man, for the poet-personality is not a second ego but a super-ego. If we look back on "The Revenge," we seem to see in it one of the functions of dramatic dialogue. In addition to creating vividness, dialogue effects a compromise between the poet's dislike of vulgarism and the man's taste for strong language: "Let us bang these dogs of Seville, the children of the devil." The dramatic character in general not only represents Tennyson's high ideals; it makes possible his enjoyment of locutions which otherwise might have seemed to him not acceptable, without sharing in the responsibility for them.

But even if we are right in attributing this function to the speech of Sir Richard Grenville, it is exercised within very mild limits. The tale of the Archbishop and the Laureate is still pertinent. After a pause Gosse said:

---

[50] *Ibid.*, pp. 102–103.

"I feel sure Your Grace heard that story!"
My father was a little off his guard.
"Well, it wasn't so very bad after all," he said.[51]

Before we summarize, now, we must admit that, having been forced to give an extreme amount of detail in this chapter, we are afraid our thesis may have been blurred. Therefore we should like to emphasize that an author, however individual he may be, is not only an individual. He is also part of a historical tradition. His style, made up of many different elements from widely differing sources and colored by his own personality, still shows a unity characteristic of his period. Even so personal a thing as Tennyson's love for and skill at rich and pretty sounds cannot be thought of as unique in a time that also produced Rossetti, Swinburne, and William Morris—not to mention the hordes of lesser figures. Clearly the Victorians in general had a taste for melody in their verse and cultivated it. A passage in Leo Spitzer's *Stilstudien* illustrates our point. Language, Spitzer says, can and should be looked at analytically, the history of each element studied by itself. But it is equally necessary to look at language as a synthesis producing unity out of diverse elements, just as we attribute a certain style to a piece of architecture, calling this building Gothic and that Tudor although both may contain elements in existence long before the date of their origin. We translate:

It is a question of looking at language as a work of art, as something finished, the details of which lock together to form a whole. A comparison may make this clear. The processions of Brotherhoods during Holy Week in Seville combine elements from the most different cultural sources. The brethren in the penitential robes of the Counter Reformation; the wooden figures from the baroque and rococo periods; the repentant Magdalen with genuine woman's hair; soldiers escorting the processions in Napoleonic or still more modern uniforms; the completely unreligious military music; ditties in the style of folk songs sounding from the balconies; the architecture of the modern houses and streets which provide the stage for the processions; the public of believers, and perhaps also of unbelievers; the gentle-

[51] *Ibid.*, p. 103.

men smoking; the perspiring seat-sellers; the water carriers crying "Hay agua!"; the peddlers of children's balloons calling "Hay globos!"; the caramel-eating youngsters; the women in mantillas—all this gives a sum which cannot be understood by enumerating its component parts, a style, a unity, a total impression that cannot be grasped by definition but only by intuition. Or one may think of the composite character of a Catholic Mass, in which the effects of color, music, word, and movement stem from different times and cultures and still make a unified impression. The most diverse waters flow together to make one stream. In the same way one is justified not only in isolating each single linguistic phenomenon and studying singly the course of the tributary springs but also the result, the river, the style.[52]

---

[52] Leo Spitzer, *Stilstudien I* (München: M. Hueber, 1928), pp. 278–279.

Chapter Fifteen

HUMOR IN LANGUAGE

EVERYONE talks about humor but what the word means, or ought to mean, has never been satisfactorily described. There is an abundance of books called *Wit and Humor, Why We Laugh,* and so forth, but many of them are merely collections of jokes held together by superficial reasoning. Others, like Henri Bergson's *Le Rire,* may be valuable as attempts to explain the philosophy and psychology of humor, but cannot be very profitable to those who are interested in its linguistic aspects. There are, however, exceptions, and one of them, Freud's *Wit and Its Relation to the Unconscious,*[1] will be employed frequently in this chapter for its great usefulness in interpreting the foundations of humor.

Ourselves hard pressed for a definition of humor, we must say that we use the word in this chapter to denote any use of language which is intended to make one laugh. We do not find it necessary to differentiate between wit and humor, and we include such verbal tricks as puns, malapropisms, spoonerisms, and other intentionally wrong forms or departures from standard language.

No theory of language can be complete that overlooks the fact that humor is the force behind a great number of linguistic creations. Many people who have neither the wish nor the ability to enrich language by offering poetic or scientific ex-

[1] Sigmund Freud, *Wit and Its Relation to the Unconscious,* authorized English ed., with Introduction by A. A. Brill (New York: Moffat, Yard and Co., 1916).

pressions never before thought of will frequently indulge for humorous effect in exceptional forms of speech, in jocular distortions of words, metaphors, coinages, or in puns which bring out new facets of meaning.

These are the outward techniques of humor, however; not its most essential element. Not how it is done but what is done by humorous speech is the basic problem. We try to get a tentative answer in our first case. The election of President Rutherford B. Hayes was so close and the means by which each of the two parties tried to swing it were so unscrupulous that half the country refused to believe in the validity of Hayes's claim. As late as 1878 a Congressional committee was instituted to investigate what was known as the great fraud. The first witness called, a crooked politician and disappointed office seeker, James E. Anderson, tried to implicate the President and his friends, but without much success. To Hayes, however, the matter was serious enough to make him write into his diary something which has all the earmarks of self-justification. Not that he can have felt that his enemies would ever succeed in proving him a cheat. But they were calling him *Rutherfraud* Hayes. And, after all, he had seen Anderson personally; the man might have construed his early friendly words as a promise. So he began the entry in his diary of June 2 in a very grave mood, carefully recalling the exact circumstance of his interview, and repeatedly pleading to his own conscience that when the interview occurred he could not possibly suspect Anderson of the disreputable actions of which he was later revealed to have been guilty. In the middle of this serious self-defense there occurs a lighter touch:

> The election investigation began yesterday with calling as a witness the scamp Anderson. . . . He also testified that he called on me soon after I was inaugurated and got from me an endorsement to Secretary Evarts to give him a consulship in a warm climate.
>
> The facts are, so far as I am concerned. . . . He had a strong recommendation. . . . Nothing was said which led me to suspect that he had been guilty of any crookedness. . . . He appeared intelligent and capable. He represented that his wife's health required

him to go to a mild climate. Our interview lasted only a few minutes. I thereupon gave him a recommendation referred to. Afterwards . . . I learned . . . facts that made me suspect him. I also learned from Senator Matthews facts that induced the belief that he was trying to levy blackmail. I then directed that nothing should be done for him until his character was investigated. . . .

. . . . .

When Anderson was recommended by me for a place in a warm climate there was nothing before me against him, and much in his favor, but after I heard the facts against him, I was satisfied we had no place as warm as he deserved, and so he got nothing! [2]

The very fact that Hayes's final indictment stands as an element isolated but strong enough to intrude itself into a context of sober argument prevents our shoving it aside by calling it a touch of humor. It evidently performs the important functions of relieving the oppressive tension under which the author is laboring, and of enabling him to assume, if for only a moment, the superior attitude of the man who can joke about serious matters. In fact, we doubt whether there is any genuine humor without a serious background. The purpose of this chapter, therefore, is not to make the reader laugh or to enrich his stock of funny stories. We are concerned with the realities, often harsh, that make humor necessary, and, of course, with the techniques language employs to create humorous outlets.

We shall return to the Hayes story after having reinforced our judgment by analyzing another. It is very similar but, written for a wide and probably not very discriminating public, it lacks the elaborate delicacy of President Hayes's circumlocution. Common to both is the tendency to turn a grave matter into a laugh. The first was written in the privacy of a personal diary solely to relieve one man; the other owed some of its great contemporary appeal to the fact that it supplied the national community with a similar catharsis. One of the classic stories of Artemus Ward is the one in which that exhibitor of

---

[2] *Diary and Letters of Rutherford Birchard Hayes* (Columbus, Ohio: Ohio State Archaeological and Historical Society, 1924), III, 485–486. Reprinted by permission of the Society.

a menagerie comes to the rescue of President Lincoln, besieged by office seekers:

"Ef in five minits from this time a single sole of you remains on these here premises, I'll go out to my cage near by, and let my Boy Constructor loose! & ef he gits amung you, you'll think old Solferino has cum again and no mistake!" [3]

What makes this a humorous way of referring to the Devil? The combination of a grave and melodious cluster of sounds with a flippantly infernal meaning has something to do with it. Another element, frequently encountered in humorous language, is the allusion to events around which contemporary popular interest centers: the name *Solferino* is that of a place where a decisive battle between Napoleon III and the Austrians was fought in 1859, only one year before Artemus Ward wrote his sketch. This device is based on the same mechanism as the first—the drawing of great events into a trivial context. The meaning of the euphemism is made unmistakable by a clever use of the sound likeness between *Solferino* and *sulfur* and by the addition of the characteristic word *old*. All these devices belong to the common techniques of humorous language. All, however, merely contribute to the satisfaction the reader or listener derives from the successful eluding of a taboo.

Old Solferino has made possible the mentioning of the unmentionable. But why do we feel that it is funny, whereas the synonymous expression *Prince of Darkness* would not be? The right context could, of course, give *Prince of Darkness* a humorous slant, but ordinarily we feel that it implies in the attitude of the speaker complete acceptance of the taboo. *Old Solferino* reveals a rebellious attitude, not that of the serious revolutionist but a schoolboy levity. Apollyon in all his grim majesty is here having his tail twisted by a boy who not only enjoys the prank for its own sake but also because he feels sure of the applause of his schoolmates—in this case an audience still under the pressure of a taboo but no longer under its ab-

[3] Charles Farrar Browne, *Artemus Ward His Book* (New York: Carleton, 1862), p. 185.

solute dominion. Evidently rebellion must never develop into open warfare. Then the play spirit would vanish. On the other hand, if the taboo becomes so weak that its violator has no longer the delightful feeling of flirting with danger, of violating a law that is a law, then violation is pointless and ceases to be funny. The outward techniques of humor may be there, but the jest will have no salt.

To return to Hayes, it may be necessary to meet the objection that, writing for himself, he was not under the same obligation to respect word taboos as if he were writing for publication. Taboos, however, are not always forced upon us against our own will. Since they form part of the cultural pattern of our society, they tend to become automatic. They are accepted as part of the unwritten law in the same way that some English gentlemen upholding the burdens of empire in remote places have dressed for dinner, even though they dined alone. Hayes was an eminently correct person. We can imagine that in the heat of debate he might tell a man to go to hell; we cannot imagine that he would in sober mood sit down and write that he would like to send that man to hell. So we need not doubt that the inhibition existed strongly enough for him to act as his own censor. On the other hand, his careful way of building up to his circumscriptive expression (the repetition of *a warm climate, a mild climate, a warm climate, no place as warm as he deserved*) is a clear indication that he did not use it as plain euphemism, but that he relished his own resulting wit. He had a quite sufficient audience in himself.

In thus stressing the connection between taboo and humor, we have adopted a point of view from psychoanalysis. As the reader will recall from the chapters on style, we have preferred to avoid using psychoanalysis as a method of interpreting linguistic fact. Not that we think it impossible to discover ways by which it might be made useful in the investigation of personal style, but whatever attempts in that direction have been made do not seem very convincing. In dealing with humor, however, we do believe that Freud's basic ideas apply to such instances as these we have quoted. What Freud says about wit in the narrow meaning of the word may also be said, with some obvious modifications, about humor in general:

Wit permits us to make our enemy ridiculous through that which we could not utter loudly or consciously on account of existing hindrances; in other words, *wit affords us the means of surmounting restrictions and of opening up otherwise inaccessible pleasure sources.* Moreover, the listener will be induced by the gain in pleasure to take our part, even if he is not altogether convinced,—just as we on other occasions, when fascinated by harmless witticism, were wont to overestimate the substance of the sentence wittily expressed.[4]

The crucial words in this passage, *wit affords us the means of surmounting restrictions and of opening up otherwise inaccessible pleasure sources* (in the original German italicized by Freud himself), offer a promising approach to the understanding of humor in language.

As for the theory expressed in the last sentence of the quotation from Freud, it is easy to find illustration. Many of the famous retorts of history have had this weight. Even to later generations such witticisms sway opinion about many famous people, and contemporaries are more susceptible still.

How effective such wit can be in argument is clear from the following anecdote. When in 1848 the newly founded Free Soil party decided to make Martin Van Buren its presidential nominee, what attitude Daniel Webster would take became an important question. Would he forget that, only a few years before, Van Buren had been the leader of the Democratic party, which he had fought during all his political career? Or would he stick to the regular Whig ticket headed by the politically untried Zachary Taylor? On the first of September in his Marshfield speech Webster gave the answer. It culminated in a pun so devastating that forty years later it was still remembered by a younger generation of politicians:

The gentlemen at Buffalo have placed at the head of their party Mr. Van Buren, a gentleman for whom I have all the respect that

[4] Freud, *op. cit.*, pp. 150–151. Reprinted by permission of Rose Owen Brill.

I ought to entertain for one with whom I have been associated, in some degree, in public life for many years, and who has held the highest offices in the country. But really, speaking for myself, if I were to express confidence in Mr. Van Buren and his politics on any question, and most especially this very question of slavery, I think the scene would border upon the ludicrous, if not upon the contemptible. I never proposed any thing in my life of a general and public nature, that Mr. Van Buren did not oppose. Nor has it happened to me to support any important measure proposed by him. If he and I now were to find ourselves together under the Free Soil flag, I am sure that, with his accustomed good nature, he would laugh. If nobody were present, we should both laugh at the strange occurrences and stranger jumbles of political life that should have brought us to sit down cosily and snugly, side by side, on the same platform. That the leader of the Free Spoil party should so suddenly have become the leader of the Free Soil party would be a joke to shake his sides and mine.[5]

Many historians will certainly be of the opinion that Webster's criticism is not fair to Van Buren. They might point out that after eight years of Jackson's Spoils politics, Van Buren had hardly any opportunity to use a broom, even had he wished to do so, and that it was not he who betrayed his party but his party who had betrayed him. But to Webster's audience, and to the average reader today, the question of justice does not arise. Whether consciously or not, one is inclined to take wit for an argument.

The following history offers a further means of gauging the effects of an apt remark, especially of how long they may endure. During the campaign to take Richmond near the close of the Civil War, General Benjamin F. Butler took up a position at Bermuda Hundred, between the James and Appomattox rivers, in which he later found himself stopped cold by the Confederate Army. Reporting the situation to Grant, General Barnard said "that the position was like a bottle and that Butler's line of intrenchments across the neck represented the cork; that the enemy had built an equally strong line immediately

[5] *The Works of Daniel Webster* (Boston: Little, Brown and Company, 1856), II, 434.

in front of him across the neck; and it was therefore as if Butler was in a bottle." [6] Grant, impressed with Barnard's figure of speech, employed it seriously and apparently without malice in his report of the operations of the army under the date of July 22, 1865: "His [Butler's] army, therefore, though in a position of great security, was as completely shut off from further operations directly against Richmond as if it had been in a bottle strongly corked." [7]

That Grant did not use the image as a joke we know.[8] Whether Barnard intended a pun—"Butler . . . in a bottle" —we cannot say. But the point is immaterial. Whoever condensed it into the formula, "Bottled-up-Butler," during the period of harsh criticism that followed Butler's failure, was deliberately exercising such wit as he had. It clung to Butler as long as he lived. Throughout his subsequent career it recurs in the mouths of his political opponents time and again.

On an occasion in 1867 when Butler asked permission in the House to make a few remarks that were out of order, Congressman Eldridge said sarcastically, "I hope the House will grant unanimous consent and not permit the gentleman from Massachusetts to be 'bottled up.' " [9] And a few days later Representative Bingham replied to an attack made upon him by Butler, "Why, sir, such a charge, without one tittle of evidence, is only fit to come from a man who lives in a bottle and is fed with a spoon [Laughter]." [10]

When as co-managers of the impeachment trial of President Andrew Johnson, Butler and Bingham fought shoulder to shoulder against the President, one of the defense council,

[6] *Personal Memoirs of U. S. Grant* (New York: Charles L. Webster & Co., 1892), II, 151–152.

[7] B. F. Butler, *Butler's Book* (Boston: A. M. Thayer & Co., 1892), p. 855.

[8] See Wilkes's letter in *Butler's Book,* p. 854.

[9] *Congressional Globe,* 40th Cong., Vol. CCLXV (March 21, 1867).

[10] *Ibid.,* March 26, 1867, p. 364. The latter part of the remark refers to the accusation that Butler had personally appropriated some of the tableware from the hotel in New Orleans which he had used for his headquarters during the occupation of the city.

William M. Evarts, read from the *Congressional Globe* Butler's attack and Bingham's retort with evident relish, and drove home his point by adding with ironic innocence, "Now, what under heaven that means I am sure I do not know." The laughter that followed showed that his audience certainly did.[11]

As late as 1872 the pun was still very much alive. The Indianapolis *Daily Sentinel* used it in a series of savage attacks. Under the date October 3: "A few years ago *Bingham,* on the floor of Congress, sneered at the military achievements of bottled Butler . . . Butler . . . bottled by Grant . . . bottled Butler." The next day the paper returned to the attack rather more wittily: "The title *Butler* is an old Norman English name, derived from French *bouteille,* a bottle. . . . The ancestors of the distinguished Benjamin F. doubtless held some such responsible position in an old aristocratic family. Many of his remarkable instincts are therefore, without doubt, hereditary. His bottling himself up at Bermuda Hundred and other playful eccentricities are thus easily explained." The following day the paper used it once more: ". . . after he had fully uncorked his bottle of wrath. . . ."

The effect of this joke upon Butler's political career was such as to cause him to say that Grant's "thoughtless" phrase "was used more to my prejudice with the people of the country than anything else he could have said." [12] This admission is the more remarkable since there were certainly much more serious charges made against Butler as a result of his war record: there was the story of the silverware, the accusation that he had misused his military position for the benefit of business transactions carried on by his brother, and there was, above all, the notorious "Woman Order" of the occupation of New Orleans (May 15, 1862).[13] In all these cases Butler was in a

---

[11] *Trial of Andrew Johnson . . . on Impeachment by the House of Representatives* . . . (Washington: Government Printing Office, 1868), II, 329.

[12] Butler, *op. cit.,* p. 855.

[13] ". . . it is ordered that hereafter when any female shall, by word, gesture, or movement, insult or show contempt for any officer or soldier of

position to fight back energetically and not without success. Wherever facts were brought out against him, he did a good job of disproving, explaining, or, at least, denying them. He tried hard to use the same techniques to prove that the bottle joke had no justification in any act for which he should be held responsible. But who can successfully cope with a witticism or a nickname?

In the chapter on the nature of word-taboos we pointed out that, apart from general restrictions like the taboos against sex, obscenity, and the names of the Deity, there are also special ones arising from the social necessity of respecting the feelings of the persons one speaks to. This is the type of word prohibition drastically characterized by the proverbial rule that one should not speak of a rope in a hanged man's house. The first examples in the present chapter—those illustrating the taboo against *go to hell* and the word *devil*—show the use of humor to avoid general word-taboo. The stories about Butler lead us into the second type. The element of hidden criticism, which could not be brought out in plain language without infringement of Congressional rules of courtesy, is very apparent in Bingham's expression, "a man who lives in a bottle and is fed with a spoon." To the uninformed reader the last half of the clause could only mean that Bingham declined to consider Butler a worthy adversary and wished him to be regarded as a babe in arms compared to himself. But this comparatively innocent criticism is only a thin veil to cover an accusation, which Bingham would no doubt have liked to make but could not, that Butler was not only an incompetent general but also a thief.

In many cases, commonplace as well as classical, wit and humor have been used for such purposes. An anecdote told by Horace Greeley about President Zachary Taylor offers an ex-

---

the United States, she shall be regarded and held liable to be treated as a woman of the town plying her avocation." Quoted from James Parton, *General Butler in New Orleans; History of the Administration of the Department of the Gulf in the Year 1862* (New York: Mason Brothers, 1864), p. 327.

cellent illustration. The problem of presidential patronage is in American politics very ticklish. Few politicians care to admit openly that the president elected by their party makes undue use of his powers of appointment. But what cannot be explicitly charged may very well be expressed by a *double entendre.* Hence the following play on *turned out:*

> General Taylor at length avowed himself "a Whig, but not an ultra Whig"; and I believe that was about the literal truth. Zealous Whigs apprehended that he might, if elected, shrink from discharging the office-holders appointed by Tyler and Polk; but, after giving him a trial, they were constrained to admit that he "turned out better than had been expected." [14]

Another tale of Greeley's, commenting on a problem which is a perpetual source of frustrating worry to Congress—the problem of how to get its pay raised without dangerously offending the electorate—illustrates again the function of humor in making criticism possible. It is true that whenever a Congress attempts such an effort, people talk bluntly among themselves about Congressional graft, but it is another thing entirely to say to a member of Congress what one says to one's nonpolitical friends, especially if that member of Congress is perhaps one's most distinguished customer. Only a touch of humor can make the impossible possible:

> Congress, in time, raised its own pay to $8 per day, and $8 for every twenty miles in coming to and returning from Washington. In 1816, the pay was changed to $1500 per annum, the mileage remaining as before; but the people revolted at this, and swept out nearly every member who had voted for it. Henry Clay had not voted at all on the question; but he was Speaker when the bill passed, and was, therefore, held responsible for its passage. . . . Opposed for reelection by one-armed John Pope . . . Mr. Clay had all he could do, by popular addresses and personal appeals, to stem the tide of discontent raised by the passage of the Compensation Act; even his barber —a naturalized Irishman, who had hitherto been one of his most enthusiastic supporters—maintaining an ominous silence on the sub-

[14] Horace Greeley, *Recollections of a Busy Life* (New York: J. B. Ford and Co., 1868), p. 215.

ject, until Mr. Clay himself canvassed him, saying: "I trust I may count on *your* hearty support, as usual?" when he responded: "Faith, Mr. Clay, I think I shall vote *this* time for the man who can get but one hand into the Treasury." [15]

The Clay story illustrates still another point. Among the important things that Freud has taught us to understand is the function of humor in permitting us to derive pleasure from other people's misfortunes or shortcomings. That John Pope was crippled is a fact which adult social custom would ordinarily require us to ignore or mention only with a show of sympathy. The same fact, however, may spice a funny story, for it supplies a little extra fillip of taboo circumvention to the situation. Freud's explanation is that in these cases we regress from the moral and social codes of the grown-up to those of the child.

In the beginning of the chapter we said that in humorous word coinage lies an important creative force even in commonplace speech. Wherever men work or live together it operates, often anonymously, to give their speech a common basis in the slang of the initiated. Very often such words involve taboo avoidances, operating if successful, however, not on the individual but upon the group. This is particularly true of soldier-words, present in the speech of every nation and flourishing during every war—words that have in them an element of criticism directed against army institutions or else make it possible to speak of dangerous things in a way that avoids, frequently by flippancy, the connotations of danger.

It is very evident that in words like *brass* (which needs no explaining to contemporary America), *chicken-officer, G I-officer* (both terms in which the common soldier sits in harsh judgment), and *big and little wheel,* as applied, for instance, to a first sergeant and a company clerk, the ordinary man is voicing a criticism against institutions which he is in no position to criticize directly and with impunity. In *crow-tracks* (stripes), *scrambled eggs* (an officer's gold braid), *fruit salad* (decorations, medals, and the like) the same critical spirit plays upon some

---

[15] *Ibid.*, p. 218.

of the outward manifestations of military grandeur. When Very Important People become *Vipers,* one senses more than just boredom in the men who transported them. Probably the offended dignity of the private is as responsible as is his frustration when a severe disciplinary talking-to becomes *chewing* (capable of very obscene and sometimes funny metaphoric development) or *reaming.*

But the soldier has *gripes* against more than his officers and army institutions. He may be driven to humorous complaint about his fellows—hence, *buzz-boy, hangar-flying* (both from the Air Corps), *sack-artist, gold-bricking, Section 8,* and such obscenities (with their vividly metaphorical avoidance of taboo) as *browning,* or *brown-nosing.* Few armies have been well enough organized to escape criticism of food, again frequently humorous: hence *grease, axle-grease, salve* (all for butter or butter substitutes), *dog-biscuit, G I turkey, battery acid* (the lemon extract, strong with citric and phosphoric acids, used so widely in the Pacific Theater).

Words like *Snafu* and *Fubar,* not confined to the ordinary soldier, of course, probably owe their popularity to their complex appeal. They avoid an obscenity taboo by the slightest of margins (avoiding it especially after they were falsified into purity by the press, theater, and radio). They furthermore parody a highly departmentalized army's habit of using initials to indicate the multiple elements of organization. And they imply a marked criticism of the standards of military efficiency.

The steady grim fear which men in combat have to control, and which affects civilians living in a danger zone equally, is nowhere better illustrated than in the joking way in which the participant avoids the connotations of danger by tabooing it in precisely the same way that humanity has always tabooed its harshest words denoting death and the other malignant forces with which it is man's lot to deal. So in England the German rocket bombs were referred to as *buzz-bombs, whizz-bangs,* and *doodle-bugs,* terms no doubt adequately supported by official policy. Taboo is often useful. The American soldier referred to his identification tag, the unique value of which under certain circumstances is grimly apparent, as a *dog-tag*. The airman spoke of *hitting the silk*. The whole army referred to a peculiarly deadly weapon as a *bazooka*—a metaphor which reminded the speaker of all the raucous gaiety of one of the favorite toys of a radio comedian much in vogue.[16]

The word lists given by Professor G. H. McKnight in *English Words and Their Background,* written just after the close of the First World War show that there is nothing exceptional in the speech habits of the 1939–1945 war. The *doughboy* father of the recent G I had as rich a humorous slang, motivated by the same psychological forces, as his son. Here by way of brief illustration is McKnight's list of food terms:

> *slum* (gullion), *mess, chuck, grub, hash,* and *chow* for "food"; *bullets* or *artillery* for "beans"; *jawbreakers* and *hard tack* for "biscuit"; *native sons* for "prunes"; *spuds* for "potatoes"; *shrapnel* for "grapenuts"; *baled hay* for "shredded wheat biscuits"; *gold fish* and *deep sea turkey* for "salmon"; *red eye* for "catsup"; *punk* for "bread"; *gooey* for "hash"; *sand and specks* for "salt and pepper"; *corn wooly; hard oil* for "butter"; *sea gull,* naval for "chicken"; *sixteen to one* for "milk"; *leather* for "meat"; *strawberries* for "prunes." [17]

The generation which fought the American Civil War had the same habit: the ironclad *Monitor* became a "cheese box," [18]

---

[16] Inquiry among veterans has proved that all the words used above were genuine soldier-words in wide use. They were also felt by our informants to be commonly humorous and to contain also a critical or taboo-avoiding element. From the same source we are assured that many words contained in current lists of army slang cannot be considered authentic, or at least in general use. However the mere fact that numbers of people seem eager to enrich the actual G.I. vocabulary with inventions of their own bears out the view that humor, real or pretended, is an extremely prolific source of word creation.

[17] George H. McKnight, *English Words and Their Background* (New York: D. Appleton and Co., 1923), pp. 55–56.

[18] "Though but a pigmy beside the Merrimac, and an entire novelty for either land or water—'a cheese-box on a raft' . . ." "The undaunted little cheese box. . . ."—Horace Greeley, *The American Conflict* (Hartford: O. D. Case & Co., 1866), II, 118.

cannon were *putty-blowers,*[19] and the language was permanently enriched with *skedaddle.*

The word *skedaddle* can, by the way, serve as a very useful reminder that words of this type offer a large field for much-needed historical research. The flippant character of these words seems to have created a feeling, even among many trained linguists, that they are not worth-while subjects for the serious investigation required of linguistic study. With relatively few distinguished exceptions like Louise Pound and Allan Walker Read, the field has been left wide open to the unbridled imaginations of amateur etymologists.

The theory that *skedaddle* is of classic origin (Greek σκεδαννυμι "scatter") has, in spite of its intrinsic absurdity, at least the advantage that the Greek word actually exists—which is more than can be said for the proposed Scandinavian derivation, connecting the word with "Swedish *skuddadahl* and Danish *skydedehl,*" neither of them words with as much reality as *jabberwock* and *borogoves.* Yet even as serious a writer as Mencken finds it necessary at least to mention the possibility of a Greek or Scandinavian source with no severer criticism than "that no likely original can be found" for the Scandinavian and that "there is no evidence for" the Greek. At the same time Mencken is entirely too severe in his criticism of the theory that *skedaddle* was originally a dialect word from Northern English. In saying that "the English *skedaddle* has not been traced beyond 1862, by which time the American *skedaddle* was already in wide use," [20] he is right only insofar as it is true that in no place has the word been found in print in England earlier than that. But we cannot argue that the first appearance in print of this word marks its origin in view of the testimony of Lord Hill in the London *Times,* October 13, 1862:

---

19 " 'I wish,' says the *petit caporal* of the Engineer Company, patting his howitzer gently on the back, 'that I could get this Putty Blower pointed at the enemy, while you fellows are bridge building.' "—Theodore Winthrop, "New York Seventh Regiment," *Life in the Open Air* (Boston: Ticknor and Fields, 1873), p. 245.

20 Mencken, *Supplement One,* p. 239.

To the Editor of 'the Times'

Sir,—Your correspondent, in an article upon the American war, tells the public that the war has brought to the surface, and added to the American vocabulary, a new word, *viz.* "skedaddle."

My object in writing this note is to correct the above error. Skedaddle is a word commonly used in Dumfriesshire, my native home. To skedaddle means to spill in small quantities any liquids. For instance, a person carrying two pails of milk,—jabbling and spilling the milk right and left—would be skedaddling the milk. An interested observer would cry at once: "You bleak buzzard, don't you see you are skedaddling all that milk!" The same word applies to coals, potatoes, or apples, and other substances falling from a cart in travelling from one place to another. But skedaddle does not apply to bodies of men scattered, under any circumstances, either in peace or in war. The Americans totally misapply the word.

It is not their invention, of that you may rest perfectly assured.

Yours faithfully,
Hill

Dartford, Oct. 9 [21]

Lord Hill's statement that *skedaddle* is a well-known Northern dialect word is born out by a similar observation in the *Atlantic Monthly* [22] and by Joseph Wright's *English Dialect Dictionary,* which lists it as to be found in Lancashire and Northumberland as well as in Dumfriesshire.

Unless one wishes to believe that there was a conspiracy of Englishmen trying to deprive America of her claim to have coined the word, we have to admit that it must have existed in Britain for a considerable period of time before the Civil War.

Furthermore, when Mencken says that it is difficult to connect the English meaning of "to spill milk" with the American meaning of "to flee precipitately," he does not take into account the attested fact that the word can also be applied to dropping coal or potatoes from a basket; while the disorderly flight of routed men could hardly be compared to spilled milk,

---

21 Quoted in *Notes and Queries,* Third Series, II (October 25, 1862), 326.

22 *Atlantic Monthly,* XL (August, 1877), 233.

the upsetting of a basket of potatoes and their rolling away in all directions would furnish a vividly descriptive metaphor. There can be no doubt that the American word is a semantic adaptation of the English one.

The form type of *skedaddle,* the playful character that everyone recognizes in the word, makes it a member of a large family of humorous word coinages. In our list of soldier-words, *whizz-bang, doodle-bug, screaming meemies, buzz-boy, G I Jesus,* and *jungle juice* all belong to the same type. Such word formations characterized by rhyme, assonance, and alliteration are, of course, no monopoly of soldier slang. Many words belonging to the stockpile of humor in the common vocabulary —*heebie jeebies, colly-wobbles* (largely replaced by *heebie jeebies*), *hotsy-totsy, hunky-dory, okey-dokey, okey-doke, razzle-dazzle, fiddle-faddle, to flub the dub, son-of-a-gun* (in which rhyme has helped to create a euphemism)—have their origin in a universal tendency toward verbal play.

Again Freud furnishes the basis for understanding this tendency. He finds in humor, or rather in that form of humor generally called wit, a strongly developed element of regression into a period probably gone through by every adult speaker, a stage of linguistic development in which language is used as a toy. Everyone remembers from his own childhood, or can test by direct observation of children, the intense relish derived from the use of nonsense language. Karl Groos in his standard work on play devotes almost thirty pages to "Receptive Sound Play" and "Productive Sound Play," respectively. He quotes the horrific example of a little Spanish girl who

> "repeated from morning till night, for fourteen days, *toro, toro, toro,* or else *rapapi, rapapi, rapapi,* and took great delight in the monotonous rhythm. Another child, nearly three years old, kept up these refrains in speaking or crying, and would take a great deal of trouble to use them in answering questions, although his parents made every effort to rid him of this vagary. For three months this little parrot continued to repeat in a loud voice the syllables, unintelligible to himself or any one else, *tabillè, tabillè, tabillè.*" [23]

---

[23] Karl Groos, *The Play of Man* (New York: D. Appleton and Company, 1901), p. 35.

This stage in infantile speech development is usually not allowed to exhaust itself naturally but is cut short by exasperated parents and teachers, who very frequently have to resort to methods of more or less violent suppression. But such suppression in matters psychological and educational is never wholly successful. Some of these childhood creations find their way into accepted use within the family as nicknames, terms of endearment, and occasional substitute words; some, like *mama, papa,* and *dad,* have even become part of the general vocabulary. Others, or the suppressed desire to create new ones after the childish pattern, come to life after a long period of latency when people have children of their own or become intimate friends with other people's children. Perhaps the most notable example is Charles Dodgson, whose friendship with a little girl resulted in *Alice in Wonderland* and *Through the Looking Glass,* both of which exhibit a conspicuous regression into infantile types of word formation: *Tumtum tree, frumious Bandersnatch, The vorpal blade went snicker-snack, O frabjous day! Callooh! Callay!*

A word probably more common in the general vocabulary than any of Lewis Carroll's creations is *namby-pamby.* It was arrived at by means of a calculated and deliberate regression into infantile speech habits, and shows how ridicule can reinforce venomous aggression by concealing it under the mask of childish play. Henry Carey coined it as a name for Ambrose Philips in 1725 or 1726, using it as the title of a poem addressed to that harmless poetaster. We quote a few lines:

Let your little verses flow
Gently, sweetly, row by row,
Let the verse the subject fit,
Little subject, little wit.
Namby Pamby is your guide,
Albion's joy, Hibernia's pride. . . .
Namby Pamby's doubly mild,
Once a man, and twice a child;
To his hanging-sleeves restor'd,
Now he foots it like a lord;
Now he pumps his little wits,

All by little tiny bits.
Now methinks I hear him say,
Boys and girls, come out to play,
Moon does shine as bright as day. . . .
Now he sings of Jacky Horner
Sitting in the chimney corner,
Eating of a Christmas pie,
Putting in his thumb, oh, fie!
Putting in, oh, fie! his thumb,
Pulling out, oh, strange! a plum.
Now he acts the Grenadier,
Calling for a pot of beer.
Where's his money? he's forgot,
Get him gone, a drunken sot.
Now on cock-horse does he ride;
And anon on timber stride,
See-and-saw and Sacch'ry down,
London is a gallant town. . . .
So much wit at such an age,
Does a genius great presage.
Second childhood gone and past,
Should he prove a man at last,
What must second manhood be,
In a child so bright as he! [24]

Something like another kind of regression to childish speech forms can frequently be observed in student circles, perhaps for the reason that in their academic activities students are forced to use serious forms of speech more or less above their natural inclinations (they are also, of course, under considerable restraint of many kinds, always, whether significantly oppressive or not, well suited to cause rebellion). Naturally they grasp eagerly any opportunity of reverting, as soon as official pressure is released, to more uninhibited speech forms. The vast amount of undergraduate slang is a natural result.

The vogue for *spoonerisms* that prevailed in England during the eighties and nineties is a case in point. The man whose

[24] Reprinted by Henry Morley, *Burlesque Plays and Poems* (London: George Routledge and Sons, 1887), pp. 136–138.

name has thus been immortalized, the Rev. W. A. Spooner, was a Fellow of New College, Oxford, and later (from 1903 to 1924) Warden of the College. It is possible that he was responsible for some of the transpositions of sound attributed to him, but it is doubtful that so distinguished a scholar and university administrator was guilty of many. What is certain is that during the later eighties and nineties spoonerisms became a fad among the Oxford undergraduates and acquired, of course, a special zest from being attributed to a distiguished don. "A column of spoonerisms became a matter of course in the lighter undergraduate journals." [25] The trick caught on, as the habits of schools attended by well-connected youth frequently do, and became conspicuous enough that in April of 1898 so fashionable a magazine as *Vanity Fair* found it amusing to publish a cartoon of Spooner with the following comment:

> His chief flaim to came lies in his genius for metathesis, for he is the inventor of "Spoonerisms." The half warmed fish has risen to his breast; He knows all about Kinkuering Congs; His Cat has popped on its drawers; He has unwearily addressed beery wenches; and he will doubtless be grattered and flatified by his appearance in *Vanity Fair*.[26]

How the device achieved popularity, how little it is really due to the linguistic habits of its putative father, and how clearly it reveals the playful rebellions of undergraduates is made clear by an anecdote told by G. H. White, who says that "rambling up the scalps" was invented not by Spooner but by Adrian Ross in verses in the early *Tatler*. An Oxford Alpine Club, whose object was to scale the heights of the colleges and houses under cover of darkness, was suppressed because of a rash excursion on the roof of Spooner's house. Ross wrote a poem on the subject in which Spooner was represented as warning the aspiring youths "not to rouse my slaughters from their deep." [27]

---

[25] *Notes and Queries,* Twelfth Series, VII (July 10, 1920), 36.

[26] *Ibid.*, p. 35. It is worth noting that the list of spoonerisms attributed to Spooner in the quotation above is supposed to be genuine, whether correctly or not the present writers cannot say.

[27] See *ibid.*, July 24, 1920, p. 79.

In sum, the significant fact is that the play spirit of youth crystallized into a humorous and deliberate linguistic trick a phenomenon of language which is, of course, not in the least new. In the earlier nineteenth century the term *Marouski* (*Marrowske*) described the same thing.[28] Medical students had used it before the Oxford boys made it fashionable.[29] Thackeray recognized it as a slang device in 1854, when he placed it in the mouth of one of the fashionable characters of *The Newcomes:* "Dine with us at the 'Gar and Starter'?" [30] And in 1882 Tourgée used it in a schoolgirl letter in a popular novel describing contemporary America: "She is such a jolly girl, and her name is Hargrove, too, and we are 'sin twisters' as we call ourselves in sport, that is, twin sisters, you know." [31] Indeed its use in literature goes back as least as far as 1634, when Henry Peacham in *The Compleat Gentleman* related how a "melancholy Gentleman" substituted "I must goe dye a beggar" for "I must go buy a dagger." [32] And it is not of course confined to English. Paul T. Lafleur provides us with some French ones:

> . . . three illustrations, here offered, are authentic, and come, singularly enough, from Swiss pulpits. In the first, the preacher meant to say, "Que Dieu vous en fasse à tous la grâce," but prayed instead "Que Dieu vous engraisse à tous la face." An old-fashioned *pasteur,* wishing his congregation to sing the eighty-fourth hymn, attempted a newer mode of diction, giving it out as "le cantique vatre-quingt-vatre; je veux dire le cantique vatre-quingt-quatre. . . . Nous chanterons, mes frères, le cantique huitante-quatre." The most remarkable instance, however, was that of a celebrated pulpit-orator of Geneva who concluded a solemn peroration with the statement that on the judgment-day, "Dieu séparera les bis d'avec les bréboucs!" [33]

And German knows them as well. Although the German vogue for spoonerisms around 1900 does not appear to have been of

[28] *Ibid.,* July 17, 1920, p. 52.
[29] *Ibid.,* August 7, 1920, p. 117.
[30] Thackeray, *The Newcomes,* Chap. L.
[31] Tourgée, *Hot Plowshares,* Chap. XVIII.
[32] *Notes and Queries,* CLXII (April 23, 1932), 299.
[33] *Ibid.,* Twelfth Series, VII (December 18, 1920), 487.

academic origin, there are a few classic examples in which the students' disapproval of this or that teacher has found expression in *Schüttelformen.* In the auditorium of the well-known and highly esteemed Professor Holthausen one of the benches bore the inscription, "Lieber Holz hauen als Holthausen," and the students of an equally distinguished medical professor in Vienna used to delight in the *Schüttelreim,* "Bei Herrn Professor Wenckebach da bleiben kaum die Bänke wach."

Spoonerisms must be as old as the use of language by tired and absent-minded people, and by those in whom the spirit of play invites to a little joke.

The rhymester who perpetrated the following poem at once reveals how the trick can be manipulated by clever people and something, likewise, of the state of mind that produces genuine verbal slips:

Lines by An Oxford Don

My brain was filled with rests of thought
No more by currying wares distraught,
As laxing dreamily I lay
In my Canoodian canay.

Ah me, methought, how leef were swite
If men could neither wreak nor spite;
No erring bloomers, no more slang,
No tungles then to trip the tang!

No more the undergraddering tits
Would exercise their woolish fits
With tidal ales (And false, I wis)
Of my fame-farred tamethesis.[34]

Of course, a large element of the child's more or less suppressed pleasure in sound effects is for the adult sublimated into art. We find it serving a major function in the poet's conscious use of alliteration, rhyme, and other patterns of sound such as we have analyzed in the chapter on the language of

---

[34] Quoted *ibid.,* August 7, 1920, p. 117, from *The Globe,* June, 1895.

poetry, but it is not always expressed in ways so conventionally acceptable. The repetitions observed in children's sound play will sometimes crop out as mannerisms suggesting a retrogression into childhood's irresponsible disregard for conventional behavior, even in adults of brilliant and sophisticated intellect. Boswell records them as characteristic of Dr. Johnson:

In the intervals of articulating he made various sounds with his mouth, sometimes as if ruminating, or, what is called chewing the cud, sometimes giving a half whistle, sometimes making his tongue play backwards from the roof of his mouth, as if clucking like a hen, and sometimes protruding it against his upper gums in front, as if pronouncing quickly *too, too, too.* . . .[35]

Although a psychological analysis of this peculiarity is not within our scope we wish to call the reader's attention to Sir Joshua Reynolds' shrewd guess at the background of another, obviously closely related, of Johnson's mannerisms.

"Those motions or tricks of Dr. Johnson are improperly called convulsions. He could sit motionless, when he was told to do so, as well as any other man; my opinion is that it proceeded from a habit which he had indulged himself in, of accompanying his thoughts with certain untoward actions, and those actions always appeared to me as if they were meant to reprobate some part of his past conduct. Whenever he was not engaged in conversation, such thoughts were sure to rush into his mind; and, for this reason, any company, any employment whatever, he preferred to being alone. The great business of his life (he said) was to escape from himself; this disposition he considered as the disease of his mind, which nothing cured but company."[36]

If Reynolds is right, and if, as must almost certainly be true, Johnson's vocal habits and gestures belong to one and the same complex (which we cannot now try to interpret) of psychological difficulties, the *too, too, too* probably indicates some form of self-criticism. In Johnson's private world they served the same function of rejecting as nonsense the idea or mood of

[35] *Boswell's Life of Johnson,* Oxford Edition (London: Humphrey Milford, 1922), I, 324.

[36] *Ibid.,* p. 99.

the moment as the German *paperlapap* or the English *fiddle-faddle* serves in two-sided communication.

Paperlapap and *fiddle-faddle* are evidently used in order to tell the interlocutor that his comment does not even warrant a reasoned reply formulated according to the laws of adult speech. In the same way, even articulate nonsense may be used as a tool of criticism. President Van Buren in his *Autobiography* tells how the removal in 1824 of Governor Clinton of New York from the Presidency of the Erie Canal Board by political enemies—a deed intended to kill his political future—actually resulted in his triumphant re-election to the governorship. Popular sympathy had been aroused and Clinton won by the largest majority that had up to that time ever been won in the state. On the morning after the election Van Buren had breakfast with Judge Roger Skinner, who had been particularly responsible for Clinton's removal and who had tried to keep knowledge of his scheme from Van Buren:

> He was standing at the window, tapping the glass with his fingers, whilst I was taking my breakfast with what appetite his news had left me. I could not resist saying to him—"I hope, Judge, you are now satisfied there is such a thing in politics as *killing a man too dead!*" an observation sufficiently absurd to the general ear, but full of significance and matter for painful reflection to him. He left the room immediately without saying a word.[37]

It seems clear the outward irrationality of *killing a man too dead* conceals the sharp criticism that *what you did is just as nonsensical as what I say.*

To produce humorous effects a man may use childish speech and by this device enable himself to defy established rules and prohibitions. That this can be done with impunity is due to two reasons: first, the speaker violates a taboo oppressive not only to himself but also to the hearer, who is therefore in a position to enjoy the forbidden fruit without shaking the tree; second, by assuming the speech habits of a child the

---

[37] *The Autobiography of Martin Van Buren* (Washington: Government Printing Office, 1920), II, 144.

speaker makes it harder to apply the full rigor of the law. He makes himself so little that criticism must pass over his head. To the bribe offered the listener is added the flattery that the speaker assumes an attitude of inferiority.

This ability of humor to create a difference of level accounts for the popularity of literary characters like Mrs. Malaprop and Ring Lardner's semiliterate baseball players. In the continued success of the Artemus Ward kind of humor, the erratic ("funnatick") spelling is not so much a source of humor as a proclamation of it. This cloak of humor is the initial bribe offered the reader. The youngsters certainly, if not their elders, who enjoy the comic strip *L'il Abner* are pleased to find someone who knows less about spelling—or most things, for that matter—than they do. The cleverer writers who have used the style have known that it was an effective means of handling subjects which ordinarily have to be handled with discretion.

The development of Artemus Ward is very characteristic. Charles Farrar Browne became city editor ("local") on the staff of the Cleveland *Plain Dealer* on October 29, 1857. Three months later Artemus Ward made his appearance with the following letter among the local columns of the paper, which Browne had been enlivening with all sorts of jesting copy, largely written, one gathers, for the amusement of himself and the younger newspaper men who formed an admiring circle about him:

LETTER FROM A SIDE-SHOWMAN

Mr. Artemus Ward, proprietor of the well-known side-show, writes us from Pittsburg as follows:

Pitsburg, Jan. 27, 18&58.

The Plane Deeler:
Sir:

i write to no how about the show bisnes in Cleeveland i have a show consisting in part of a Calforny Bare two snakes tame foxies &c also wax works my wax works is hard to beat, all say they is life and nateral curiosities among my wax works is Our Saveyer Gen taylor and Docktor Webster in the ackt of killing Parkman. now mr. Editor scratch off few lines and tell me how is the show bisnes in your good city i shal have hanbils printed at your offis you scratch my back and i will scratch your back, also git up a grate blow in the paper about my show don't forgit the wax works.

Yours truly,
Artemus Ward
Pitsburg Penny

p S pitsburg is a 1 horse town. A.W.

We believe Mr. W. would do well with his show here, and advise him to come along immediately.[38]

The humor of this letter is almost entirely derived from the satire upon its supposed author. The reader is enabled to hold himself very superior to Ward not only because of his illiteracy, but also because of his naïve unscrupulousness and his business principles. The touch of irreverence perceptible in the juxtaposition of Our Savior with Parkman and Webster involves taboo circumvention, and there is in addition a lighthearted appeal to local Cleveland patriotism in the postscript, but these are minor sources of appeal.

Three weeks later (letter dated from Tiffin, "Febey the 23th, 18&58"), we find him developing his tabooed theme. Without the covering mask of illiteracy many of his readers would certainly have considered it bordering on the blasphemous:

the peple air delited with my show. my wax works is the prase of all. Among my wax works is the Lords last supper. the characters bein as large as life. A feller from the east part of Seneky County cum to my show and thot my Judus Iscarrot was alive. Sez he to me, yu jus take that sneakin cuss out this haul er ile smash his hed in. Sez i yung man that air is a wax work. Sez he wax work be darned, thats old Judus Iscarrot and if heze a man he will step out here and fite me. i kan stan a good deel but i gut all fired mad, and sez i yu ornary cuss keep away from my wax works or ile fall on ye. At that he made a lunge cross the table and seised Judus by the neck and dragged him out inter the middel of the haul and kommensed a poundin him. Sez he Judus Iscarrot cant show hisself with impunerty in tiffin by a Dam site. I finerly convinsed the pesky fool that it was a wax work. He

[38] Quoted in Don C. Seitz, *Artemus Ward* (New York: Harper & Brothers, 1919), p. 24. Reprinted by permission of Harper & Brothers, publishers.

larfed and said he would stan the old rye for he and me. Tiffin is a grate sity.[39]

By May 29 of the same year the little anecdote is expanded into a much more elaborate and daring form. No longer confining his jest to Judas alone, Browne broke the taboo surrounding all the apostles (not to speak of that protecting such historical heroes as George Washington, Generals Taylor and Winfield Scott, and Napoleon):

No man evir seen me intossikated but onct and that air happind in Pittzbug. A parsel of ornery cusses in that mizzerable sity bustid inter the hawl durin the nite and aboosed my wax works shaimful. I dident obsarve the outrajus transacshuns ontil the next evenin when the peple begun for to kongregate. Suddinly thay kommensed for two larf and holler in a boysterious stile. Sez i good peple whats up? Sez thay thems grate wax works isnt thay old man. I immejitly looked up ter whare the wax works was and my blud biles as i think of the site which then met my Gase. I hope two be dodrabbertid if them afoursed raskals hadent gone and put a old kaved in hat onter George Washington's hed and shuvd a short black klay pipe inter his mouth. His noze thay had paintid red and his trowsis legs thay had shuvd inside his butes. My wax figger of Napoleong Boneypart was likewize mawltratid. His sword was danglin tween his legs, his cockd hat was drawn klean down over his ize and he was plased in a stoopin posishun lookin zactly as tho he was as drunk as a biled owl. Ginral Tayler was standin on his hed and Wingfield Skott's koat tales were pind over his hed and his trowsis ware kompleetly torn off frum hisself. My wax works representin the Lords Supper was likewize aboozed. Three of the Postles ware under the table and two of um had on old tarpawlin hats and raggid pee jackits and ware smokin pipes. Judus Iskarriot had on a cocked hat and was apperently drinkin, as a Bottle of whisky sot befour him. This ere specktercal wuz too much fur me. i klosed the show and then drowndid my sorrers in the flowin Bole.[40]

As Browne went on he became conscious of the social function of the satirist. The light and undeveloped notes heard in his very early account of how members of the Ohio State Legislature in Columbus tried to "cum a Gouge gaim on me and

[39] *Ibid.*, p. 31.
[40] *Ibid.*, pp. 40–41.

kraul in to my show without Payin"; or of how Sandusky believed that Bunyan's *Pilgrim's Progress* was written in that city and first appeared in the pages of the local newspaper, or the satire on business and newspaper ethics implied in the very characterization of Ward himself rapidly became full criticism of the whole circle of contemporary habits, ignorances, and beliefs. And they soon included those time-honored follies which have been targets for all satirists since Aristophanes and Juvenal. His subjects ranged from the vulgarity of boasting advertisement and the absurdity of singing coloratura arias in foreign languages to the secessionist movement and the personalities connected with it.

Even as early as March 20 of his first year Browne had used Ward to satirize what he considered pompous sentimentality in Oberlin:

> So I opened in Kolonial Hall, which was crowded every nite with stujents, &c. Perfesser Finny gazed for hours at my Kangaroo, but when that sagashus but onprincipled little cuss set up one of his onarthly yellins and I proceeded to hosswhip him, the Perfesser objected. "Suffer not your angry pashuns to rise up at the poor annimil's little excentrissities," said the Perfesser.
>
> "Do you call such conduck as *those* a little excentrissity?" I axed.
>
> "I do," sed he, sayin which he walked up to the cage and sez he, "let's try moral swashun upon the poor creeter." So he put his hand upon the Kangaroo's hed and sed, "poor little feller—poor little feller—your master is very crooil, isn't he, my untootered frend," when the Kangaroo, with a terrific yell, grabd the Perfesser by the hand and cum very near chawin it orf. It was amoozin to see the Perfesser jump up and scream with pane. Sez I, "that's one of the poor little feller's excentrissities!"
>
> Sez he, "Mister Ward, that's a dangerous quadruped. He's totally depraved. I will retire and do my lasserated hand up in a rag, and meanwhile I request you to meat out summery and severe punishment to the vishus beest." [41]

In September appeared the *Celebration at Baldinsville in Honor of the Atlantic Cable,* in which pretentious local pa-

[41] *Artemus Ward His Book, ed. cit.,* pp. 66–67.

triotism is shown in all its naïveté, and in which the advertising uses to which business can put patriotism are made equally evident:

The Skool house was lited up in grate stile and the winders was filld with mottoes amung which I notised the follerin . . . sentimunt written by the skool master, who graduated at Hudson Kollige. "Baldinsville sends greetin to Her Magisty the Queen, & hopes all hard feelins which has heretofore previs bin felt between the Supervizers of Baldinsville and the British Parlimunt, if such there has been, may now be forever wiped frum our Eschutchuns. Baldinsville this night rejoises over the gerlorious event which sementz 2 grate nashuns onto one anuther by means of a elecktric wire under the roarin billers of the Nasty Deep. QUOSQUE TANTRUM, A BUTTER, CATERLINY, PATENT NOSTRUM. . . . Doctor Hutchinsis offiss was likewise lited up and a Transpirancy on which was painted the Queen in the act of drinkin sum of "Hutchinsis invigorater," was stuck into one of the winders. The Baldinsville Bugle of Liberty noospaper offiss was also illumernated, & the follerin mottoes stuck out—"The Press is the Arkermejian leaver which moves the world." "Vote Early." "Buckle on your Armer." "Now is the time to Subscribe." "Franklin, Morse & Field." "Terms $1,50 a year—liberal reducshuns to clubs." [42]

In a time like the years preceding and during the Civil War the satiric attitude would inevitably carry Browne into a position where he would have to say serious things. He managed to say them in an effective way because his by that time stereotyped disguise proved a means of correcting the excesses of exaggerated rhetoric. We quote from his "Fourth of July Oration":

I'm not a politician and my other habits air good. I've no enemys to reward, nor friends to sponge. But I'm a Union man. I luv the Union—it is a Big thing—and it makes my hart bleed to see a lot of ornery peple a-movin heaven—no, not heaven, but the other place—and earth, to bust it up. Too much good blud was spilt in courtin and marryin that hily respectable female the Goddess of Liberty, to git a divorce from her now. My own State of Injianny is celebrated for unhitchin marrid peple with neatness and dispatch, but you can't

[42] *Ibid.*, pp. 37–38.

git a divorce from the Goddess up there. Not by no means. The old gal has behaved herself too well to cast her off now. I'm sorry the picters don't give her no shoes or stockins, but the band of stars upon her hed must continner to shine undimd, forever. I'me for the Union as she air, and whithered be the arm of every ornery cuss who attempts to bust her up. That's me. I have sed! . . .[43]

In the same vein after the war had broken out Browne wrote the dialogue between Jefferson Davis and Artemus Ward from which we quote these few lines, calling special attention to the phrase, *the piece of dry-goods:*

"Wall, wall, Mister Ward, you air at liberty to depart; you air frendly to the South, I know. Even now we hav many frens in the North, who sympathise with us, and won't mingle with this fight."

"J. Davis, there's your grate mistaik. Many of us was your sincere friends, and thought certin parties amung us was fussin about you and meddlin with your consarns intirely too much. But J. Davis, the minit you fire a gun at the piece of dry-goods called the Star-Spangled Banner, the North gits up and rises en massy, in defence of that banner. Not agin you as individooals,—not agin the South even—but to save the flag." [44]

Our analysis of Artemus Ward, undertaken with a view to establishing the inseparability of the linguistic aspects of humor and its general technique and content, will have made the reader conscious of the fact that there can be a form of speech which we might almost call the "dialect" of humor. In this dialect all the laws of well-regulated linguistic use from the conventions of spelling and word formation to ethics may be suspended—and frequently are. Of course the thing we call the logic of language is likewise put out of use: "I tell you, feller-citizens, it would have bin ten dollars in Jeff Davis's pocket if he'd never bin born!"

As with any other dialect only a minority can use it with dexterity and to good effect. Not everybody can even understand it. When the great John Bright heard one of the Artemus Ward lectures in London, he could only comment that "its

[43] *Ibid.,* pp. 209–210.

[44] *Ibid.,* pp. 195–196.

information was meager, and presented in a desultory, disconnected manner."

We included Bright's comment to remind the reader that whoever talks about humor must be prepared to have others disagree with him about the very heart of the matter—what is, or is not, funny. To make sure ourselves what other people find of the humorous and of the contributing elements of humor, we conducted a little experiment. A class of forty-one patient students was given the following two versions of the same story to judge their humorous effectiveness. The first is General W. T. Sherman's account as polished formally for his *Memoirs:*

During this interview I inquired of the President if he was all ready for the end of the war. What was to be done with the rebel armies when defeated? And what should be done with the political leaders, such as Jeff. Davis, etc.? . . . As to Jeff. Davis, he was hardly at liberty to speak his mind fully, but intimated that he ought to clear out, "escape the country," only it would not do for him to say so openly. As usual, he illustrated his meaning by a story: "A man once had taken the total-abstinence pledge. When visiting a friend, he was invited to take a drink, but declined, on the score of his pledge; when his friend suggested lemonade, which was accepted. In preparing the lemonade, the friend pointed to the brandy-bottle, and said the lemonade would be more palatable if he were to pour in a little brandy; when his guest said, if he could do so 'unbeknown' to him, he would not object." From which illustration I inferred that Mr. Lincoln wanted Davis to escape, "unbeknown" to him.[45]

The second is the same story given orally by Sherman to Whitelaw Reid, "as General Sherman said Lincoln told it":

"I asked Mr. Lincoln explicitly, when I went up to City Point, whether he wanted me to capture Jeff. Davis, or let him escape, and in reply he told me a story."

. . . . .

"I'll tell you, General," Mr. Lincoln was said to have begun, "I'll tell you what I think about taking Jeff. Davis. Out in Sangamon

[45] Wm. T. Sherman, *Memoirs* (New York: D. Appleton and Company, 1875), II, 326–327.

County there was an old temperance lecturer, who was very strict in the doctrine and practice of total abstinence. One day, after a long ride in the hot sun, he stopped at the house of a friend, who proposed making him a lemonade. As the mild beverage was being mixed, the friend insinuatingly asked if he wouldn't like just the least drop of something stronger, to brace up his nerves after the exhausting heat and exercise. 'No,' replies the lecturer, 'I couldn't think of it; I am opposed to it on principle. But,' he added, with a longing glance at the black bottle that stood conveniently at hand, 'if you could manage to put in a drop *unbeknownst* to me, I guess it wouldn't hurt me much!' Now, General," Mr. Lincoln concluded, "I'm bound to oppose the escape of Jeff. Davis; but if you could manage to let him slip out unbeknownst-like, I guess it wouldn't hurt me much!" [46]

Nearly all the students preferred the Sherman-Reid version. Only two favored the Sherman. One of them placed himself beside John Bright in imperviousness, if not in intellectual and moral structure and grammatical skill, by commenting, "The first of the two paragraphs is the better of the two. The choice of words are by far the better than those chosen in the second paragraph. For example the word used in the illustration, *unbeknown,* is more effective and is better than the corresponding word in the second paragraph."

The reasons given by the thirty-nine students for preferring the second version over the first were sometimes general —"more vivid," "more characteristic of Lincoln stories"—but usually acknowledged that the different effect of the two stories is due largely to the way in which linguistic detail is handled. There was a general consensus of opinion as to the narrative value of the mention of *Sangamon County, old temperance lecturer, mild beverage, the black bottle,* and of colloquialisms like the repeated *I'll tell you, unbeknownst,* and *unbeknownst-like,* and colloquial understatements like *the least drop of something stronger.*

No one, however, seemed fully to realize why these details were felt to be improvements. We have to give our own theory

---

[46] Whitelaw Reid, *After the War: A Southern Tour* (Cincinnati, Ohio: Moore, Wilstach & Baldwin, 1866), pp. 32–33.

about this point. The style of the story is subservient to its purpose. Once more humor is used to make possible the saying of something that couldn't be said bluntly. The speaker does not find it possible to give the order to let Davis escape. His way out is to create a double of himself—a man in a similar dilemma —in the person of the temperance lecturer, who has an excusable thirst for something stronger than lemonade, but is in a position to suffer only frustration if he allows his ostentatiously publicized principles to guide his conduct. Therefore every detail which makes this man and his problem vivid (*very strict in the doctrine and practice of total abstinence, long ride in the hot sun, exhausting heat and exercise*), and every detail that lessens the distance between Lincoln and him (*Sangamon County,* where Lincoln himself once lived, and such familiar details of the Illinois setting as *the black bottle*) is a way of saying: "I am in the same position as this old man, and I am prepared to go any length to force my eyes shut in order not to see a problem I earnestly wish to ignore—but which also the country probably expects me, because of my position and principles, to see and act upon." The analogue also has a tendency to lower the importance of the Davis problem until the listener is tempted to regard the escape of the President of the Confederacy as no more important than the question of indulging in a drink of liquor.

The expression in language of this tendency toward identification is evidently to be found most clearly in the close parallelism between the concluding sentences: *I am opposed to it on principle. But if you could manage to put in a drop unbeknownst to me, I guess it wouldn't hurt me much!* as against, *Now, General, I'm bound to oppose the escape of Jeff. Davis; but if you could manage to let him slip out unbeknownst-like, I guess it wouldn't hurt me much!* The one important point breaking the parallelism (apart from the necessary variations required by the two situations) is the *unbeknownst-like* in place of *unbeknownst.* Nothing makes Lincoln's reason for using the story more obvious. The *-like,* a common dialect feature of general American (Wentworth's *American Dialect Dictionary* lists it North and South from the Atlantic Coast to California), was common in Lincoln's Illinois. Used here, however, out of its usual illiterate or semiliterate environment by an accomplished stylist and added deliberately to the *unbeknownst* of the temperance lecturer, it introduces a new element. It suggests an enhanced degree of self-consciousness, a note of humorous embarrassment, if not of guilt; Lincoln seems unwilling to admit completely to himself as well as to his listener the full force of what he is suggesting that that listener do. His dilemma, despite his analogue, is of course stronger than the moral crisis of the old temperance lecturer, and so is his resulting discomfort.

To reinforce our interpretation of the suffix *-like* we quote from a book which describes with considerable fidelity a culture in time and place very close to that of Lincoln. Edward Eggleston clearly felt the note of embarrassed understatement in *-like,* as he uses it in the following scene from *The Hoosier Schoolmaster:*

> Ralph came in sight in time to see the beginning of the fight, and he arrived on the ground just as Pete Jones went down under the well-dealt blow from the only remaining fist of Bud Means.
>
> While Ralph examined Bud's disabled left arm Pete picked himself up slowly, and, muttering that he felt "consid'able shuck up like," crawled away like a whipped puppy. To everyone whom he met, Pete, whose intellect seemed to have weakened in sympathy with his frame, remarked feebly that he was consid'able shuck up like, and vouchsafed no other explanation. Even to his wife he only said that he felt purty consid'able shuck up like, and that the boys would have to get on tonight without him.
>
> . . . . .
>
> Gideon did not feel any more honest pleasure in chastising the Midianites than did Bud in sending Pete Jones away purty consid'able shuck up like.[47]

Here at last we make an end, conscious that we have not exhausted our subject but believing that anyone who writes on humor will have to leave his chapter sort of unfinished-like.

---

[47] Edward Eggleston, *The Hoosier Schoolmaster,* Chap. XVI.

Chapter Sixteen

STANDARDS OF USE

HERE is a bit of streetcar conversation overheard in Columbus, Ohio, during the summer of 1943. Two girls were complaining about the scarcity of men and the general dullness of life. "Any more," sighed one, "I just ain't havin' no fun!"

"Well," came the crisp reply, "tain't cause you ain't went much lately."

To the average citizen who does not happen to use such locutions himself they are merely "bad" grammar, and the extent of his analysis is to wonder what is the matter with our public schools. The language training of most people is usually rather severely limited to learning how to make choices between what we are taught to regard as acceptable and unacceptable forms. If we are members of certain classes of society, we have undergone a lengthy conditioning in spelling, pronunciation, grammatical forms, word choice, and so on. Naturally then after we have spent years of our lives learning to differentiate between *ei* and *ie* spellings, for example, or words like *lay* and *lie,* and in acquiring a set of pronunciations similar either to that in vogue around us or, as we sometimes hope, to that prevailing in an area or class culturally or socially superior to our own, our curiosity about language is apt to be limited to one query: What is *correct?* We sometimes make the naïve assumption that if two ways exist of saying something, one of them must be wrong. And if we suffer from the common inferiority complex about our speech, we may even buy a book entitled *Five Thousand Words Frequently Mispronounced* or *You Don't Say!*—

with no guarantee that the opinions therein expressed are more than the author's own, or that they are any better than the reader's.

But the linguistic scholar brings quite different points of view to his study of usage. First of all, whatever forms people use for expression and communication are of interest to him in his search for scientific knowledge; he does not limit himself to middle- and upper-class canons of social acceptability or to the literary over the many types of the colloquial. His interest in regional dialect may be as great as his interest in the language of the political and commercial capital. He recognizes the jargon of the underworld. His concern is for the past as well as the present. And his work with pronunciation or the forms of grammar need not include any statement of preference whatever. Indeed he may be interested only in such a science as the mechanics of the production of vocal sound.

What place has the study of "standards" of usage, then, in such merely descriptive and scientific analysis of linguistic fact? And what is the approach of the scientific linguist to these problems?

Realizing that although they certainly are not standard English, "I just ain't havin' no fun" and "Tain't cause you ain't went much" are in their humble way still *good* English—clear, crisp, pointed expression, communicating immediately just what the speakers desired to say—the linguist would like to know why they are not standard, especially since they and other locutions like them are to be heard wherever English is spoken. What makes us call them illiterate? Why have they been condemned? And why with the enormous spread of popular education are they still heard so widely? Is there anything in their history to explain their vitality?

The three striking "illiteracies" in the conversation quoted are the double negative, the use of the past tense *went* for the participle *gone,* and the use of *ain't.* The provincialism *any more* for *of late, lately* belongs, however, so far as standard English is concerned, in much the same category.

Why after generations of teachers have labored the point

is the double negative still with us? Here history sheds much light. For it is not the double negative but the standard so-called logical form (usually described with the formula that two negatives make an affirmative) which is the intruder, and a rather recent one at that. The double negative is not a corruption of a more correct form: it is simply the old standard still preserved in popular speech despite a newer literary fashion. Anglo-Saxon used it regularly, used even triple and quadruple negatives: *ac he ne sealde nanum nytene ne nanum fisc nane sawle*. In modern standard English we must express it, "But he did not give a soul to any animal or fish." Literally translated, however, it reads, "But he gave not to no animal not to no fish no soul." In Chaucer's time the pattern was still the same. He used double, triple, or even quadruple negatives:

> But he ne lefte nat, for reyn ne thonder,
> In siknesse nor in meschief to visite
> The ferreste in his parisshe. . . .[1]
>
> . . . . .
>
> He nevere yet no vileynye ne sayde
> In al his lyf unto no manner wight.[2]

And centuries later Shakespeare still found a resounding double negative one way of exhibiting Mercutio's stubborn determination—"I will not budge for no man's pleasure, I." [3]

The native English pattern clearly called for a negative particle modifying the finite verb in negative statements. Such other negatives were then added as emphasis made desirable, the grammatical process being one of cumulative emphasis, not of logic.

But in the seventeenth century, under the influence apparently of formal Latin style where the "logical" concept that two negatives cancel each other prevails, English writers began to use only one negative to express a negative statement. Under

---

[1] *Canterbury Tales, Prologue,* lines 492–494.

[2] *Ibid.,* lines 70–71.

[3] *Romeo and Juliet,* Act III, scene 1.

the pressure of our vast complex of books, papers, popular education, and so on, the literary has become unquestionably the standard. Yet wherever speakers of English are not under a very strong book influence, the multiple negative is still a major pattern of negation. And not even the man who prefers the logical point of view would claim that the two negatives of "I ain't havin' no fun" make the affirmative, "I'm having fun."

The second problem we have to consider is the use of the past tense "went" for the past participle *gone* of standard English in "Tain't cause you ain't went much." Perhaps an added illustration will make the extent of the usage more apparent. George Cary Eggleston in the charming opening chapters of *The First of the Hoosiers* describes the efforts of the Methodist church to train its backwoods preachers of a century and more ago. A major study required by the Presiding Elders

> was English grammar, through the diligent study of which it was hoped that every young minister would presently learn to use a better English than that which he had learned from association. This result was not always realized. I well remember that one able and even eloquent preacher, past middle life, and sufficiently prominent to be assigned successively to the charge of the best churches in the larger towns, always said that "John the Baptist had went out into the wilderness." [4]

---

[4] George C. Eggleston, *The First of the Hoosiers* (Philadelphia: Drexel Biddle, 1903), pp. 98–99. Two other stories told by Eggleston in the same book reveal something of the social and psychological aspects of the problem of usage. The student of language can profitably consider both—in fact, the linguist must not ignore the soil from which language situations grow. If the reader still doubts that they are outside the range of the study of language, then we are afraid that we have written in vain. "I remember one case related in my presence by an old Presiding Elder. He said that upon one occasion, when going down the Ohio river on a steamboat, he had for companion a youthful minister whose bringing up had been of the rudest kind. The two were assigned to a single stateroom, and the Presiding Elder, observing in the young man a regrettable neglect of personal cleanliness, gently reproved him. Among other things he told the uncouth youth that he should brush his teeth every morning. The young man meekly accepted the chiding as a godly admonition, and in the morning when

Any native speaker of English recognizes that *have went* and the many similar expressions like *I've saw* and *I seen* are in very common English use. Among groups who agree to say *have gone, I've seen,* and *I saw,* however, such forms are condemned as symbols of at least an untutored, and probably a lower-class, background. Don Marquis neatly categorized the prevailing situation in the person of Aunt Matilda Stevens:

Aunt Matilda knew about "seen" and "saw," but she was a little shaky herself where "who" and "whom" were concerned.

There is a definite line of separation between persons who make mistakes about "seen" and "saw," and persons who make mistakes about "who" and "whom." Those persons who make mistakes about nothing more serious than "shall" and "will" are obviously superior to both. It is just as well to place Aunt Matilda at once, firmly in the grammatical middle classes.[5]

Nevertheless readers of the literature of the past do not condemn that great lady and bluestocking, Lady Mary Wortley Montagu, for writing, "All the verses were wrote by me." Lord Chesterfield remains the symbol of elegant fastidiousness despite his use of *spoke* for *spoken.* And Thomas Love Peacock, who wrote a century later, is still granted much learning and a pleasant style although he seems to have preferred such past tenses as *sprung* and *drunk.* Nor do Shelley, Thackeray, and Cardinal Newman lose their places as masters of English because they, on the other hand, sometimes used *drank* as a past

the two arose, he said to his mentor, 'I'm going to begin at once, and this morning I have used your tooth-brush. When we go ashore I'll buy one for myself.'

" 'No,' answered the older man, scarcely able to suppress a laugh, 'you may spare yourself that expense. In recognition of your effort to profit by my suggestions, I'll make you a present of that tooth-brush.' "—Pages 97–98.

The other tale referred to is "of a minister who, when called to account for his persistently ungrammatical speech, tearfully expressed regret, and added: 'Brethren, I can't help it. For years I have carried a grammar in my hat, but for the life of me I can't get it into my head.' "—Page 99.

[5] Don Marquis, *Sons of the Puritans* (New York: Doubleday, Doran and Company, 1939), p. 2.

participle. We recognize a strain of elegant mock-heroics, polished as polite irony is required to be, when Trollope writes of Mrs. Proudie, ". . . she did not even dream of the treacherous resolves which those two false men had made together to upset her in the pride of her station, to dash the cup from her lip before she had drank of it. . . ." [6] We even accept inconsistency of forms. During the last half of the eighteenth century Dr. Alexander Carlyle was one of the leading divines in the Established Kirk of Scotland, a learned and admired preacher, as well as an influential figure in the literary life of Edinburgh. In an oration full of formal rhetoric, delivered before the General Assembly of the Kirk, he said:

> Who have wrote the best histories, ancient and modern?—It has been clergymen of this Church. Who has wrote the clearest delineation of the human understanding and all its powers?—A clergyman of this Church. Who has written the best system of rhetoric, and exemplified it by his own orations?—A clergyman of this Church. Who wrote a tragedy that has been deemed perfect?—A clergyman of this Church. . . .[7]

Clearly with writers like Lady Mary Montagu and Anthony Trollope one recognizes a fact of history: this is the way they said it then. One perceives that usage here depends not upon logic but upon a convention—upon a changing convention. And the reader accepts the grammatical conventions of the past as he accepts the conventions of manners. But if there is a history behind these forms as used by distinguished people in the past, then there is a history behind the unschooled uses of the present. And today there is no reason why one form should be substandard, the other accepted, save the accidents of that history. In fact, in a considerable number of verbs usage among even the educated is still so fluid that great dictionaries like the Merriam-Webster list *sung* and *sang, sunk* and *sank, dove*

---

[6] Anthony Trollope, *Barchester Towers,* Chap. XVIII.

[7] *The Autobiography of Dr. Alexander Carlyle of Inveresk,* ed. by John Hill Burton (London: T. N. Foulis, 1910), "Supplementary Chapter," p. 589.

and *dived* as acceptable past tense variants in standard English.[8]

Why then have we made a shibboleth out of past tense and past participle forms? The history of the English strong verbs (those which form their past tenses and past participles by means of vowel change rather than by adding a final *-d* or *-t* sound to the infinitive) reveals a tendency toward simplification. Many have beome weak (i.e., they now, like the vast majority of all verbs in English, form their past tenses and past participles by adding a final *-d* or *-t*). The few that remain show a tendency toward making their past forms agree, as in *bind, bound, bound.* Some, however, maintain a threefold pattern like *drink, drank, drunk* and *write, wrote, written.*

When we read eighteenth-century writing, we recognize that the tendency to reduce verbs of the latter type to identical forms like the former was very strong, even among educated people like Lord Chesterfield. Analogy, the principle of making like things agree, is very powerful in language, and in these instances the principle of agreement has behind it the weight of not only the two-form strong verbs but also the thousands of weak verbs in which the past tense and past participle must agree with each other. *Went* as a past participle, then, represents a well-established tendency in English verbs. Had the tendency been allowed to continue unchecked, English might have reached a place where all past tenses and past participles would have become identical.[9]

The third of the illiteracies we have to analyze is *ain't,* used here in three ways, all "vulgar"; *I ain't* for *I haven't, it ain't* for *it isn't,* and *you ain't* for *you haven't.* But this by no means exhausts the possible uses of the word. It may be used in place of *am not,* and of *are not* in both numbers and all

---

[8] It is interesting, however, that although some good dictionaries still list *drank* as a past participle and we all admit that we occasionally "slip" into its use, no proofreader for a reputable publishing house would today permit so egregious an "error" to pass "uncorrected." It would be regarded as almost as bad as *had went.*

[9] The fact that *go, went, gone* is an anomalous verb, made up of two verbs originally quite independent of each other, while it complicates the early history of the verb, does not alter at all the problem of its modern use.

persons; the form *hain't* is also common; and *bain't* (*be not*) has had a long history. Any reader of eighteen- and nineteenth-century plays, fiction, diaries, and correspondence recognizes that not very long ago such forms were in standard colloquial use among well-bred people. Dean Henry Alford, an acute observer of mid-nineteenth-century usage, remarked it as in respectable use in his time, even though he disapproved:

> One word with regard to the colloquial contractions. . . . We occasionally hear some made use of, which cannot be defended. For instance, *"I ain't certain," "I ain't going."* This latter, in the past tenses, degenerates still further into the mere vulgarism, *"I warn't* going." This latter is heard *only* as a vulgarism; but the other two are very frequently used, even by highly educated persons.[10]

Dr. F. J. Furnivall (1825–1910), to whom more than anyone else English linguistic science owes its splendid collections and tools, was conspicuous for his habitual use of *ain't*.

Ain't, like the other forms we have been studying, is a natural phonetic development and no more a "corruption" of language than the other contracted verb plus negative forms—*don't, won't, shan't, can't,* and so on, words which are still regarded as good colloquial English, just as *ain't* was regarded not so long ago. Professor Otto Jespersen gives a fairly detailed history of the origin and extent of contracted negative forms including *ain't* in his *Negation in English and Other Languages*[11] and in Volume V of his *Modern English Grammar.*[12] Here it is enough to say that the thoroughly normal contraction of *have not* to *ha'n't* gives in modern English *hain't* by the same process of sound change that gives us our present pronunciation of the *a* in *behave* (*be* plus *have*). The *h*-sound in English, a mere aspiration, a rough breathing, is, as the history of dialects and of divided usage in the pronunciation of many words shows, one of the most easily lost sounds. This fact plus

---

[10] Henry Alford, *A Plea for the Queen's English* (London: Alexander Strahan, 1864), p. 95.

[11] Copenhagen: 1917.

[12] *A Modern English Grammar on Historical Principles* (Copenhagen: Ejnar Munksgaard, 1940), V, 426 ff.

the analogical pull of the other *ain't* forms (to be discussed immediately) makes *ain't* for *have not* a form simply to be expected. Much the same sort of thing happened to the vowel of *are not,* which, together with the loss of the *r* (in the same way that we lost the *r* of *forecastle, worsted, Worcester,* and the *r* of *cursed* and *burst* to give us *cussed* and *bust*), gives us *ain't* for *are not* in all situations. In *isn't, wasn't,* and *doesn't* the *s* tended to vanish (incidentally explaining *he don't* as well as the dialectal *wan't,* Dean Alford's vulgarism, *warn't*), and with *isn't* the shifting vowel pulled the word through *e'n't* to *ain't. Am not* contracted to *an't,* and then moved on to regularity with the other *ain't* forms. As a result of all the shifts we have one word *ain't* which may be used for all persons and both numbers for the present of *have* and *to be,* and naturally then in a variety of combinations with other verbs as in *ain't went.*

Our negative contractions have never been widely used in formal writing. They have remained colloquial. (The increasing frequency of their use in print in recent years is a sign of our own increasing tendency to favor informal expression.) Especially the contractions like *wa'n't, ain't,* and *don't* for *doesn't,* which vary greatly from their originals in sound and appearance, have been little used by the cultivated save in intimate writing. As a result the same processes that regularized our strong verbs and changed our system of negation eventually blotted *ain't* out of even the colloquial speech of the literate.

The whole matter, then, boils down to this: There is nothing that can be called corruption in any of our contractions. They are all phonetically regular; they are all amply supported by analogy. Furthermore, they have been degraded to characteristics of vulgar speech only more or less recently—as Jespersen's material shows. The situation is very similar, therefore, to that prevailing in the other two problems discussed in this chapter. A process was somehow stopped with very moderate success in regard to *don't* for *doesn't,* with almost complete success with *bain't,* with something in between so far as *ain't* is concerned. An important factor in the resistance appears to be the degree of deviation from the uncontracted form. Probably with *bain't* the fact that *be* itself is less used than formerly in common conjugational patterns is a major reason for its disappearance. Our language is probably impoverished by the rigidity of current dogma about *ain't* at least, for the usefulness to English of an equivalent to the French *n'est-ce pas* seems obvious. Nonetheless it would require a bold man to defy the convention. Even a scholar of Furnivall's redoubtable enthusiasm would find it almost impossible to use *ain't* habitually today. And the storyteller who now puts it in the mouth of one of his characters definitely intends his reader to understand that the character does not possess the conventions of contemporary linguistic culture, lives in a society where he may not use them successfully, or is one of those brave or neurotic rebels whose personal integrity requires him to flaunt all convention.

We must now assure our reader that these are not picked examples. Wherever one touches upon nonstandard forms one finds historical evidence of a valid development. That history is just as sound as the history of the standard. Many uses that we have lost or are losing have been just as widely current as these here discussed, were just as logical, just as euphonious, just as nicely adapted to the purposes of communication. But in the process of selection that derives from our human need to speak like our fellows, and especially to speak like those we admire as being above us socially or intellectually, the substandard uses have simply fallen into disrepute, for no other reason than that they have not received the sanction of the people who led. They have not belonged to the dialect which for purely nonlinguistic reasons was spoken by the powerful groups who have represented society's organized business and whose play has been most conspicuous. Or, and this is especially true of the last two hundred years, they have not fitted into the theories of those people whom a middle-class society found it profitable to employ to condition its children into the behavior patterns which have the special utility of being indistinguishable from everybody else's.

It was at that point in the mid-eighteenth century when a rising and wealthy middle class began to educate its children into conformity that there developed one of the most extraordinary combinations of forces ever to act upon language—the schoolteacher, the dictionary maker, and the writer of grammar, who no doubt with the help of the editor and printer (always looking out for the ease to be provided by systematized rules), undertook to codify these matters. Their decisions were often based not on the speech habits of even the educated, but upon written use, and that of a very small segment of the population; sometimes they represented no actual use but only the critic's theory as to what was more logical (that is, usually, analogical), more in keeping with "right reason" than actual use. On the literary level of our language the correctors in some cases succeeded amazingly, and nowhere to a greater degree than in the three problems we have just reviewed.

The extent and vigor of the movement toward "correctness" can well be seen in the pages of one of the most influential grammars of the eighteenth century, Bishop Robert Lowth's *A Short Introduction to English Grammar*. Here is part of the Bishop's comment on strong verbs:

> There are not in English so many as a Hundred Verbs, (being only the chief part, but not all, of the Irregulars of the Third Class) which have a distinct and different form for the Past Time Active and the Participle Perfect or Passive. The General bent and turn of the language is towards the other form, which makes the Past Time and the Participle the same. This general inclination and tendency of the language, seems to have given occasion to the introducing of a very great Corruption; by which the Form of the Past Time is confounded with that of the Participle in these Verbs, few in proportion, which have them quite different from one another. This confusion prevails greatly in common discourse, and is too much authorised by the example of some of our best Writers. Thus it is said, *He begun,* for *he began; he run,* for *he ran; he drunk,* for *he drank:* the Participle being used instead of the Past Time. And much more frequently the Past Time instead of the Participle: as, *I had wrote, it was wrote,* for *I had written, it was written; I have drunk,* for *I have drank* [*sic*]; [13] *bore,* for *born; chose* for *chosen; bid,* for *bidden; got,* for *gotten;* &c.

[13] That this slip is of course only a printer's error, and not the Bishop's, is amply clear from the rest of the chapter.

This abuse has been long growing upon us, and is continually making further incroachments: as it may be observed in the example of those Irregular Verbs of the Third Class, which change *i* short into *a* and *u;* as, Cling, clang, clung; in which the original and analogical form of the Past Time in *a* is almost grown obsolete; and, the *u* prevailing instead of it, the Past Time is now in most of them confounded with the Participle. The Vulgar Translation of the Bible, which is the best standard of our language, is free from this corruption, except in a few instances; as, *hid* is used for *hidden; held,* for *holden,* frequently: *bid,* for *bidden; begot,* for *begotten,* once or twice: in which, and a few other like words, it may perhaps be allowed as a Contraction. And in some of these Custom has established it beyond recovery. In the rest it seems wholly inexcusable. The absurdity of it will be plainly perceived in the example of some of these Verbs, which Custom has not so perverted. We should be immediately shocked at *I have knew, I have saw, I have gave,* &c: but our ears are grown familiar with *I have wrote, I have drank, I have bore,* &c. which are altogether as barbarous.[14]

Words like "wholly inexcusable," "absurdity," "perverted," and "barbarous" seem emphatic enough to convey Lowth's point of view, but it is still worth adding that he appends to this discussion a footnote listing thirty-two examples of error committed by "some of our best Writers." The authors thus stigmatized as guilty of barbarisms are Milton, Dryden, Atterbury, Clarendon, Addison, Pope, Prior, Swift, Bolingbroke, and Gay.

This movement toward fixity rather than fluidity of use has been until very recently basic to every grammar and handbook since the time of Lowth and his contemporaries. The unschooled have not been troubled by it, the great aristocrat has often ignored it, and accomplished writers have frequently exercised the rights of talent to regard whatever has been at all times English as English undefiled still. Nonetheless teachers and proofreaders and writers of textbooks have insisted upon it. A hundred years after Lowth we find the American critic Richard Grant White condemning Tennyson's delicate and

[14] Robert Lowth, *A Short Introduction to English Grammar* (London: J. Hughs, 1762), pp. 85–90.

skilled use of *sung* and *sang* as equivalent past tenses, even though he recognized the variation as a part of a conscious artistic effect. Having devoted pages to criticisms of Pope ("He writes, at pleasure, *you rid* or *you rode, they writ* or *they wrote, you was* or *you were*"), White continues:

His authority is evidently nothing worth in this respect; and the same may be said of poets generally, who, if they can make themselves understood, and get the flow and the sound of their verses to please their ears, shrink little from any perversion of the form, or even of the sense, of language. This is particularly true of the poets who preceded Dryden; but even Tennyson, in his most carefully finished poem, "In Memoriam," writes thus:—

"Then echo-like our voices rang;
We *sung,* tho' every eye was dim,
A merry song we *sang* with him
Last year; impetuously we *sang.*" [15]

While the current manuals of style and grammar usually admit the right of the creative artist to his own manipulation of language, the cautions prescribed by Lowth still prevail in their advice to the student and the average writer. Choice is allowed in only a few instances. Hours are still devoted to fixing the "correct" verb patterns in our schools and to sternly repressing *ain't* and double negatives. Yet the old patterns continue as normal in untrained speech—and often, naturally enough, in the utterance of the trained. The only difference is that, if we are trained, we feel we must apologize for them, and, if we hear them in someone else's speech, we call them illiterate.

The linguist has a perfect case in making the statement that our standards are often mere differences from another way of speech and by themselves neither more nor less lucid, euphonious, and logical, but he can say this only as a linguist. Conformity to the standard, however defective the reasoning on which it is based, is another matter. For certain standards of use now exist as speech forms characteristic of a community.

[15] Richard Grant White, *Words and Their Uses,* 3d ed. (Boston: Houghton Mifflin Company, 1881), p. 404.

Can one with impunity depart from them? Our schools, of course, have traditionally and with a greater or less degree of success maintained that only a rigidly defined standard is acceptable. As a result many people are in much the same cheerfully despairing frame of mind as the young man in Jack London's *Burning Daylight* known to be college bred because of his football reputation. The hero goes to him for a certain bit of linguistic information which has long troubled Americans, Scots, the Irish—in fact, most of the English-speaking world save perhaps that group of southern Englishmen who speak the "Received Standard" of Eton, Harrow, Winchester, and Rugby.

"Look here, Bunny," Daylight demanded, "which is right, *I shall be over to look that affair up on Monday,* or *I will be over to look that affair up on Monday*"?

The ex-football captain debated painfully for a minute.

"Blessed if I know," he confessed. "Which way do I say it?"

"Oh, *I will,* of course."

"Then the other is right, depend upon it. I always was rotten on grammar." [16]

Perhaps our question may find a partial answer by further illustration from the same romance. London's unsophisticated and unlettered hero, after striking it rich in the Alaskan Gold Rush went to San Francisco, there to play the role of a man of vast wealth. To prepare to do so, says London,

he studied the game and its rules, and prepared himself to take a hand. He even took private instruction in English and succeeded in eliminating his worst faults, though in moments of excitement he was prone to lapse into "you all," "knowed," "sure," and similar solecisms. He learned to eat and dress and generally comport himself after the manner of civilized man. . . .[17]

London's understanding of the social meaning of language is exact. To acquire standard speech forms, to learn not to say

[16] Jack London, *Burning Daylight* (New York: The Macmillan Company, 1910), pp. 166–167. Excerpts from this work are reprinted by permission of Charmian K. London.

[17] *Ibid.*, p. 125.

"knowed," is a part of the "game" for a man who intends to move in certain economic and social groups and to such a man they belong in the same category with learning to eat and drink and generally "comport himself after the manner of civilized man." [18]

The ways in which pressure may be applied to produce conformity are further illustrated by the *I shall* just referred to. The episode began when Daylight's secretary changed the grammar of a letter:

> One morning, signing up letters, he came upon an *I shall.* Glancing quickly over the page for similar constructions, he found a number of *I wills.* The *I shall* was alone. It stood out conspicuously. He pressed the call-bell twice, and a moment later Dede Mason entered.
>
> "Did I say that, Miss Mason?" he asked, extending the letter to her and pointing out the criminal phrase.
>
> A shade of annoyance crossed her face. She stood convicted.
>
> "My mistake," she said. "I'm sorry. But it's not a mistake, you know," she added quickly.
>
> "How do you make that out?" challenged Daylight. "It sure don't sound right in my way of thinking."
>
> She had reached the door by this time, and now turned, the offending letter in her hand.
>
> "It's right just the same."
>
> "But that would make all those *I wills* wrong, then," he argued.
>
> "It does," was her audacious answer. "Shall I change them?"
>
> *"I shall be over to look that affair up on Monday."* Daylight repeated the sentence from the letter aloud. He did it with a grave, serious air, listening intently to the sound of his own voice. He shook his head. "It don't sound right, Miss Mason. It just don't sound right. Why, nobody writes to me that way. They all say *I will*—educated men, too, some of them. Ain't that so?"

---

[18] In his details, however, London is certainly wrong. To bracket the dialectal *you all* and the colloquial *sure* in the same class with the illiterate *knowed* would be done by very few social groups indeed, and never by a competent student of language. London here shows a little hypersensitivity on his own part, probably because of his timorousness in the face of books written in the pedantic Richard Grant White tradition.

"Yes," she acknowledged, and passed out to her machine to make the correction.[19]

But at lunch Daylight heard an educated young Englishman use *I shall* several times, discussed the matter as we have seen with his friend Bunny, and on his way back to the office bought a grammar, "and for a solid hour, his feet up on his desk, he toiled through its pages."

" 'Knock off my head with little apples if the girl ain't right,' he communed aloud at the end of the session." The next day he dictated, "I shall meet you half way in this proposition . . . ," but not without, as London shrewdly observed, "a sheepish grin" as he confessed that his secretary was right.[20]

The obviousness of the illustration leaves little room for the commentator. The linguist can point out the failure of the standard to be necessarily "better" than the nonstandard, but only as a linguist. He may even on the basis of scientific gathering of the facts of usage question whether the standard is actually what it claims to be. But conformity, however defective the reasoning which supports it, is another matter. Insofar as a speech form is truly characteristic of a community one cannot with impunity depart from it—if one wishes to belong to that community. If one is to live, work, and play among people whose language follows standard patterns, or who think it does, one must learn to use them too under the threat of embarrassment—and sometimes of something more.

The handicap of not knowing the conventional forms is put with miserable clarity in the official account of the *Trial of Andrew Johnson, President of the United States, before the Senate of the United States, on Impeachment by the House of*

---

[19] *Ibid.*, pp. 165–166.

[20] *Ibid.*, p. 167. It is worth noting that if Daylight's educational career had taken place approximately forty years later he and Bunny would have found learned and staunch authority for their preference in such books as Albert H. Marckwardt's *Scribner Handbook of English* and Charles C. Fries's *American English Grammar.* The studies of each bear out Daylight's observation that educated Americans do say *I will,* and therefore each recommends the expression as standard in American English.

Representatives for High Crimes and Misdemeanors.[21] In testing the credibility of a newspaper reporter, Henry F. Zider, as a witness to, and the reliability of the newspaper accounts of a speech delivered by the President in St. Louis on September 8, 1866, Benjamin F. Butler, conducting the cross-examination for the House of Representatives, managed to fill nearly two and one half pages of the official report with questions about and discussion of the President's nonstandard grammar and provincial pronunciation. Despite the witness's firm denial that the President pronounced *Judas:* "Jud-a-as," *yes:* "y-a-s," *were:* "ware," and substituted the plural *ware* for the singular *was,* Manager Butler succeeded in placing the competency of President Johnson's oral speech under question. Butler's forensic skill, shown in the following summarizing quotation, is no more deadly than the implication of incompetence he managed to cast over Johnson:

Q. Then all your corrections are of pronunciation and grammar, are they not?
A. The President did not use those words.
Q. Do you say that the President does not pronounce *were* broadly, as is sometimes the southern fashion?
A. I say that he did not use it as used in that paper.
Q. Did he not speak broadly the word *were* when he used it?
A. Not so that it could be distinguished for *ware.*
Q. Then it is a matter of how you spell pronunciation that you want to correct, is it?
A. The tone of voice cannot be represented in print.
Q. And still you think *were* best represents his tone of voice, do you?
A. I think it did.
Q. Although it cannot be represented in print. Now, sir, with the exception of these corrections in pronunciation and grammar, is there any correction as the speech was printed in the Democrat on Monday from that which was printed in the Republican? [22]

Ostensibly the contest between Butler and Zider has been about the relative reliability of two newspaper accounts. Actu-

---

[21] Published by order of the Senate, Washington, 1868.
[22] *Trial of Andrew Johnson . . . ,* I, 652.

ally Zider does not challenge other unimportant verbal variants but emphatically insists that the President did not use the "ungrammatical" forms and dialect pronunciations attributed to him in one of the accounts. The inference can only be that he regarded the use of these forms as lowering the dignity of the presidential office—an opinion obviously shared by the inimical Butler, as his ingenious way of leaving them in the record as if proved makes clear. Again the principle emerges that, even though not every poor American boy will become president, it is well to speak the speech of those who will sit in judgment upon you.[23]

But if that generalization is true, then it also follows with very simple logic that whenever those who will sit in judgment upon you do not themselves employ a standard dialect, you may use it yourself only at some risk of offending them. You put yourself outside their speech community by using a speech more literary than theirs. Politicians have long known the truth of that. While we recognize the skill with which popular language has been handled by certain well-known political figures in our own time, we are inclined to be surprised to find that some of the traditionally great masters of oratory from the American past have, it would seem, practiced the art of popular communication with equal effectiveness.

Patrick Henry, whose one most famous speech we know only in the polished form tradition has left us, emerges from the pages of his biographer as a man as much at home in the vulgar tongue as he was in the standard. That his great oratorical gifts really did include elegance and polish, however, we know from the effect he had upon such judges as Thomas

[23] As a matter of historical fact we have the sworn testimony of an expert stenographer that President Johnson did at other times, even on the occasion of a formal address, use such forms as "you and I has saw," corrected by the reporters for newspaper publication. This testimony was unchallenged by other expert witnesses (See *Trial,* I, 285). We also have stenographic testimony of his use of the dialect form *wa'n't* (I, 329) and *don't* for *doesn't* (I, 332), likewise in a major speech, likewise corrected by the newspapers, and likewise unchallenged as evidence in the impeachment trial.

Jefferson and the delegates to the Continental Congress in 1774. He could sway the most critical audiences of his day with an eloquence which they found comparable to that of Demosthenes and the Bible. But he was also an adept at backwoods colloquialism. His biographer, William Wirt, says:

> . . . he saw very distinctly, that all his hopes rested on the people's favour. He therefore adhered to them with unshaken fidelity. He retained their manners, their customs, all their modes of life, with religious caution. He dressed as plainly as the plainest of them; ate only the homely fare, and drank the simple beverage of the country; mixed with them on a footing of the most entire and perfect equality, and conversed with them, even in their own vicious and depraved pronunciation.[24]

To this last disapproving phrase Wirt adds a footnote:

> Governor Page relates, that he once heard him express the following sentiments, in this vicious pronunciation:—"*Naiteral* parts *is* better than all the *larnin* upon *yearth;*" but the accuracy of Mr. Page's memory is questioned in this particular, by the acquaintances of Mr. Henry, who say, that he was too good a grammarian to have uttered such a sentence, although they admit the inaccuracy of his pronunciation, in some of the words imputed to him.[25]

We cannot at this late date vouch for the accuracy of the Governor's linguistic observation, but it matters little whether these words were used precisely as here recorded. Henry's friends admitted that "he was frequently careless and sometimes incorrect." And since Governor Page's comment fits so perfectly into his general pattern of behavior as described by Wirt, we feel justified in believing it to be probably more true than Wirt's uncomfortable denial.[26] The lawyer and politician who had to deal both with Lees and Randolphs and with the

---

[24] *The Life and Character of Patrick Henry, ed. cit.*, pp. 52–53.

[25] *Ibid.*

[26] As often, the critic tells as much about himself as about the man he describes. Wirt's sense of shock reveals that as a child of his age he was accustomed to thinking of dialects as "vicious and depraved" speech and also that a man who knows the literary standard and deliberately condescends to use a "lower" speech form demeans himself.

plain people who elected him and who sat on the juries before which he tried his cases, shaped his language as he chose his food, drink, manners, and clothes. Wirt's account of his dress, indeed, helps us to understand his linguistic range and variety in its proper context. At home and in the country Henry was negligent of his dress, but,

At the bar of the general court, he always appeared in a full suit of black cloth, or velvet, and a tie wig, which was dressed and powdered in the highest style of forensic fashion; in the winter season, too, according to the *costume* of the day, he wore over his other apparel an ample cloak of scarlet cloth; and thus attired, made a figure bordering on grandeur.[27]

The implied analogy is sound. Standards of speech are like clothes, and the wise man has more than one suit.

When we acknowledge "correct" speech habits as a social asset, however, we must never forget that there is a difference between "correct" expression and good style. Style is the art of effective and efficient expression, of leaving with an audience the exact impression you wish. Here is an example of "bad" English as very good style. Judge Priest leaves exactly the impression he wishes and achieves the popularity he is after. To use literary English for the concluding remark would be as unfortunate stylistically as to use dialect grammar and pronunciation for the first:

"Such being the case, this term of Circuit Court stands finally adjourned." In the midst of a scrape of feet and a rustle of moving bodies, he ponderously labored down the two steps of his stubby dais, on the instant ceasing to be the earnest and seasoned jurist, most careful in speech and most punctilious in behavior, that unfailingly he was when on the bench and, in this same magical instant, became the homely, deliberately ungrammatical, dram-drinking lover of all good things, that he was when off the bench. From the doorway of his private chambers he whimsically addressed the spinal columns of the departing crowd: "I mout add that ef any one of you-all should keer to communicate with me durin' the next few days, you'll

[27] *Life and Character of Patrick Henry,* ed. cit., p. 423.

probably find me sojournin' by the placid waters of Moundbuilder Creek." [28]

The way in which good style—i.e., style adapted to the needs of communication with a particular audience—must take precedence over mere correctness is even more effectively illustrated in the autobiography of Wilbur L. Cross. After a long and distinguished career as an author, Professor of English at Yale, and Dean of Yale's Graduate School, Cross entered politics to become for eight years Governor of Connecticut. As a literarily trained professor used to the ways of academic discussion he did not in his campaign speeches "hit the trail at once" (p. 230). But he soon learned to deliver "a familiar cracker-barrel talk seasoned with the native dialect which they all liked to hear." [29] His new art he illustrated with the following inelegant but for that very reason skilled and effective bit of rhetoric:

This conversation led to the trouble I had with settin' hens. "Take the eggs out from under one," I said, "and throw her out of the nest, and she will come back as soon as she is left alone. Put chestnut burrs into her nest in place of eggs, and she will still come back. The only way to get rid of a settin' hen is to kick her out of the coop. Likewise the Republican organization and its leader have been settin' on rotten eggs for fifteen years without hatching out any chickens. The only way you can get rid of this old hen is to throw her out into the snows or cold rains of next November." [30]

---

[28] From *Judge Priest Turns Detective,* by Irvin S. Cobb, p. 126, copyright 1934, used by special permission of the publishers, The Bobbs-Merrill Company, Inc.

[29] *Connecticut Yankee, ed. cit.,* p. 231. Further definition of what Cross means is to be found on page 36 where, describing the political forum nightly congregated in a rural general store, he says, "There was no parliamentary restraint in that Yankee House of Commons. Everyone spoke the language to which he was accustomed, however profane or indecent it might be. Never before nor since have I heard so many double negatives for emphasis; never before so many allusions to sexual and other functions of the human body or to the hencoop or barnyard. It was the raciest speech God or Satan ever put into the mouth of man."

[30] *Ibid.,* p. 232. Reprinted by permission of the Yale University Press, publishers.

Apart from the undeniable popularity value of "incorrect" speech to those who must live on the favor of the democratic masses, it must also be pointed out that school language is often weak and anemic in comparison with the living speech of the people. Even grammar, quite apart from crisp metaphor and pungent phrase, can illustrate that. No doubt the late Secretary of the Navy, Frank Knox, knew the conventions of grammar as well as the next man. Nevertheless in a speech early in World War II he used the expression, "It's them or us," and was justly praised for committing this "mistake" by a radio commentator (over WHKC, Columbus, Ohio, May 8, 1942), who stated that in this connection he preferred *them* to *they* "because it packs a big wallop."

The scholarly and fastidious A. E. Housman recognized the superior, mouth-filling sound of *them* for emphatic statement (for packing a wallop) just as surely as did Secretary Knox. Consequently his famous poem, "Terence, this is stupid stuff," includes the two lines,

> They shook, they stared as white's their shirt:
> Them it was their poison hurt.[31]

With the same shrewd understanding that grammatical orthodoxy must not be allowed to interfere with style, E. M. Forster begins his very literary causerie on *Anonymity* (in literature) with the sentence, "Do you like to know who a book's by?"—and immediately establishes the tone he seeks, that of a cultivated gentleman talking in friendly, casual fashion with other cultivated people.[32]

Lest the reader think that the habit of disregard of con-

---

[31] From A. E. Housman, *A Shropshire Lad* (New York: Henry Holt and Company, 1900). Reprinted by permission of Henry Holt and Company, publishers.

[32] *Anonymity* (London: L. and Virginia Woolf), 1925. Since the problems of a standard of usage are so clearly sociological in nature, it is worth noting that the question bothersome to Marquis's Aunt Matilda is here casually brushed aside by an upper-class English artist. Probably Mr. Forster would find the essence of the grammatical (and social) middle class not in uncertainty about *who* and *whom* but in worrying about it.

vention is one developed either by democratic politics or by modern informality, here is one more illustration, one from a founder of Western civilization fifteen hundred years ago. The educated man who has something to say and a passionate conviction about the importance of saying it may choose non-standard expression because he knows that thereby he will reduce the distance between his thought and that of his less well educated audience. So Augustine knew that spiritual salvation was more important than verbal elegance, and in his commentary upon Psalm 138:15, in order to be clear to the illiterate he adopted the popular *ossum* for the standard *os,* "bone":

> *Non est absconditum os meum a te, quod fecisti in abscondito.* Os suum dicit: quod vulge dicitur ossum, latine os dicitur. . . . Habeo in abscondito quoddam ossum. Sic enim potius loquamur: melius est reprehendant nos grammatici, quam non intelligant populi. Ergo est, inquit, quoddam ossum meum intus in abscondito; tu fecisti intus ossum mihi in abscondito, et non est absconditum a te.[33]

Leaving out considerations of literary effectiveness, political necessity, or religious fervor, one's speech may still be too elegant for the purposes of ordinary social living. One fails to conform to the standards of one's community—whatever those standards may be—at one's peril. If its members are less fastidious or less well trained than the speaker, they may resent superior speech. Joseph Kirkland in his novel, *Zury: the Meanest Man in Spring County,* an early and authentic effort at the

[33] Migne, *Pat. Curs. Com., Patres Latini,* Vol. XXXVII, col. 1796. According to the numbering of the King James version the psalm is 139, and in place of *os* the English version reads *substance.* Augustine's words are translated in the *Library of the Nicene and Post Nicene Fathers: Saint Augustin,* VIII, 638, as follows: " 'My bone is not hid from thee, which Thou has made in secret' (ver. 15). 'His bone,' he saith. What the people call *ossum,* is in Latin called *os.* . . . He saith, then, I have a certain bone (*ossum*) in secret. For this word let us prefer to use; better is it that scholars find fault with us, than that the people understand us not. 'There is then,' saith he, 'a certain bone of mine, within, hidden; Thou hast made within a bone for me in secret, yet is it not hidden from Thee.' "

realistic description of frontier life, uses the idea skillfully. The educated heroine at the end of her first day of teaching in a pioneer Illinois school is in tears because she thinks she is laughed at. She is advised:

" 'Course some o'yer high-up scollops took daown offen th' top shelf way back—pronouncin' yer words so carefle, wearin' yer Sunday clo's a week days, 'n' so f'rth—dooz make most folks larf wunst in a while." [34]

And the same adviser years later, after he has married the schoolteacher and changed some of the habits that had made him so generally admired in Spring County, has to face the same charge. An old friend has to tell him the painful truth that the "hoss-shedders" think he is "A-PUTTIN' ON SCOLLOPS" (nothing less than capitals suffice to convey the gravity of the indictment). First among the specific charges, taking precedence over his servants, his stand-up collar, the "straps" to his pants, and his daily clean shirt, is his language:

"Why, fer one thing, the' 'llaow ye don't ollers talk country-fashion. When ye pass th' time o' day er what not with yer ol' neighbors; why then it saounds pooty much th' same's ever; but when ye talk t' strangers—conf'rence delegates, city-folks a visitin' yer wife, er what not; why then ye kind o' clip yer wurds like stuck-up Eastern folks, 'n' 'ffected Europian furriners th't plain English ain't good enough fer." [35]

Precisely the same sort of charge was hurled by political opponents against the group of young reformers among whom Theodore Roosevelt began his career. Joseph B. Foraker quotes a characteristic description from a contemporary newspaper:

. . . Wm. Walter Phelps, who appeared in banged hair, was properly English in appearance. So was Lodge, after the manner of the young Anglomaniac, along with Roosevelt. But in this respect all were laid

---

[34] Joseph Kirkland, *Zury: the Meanest Man in Spring County* (Boston: Houghton Mifflin Company, 1888), p. 164.

[35] *Ibid.*, p. 526.

in the shade by Curtis, with his intensely intellectual John Bull face, mutton chop whiskers and hair, parted evenly in the center and slightly banged.

. . . . .

It was noticed that all the men of this section had their hair parted in the middle, banged in front, wore an eyeglass, rolled their r's and pronounced the word *either* with the *i* sound instead of the *e*.[36]

To deduce from such mannerisms that these men were not sincere in their wish to introduce higher standards of political behavior, and that their cry for reform was but another way of vindicating their assumed superiority over the rest of the people, may have been neither logical nor fair. But it was too promising a method not to be tried. Among the many abusive terms bandied against the group the "Anglomaniac" theme recurs loudly. It was steadily used in conjunction with words like *pharisee, holier-than-thou,* and *goody-goody,* which were directed against the group's alleged self-righteousness and conceit.

Lest we make the issue seem more important than it should be, let us add three anecdotes from the career of Lincoln, a master of both written and oral expression and keenly aware of the effects of his language:

The same care which Lincoln bestowed on his messages and letters was given to his speeches. . . . He was afraid, it seemed to me, of being betrayed into using undignified expressions when called out without due preparation. Once, being notified that he was to be serenaded, just after some notable military or political event, he asked me to come to dinner, "so as to be on hand and see the fun afterward," as he said. He excused himself as soon as we had dined, and, while the bands were playing, the crowds cheering, and the rockets bursting, outside the house, he made his reappearance in the parlor, with a roll of manuscript in his hand. Perhaps, noticing a look of surprise on my face, he said, "I know what you are thinking about. You think it mighty queer that an old stump-speaker like myself should not be able to address a crowd like this outside without a written speech. But you must remember that I am, in a certain sense, talk-

[36] *Notes of a Busy Life* (Cincinnati: Stewart & Kidd Co., 1916), I, 167.

ing to the country, and I have to be mighty careful. Now, the last time I made an off-hand speech, in answer to a serenade, I used the phrase, as applied to the Rebels, 'turned tail and ran.' Some very nice Boston folks, I am grieved to hear, were very much outraged by that phrase, which they thought improper. So I resolved to make no more impromptu speeches if I could help it." [37]

In the July following Mr. Lincoln's inauguration, an extra session of Congress was called. In the message then sent in, speaking of secession, and the measures taken by the Southern leaders to bring it about, there occurs the following sentence:

"With rebellion thus *sugar-coated,* they have been drugging the public mind of their section for more than thirty years." Mr. Defrees, the government printer, told me that, when the message was being printed, he was a good deal disturbed by the use of the term "sugar-coated," and finally went to the President about it . . . he told Mr. Lincoln frankly . . . that a message to Congress was a different affair from a speech at a mass-meeting in Illinois; that the messages became a part of history, and should be written accordingly.

. . . . .

"Defrees," replied Mr. Lincoln, "that word expresses precisely my idea, and I am not going to change it. The time will never come in this country when people won't know exactly what *sugar-coated means!* [38]

The third story records the impression made upon at least one member of the audience by Lincoln in his famous Cooper Union speech during the 1860 campaign:

He began in a low tone of voice—as if he were used to speaking outdoors and was afraid of speaking too loud. He said "Mr. *Cheerman,*" instead of "Mr. Chairman," and employed many other words with an old-fashioned pronunciation. I said to myself: "Old fellow, you won't do; it's all very well for the wild West, but this will never go down in New York." But pretty soon he began to get into his subject; he straightened up, made regular and graceful gestures; his face lighted as with an inward fire; the whole man was transfigured. I for-

---

[37] Noah Brooks, "Personal Reminiscences of Lincoln," *Scribner's Monthly,* XV (February, 1878), 567.

[38] F. B. Carpenter, *Six Months at the White House* (New York: Hurd and Houghton, 1867), p. 126.

got his clothes, his personal appearance, and his individual peculiarities. Presently, forgetting myself, I was on my feet with the rest, yelling like a wild Indian, cheering this wonderful man. In the close parts of his argument, you could hear the gentle sizzling of the gas-burners. When he reached a climax, the thunders of applause were terrific. It was a great speech. When I came out of the hall, my face glowing with excitement and my frame all a-quiver, a friend, with his eyes aglow, asked me what I thought of Abe Lincoln, the rail-splitter. I said: "He's the greatest man since St. Paul." And I think so yet.[39]

As a result of having used the first of these popular expressions, the President bowed to criticism and sought to avoid further inelegancies that might offend the fastidious. The second he firmly retained for its apt and vivid expressiveness; undignified or not, nothing else would do as well. Of the third we, like his audience, recognize that it was totally unimportant. Neither awkwardness nor dialect has significance in the presence of real power. Andrew Johnson may have injured himself by the use of dialect probably very like Lincoln's. But the great man with something to say could afford to be ignorant of a fashionable pronunciation. It was a fact his listeners simply forgot.

[39] Quoted from Noah Brooks, "The Life of Lincoln," in *The Writings of Abraham Lincoln,* ed. by A. B. Lapsley (New York: Lamb Publishing Co., n.d.), VIII, 186–187.

CONCLUSION

FIRMLY believing that we cannot understand language in the abstract without observing its concrete manifestations, we do not feel like apologizing for the mass of examples with which we have showered our readers. They are essential to our work. But we must not take the risk of letting our shrubbery hide the path we intended to follow. It is now necessary to bring out some theoretical positions unencumbered by the data that support them.

The study of language is largely a matter of psychology. If some readers, however, feel inclined to insert a sceptical "whatever that may mean," we admit their perfect right to do so. Psychology embraces such a variety of notions and terms that words like *mind, soul,* and *psyche* have become ambiguous and to some students devoid of meaning. Almost every term referring to what in the vernacular is called *feeling* or *will* or *impression* suffers from the same weakness. Let us then try to state our meaning in a way acceptable to both the "mentalist" and the "materialist." In calling language psychological we are using a short formula for two basic things. First, any individual use of language, whether it is an act of original creation or just a selection from the large store of traditional words and structures, is an outcome of individual conditions and behavior. Second, any development in language as a group phenomenon begins with an individual act of creation or of modification of the traditional, but continues and is achieved through the acceptance of the individual act by a speech community. It is a process, in other words, of mass reaction. Since emotions are even less subject to rational control in the reactions of a group than in the individual, the feeling aroused by words becomes a dominant factor in their history. Emotional situations are not only in part created by words but themselves are a creative force in language, constructing new words, expanding meanings, imposing selections, and what not.

The picture developed here is the one we get, however, when there are no appreciable obstacles to the utterance of feelings. It may happen that the speaker knows or feels that unobstructed expression of his emotions—or of the facts of a case—will affect the community of hearers unfavorably. In such instances we get compromises in the shape of taboos of all sorts, ranging from substitute words, understatement, and hints, to humor. Furthermore, man is not a free agent in these matters. His behavior is defined and restricted by laws, mostly unwritten but nevertheless so potent that they continue in force even after the conditions that created them have disappeared.

To acknowledge that large parts of linguistics have to deal with mass psychology, or even to say that linguistic behavior can be governed by the impact language makes on others, is to say that language is not only a psychological but also a social phenomenon. Apart from the relatively rare cases of monologue language, there are always a speaker and an audience. Sometimes the speaker has the direct intention of influencing his audience, but whether he does or not he still cannot help making some kind of impression. So long as there is an audience language establishes a social relation. The social factor pervades the whole structure of language, but it is particularly conspicuous in groups of words like titles and stereotyped formulas of greeting, apology, expressions of wishes, and so forth that have the special task of helping to establish and define these relationships. The social element is present even in many cases where it usually has been ignored, as in the metaphor which can be used to establish a link between the purpose of a speaker and the interest of his audience. Whenever social circumstances of any sort, moreover, lead to the formation of a distinct group within the whole body of a society, the members of this group will tend to develop speech habits of their own. In return such social dialects will, as the history of Quaker speech shows, strengthen the cohesion of the group. What we mean by insisting on language as a psychological phenomenon, then, is that all these forces of individual and mass reaction have to be taken into consideration whether we label them with terms taken from mentalistic psychology or prefer to describe them behavioristically.

Everybody knows that language has a history. But this history does not consist exclusively of the record of changing sounds and forms. Its aim must be to tie every development within language to those events in the life of the people which created the special cultural conditions that in turn made necessary the use of new words or forms. Quaker language is, as we have seen, the product of the seventeenth century and of no other period. We cannot understand it unless we know how this one period reacted to a man's keeping his hat on in the presence of his social betters. In the many instances where we cannot point to such an obvious connection we ought not be satisfied with our ignorance but recognize the existence of unsolved problems. New words and meanings are not brought by the stork, and the question of paternity has to be raised. Frequently it is not enough to think of history as a system of dated events. There is also a history of culture, and often we have to dip into it to explain the names given to this and that.

While it is doubtless a relevant and attractive task to trace linguistic facts back to their origins, we must not forget that whatever is introduced into language has not only a past but likewise a future. Whatever we say produces effects, some of them outside language (your nonverbal reaction in movement to "close the window"), some of them within language (your word "certainly" or "with pleasure" in answer to "close the window"). Both types of reaction, but particularly the latter, must be studied by the linguist. When a manufacturer adopts a name designed to help the sale of his product, he creates a linguistic problem deserving of study. But more important is the situation in which a new word acts as a stimulus to the creation of a sometimes considerable body of new expressions, as with the metaphor *Underground Railroad.* The existence of *Red* as a political label has made *Pink* inevitable.

What we have here said applies in a body to all the materials of our book. It is, of course, clear that in any given instance one aspect rather than another will seem more obvious—or to the commentator more immediately useful. Hence we have not always brought out the complexity of the many illustrations we have used in this book. Most often we have sought to place them in only one context to make clear one special problem. But fully understood nearly all of them involve many different forces. We now take one example, *copperhead,* from the many we have discussed, to show how intricate the interplay of psychological, social, and historical factors may be in a single word. The influence of historical events upon this word is, in the main, perfectly clear. But apart from its general connection with the parties of the Civil War we want to remind the reader also that the tempo with which it was accepted was accelerated by the 1862 Congressional elections. And we should note that in the First World War it was revived. To turn from the historical to the social, we cannot prove that a man was entirely ostracized by being declared a *copperhead,* but it is a fact that Augustus Thomas found the theme of ostracism (as told in Frederick Landis' *The Glory of His Country*) so real that he could use it as the subject of his play, *The Copperhead.* He has told us in the preface to the play that one reason it appealed to him was his vivid memory of the political bitterness of the time in southern Illinois. And the record of the play's success is there to show that the audiences of 1918 found it credible. There can be no doubt of the social meaning of Blaine's admission that his use of *copperhead* in Congressional debate was bad taste. Bad taste means bad manners. Manners are a result of social regulation—in this instance apparently almost of social taboo. As for the psychological side, we would stress that the word brings out with the utmost clarity what we have said about the place of both individual psychology and mass psychology in the linguistic process. The emotional background of the history of a word could not possibly be clearer. The first known appearance of *copperhead* suggests that it was created in order to satisfy a degree of embittered passion which found even *rattlesnake* inadequate. In a very few instances only can we follow the spreading of a new expression with enough exactness to see how the community makes an individual creation its own property. Here we can date it precisely. In addition the word offers an excellent example of change of meaning based on an emotional force so strong as to drive it out of its originally restricted field of application; it soon came to mean Democrat in general. Again *copperhead* shows how a new word may in turn become the stimulus for still further developments both within and outside the language. All these heterogeneous elements enter into the history of *copperhead,* but they do not exhaust it. Since we wrote the chapter on change of meaning, we have found the following new coinages resulting from it: "a dead-beat copper soldier," 1867 (Dennett, *Lincoln and the Civil War in the Diaries and Letters of John Hay,* 276); "Copper votes," 1863 (Dennett, 109); "Copperheadism," 1864 (F. Ward, *Copperhead Catechism*); "To be a Democrat in Ashtabula is not only to be Copperheaded but copper-bottomed and copper-plated," 1866 (Cleveland *Leader,* September 15). Indeed the linguistic consequences may range from the introduction of new words to the appearance of literary productions wholly dependent, like the poem quoted from Bret Harte, on the metaphorical adaptability of the word. And a nonlinguistic consequence was the effort of the northern Democrats to neutralize it by making a liberty symbol of the copper penny.

From all this it appears that the theoretical study of language is apt to be a complicated affair. It becomes still more involved when to all these theoretical questions we add the problems of the practical use of language. It is not the duty of the scientific linguist to tell men how they ought to use their language. Still we have felt that in a book addressed to the general reader as well as to the professional linguist some consideration should be given to the fact that skill and versatility in the use of language obviously can smooth a man's way as surely as tongue-bound ineptitude and lack of familiarity with accepted standards can handicap him. If our opinions can be of any help to the reader it ought to be in regard to these points: that much of what is passed on as inviolable rule has no foundation whatever in linguistic history or theory; that many of these "rules" have never had the importance their supporters claimed because of the frequency of infractions by people of good educational and social standing; that in many cases a vigorous ungrammatical phrase can be incomparably more effective than a correct but colorless expression ("It's us or them"); and finally that strong personality will make itself felt behind the ungrammatical as well as the grammatical expression. Anything that a man decides to do about his own language depends upon his powers of observation, but serious thinking about it is one means of developing such power.

To our fellow linguists we want to say that linguistics to us means the study of all the problems of language and that we do not limit the range of this discipline to those that can be approached by the methods of natural science. We have ourselves omitted many because we did not feel prepared to deal with them and because we were writing one volume, not an encyclopedia—but that is an entirely different matter from claiming that a problem which is not readily amenable to treatment by a given method is not a legitimate part of scientific linguistics.

That all the major uses and manifestations of language are essentially unified is a concept that has grown on us as we have written. Taboo, meaning and change of meaning, word creation, forms, phonetics, stylistics, standards of use, even humor are closely intertwined. They take their shape and function as results of the impact of the speech community upon the individual and the individual upon his community or communities. They cannot be studied wholly in isolation. And they cannot be broken apart. There is plenty of room for the restricted and specialized study, of course, but the meaning of that study will never be complete unless we see it as part of the whole rich complex which is language—and, in turn, see this complex as part of the total pattern of human behavior.

INDEX OF WORDS

S

T

GENERAL INDEX

D